VANQUISHED

CRUSHING DEFEATS
from ANCIENT ROME
to the 21ST CENTURY

OSPREY
PUBLISHING

VANQUISHED

CRUSHING DEFEATS
from ANCIENT ROME
to the 21ST CENTURY

MIR BAHMANYAR

First published in Great Britain in 2009 by Osprey Publishing,
Midland House, West Way, Botley, Oxford OX2 0PH, United Kingdom.
443 Park Avenue South, New York, NY 10016, USA.

Email: info@ospreypublishing.com

A CIP catalog record for this book is available from the British Library.

ISBN-13: 978 1 84603 327 8

Mir Bahmanyar has asserted his right under the Copyright, Designs and Patents Act, 1988,
to be identified as the author of this book.

Page layout by Myriam Bell Design, France
Index by Margaret Vaudrey
Typeset in Adobe Caslon Pro
Maps by Peter Bull Art Studio
Originated by PPS Grasmere Ltd
Printed in China by Worldprint

09 10 11 12 13   10 9 8 7 6 5 4 3 2 1

In each of the maps in this book, blue denotes the victor, and red the vanquished.

For a catalog of all books published by Osprey please contact:

NORTH AMERICA
Osprey Direct, c/o Random House Distribution Center
400 Hahn Road, Westminster, MD 21157, USA
E-mail: uscustomerservice@ospreypublishing.com

ALL OTHER REGIONS
Osprey Direct, The Book Service Ltd., Distribution Centre, Colchester Road, Frating Green,
Colchester, Essex, CO7 7DW
E-mail: customerservice@ospreypublishing.com

Osprey Publishing is supporting the Woodland Trust, the UK's leading woodland
conservation charity, by funding the dedication of trees.

www.ospreypublishing.com

CONTENTS

ACKNOWLEDGMENTS

I should like to thank Ruth Sheppard, Emily Holmes and Michelle Ricci for without them this book would never have been finished.

Special thanks to my contributors on this book:

Odin Benitez, who loves all things Byzantine and is an expert on many other eras unknown to mortal man, for writing with such great care and attention to detail on Adrianople and Pliska.

Matthew Rigdon for his terrific work on Jena-Auerstädt, the epic Napoleonic battle which reinvigorated the Prussian military and its staff most notably among them the great philosopher of war Carl von Clausewitz.

Ethan Reiff, who may have been a colonial war correspondent or British officer or perhaps even an Afghan warlord or mullah in his previous life, for Jugdulluck.

Last but not least Giacomo Ghiazza, my long time artist friend, for his beautiful sketches.

All of them came to my rescue. Their contributions and insights have made this a far better book. Any mistakes or oversights are of course mine.

Mir Bahmanyar, Los Angeles

INTRODUCTION

I was discussing the current state of the modern Western military with a good friend of mine who had participated in the combat parachute assault on the Rio Hato military airfield, Panama, in 1989 while serving with the 3rd Battalion, 75th Ranger Regiment. Our discussion concluded with a criticism of the American senior military leadership, or more specifically, its lack of leadership from the front. It is shocking to consider how inconclusive modern wars have become compared to those of history, and how actions promising to be "battles of annihilation" instead turn into quagmires of drawn-out stalemates and compromise. How did the United States, the most powerful country on earth, fail to achieve decisive victories on tactical and strategic levels? From this discussion of very modern military history was born the idea for this book, a book examining battles of annihilation, the ultimate conclusive action, and why they occur so infrequently in modern warfare.

Although large numbers of people have been killed during war in the 20th and 21st centuries, few battles of annihilations have been fought since the middle of the 20th century. Outside of a large-scale conventional war or a state-led genocide against a vastly technologically inferior people, battles of annihilation are now mainly found in history books. Today's wars are fought in urban or mountainous environments, waged primarily by non-uniformed personnel against conventional forces. Guerrilla fighters worldwide can easily intermingle with the local populace or retreat into inaccessible areas, only to reemerge when suitable making it difficult to destroy a guerrilla force in combat. Conventional forces often desert when facing overwhelming firepower, as was seen in the case of the Iraqi Army during the two Gulf wars.

Currently, the interests of public image and perhaps the desire of a few to reduce collateral damage, prevent complete obliteration of cities in Iraq or the Occupied Territories such as Palestine, unlike the strategic bombing campaigns against civilian targets utilized during World War II. Still, "annihilation" occurred most frequently in the 20th century not in conventional battles involving regular troops, but through actions against civilians. These events were mainly acts of genocide, from the concentration camps built by the British to hold the Boers, through the Turkish genocide of more than one million Armenians, to the most infamous mass murder, the Holocaust (Judeocide) during World War II. These types of "actions" are the modern "battles of annihilation," though one side is often unarmed, untrained, and possibly even unaware a battle is being fought.

Military history is littered with decisive campaigns, battles, or sieges between regular armies seeking a conclusive battle, and when those engagements ended with

"Knight, Death and the Devil" by Albrecht Dürer (1471–1528), shows the true face of war. (Anne S.K. Brown Military Collection, Brown University Library)

one side obliterated, the commanders, who were often right in the main battle line, died with their men. In some societies, defeated commanders, after realizing all was lost, sought death for their failures rather than face punishment – the defeated Roman commanders Paullus at Cannae and Varus at the Teutoburg Forest are two examples. Nearly a hundred senators died at Cannae. Hannibal, the great Carthaginian commander, fled when all was lost at Zama, but he was there in command, finally committing suicide after years of being hunted by Roman agents. One cannot imagine such things nowadays. When more conventional battles of annihilation have occurred in recent years (i.e. between two conventional armed forces), very few senior military commanders were present on the battlefield and perhaps this absence of leadership is part of the reason that conclusive battles are now rare.

Vanquished focuses on a selection of battles where the commander of one side got it right and won an overwhelming victory, or where the other side got it terribly wrong. Although "annihilation" implies a focus on very high casualties, within at least one of the armies present and quite often in both, one should of course be wary of a simplistic tallying of dead to judge a victory. Victories cannot always be judged by numbers, or other traditional methods of evaluating them – a battle of annihilation could include one force managing to destroy the enemy's morale completely, even though by some evaluations they might be considered to have lost the fight. In general terms, however, a battle of annihilation such as those in this book requires one side to destroy the other completely, at least in terms of combat ability. The broader context, of course, can make the victory or defeat more complex. For example, most people will agree that the battle of the Alamo in 1836 was a complete victory for the Mexican forces, yet it served as such a potent rallying cry for the Texians that it pretty much won the war for them. Cannae, fought more than 2,000 years ago, is still considered by many to be the greatest of all battles of annihilation and its impact on Prussian and German militarism was significant, yet Hannibal, the victor on the battlefield, lost the war.

It is unfortunately rather easy to forget when writing or reading about these battles the misery and horror wars inflict on people and in particular on the men who fight them. The casualty numbers for some of the battles included in this book are almost incomprehensible, with the result that the experience of the individual, or the true human cost of the battle, is at times hard to consider. Chris Cocks' *Fireforce: One Man's War in the Rhodesian Light Infantry* is a wonderful addition to a handful of meaningful war literature that includes such notable authors as Paul Fussell, Eugene Sledge, and Guy Sajer. His after-battle thoughts might well have been those of the survivors, on either side, in any number of the battles in this book:

It was just a big adventure which slowly began to turn sour when I discovered that upwards of forty thousand people had been killed in the conflict. "What the f*** was it all for?" That is the bitter sentiment generally heard today and I cannot even try to answer. In 1977 I was just a young man – a boy, and in all wars it is always the youngsters who are caught up in the fights of the fathers – not of their own making.[1]

War is hell and yet as journalist Chris Hedges points out with the title of his excellent book, *War is a Force that Gives Us Meaning*. It is a sobering thought.

Carl Philipp Gottlieb von Clausewitz (1780–1831), was arguably the greatest philosopher in the history of warfare and his unfinished manuscript, *On War*, attempts to analyze the tangible and intangible elements of war. His thinking was influenced by his military experience; he was captured during the battle of Jena-Auerstädt. (Author's Collection)

Deciding which battles of annihilation to cover in this book was not an easy task. Months were spent researching and two books in particular are noteworthy: David Eggenberger's *An Encyclopedia of Battles – Accounts of over 1,560 Battles from 1479 BC to the Present* and Thomas Harbottle's *Dictionary of Battles from 743 BC to the Present.* The list of battles underwent many revisions; often a battle of annihilation turned out not to be such or was simply a complete fabrication. The often cited battle of annihilation fought at Cajamarca, Peru, in 1532, pitting Spanish soldiers against the Incan king and his personal attendants, seems instead to have been the slaughter of unarmed Incans. The ground battle of Longewala in 1971 between Pakistani and Indian forces seems to have been completely fabricated by the victorious Indians. Other times a lack of scholarship in English prevented a battle from being included including the battle of Xinkou in the second Sino-Japanese War.

The limitations of the book meant that it was impossible to include all the battles of annihilation through history. Those included have been selected to provide a variety of types of battle of annihilation, showing both similarities between battles centuries apart, and also fundamental differences in how crushing defeats have come about.

BATTLES IN THE BOOK

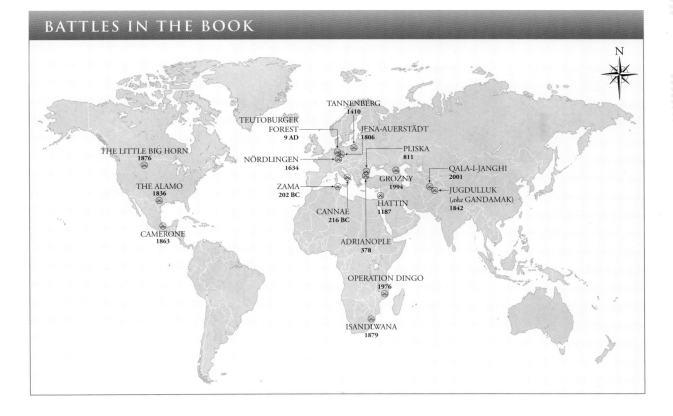

Although battles of annihilation are rare in modern times, this is not to say that modern warfare is any less horrific for the combatants. This drawing of the famous "thousand-yard stare" dates from World War II, a war with more than its fair share of horror. (Anne S.K. Brown Military Collection, Brown University Library)

Though there are fewer modern battles that can be classed as having ended in annihilation, there are some that could have been included from 20th-century conflicts, such as Tannenberg, 1914, or Cisterna, 1944, if space had allowed. However, the scholarship on these conflicts is vast and anyone interested in battles of annihilation from these or similar conflicts should have few problems in accessing the research.

The interpretations of the battles that you will find in these pages are just that – interpretations. Even a discussion of Cannae, one of the best-documented ancient battles, must contain many estimates, surmises, and guesses. For although Cannae was recorded by both Greek and Roman historians, no Punic records of the gargantuan struggle between the powerful cities of Carthage and Rome survive, and each surviving source inevitably has its biases or flaws. As Professors Yozan Mosig and Imene Belhassen warn:

History was written by the victors. As it is, historical records that were produced by the Carthaginian side have been totally obliterated or lost, and most of what we have was penned by pro-Roman sources. Polybius was enslaved by the Romans, and came to serve the Aemilian/Scipionic family, becoming friend and mentor of Scipio Aemilianus, the destroyer of Carthage. He wrote about 50 years after Cannae, and his works are generally regarded as more reliable than those of Livy. Nevertheless, his objectivity and accuracy becomes suspect when he writes about members of the family he served. Livy was essentially a Roman moralist and propagandist, whose historical accounts, although beautifully written, contain many fictionalized incidents, such as speeches (which he pretends to quote verbatim) and anecdotes, clearly invented to embellish the record and provide an inspirational and patriotic narrative for his Roman audience.[2]

Given the truth of Mosig and Belhassen's statement that history is always written by the victors, uncovering the whole truth behind accounts of battles where the defeated force was annihilated is an impossible task. Thus, my conclusions are not to be considered final.

CANNAE, 216 BC

BACKGROUND

The titanic struggle for supremacy in the Mediterranean between the metropolis of Carthage, founded by Phoenician colonists on the shores of North Africa, and the rapidly growing city of Rome began in earnest with the First Punic War (264–241 BC), when both city-states answered a call for help from the island of Sicily. Historically, Sicily had been a major trading partner with Carthage. Hiero II of Syracuse was at war with another Sicilian city, Messina, whose citizens duplicitously asked for help from first Carthage, then Rome. Both city-states responded with an attempt to dominate the strategically placed island. Carthage, confronted with a betrayal, decided to fight Messina, while Rome continued to support the city. The local conflict thereby engulfed the Mediterranean in a war that lasted until 241 BC. The outcome was a clear-cut victory for the Romans, who surpassed the Carthaginians in the art of seamanship. Carthage accepted the terms demanded by Rome and ceded Sicily. The Carthaginians then fought a war against their own mercenaries, who had risen against their paymasters for failing to deliver promised wages – Carthage's financial resources had been slashed by a large indemnity owed to Rome. During Carthage's struggle to control its mercenaries, Rome, none too subtly, seized Sardinia and Corsica, provoking another war with the North African city.

Rome had expanded at Carthage's expense. The Carthaginians, however, took the path of least resistance by consolidating their hold in Africa and then expanding into the Iberian peninsula, where rich silver mines reestablished Carthage's status in the ancient world. Rome eyed Carthaginian expansion in the Iberian peninsula with suspicion and envy, for their opponents were doing remarkably well in subjugating and exploiting the region. Carthaginian general and statesman Hamilcar Barca and, upon Barca's death in 229 BC, Hasdrubal, his son-in-law, were the principal men responsible for the expansion in Spain. The Ebro river in the northern part of Iberia

Hannibal's crossing of the Alps has inspired artists for centuries. (Liebig cards printed with permission of Campbell's Soup Company)

was the ratified yet unofficial border between Hasdrubal and Rome. One condition of the fragile peace was that neither was to advance into the other's region. In 228 BC, however, Rome signed a friendship treaty with Saguntum, which lay well south of the Ebro.

In 221 BC, Hasdrubal was assassinated in Spain.[1] The popular Hannibal (247–183 BC), son of Hamilcar Barca, was given command of the army in Spain at the age of 26. Hannibal was only ten years old when he had joined his father in the Iberian peninsula, and although his allegiance was to Carthage there can be little doubt that he was a Spaniard at heart as well. He went about consolidating his holdings and reasserted Carthaginian dominance over various Spanish tribes south of the Ebro river.

Internal rival politicking in Saguntum, possibly encouraged by Rome, led to heightened tensions between Carthage and Rome and subsequently to a meeting between Hannibal and a Roman legation. The meeting, however, proved fruitless and resulted in an eight-month siege of Saguntum by the Carthaginians and its eventual reduction to rubble. Hannibal was wounded during the siege. Rome, either by design or incompetence, failed to render aid to the city while busy fighting a second war against Illyria. Subsequent Roman demands to Carthage for the surrender of Hannibal went unheeded. Thus the Second Punic War, 218–201 BC, (also known as the Qarta-Romano War) began, with old men opting for war while young men sought to experience the supposed glory of killing one another.

Hannibal Barca (248–183/2 BC). Rome's greatest enemy and Carthage's brilliant commander. (Author's Collection)

The Second Punic War overshadowed the previous Roman/Carthaginian conflicts completely. Hannibal's audacious decision to take the war to Rome herself fired historical imagination for many for centuries to come. The story of elephants crossing the Pyrenees and the Alps, alongside tens of thousands of ethnically diverse mercenaries, became a favorite for romantically minded writers and artists. Hannibal, born Carthaginian but Iberian in spirit, showed the world that one man's dedication and vision can forever alter the landscape of war.

Throughout the winter and spring months in 216 BC, the opposing armies were encamped, living off their stored supplies. Once winter turned to spring, Hannibal needed to move on to find new food supplies for his army. He therefore broke camp at Gerunium and marched toward a large Roman depot at the citadel of Cannae near the River Aufidus, in Apulia, southeastern Italy. The city had been previously razed, and Hannibal now seized the citadel and supplies. Polybius writes that the seizure of Cannae caused great concern to the Romans, since the countryside was being ravaged and some of their regional allies were wavering in their loyalties to Rome.[2] The generals requested instructions from Rome, as moving major land forces toward the tactically important city of Cannae would bring about a battle in the surrounding plains.

The Senate in Rome chose battle – Cannae it would be.

THE ROMAN ARMY

Following successive defeats at Trebbia in 218 BC and Lake Trasimene in 217 BC, together inflicting approximately 60,000 Roman casualties, Rome was forced to rebuild its armies. While it did so, it had to avoid other pitched battles with the seemingly undefeatable Hannibal. The Senate elected Quintus Fabius Maximus as dictator of Rome to oversee the rebuilding of the army, and Maximus' strategy was one of delay. Instead of seeking out another battle with the Punic forces and thus possibly suffering another disastrous defeat, he stayed in close proximity to the Carthaginian Army, shadowing it without ever committing to a pitched battle. This "Fabian Strategy" accomplished its mission perfectly, creating enough time to raise and train new legions.

In 216 BC, Lucius Aemilius Paullus and Gaius Terentius Varro were elected as Roman consuls, replacing the dictatorship of Maximus. Rome decided to force the Carthaginian issue once and for all by raising a war-ending army of unprecedented scale. To accomplish this feat, Paullus was tasked not only with increasing the number of legions, but also with raising the strengths of all the individual legions by another 800 men.

The army was composed of eight reinforced Roman legions accompanied by an equal number of allied legions. Each legion had grown from 4,200 to 5,000 infantrymen, although the cavalry arm stayed at 200–300. The Italian Allied legions had a similar number of soldiers, but their cavalry arm was between 600–900 per legion. All told, the Romans forged 16 reinforced legions numbering around 80,000 infantrymen and a 6,000-strong cavalry contingent. To put this and the subsequent slaughter into perspective, we can look at total Roman manpower. Rome at this time had 17 Roman legions deployed, and the same number of allied legions. Mark Healy writes that Rome's "total citizen manpower deployed [worldwide] would have exceeded approximately 150,000 men. A similar quantity of allied troops was also deployed, making a total Roman and allied deployment in excess of some 300,000 men."[3] Legions I, II, XII, XIII, XIV, XV, XVI, and XVII were at Cannae; V and VI were stationed in Spain; VII and VIII in Sicily; Legion IX was deployed in Sardinia; Legions XVIII and XIX in the Po Valley; and lastly, XX and XXI were stationed in Rome.[4]

There has been much scholarship on the total numbers of troops present at Cannae. Various arguments have indicated that the Roman legions were not as numerous as suggested by the ancient chroniclers. Peter Connolly favors the numbers mentioned in Livy and J. F. Lazenby points out that the strength of the Romans listed by Polybius, for example, may very well have been paper strength only.[5] Yet most ancient sources are clear that the Romans were numerically superior to the Carthaginians.

An important question is why the Romans, realizing the superiority of the enemy's cavalry both quantitatively and qualitatively, had not increased their own cavalry arm during the recruiting drives to enlarge the legions. Republican Rome had risen to dominance through political astuteness coupled with infantry strength and tactical adaptability. Certainly the Romans had previously demonstrated an ability to learn from their enemies and redress any of their own deficiencies. They were able to best the Carthaginian fleet, one of the finest of its time, during the First Qarta-Romano War (also known as the First Punic War, 264–241 BC) when they had had no background in maritime operations. However, during the second campaign of the 'Long War' with Carthage, they seemingly failed to adapt their military organization to counter Hannibal's clear superiority in cavalry. Perhaps the Romans believed in their land forces' dominance; after all, it had served them exceedingly well. Perhaps they did not believe that they could have raised a quality cavalry arm. Surely the Romans must have been able to increase their cavalry contingent, but they probably felt confident enough in sheer size, a confidence supported by the opportunity to train and thus become more cohesive. The Roman command staff and non-commissioned officers (NCOs) were certainly experienced, and they were fighting on native soil.

Alternatively, some scholars, such as Mosig and Belhassen, speculate that the Romans did strengthen their cavalry alongside their infantry, arguing that cavalry complements for each enlarged legion probably were increased to at least 300 per legion, if not 350 or 400, based on Polybius' statement that cavalry was increased "on occasions of exceptional gravity."[6] Such expansion would give a combined cavalry of at least 9,600, and perhaps even as high as 12,800, meaning the Romans not only outnumbered Hannibal in infantry but had at least "practical numerical equality with Hannibal's horsemen," if not superiority. They suggest the lower numbers in the sources are due to the fact that the Romans "consistently rationalized their defeats by attributing them to Hannibal's superior cavalry numbers, so that accepting that they actually held superiority, or at least parity, in cavalry, at the moment of their greatest disaster, would have made their defeat that much more shameful."[7]

In addition to raising the strength of his army, Paullus had to ensure that the quality of the legionaries was improved, for the Senate believed that previous defeats were due to the poor standard of Rome's troops.[8] Roman legions in the field, led by the previous year's consuls Marcus Atilius Regulus and Gnaeus Servilius, shadowed Hannibal. They were prohibited from engaging the Carthaginians in anything but minor harassment operations, while simultaneously turning the new recruits into combat-capable legionaries.

There are modern authors who argue that the Romans, including command staff, were not professional soldiers at this time. Instead, it is theorized, they were citizen militia, turning out for duty for several months a year and hence not the soldiers one associates with the glory of the later Roman Empire. On this basis, we could assess that inferior, unprofessional troops caused defeat in Hannibalic battles in general and Cannae in particular. There is some validity to the argument that the Romans were not producing the professional armies of later years.[9] Technically speaking, they did not stay on duty year-round, as is associated with a regular standing army. However, they were professional enough to have dispatched a great number of enemy warriors in battle, including the Carthaginians several decades earlier. Roman legionaries spent consecutive months together once recruited and deployed in the field. (By contrast, modern reserve and guard units do not serve for months on end unless deployed during national emergencies.) Once they were deployed, they naturally learned valuable combat lessons – war is the ultimate training ground. Furthermore, we can reasonably assume that the Roman legions contained a core of competent soldiers and leaders. As with any army being brought up to strength, the quality of the troops would have varied, and newer recruits may have lacked the social bonds developed by the members of the unit. Yet the new men were integrated into the legions over several months prior to the battle, and enough time was spent observing and harassing Hannibal to bring even raw recruits up to competence. In addition, the Roman legionaries were fighting on native soil to protect their families and society.

We should also recognize that the men who ultimately fought at Cannae lived in an agrarian society, and in general terms were fit and hearty, capable of carrying and wielding weaponry. They were also steeped in military tradition. There can be little doubt, therefore, that by the time the legions clashed with the African invaders, they had been bloodied enough and trained enough to be considered fit for battle.

THE CARTHAGINIAN ARMY

The Carthaginian Army was completely the opposite to that of the Romans. Few citizens of Carthage actually fought in Hannibal's Italian Army. The vast majority of his troops in the Italian campaigns were recruited from among the Celtic and Gallic tribes who had and would continue to have long-running hostilities with the Romans, eventually resulting in the death or enslavement of several million of them by the Romans.[10] These warriors formed the core of Hannibal's armies and were used primarily in the front ranks to blunt the swords of the legionaries. Most fought naked, although some must have equipped themselves with Roman armor and equipment after their victories at Trebbia and Lake Trasimene. Their traditional shields were large and their primary weapon was a long slashing sword that required "a wide sweep."[11] Some caked their hair with lime to make it stand up, giving them an even fiercer, wilder look.

The Spaniards, like the Celts and Gauls, provided Hannibal with cavalry and infantry. The infantry had similar shields to the Celts, although some of their lighter

Ancient coin believed to depict Hannibal and one of his legendary war elephants. (Author's Collection)

troops carried smaller round ones. Their main weapon apart from spears (including throwing spears similar to the Roman *pilum*) was a slightly curved short sword called the *falcata*. The Spanish troops wore white tunics bordered in purple, which Polybius identifies as their national dress.[12] Personal body armor, if worn at all, may have been composed of indigenous as well as captured or purchased varieties. These included captured chest plates and possibly some mail as well. One beautifully engraved Samnite triple-disk cuirass was discovered in North Africa and may have been produced in southern Italy.

The Liby-Phoenician[13] or African troops at Cannae were equipped similarly to the traditional Roman infantryman (courtesy of spoils from recent victories), but remnants of older armor must have survived as well. Mail, chest plates, and Greek-styled linen cuirasses as well as *scutum* (Roman-type rectangular, convex body shield) and round shields must have intermixed in these units.

Several modern scholars, including Peter Connolly, argue for the existence of pikemen units (*phalangites*) within the Carthaginian Army, based in part on the Macedonian and Greek dominance in ancient warfare and its influence throughout the Mediterranean.[14] Connolly describes his version of the Liby-Phoenician pikemen as such: "These half-castes formed a Macedonian type phalanx. The phalangites would have had the armour and weapons of a typical Hellenistic [late Greek] infantryman: a small round shield, a heavy two-handed spear 5m to 7m long and a short sword for hand-to-hand fighting. These pikemen would line up many ranks deep with several rows of spears projecting beyond the front rank."[15]

Whether or not the Liby-Phoenicians carried pikes or spears is actually still hotly debated. Gregory Daly does not believe that they actually ever served as infantry, but provided the heavy cavalry instead.[16] One argument against pikes is that the captured Roman shields were unsuitable to allow a pikeman proper handling of his long weapon. In fact, Daly argues that Libyans were swordsmen armed almost identically to the Roman legionary at Cannae.[17] Of course, this argument rests on the assumption that the captured *scuta* were carried by these Liby-Phoenician pikemen. He states:

> A thornier issue is whether or not the Libyans were armed with *pila* and *gladii* [swords]. If they were, it would seem almost certain that they were used to fighting as swordsmen rather than like Greek or Macedonian-style spearmen, since it is unlikely that Hannibal would have risked retraining his men while on campaign. The absurdity of simply assuming that there had been no significant changes in Libyan equipment since 341, when they certainly were spearmen, has been noted [in an earlier section], and the fact that they clearly used the large, heavy, Roman shield at Cannae surely indicates that they

had not adopted the Macedonian-style pike – such a weapon could be extremely heavy and required both hands for use, something which would have been impossible carrying a Roman *scutum*.[18]

The assertion that pikemen existed within Hannibal's army does not necessarily contradict Polybius, but there is also no direct evidence to suggest the existence of them in their traditional role made famous 100 years earlier by Alexander the Great of Macedon either. However, the battle of Pydna in 168 BC saw Roman legions cut the Macedonian pikemen to pieces. Is it then impossible to assume that Hannibal indeed had a core of veteran pikemen, since similarly equipped units functioned for well over 50 years after Cannae? A phalanx of pikemen could certainly keep enemy cavalry and infantry at bay. Their ranks would have been much deeper than the rest of the Carthaginian line to accommodate a traditional phalanx, which was at least 16 men deep by 16 men wide.[19] In any case, the North African infantry should be considered more heavily armored than the Spaniards and Celts/Gauls.

The Numidian cavalry was considered the best light cavalry of its time. They were fearsome predators, armed with small round shields and several types of throwing spear. The Numidians were expert at attacking from various sides without ever closing with the enemy, exploiting gaps and encircling their opponents. Often these horsemen were used to hunt down retreating units. Their value as a "combat multiplier" (an element that increases the combat potential of a force without necessarily increasing force numbers) during the Punic Wars should not be underestimated. Livy recounts a story from the battle of Cannae in which 500 Numidians surrendered to the Romans, only to reappear after killing their guards and spreading confusion among the Romans at a crucial time in the battle.[20] This account may not be true, but it does suggest the fear the Numidians spread among their enemies. The Numidians were to be instrumental at Cannae by stalemating the enemy cavalry and at Zama they were Rome's salvation and Hannibal's damnation.

If the Carthaginians were awed by the mass of Roman legions, one can only wonder what the Roman *velites* (light infantry) and *hastati* (spearmen/swordsmen) in the front rank must have thought as the Spanish and Celts were drawn up opposite them in alternating companies. Polybius appreciated it best when he wrote "that the line presented a strange and terrifying appearance."[21]

The challenges of commanding a multi-ethnic army do not seem to have handicapped Hannibal. His art of war was not exclusively Carthaginian, as the overwhelming majority of his campaigning life had been spent on the Iberian peninsula and mainland Italy. Though, like other commanders, he was educated in Greek and Macedonian warfare, his real-world combat experiences were formed under the tutelage of his Carthaginian predecessors in Spain and refined during the years of hard campaigning in Italy.

Victor Davis Hanson describes the Punic Army as "poorly organized but brilliantly led."[22] Such a judgment seems rather hasty, for no disorganized but well-led mob could have been as successful as Hannibal's army was for so many years. Success on the battlefield has many fathers, but poor organization is not one of them.

We can certainly presume communication difficulties within the Carthaginian camp, with different tongues babbling everywhere and interpreters accompanying command staff in their discussions with various ethnic tribal leaders. However, Nic Fields points out that "Hannibal, a pure blooded Carthaginian, spoke several tongues and no doubt his veteran army of Italy developed a sort of bastard tongue [akin to] Creole or pidgin used by slave societies, perhaps some form of camp Punic. Carthage had centuries of experience dealing with foreigners both as traders and employers of mercenaries."[23] There is no reason to doubt effective communication with the various tribal contingents that comprised Hannibal's army.

Hannibal's officers undoubtedly were of similar ilk and disposition as their commander and hence equally experienced in integrating mercenaries from the Iberian and Italian peninsulas. The Hannibalic army, prior to the invasion of Italy, was composed of veteran North Africans and Spaniards. Once in Italy, Hannibal's depleted army retained its core of veterans and capable commanders and was reinforced by Celtic warriors. They were certainly good recruits, capable of learning the Cartho-Iberian art of war while retaining their own peculiar style of combat. In essence, the Punic Army incorporated the various distinct fighting styles into one coherent force. As the years passed and more veterans died or left, the Celts became the primary anvil to dull Roman blades, and their enthusiasm for plunder and war, particularly against the Romans, was undiminished. Celtic warriors, mostly accustomed to raids or sporadic battles, became adept at campaigning under the watchful eyes of their war-hardened paymasters. Indeed Connolly writes that the success of the Hannibalic army is "a tribute to the Carthaginian system. No attempt was made at uniformity. Each native group fought in its own way and had to be used to its best advantage. Hannibal's relationship with his troops was remarkable. In spite of their mixed backgrounds they stuck with him for fifteen years with never the whisper of a mutiny."[24]

THE ROAD TO CANNAE

With their super-army gathered, this time the Romans intended to teach the audacious young Hannibal a lesson. No doubt some politicians were envisioning a spectacular triumph and cruel torture for the foreigners, especially their leader.

Paullus and Varro united their legions and moved via a two-day march to within 8–9km of the Carthaginian camp situated near the citadel of Cannae, arriving nearby on July 28, 216 BC.[25] Here they built a fortified camp. No doubt the Roman staff reconnoitered the area and found the terrain to be suitable for cavalry operations, which would give the African Army an edge in maneuverability. The plains around Cannae were "flat and treeless," records Polybius, and Paullus argued that the legions ought to march to a more suitable area to negate Hannibal's cavalry superiority.[267]

The Roman Army at Cannae was commanded on alternate days by Paullus and Varro. Varro receives highly unflattering if not insulting commentary from the ancient sources for his brashness and his failure to heed Paullus' advice on terrain. In history, therefore, he thus becomes the one at fault for the impending debacle. However, everything in the battle stemmed from the Senate's order to close with Hannibal and to destroy him forever. The Senate provided the power and will of the people of Rome and all Varro and Paullus had to do was to unleash their hordes of revenge-seeking legionaries. Differences of opinions between Roman commanders must have commonplace, yet they and their senior officers would have debated every single aspect of operations prior to combat. Many scholars have cautiously followed the lead of the ancient sources in viewing Varro as unwilling to listen to wiser or more experienced council, and as we shall see, Varro had opportunities to engage Hannibal earlier but chose not to do so. Yet however we view the Roman commanders, ultimately the highest Roman leadership bears much responsibility for any failures or successes.

On July 29, Varro, in command, broke camp and advanced. Hannibal responded with light troops and cavalry to harass the advance. The Romans contained the Carthaginians comfortably by supporting their own light troops with heavy infantry as well as cavalry. Polybius notes that the Roman light and heavy troops fought intermixed.[27] Night ended the early round of skirmishing on the first day. The Roman advance probably covered a couple of kilometers, before they again fortified their position for the evening only a short distance from the Carthaginian camp across the river.

On the morning of July 30, Paullus took command of the army from Varro. We are told by Polybius that Paullus faced two problems. The first was that the surrounding terrain was still too advantageous to the Carthaginian cavalry and therefore it was not ideal for the Romans to offer battle. Second, Paullus believed the Roman Army could not withdraw in the face of the enemy.[28] He reasoned that his men, while decamping, could be harassed by the Carthaginian light troops and the Numidian light cavalry until Hannibal's main force engaged them in a battle on not just unfavorable terrain, but more importantly while the Romans were in disorder.

Potentially this could be disastrous, but even more calamitous than going down in a fight would be withdrawing in the face of an enemy, thereby incurring the shame and wrath of the Roman people and Senate. The morale of the ordinary soldier would have reached a new low.

Paullus therefore decided to pitch a camp with two-thirds of his army on the bank of the River Aufidus, while the remaining third of the legions "fortified a position on the far side of the river to the east of the ford. This was situated nearly a mile and a quarter from his main encampment and rather further from that of the enemy."[29] The intended purpose was to forage as well as harass Punic foragers. The Carthaginians had to cross the river to do this. The main opposing camps were less than 2km apart. Peter Connolly notes "the positioning of the camp on the south bank now makes sense: it is to stop Hannibal foraging on that side of the river and is clearly part of the overall Roman strategy. This makes nonsense of the theory that the two consuls were in bitter conflict."[30] Some time during the day, and probably in response to Roman movement, Hannibal moved his entrenchments to the same side as the larger Roman camp.[31] Immediately after the Romans established the smaller second camp, Hannibal exhorted his men to have confidence, stressing the favorability of the battle ground and also reminding them that they had already defeated the Romans in three consecutive battles at Ticinus, Trebbia, and Lake Trasimene.[32]

Romantic lithograph of Hannibal's famed crossing of the Alps. (Author's Collection)

A 19th-century lithograph of the battlefield of Cannae. The River Aufidus would have changed course substantially from the time of the battle. (Author's Collection)

One of the most interesting points from the narrative of the ancient sources is Paullus' hesitancy in withdrawing his army. However reasonable his concerns may have been, he would have fully aware of instances in which this had been successfully accomplished in the past by other forces.[33] Therefore, given that the Romans had driven off a Carthaginian attack of skirmishers and cavalry, they could easily have withdrawn if they had felt it necessary. Caution was prudent, as the Roman commanders were well aware of Hannibal's use of ruses and ambushes, which had destroyed an army under the generalship of Gaius Flaminius at Lake Trasimene in 217 BC. Paullus and Varro must have felt confident in a straightforward battle, however, and saw no need to retreat or for a hasty engagement. One wonders, though, how Hannibal managed to move his entire army across the Aufidus to build his entrenchments without being harassed or put into disorder by the Romans.

In any event, the next morning Hannibal issued orders to his command staff to prepare the army for deployment on the following day, August 1, 216 BC. Foraging was always going to be difficult and the sooner he could bring the Romans to battle the better for his army. The Romans under Varro did nothing. The Carthaginian general duly offered battle on the morning of August 1, but Paullus, now in command again, refused to deploy his army to fight. Instead he increased the guards at the two Roman camps. Hannibal withdrew his forces, relying on the Numidians to harass the Roman foragers at the smaller camp. In fact, they were so audacious that the North

African light cavalry rode straight up to the palisades, only for the Romans to remain behind their entrenchments. Such actions must have had a terrible impact on the morale of the Roman soldiers and their allies. There is little worse for soldiers than inaction and having to suffer through the insults of their enemies, as Polybius notes.[34] The time for battle, however, was at hand.

INTO BATTLE – THE ROMAN DEPLOYMENT

On August 2, the Roman Army finally advanced under the command of Varro. It crossed the Audifus, probably some time after sunrise, and deployed facing south. There is controversy regarding the exact location of the river, as it has shifted its course over time and thus scholars have argued for varying locations. For our purposes, it is sufficient to follow Polybius' account that the Romans crossed the river and that it flanked the Roman Army's right wing. The Roman cavalry under Paullus anchored the right flank at the river bank, next came the tactical units, the *maniples*, of the Roman and allied legions from the main camp, followed in line by the maniples of the smaller camp. Finally the Roman left flank was anchored by the larger allied cavalry under Varro. The light troops, the *velites*, were spread out in front of the army.[35]

The Roman Army, anchored on each flank by cavalry, set up on the battlefield in a pattern similar to a three-deep checkerboard. The infantry proper was composed of three ranks. The front rank, made up of some of the youngest men, were the *hastati* (spearmen, though they were using the throwing *pila* and not spears), and traditionally were equipped with *scuta* shields. For body armor they wore a square metal chest plate and a helmet as well as a metal shin guard, a greave, common to all legionaries, on their leading left leg. For offensive operations, the hastati carried possibly two *pila*, one lighter than the other, and the sharp sword commonly known as the *gladius* for close-in work. The second rank was the *principes* (chief men), who were slightly older and were similarly armed, though some of them may very well have been wearing mail body armor. The *triarii* (third-rank men) comprised the last line of the legion and here stood the veterans of Rome. Older and more experienced, these men carried 2.5–2.7m-long spears, wore mail and helmet and carried a *scutum*. Their personal side arm was also the short sword common to all legionaries. One can hardly imagine the experience of an enemy who cut his way through the two first Roman lines then having to face the hedgehog of triarii spears. The cavalry was most likely rather small, composed of well-to-do Romans who could afford the purchase and maintenance of the animals. In front of the army were the young and poor, the *velites*, armed only with throwing spears and small round shields.

The traditional Roman legion numbered roughly 4,000–4,200 men, of which 200–300 comprised the cavalry. There were ten maniples (units) of each of the line: hastati, principes, and triarii. Each unit had an approximately 20-man front with six ranks deep, totaling 120 hastati or principes. The triarii were half that size, comprising three ranks. In effect 3,000 heavy infantrymen, 1,000 light troops, and 200–300 cavalry represented a regular legion strength. Each maniple was administratively subdivided in two *centuriae* equal in strength. The front *centuria* was called the *centuria prior* and the rear one the *centuria posterior*.[36]

As we have seen, the legions at Cannae had been bulked up and the traditional Roman legion's tactical disposition consequently changed. "Here," Polybius writes, "the maniples were grouped more closely than in their formation, so that the depth of each was several times greater than its width."[37] Connolly, among other modern-day scholars, argues that each maniple presented a five-man front with a 30-man depth – in effect 150 legionaries per maniple, with the extra men sent to be velites.[38] Gregory Daly also favors the straight-across-the-board addition of manpower, bringing each maniple to about 144 men and the Roman legion then presenting a table of organization that includes 300 cavalry, 1,520 velites, 1,440 hastati, 1,440 principes, and the 600 triarii.[39] One can argue, however, that given the significance of Rome's decision to end the war with one battle, the additional manpower might very well have been evenly distributed between the principes and hastati, as they were the ones who would decide the engagement. It seems not unreasonable to assume, therefore, that the additional 800 men per legion were distributed among the first and second lines. The 'super maniple' may have numbered 160 hastati or principes. These maniples retained a 20-man front, but were eight ranks deep. Be that as it may, the important point to address is that the maniples were grouped closer and their depth was many times their width because of the terrain. We can assume, figuratively, that the maniple simply turned 90 degrees and presented an eight-man front with 20 ranks deep.

The reasoning behind this compact front is open to several interpretations. First and foremost, the Romans anticipated a straightforward brawl. There was not going to be anything sophisticated about this battle from the Roman perspective and tactical flexibility or maneuvering was not necessary. Instead, they were going to rely on the historical strength of their infantry and were simply going to crush the enemy with superior numbers. Second, the deployment was affected by the narrow battlefield. The Roman commanders chose the battlefield and it suited their needs. Historians estimate the length of the battle line to have between 1 and 1.6km long.[40] A longer line would have allowed a 1,100-man front rank, with each Roman legion occupying approximately a 100m front, three lines and at least 50 men deep, based on 55,000 total infantry, excluding velites.[41] Connolly also believes the infantry frontage to have been about 1,500m, but the entire frontage to have required 3km and hence the battle line shifted diagonally, facing south as Polybius notes, to accommodate the ranks of men.[42]

If the deployment of the legions was restricted by the terrain, then we would expect that the Roman staff had conducted reconnaissance and realized the restrictions. It would be hard to believe that an army would simply march out of its entrenchments and haphazardly form up. The mounting pressure of Numidian raiding parties, however, may have forced the Romans into action sooner than preferable. The Roman commanders were aware of the ambushes that had previously destroyed their legions, and a plain was their preferred choice to prevent any repeat of such engagements.[43] This was also the largest army ever fielded by Rome, so its commanders may very well have felt the need to stay compact in order to maintain control.

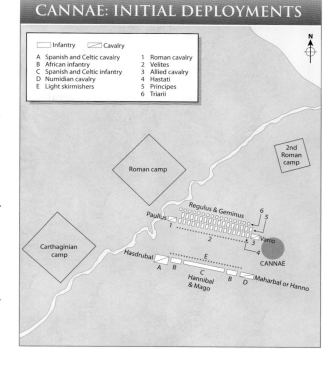

CANNAE: INITIAL DEPLOYMENTS

Infantry   Cavalry

A Spanish and Celtic cavalry
B African infantry
C Spanish and Celtic infantry
D Numidian cavalry
E Light skirmishers

1 Roman cavalry
2 Velites
3 Allied cavalry
4 Hastati
5 Principes
6 Triarii

The Roman Army that faced the Cathaginians must have presented an awesome sight. The far Roman right, anchored at the river, was comprised of 2,400 Roman cavalry commanded by Paullus himself. Next to them were the Roman and allied legions from the big camp. The allied legions may well have flanked each Roman legion as was customary, meaning the heavy infantry line may have started with an allied legion closest to the Roman cavalry, then two Roman legions, followed by another allied legion, thus retaining the traditional organization of a consular army. Alternatively, the deployment may well have alternated between Roman and allied units.[44] The line continued with the Roman and allied infantry from the second, smaller camp, who previously had to endure the taunts of the Numidian cavalry harassing their foragers. According to Polybius, the Roman center was commanded by Regulus and Servilius; the latter had done a commendable job in shadowing Hannibal's army and training the Roman legions. Goldsworthy notes, however, that Regulus was recalled to Rome just prior to the battle.[45] The allied cavalry guarding the left flank was under the command of Varro and fielded about 3,600 horse according to the ancient sources. The controversy over cavalry numbers has already been noted, and in general terms the allied cavalry ought to have been three times the size of the Roman cavalry. Nonetheless, according to Polybius 80,000 infantry and 6,000 cavalry were available to the Romans. Of that number about 10,000 were used to garrison the two camps and these troops may have consisted of one Roman and one allied legion, thus leaving 14 legions to deploy on the plains of Cannae. Lazenby believes that the Roman right wing under Paullus probably consisted of the 2,400 Roman cavalry, and one Roman legion and one allied legion. The 10,000 legionaries left behind to guard the camps were also under Paullus' command. Paullus was not just in command of the cavalry. Lazenby further argues that the center of the Roman main battle line, commanded by Geminus, was composed of veteran legionaries who had already seen action against Hannibal in Apulia and Campania under these commanders. The left wing featured two powerful consular armies, including allies as well as the 3,600-strong allied cavalry under Varro.[46] In essence, each commander officered his own units to maintain leadership continuity throughout the battle line. Mosig and Belhassen argue that it was Roman elitism that placed the Roman cavalry in the position of honor, the right wing, instead of splitting their cavalry, explaining "If the Romans had divided their total cavalry into two equal forces, deployed on either side of the field, the outcome of the battle might have been quite different. But they predictably placed the smaller elite Roman force on the right, and Hannibal was able to deploy against them the heavy Celtic and Iberian cavalry under Carthaginian officer Hasdrubal, outnumbering them by more than two to one, and practically assuring victory on that side."[47]

THE CARTHAGINIAN DEPLOYMENT

Once Varro had ordered his legions to cross the Aufidus, Hannibal deployed. The Carthaginian staff were doubtless competent and capable enough to have had contingency plans in place for the Roman move, as Daly points out: "Although the regular troops are described as being surprised by the Romans being led out, Plutarch attributes no such surprise to Hannibal, who calmly ordered his men to prepare for battle and then rode with some companions to a nearby vantage point to study the Roman dispositions."[48]

The Carthaginian general ordered his slingers and spearmen to cross the river in order to cover his army's advance. The Punic Army, so Polybius writes, crossed the Aufidus at two spots and deployed in battle formation. On the left flank, directly opposite Varro's Roman cavalry, the Spanish and Celtic cavalry commanded by Hasdrubal took up position, "Closer to the centre were placed half the Africans, then the Spanish and Celtic infantry, next to them the other half of the Africans, and finally on his right wing the Numidian cavalry."[49] Hannibal and his brother Mago directed the main battle line and the Numidian right wing was led by Hanno. At Cannae, the Carthaginian cavalry numbered 10,000 strong and the infantry "not much above 40,000," the vast majority being mercenary Celts and Spaniards.[50]

The Roman Army faced south and the Punic one north. Connolly argues the battle lines were at an angle to accommodate the narrow frontage of the armies dictated by the terrain[51] with "neither side disadvantaged by the sun," as Polybius notes.[52] The Romans, though, "were troubled by the Volturnus, a south-east wind, blowing in their faces."[53] Both armies were also wet from the river crossings. Nevertheless, both were determined to exterminate their opponents.

The Deployment Controversy

At this point in the battle analysis, there is an interesting controversy. The Punic Army formed in a straight battle line behind the protection of the pikemen (spearmen) and light skirmishers. According to Polybius:

> Hannibal at the same time sent his slingers and pikemen over the river and stationed them in front, and leading the rest of his forces out of camp he crossed the stream in two places and drew them up opposite the enemy. On his left close to the river he placed his Spanish and Celtic horse facing the Roman cavalry, next to these half his heavy-armed Africans, then the Spanish and Celtic infantry, and after them the other half of the Africans, and finally, on his right wing, his Numidian horse. After thus drawing up his whole army in a straight line, he took the central companies of the Spaniards and Celts and advanced with them, keeping the rest of them in contact with these companies, but gradually falling off, so as to produce a crescent-shaped formation, the line of the flanking companies growing thinner as it was prolonged, his object being to employ the Africans as a reserve force and to begin the action with the Spaniards and Celts.[54]

It is unclear which troops composed the screening elements covering the deployment of Hannibal's army. If the Liby-Phoenician units were the pikemen (spearmen) Polybius mentions, then they must have numbered between 10,000–12,000 heavily armed men, bearing Roman equipment; Polybius mentions that the army still included 12,000 Africans when it entered Italy, and certainly some of them must have become casualties of Trebbia and Lake Trasimene. But more important than their numbers is whether or not they were part of the screen. Connolly interprets the African pikemen as being on either side of the slingers while covering the deployment, then retreating behind the cavalry and forming into a phalanx on either side of the main battle line.[55] The pikemen and skirmishers then must have numbered approximately 18,000–20,000, literally half of the infantry's total, if the general consensus of 8,000 slingers is accepted and the infantry total included the 8,000. Even if the 8,000 slingers were in addition to the 40,000 infantry, it would still seem disproportionate to have so large a force as a covering screen even if they faced a larger Roman skirmishing force of perhaps 15,000. Hannibal also had to guard his camp, and thus his infantry numbers may have been further depleted. It is impossible to know for certain, and so there has to be some reliance on Polybius and his numbers at this point.

It seems difficult to imagine 10,000–12,000 armored men, possibly with pikes, being able to move behind the Carthaginian cavalry units anchoring the flanks in so limited a space without, as Connolly states, a good chance of collision and disaster. Let us suppose, however, that the Liby-Phoenician units eventually anchored the flanks of the skirmish line, if they were not intermingled as Connolly argues. It is also possible that these units were not directly in the path of their own cavalry as the main battle line started to form, because they and the skirmishers did not occupy the entire front. Such is in contrast to Connolly's argument that favors a complete screen in front of the

A hypothetical depiction of the Roman legions' deployment on the plains of Cannae. (Author's Collection)

main battle line. Instead the African formations could have stood their ground as the main battle line fell into place to the rear. The line then moved forward between the African units while simultaneously the skirmishers withdrew to the rear of the line. It is possible that the Liby-Phoenician units served as field markers for the Punic Army. Once the main battle line was formed to Hannibal's satisfaction, he then advanced the center units forward to create a crescent-shaped formation. The center then passed beyond the African flanking companies as it formed its bulge.

Many historians have argued that the pikemen were a completely different unit to the African heavy infantry. Daly proposes that the covering spearmen were not a racially homogeneous unit.[56] Lazenby too believes the skirmishers to have been specialty troops numbering about 11,400, leaving 28,600 for the main battle line with 10,000 African and 6,000 Spaniards from his original army and the remaining numbers being composed of Celts.[57] Certainly these more lightly armed skirmishers could easily fight intermingled with the slingers and it seems more reasonable to assume that in fact these spearmen provided the extra muscle for Hannibal's screen. Behind this screen, the Spanish/Celtic cavalry was on the far left flank next to the river, then one-half of the African heavy infantry, dressed similarly to the Romans, followed by the Spanish and Celtic center units, the remaining half of the Africans, and lastly the Numidian cavalry on the far right flank. Lazenby believes that the spearmen and slingers aided the subsequent flank attack.[58] They could also have been ultimately instrumental in presenting a reserve line.

Several historians who believe the Liby-Phoenicians to be part of the main battle line have placed their units in rectangular formations, with the shorter side facing the Romans, although Polybius makes no mention of their particular depth or formation. Hans Delbrück claims that these units were deployed in column, behind the cavalry, to reinforce the center or flank the opponent.[59] Adrian Goldsworthy depicts the Liby-Phoenicians in column as well.[60]

We do not know whether the Carthaginian heavy infantry carried spears, pila, or pikes. The weapons they carried would necessarily have informed the battle

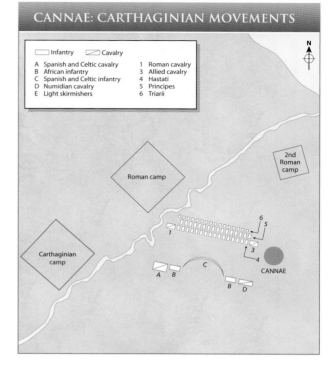

CANNAE: CARTHAGINIAN MOVEMENTS

Infantry   Cavalry

A Spanish and Celtic cavalry   1 Roman cavalry
B African infantry   3 Allied cavalry
C Spanish and Celtic infantry   4 Hastati
D Numidian cavalry   5 Principes
E Light skirmishers   6 Triarii

Roman camp

2nd Roman camp

Carthaginian camp

CANNAE

formation, as would the terrain upon which they were arrayed. Polybius does not mention their deployment, and historians have suggested several different possibilities.[61] What we do know is that they were divided into two distinct units, flanking the center composed of Spaniards and Celts.

Hannibal's infantry numbered 40,000, including 11,400 skirmishers. Although Polybius says the two African units totaled 12,000 at Cannae, it seems likely that the 12,000 who had reached Italy would have been reduced by the time of Cannae, due to the previous major battles they had fought. If they presented a very narrow front as many scholars suggest, then the majority of the battle line would have been manned by around 18,600 men. One meter per man would indicate roughly 1,860 to the front and ten deep, allowing for the cavalry and the narrow Liby-Phoenician units to occupy the remaining spaces on either flank. Lazenby's much shorter frontage would allow a main battle line of approximately 900 men across by 20 men deep. He argues that the Africans covered in total the same frontage as two Roman legions and that they were much deeper in formation, as they were to be the jaws of the trap. The rest of the Carthaginian line covered the remaining five Roman legions, including allied infantry, and thus leaving the Spanish and Celtic central units at about half the depth of the legions they were facing.[62] If the main battle line was that shallow, then it is possible that the Punic light troops could literally stand behind the main battle line and hurl their spears at the Romans engaged in hand-to-hand combat. They had only a dozen or so yards in distance to cover and if, as some scholars have argued, the effective range of a Roman *pilum* was 30m then the Carthaginian light troops could have launched numerous salvos unmolested. In Lazenby's interpretation, the main battle line would have stood more than 20 men deep, which may very well have prevented any volleys by the skirmishers to their rear.[63]

Hannibal's army first deployed in a straight line, as Polybius does not note a deeper formation of the African heavy infantry. The entire frontage was likely to have stretched 3km, with one full kilometer needed to accommodate the cavalry, leaving the infantry about 2km to accommodate fewer than 30,000 men. The entire center would have stretched thinner as the crescent occupied more space, more so on the flanks then the center companies – this configuration makes sense as the central, most forward, units were to bear the brunt of the fighting. We also know that Hannibal advanced the central line forward while the Liby-Phoenicians stayed in place, never advancing across the main line of departure during the battle. Thus the African infantry presented a reserve that would crush the Roman maniples in a vice grip from their respective flanks.

THE BATTLE

The battle opened with thousands of light skirmishers engaging one another. Slingers, armed with a variety of stones for varying distances, unleashed deadly salvoes while others threw or jabbed their spears. Occasionally, courageous light-armed men clashed. Often these skirmishes are dismissed too quickly as ineffective or trivial parts of an ancient battle. Yet we should not underestimate their significance, for they started the engagement proper and could ease the nerves of the armies while simultaneously setting the tone for the clash – a bad showing here could affect the morale of the troops behind. Not engaging the opposing skirmishers would certainly allow them to inflict far more casualties on the front rank of the main infantry. The skirmishers must also have participated in the removal of the wounded and dead whenever the opportunity presented itself. Perhaps they even re-emerged to the front later in the battle when the battle lines reformed or were replaced by the second rank, buying valuable time for their comrades to reorganize their ranks. Some scholars have argued that these troops may well have supported flanking units. It would be hard to accept that the skirmishers performed no other role in battle then to initiate contact.

The Roman Army advanced methodically toward the Punic lines as the light troops disengaged and disappeared back within the bowels of their respective forces. It is quite possible that at this time, once the velites were absorbed within the army, the hastati closed ranks by shifting their rear centuries to fill in the gaps and thus presented a solid unbroken battle line to the enemy. The hastati launched their pila within a few dozen meters of the enemy units, who in turn launched their own spears if they had any. Once the pila were discharged, the hastati front rank drew their swords and closed with the enemy or met the enemy's charge. Nic Fields suggests that once the battle was joined, the fighting lines were in it for the long haul:

> ...to disengage in active hand-to-hand combat is almost a no-no. So, second and third lines would reinforce the existing fighting line when needed. Remember, the art of a good Roman commander was to judge when to commit his reserve lines. Of course, if your fighting line broke, you hope the second and third held firm, survivors of the first being scooped up, if all things are equal of course, as they passed.[64]

The maniples engaged the crescent-shaped Spanish and Celt/Gaul units one after another. Much like a shock absorber, the attacking maniples' blows were cushioned by successive engagements. There was no single clash of the entire line. It is unclear whether or not the entire line of the Roman heavy infantry closed with the staggered Punic units – in effect hugging the entire line in a corresponding crescent shape. For doing so would certainly have exposed the flanks of some Carthaginian and Roman units, if in fact the individual units did not constitute one continuous crescent-shaped line. It would make sense that the Roman battle line only advanced forward far enough to allow contact with the outermost units of Hannibal's Celts and Spaniards. In fact, as the battle progressed individual Spanish and Celtic units withdrew, and as the line straightened out more and more maniples and Celt-Iberian units became engaged, and thus the initial clash was not cohesive. Polybius writes that "the Carthaginian centre and wings did not go into action at the same moment."[65]

Once contact was made, the fighting probably ebbed and flowed for a short while, as no man could conceivably engage in hand-to-hand combat for very long. Eventually, however, the entire main battle lines of the opponents were locked together in combat. The battle of heavily armed legionaries versus mostly naked Gauls and some Spaniards was in its opening stages when the 6,500 Spanish and Celtic cavalry under the Hasdrubal advanced on the left against Varro's cavalry on the Roman right. The resulting fight was "truly barbaric."[66] Polybius gives the modern reader an insight into the nature of cavalry warfare at the time when he notes that there was none of the formal advance and retreat. Instead the sides met, dismounted, and fought man to man. Most of Varro's Romans were killed, though they "resisted with desperate courage."[67] The survivors were driven off along the riverbank where they were being slaughtered by the pursuing Carthaginian cavalry. Paullus, though defeated, rejoined the center command where the battle needed to be won – at least that's what the Romans had hoped. The charge led by Hasdrubal was a desperate one, but it was crucial to the success of the overall Carthaginian battle plan. In effect, by Hannibal's advancing and then withdrawing the central line, he bought valuable time for his Spanish and Celtic cavalry to rout the Roman horsemen. Once they had done so, they could continue with their mission to disperse the allied cavalry on the other flank as well, and then to return to the battle in the fight against the superior legions. Hasdrubal's 6,500 men were needed against the Roman juggernaut.

As the cavalry clashed on the flanks, the Roman heavy infantry had moved up into close quarters, and for a while the combined Spanish/Celt center held and "fought with great gallantry but then they turned tail, forced back by the sheer weight of the legions and the convex centre of the Carthaginian line was driven in."[68]

The Romans surged "forward triumphantly and easily pierced the enemy's front, since the Celts were extended in a thin line."[69] On the Roman right, the Roman cavalry had been defeated but here in the center overwhelming force seemed about to bring them a decisive victory. No doubt the pressure of the hastati and principes took its toll on the hard-pressed Carthaginian center. And it seems, according to Polybius, that the center units turned tail, broken by the power of the legion. Yet this turn of events might not be as straightforward as it seems. There are three key components worth reexamining in some more detail: First, the center of the Punic Army; second, the outermost Spanish units; and third, the Liby-Phoenician heavy infantry.

The mainly Celtic troops in the Punic center gave a good account of themselves for some time during the battle, until they fled. Polybius does not mention their return to the battlefield, yet they must have done so otherwise the Romans surely could have repeated another escape, as some 10,000 had done during the battle of Trebbia where they cut their way through the weak center. Hannibal and Mago were stationed in the middle of the battle line from the beginning of the clash. A pure rout by the Celts would have seen the Carthaginian leadership swept up with them, thereby creating panic among the other troops and providing an escape route for the legionaries. Conversely, the Romans could have reformed and charged back into the fray, thereby destroying the remaining Spanish and Liby-Phoenician units. Mosig and Belhassen write that "the Carthaginian center did not break, and reversed its

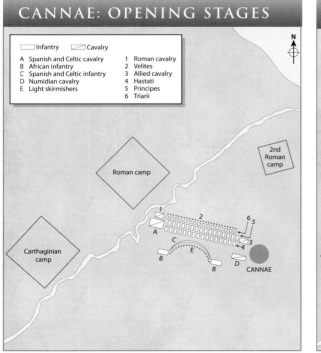

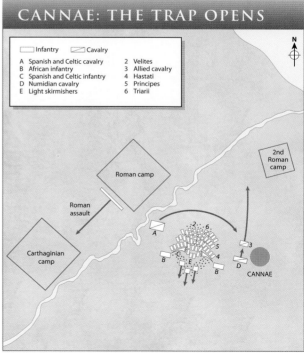

retreat as the Roman Army became gradually immobilized."[70] It is a likely possibility that Hannibal, on command, ordered a retreat of his center at a crucial time during the battle, and reformed them to plug the gaping hole subsequent to the charge of the African *phalangites*. And since Polybius does not mention any reserves per se, other than the Africans, we can argue that the slingers and other light Carthaginian troops harassed the forward-surging legionaries and presented a line that was ultimately reformed with the Celts. This reformed line then prevented the Romans from continuing their surge forward, or from reforming, turning about, and charging into the exposed flanks of the Liby-Phoenician veteran troops, who at this point had advanced and engaged the maniples.

Some historians have argued that the skirmishers and slingers enveloped or aided the flank attack of the Liby-Phoenicians. Delbrück, in fact, stipulates that the Punic lights joined Hasdrubal's cavalry in their attack on the Roman rear and were instrumental in obstructing further movement forward by the entire army.[71] There are many possibilities for their subsequent use. For example, the light troops could have divided, the slingers supporting the flanks of the Africans and harassing the legionaries, forcing them to move toward the crowded center, while the skirmishers stayed behind as a reserve line to plug the gaping hole vacated by the fleeing Celt-Iberian companies. It makes more sense to argue, however, that these skirmishing units fought together cohesively and prevented the Romans from rolling up the remaining Carthaginian units.

Although the Carthaginian center seemed to have given way, events further out were rather different. The wings composed of other Celt-Iberian units continued to absorb the pressure of the maniples they faced. The African units, which were nearest to the cavalry flanks, seem not to have become engaged in the battle at this point, perhaps because the crescent was so far to their front. If the Liby-Phoenician units were only lightly engaged or even not at all, the remaining Spanish and Celtic units closer to the center certainly held firm. "The Romans were pursuing the Celts and pressing inwards against that part of the front which was giving way, they penetrated the enemy's line so deeply that they then had both contingents of the African heavy infantry on their flanks."[72] Maniple after maniple of the rear ranks followed the path of least resistance and advanced through the Carthaginian main line. Other maniples continued their hand-to-hand combat facing the remnants of the enemy's central line.

It is possible that, flushed with excitement, even senior men and officers encouraged this mass pouring through the enemy line. Paullus must have arrived at some time before the collapse of the Punic center and if not he, then certainly the experienced consuls, ought to have taken better charge. And what of the triarii?

Veterans should have known better. Yet the canvas of the battlefield is painted by many brushes. Each individual action is part of the overall outcome. Perhaps we are too harsh on the Roman leaders, expecting less emotion and more discipline on the field of battle. Most legionaries would not have known that the Roman cavalry was destroyed on the right flank, that the center had pierced the main Carthaginian battle line, and that the allied left cavalry wing was skirmishing with the Numidians. Perhaps they only knew to move forward as they heard a great shout from their comrades. Victory seemed at hand.

As the Roman soldiers rushed toward the center and lost their cohesion, the remaining Spanish and Celtic units further away from the center stayed and fought. Indeed we can argue that it was these troops who pivoted, forcing the Romans more into the center as the furthest Spanish units advanced into the open spaces yielded by the Romans rushing forward. In effect, the Spanish units closest to the center were also slowly giving ground, as their most outward units advanced into the spaces being vacated by the legionaries (or at least they did not give way). In effect, the Spanish units were becoming swinging doors. The Roman lines were thinned out due to casualties, exhaustion, and the simple fact that their replacements were moving toward the center and not toward their front. By implication, the Spanish units closest to the Africans either stayed in place or advanced as they encountered less resistance. Consequently, these troops enveloped ever so slightly the legions' outermost maniples, encouraging or forcing the remaining Romans toward the hole in the center.

The collapse of the center and the eventual arrival of the Carthaginian cavalry probably caused some of the Roman maniples in the rear to move together, further helping the Spanish units to execute pincer-like movements by sheer default. They and the cavalry shut the back door on the Roman Army. Certainly, the maniples must have attempted to spread out to reorganize or to seek out any enemy once they punched through the enemy's main battle line. Paullus was in the center, for Polybius notes that "he saw that the outcome of the battle was likely to be decided by the legions."[73] If this was prior to the massive Roman surge, Paullus too must bear responsibility for the ill-disciplined forward movement of the legions. What seems most likely is that the specialty skirmishers, possibly including the slingers, presented a reserve component that either formed a line or harassed and thus slowed down the Roman push. In either case, the African blocks of 5,000 men each were to be Hannibal's reserve, according to Polybius:

The Romans, however, following up the Celts and pressing on to the centre and that part of the enemy's line which was giving way, progressed so far that they now had the heavy-armed Africans on both of their flanks. Hereupon the Africans on the right wing facing to the left and then beginning from the right charged upon the enemy's flank, while those on the left faced to the right and dressing by the left, did the same, the situation itself indicating to them how to act. The consequence was that, as Hannibal had designed, the Romans, straying too far in pursuit of the Celts, were caught between the two divisions of the enemy, and they now no longer kept their compact formation but turned singly or in companies to deal with the enemy who was falling on their flanks.[74]

The Liby-Phoenicians never advanced past the main line of battle. According to Lazenby's interpretation, the Africans turned individually, dressed ranks, and attacked. In fact, they did not wheel into action.[75] F. W. Walbank describes the commands given to the Africans as: "Right (left) turn! Dress ranks on the left (right)!" and that these commands "were enough to bring the Libyans [Africans] into a position to attack the Romans on the flank."[76] The Liby-Phoenicians presented something like a 330-man front by 15 or 16 deep, probably divided into companies. These companies then executed an immediate action drill via a facing maneuver and then fell into line, presenting yet again a 300-man front toward the Roman legionaries flooding through the Punic center.

The Liby-Phoenician blocks flanking the Spanish and Celtic center companies were certainly veteran units capable of complex maneuvers. Polybius does not say that they advanced forward and then turned inward to attack the legionaries, though many battle schematics show this type of tactical movement.[77] The intentional withdrawal, if indeed it was that, spurred the African units into action.

Numbers were still on the side of the Roman Army, as maniple after maniple flooded forward, but now they were hit hard in their flanks. It is hard to imagine the terror of the legionaries, who were now cruelly exposed on their sides. The scutum was carried on the left arm and the Romans on that side had a few more minutes to live, as their flank was protected. The Roman legions on the right side of the surge must not have been so lucky. On both flanks of the surge, veteran African troops, heavily armored and in orderly fashion, clashed with the disordered maniples of hastati and principes. And if, as Connolly argues, they were pikemen, then they must have presented a wall of sharp steel pointed pikes, crushing everything in their paths until their long weapons became useless and they resorted to the short swords. Even without pikes, these veteran units executed their facing movement expertly. Connolly believes the Punic light troops flooded around the flanking African troops and assaulted the Roman Army's rear, but this seems rather implausible, as the center of Hannibal's army was wide open and needed some kind of obstacle to slow down the

Romans for ever so brief a moment to allow the reformation of the fleeing or withdrawing central Spanish and Celtic companies.

The most important discussion concerns the Carthaginian deployment on the main battle line and subsequent movement. Polybius says they turned inward, implying a facing maneuver. Hannibal realized from previous engagements that his center was the weak point for enemy forces to punch through, and thus effectively escape the trap he had carefully laid out. It seems reasonable to argue that the Liby-Phoenicians executed an about-face and wheeled into position, although Lazenby (among many) disputes this based on the technical terminology used by Polybius to describe their movement.[78] Approximately 20,000 Spaniards and Celts composed the battle line no more than 2km long, and they then advanced, thinning out the flanking units. The African units on the far flanks provided additional strength and experience to aid their immediate neighboring Spanish companies in case the Romans assaulted them sooner rather than later. The Africans numbered 5,000 per block. There are two possibilities for their intended purpose; one theory is that the Africans were supposed to execute pincer movements when needed against the flanks of the Romans, the other theory is that they were tactically positioned to support the center should it give way unexpectedly, as Polybius notes their use as a reserve. Once the center started to give way, the African blocks only had to face inward and advance, joining in the middle to form a single line of 10,000 veterans. Most scholars favor Polybius' interpretation, which maintains that: "the result was exactly what Hannibal had planned: the Romans by pressing too far ahead in pursuit of the Celts were trapped between the two divisions of Africans."[79] Hannibal had laid a trap and intended to use his

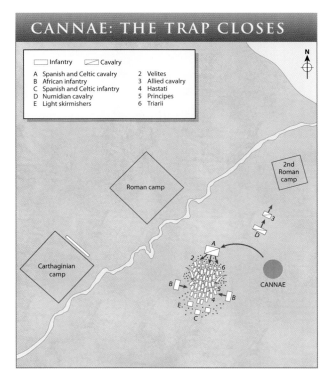

CANNAE: THE TRAP CLOSES

Infantry   Cavalry

A Spanish and Celtic cavalry   2 Velites
B African infantry   3 Allied cavalry
C Spanish and Celtic infantry   4 Hastati
D Numidian cavalry   5 Principes
E Light skirmishers   6 Triarii

Roman camp

2nd Roman camp

Carthaginian camp

CANNAE

veterans to deal the Romans a crippling blow, buying enough time for his cavalry to sweep away their opposition and in turn encircle the Roman Army with as many men as he could possibly use. Ultimately, the only thing that mattered was that they executed a drill and slammed into the forward rushing legionaries. How they deployed and achieved this remains controversial.

Meanwhile, on the Roman left the Numidians skirmished with the large allied cavalry force, "attacking them from one quarter and now from another."[80] They did so until Hasdrubal with the exuberant Spanish and Celtic cavalry approached, having virtually destroyed all Roman horsemen they had encountered earlier. The allied cavalry under Varro fled the field. "He [Hasdrubal] saw that the Numidians had the superiority in numbers" and left them to deal with the pursuit as "they were at their most effective and formidable when they had the enemy on the run."[81] Hasdrubal wheeled his cavalry around and returned to the main battlefield where he supported the hard-fighting Africans by "launching a number of charges from several directions [and] he at once put fresh heart into the Africans and dealt yet another blow to the sinking spirits of the Romans."[82] Polybius recounts a bitter and difficult fight up until this point. So the battle could still have been won by the Romans, even though they were attacked on their flanks, and quite possibly had to deal with Carthaginian skirmishers and the rallied central companies. The Punic cavalry did not charge into the masses, but their arrival probably forced the Roman legionaries either to attempt to flee in small groups, which were easily destroyed, or to seek safety in numbers by clustering together, further encumbering the fighting ability of the packed mass of the legions.

Whatever the intended purpose of the Africans, the battle was in the balance until the arrival of the Carthaginian cavalry. It seems reasonable to assume that Hannibal and Mago intended for the center to give way, but then the Celtic units reformed and reentered the fight, presenting a battle line supported by light troops to the front of the Roman legions, which were now being attacked from all sides.

The Romans were unable to maintain a front as their outer ranks, including Paullus himself, were cut down. Simultaneously the Numidians pursued the fleeing allied cavalry. The detail of Polybius' narrative is stark:

Attacking the Roman legions in the rear and delivering repeated charges at various points all at once, he raised the spirits of the Africans and cowed and dismayed the Romans. It was here that Lucius Aemilius [Paullus] fell in the thick of the fight after receiving several dreadful wounds, and of him we may say that if there ever was a man who did his duty by his country both all through his life and in these last times, it was he. The Romans as long as they could turn and present a front on every side to the enemy, held out, but as the outer ranks continued to fall, and the rest were gradually huddled in and surrounded, they finally all were killed where they stood, among them Marcus and Gnaeus, the consuls of the preceding year, who had borne themselves in the battle like brave men worthy of Rome. While this murderous combat was going on, the Numidians following up the flying cavalry killed most of them and unseated others.[83]

The 10,000 Romans left to guard Paullus' camp had been ordered to attack Hannibal's entrenchments if he failed to protect them. Once battle commenced the Roman guards assaulted the Carthaginian camp, but were held off until the end of battle when Hannibal came to the rescue. The Romans fled back to their camp where they were captured. Subsequently, the Numidians "stormed various strongholds in the district" and captured 2,000 cavalry, who must have been allied cavalry as the majority of the Roman cavalry arm lay dead on the Aufidus river bank. Varro escaped to Venusia with 70 out of 6,000 Roman cavalry, and 300 allied cavalry managed to escape as well. Some 10,000 Roman infantry were captured, 3,000 escaped, and 70,000 died. Lazenby, by contrast, concludes that the casualties suffered were:

> 45,00 Roman infantry killed along with 2,700 cavalry, 19,300 enemy prisoners of war comprised of 4,500 captured on the field, 2,000 who fled to Cannae and 12,800 from the two Roman camps. 14,550 escaped. Several commanders died including Paullus, Geminus and Rufus, as well both the Consul's Quaestors, 29 out of 48 tribunes and no fewer than 80 senators or expected to become senators were killed as well.[84]

Mosig and Belhassen conclude, based on the real number of Roman and allied cavalry being far greater than Polybius likes us to believe, that it is indeed probable that 70,000 Romans died on the battlefield.[85] "At Cannae, as in previous encounters, it was the superior numbers of the Carthaginian cavalry that contributed most to the victory, and the battle demonstrated to posterity that it is more effective to have half as many infantry as the enemy and an overwhelming superiority in cavalry than to engage him with absolutely equal numbers."[86] A total of 4,000 Celts, 1,500 Spaniards/Africans, and 200 Carthaginian cavalry died. Certainly in comparison to Roman casualties these numbers are small, but in the overall scheme of the Carthaginian strength these casualties were nearly impossible to replace.

A few days later, a Roman Army under Lucius Postumius was annihilated by Cisapline Gauls in an ambush, but yet Rome stood firm and refused to sue for peace.

Only Rome could survive such an unmitigated disaster. Instead more armies were raised and the slaughter continued for years to come, ending only after another battle of annihilation, this time on the continent of Africa.

ZAMA, 202 BC

The final epic battle of the Second Punic War (218–201 BC) was fought on the North African continent west of Carthage. Zama-Naraggara has been generally accepted as the site for the battlefield, although J. F. Lazenby believes it to be near the town of El Kef.[1] The battle pitted the visionary Carthaginian commander Hannibal and a ragtag army against Publius Cornelius Scipio, the leader of a veteran Roman force and of new-found Numidian allies. Hans Delbrück writes that:

> Naraggara is the first battle in the history of the world in which we find echelon tactic significantly and decisively applied in the conduct of the battle as a great, newly discovered principle. In the echelon formation the tactical units are placed one behind the other, far enough apart so that each can move independently, near enough so that they can directly support each other.[2]

BACKGROUND

Meaningful analysis of Zama (as the battle is generally known) is made very difficult by the ancient accounts of the battle. The problem is discussed by several scholars, among them Mosig and Belhassen, who view the existing accounts as being propaganda for the Romans. Rome's humiliation at the hands of Hannibal at Cannae required an equally great humiliation of the Carthaginian general at Zama. In the records that was done by manipulating the numbers of the combatants to favor the Carthaginians and by presenting Scipio as the tactical genius.

Hannibal had waged a campaign from 218 BC until 203 BC in the heart of the Roman territory, without ever suffering defeat in a major battle. He was able to sustain his campaign with limited support from Carthage, a city he had left before he reached his teens. Hannibal had sacrificed all in his endeavor to keep Carthage safe from Roman imperial desires. He had been wounded, suffered the loss of an eye, and had mourned the death and decapitation of his brother Hasdrubal at the battle of Metaurus in 207 BC. Hannibal also lost his youngest brother Mago, who succumbed to wounds obtained in battle at Cisalpine, while en route to join Hannibal in North Africa in 202 BC. Yet Hannibal was unyielding in his efforts to effect a peace with Rome through the force of arms. He knew that only his presence in Italy assured the safety of Carthage.

At long last, after having lost the early strategic initiative to Hannibal, Rome subdued the Iberian peninsula and felt secure enough to launch an attack into the heartland of their rival. In 204 BC Publius Cornelius Scipio took his veteran army, composed of Cannae survivors who had waged a successful campaign in Sicily, and invaded Carthaginian land. Scipio understood that by invading the North African continent and by controlling the sea lanes he would have the strategic and tactical advantage over Hannibal. The Carthaginian general would stop being a threat to the city of Rome and would have to leave the majority of his army behind in Italy to face Scipio with unknown local troops near Carthage.

Fear of the Roman invasion spread throughout the countryside. The Carthaginians were able to muster two armies prior to Hannibal's arrival, both of whom were defeated by Scipio and allied Numidians in 203 BC. One army was destroyed during a daring night-time raid after peace negotiations had started. Although one often reads Roman accounts about Punic Faith, meaning a promise one cannot trust, Scipio's actions speak louder than any Roman propaganda. Mosig and Belhassen describe Scipio's night-time attack on the Punic camp as "one of the most treacherous attacks recorded in human history."[3] Scipio's delegates had mapped out the rival camp from their visits, and then when the Carthaginians were expecting an imminent settlement, he launched an attack. The camp was set alight, and as the unarmed soldiers emerged from their tents to put out the fires, the Romans cut them down. As Mosig and Belhassen conclude:

So much for good faith and "Roman fides." Through fire and sword, the unarmed and defenseless Numidians and Carthaginians were slaughtered by the thousands. No honor could be attached to such treachery, but Roman historiography tries to justify the actions of their hero by stating that he feared some Punic trick, and that he had indicated that the negotiations were off prior to the sneak attack, both highly unlikely.[4]

Another Carthaginian force was annihilated at the battle of the Great Plains, when the Romans executed a double enveloping maneuver against raw Liby-Phoenician recruits whom Livy describes as a "half-armed mob of peasants hastily collected from the fields."[5] Lazenby says that at this battle the hastati pinned or held in check the enemy front, "while the principes and triarii moved out to the left and right and fell upon the their [enemy's] flanks."[6]

Meaningless peace negotiations by Rome and Carthage then yielded little, as Carthage had anxiously recalled Hannibal earlier – although blaming him publicly for the war, he was their only hope. The usually impotent Carthaginian fleet had raided Roman vessels as well during the talks. War was to be had no matter which side may or may not have violated the supposed peace treaty.

THE ROMAN ARMY

Scipio's army was in part composed of the disgraced veterans of the battle of Cannae. The Senate of Rome argued that prior to Cannae the Roman legionaries were lacking in quality – how else, in their view, could the Romans have lost? Scipio had escaped the slaughter and so must have been more sympathetic to the losers' plight than most Romans. After Cannae, the two surviving Roman legions were banned from mainland Rome and waged a successful campaign in Sicily, redeeming their tainted status. Lazenby notes that "they were the most experienced soldiers in the Roman Army, and Scipio knew that Cannae had not really been lost through any cowardice of theirs – having served with them at that battle, he may well have had a fellow-feeling for them."[7]

The size of the Romano-Numidian Army remains unknown. Traditionally, a Roman legion normally comprised 4,200 infantry and 200–300 cavalry, and an allied legion offered the same number of foot soldiers but 600–900 cavalry. A consular army, featuring two Roman and two allied Italian legions, would be no less than 16,800 legionaries and at least 1,600 horsemen. A Polybian legion (a Roman legion as described by Polybius) was composed of 3,000 infantry, 1,000–1,200 skirmishers, and 200–300 Roman cavalry. Adding to this total the lowest numbers of Numidians – 6,000 foot and 4,000 cavalry – we arrive at 22,800 for the foot soldiers and 5,600 for the mounted contingent. This would be the lowest theoretical size of Scipio's Romano-Numidian Army. Hence the consular army technically could not have exceeded 20,000 in paper-strength terms.

At Cannae the Roman legions numbered well over 5,000 per legion, and perhaps for the North African campaign the legions were bulked up as well. Lazenby deduces the total numbers for Scipio's army to have been 28,000 foot and 6,100 horse.[8] Livy states:

as to the number of troops ... there is considerable divergence among the authorities. I find that some state it to have amounted to 10,000 infantry and 2,200 cavalry; others give 16,000 infantry and 1,600 cavalry; others again double this estimate and put the total of infantry and cavalry at 32,000 men. Some writers give no definite number, and in a matter so uncertain I prefer to include myself amongst them.[9]

Lazenby's argument rests on the assumption that a greater number of allied troops stationed in Sicily accompanied Scipio's African Army. Struggling with the different numbers given by Livy, he argues that 10,000 Roman infantry, 600 Roman cavalry,

Stele on Carthage's Tophet. One of the few remaining artifacts at the site of the ancient city. (Courtesy of Bishkek)

16,000 allied infantry, and 1,600 allied cavalry totaling 28,200 Italians were part of Scipio's consular army and that the legions were roughly 5,000 in strength, not the 6,200 foot Livy mentions as well.[10]

It is documented that Masinissa, a Numidian prince and master of horse, son of Gaia, king of the Maessylii, brought the aforementioned 4,000–6,000 horse (Polybius mentions 6,000 whereas Livy lists 4,000) along with 6,000 Numidian foot soldiers. Assuming the higher number for Masinissa's Numidian cavalry, the Roman/Numidian forces at Zama would have totaled 32,000 foot and 8,200 horse, subtracting casualties incurred during their campaign prior to the battle at Zama. Perhaps there was an additional legion, perhaps the legions were bulked up just like they had been prior to Cannae. A conservative estimate would be that at least 30,000 foot and 6,000 cavalry were present for the engagement. Polybius' silence on the size of the Roman Army is interesting. When considering this and other points of his narrative it is important to consider his relationship with the Cornelian clan. There is no doubt that the Roman general's victory was important and decisive but there is lingering doubt about the reality of the numbers and the undercurrent of Scipio's greatness in this campaign.

Scipio was a fortunate man for despite his relatively small army, he was able to exploit internecine Numidian conflict to shift the loyalty of some Numidians away from Carthage. The Numidian switch gave Scipio the best cavalry force in the world, under Masinissa.[11] Scipio's cavalry and infantry forces were to play the most important part in the battle of Zama. After the meaningless peace negotiations with Carthage, Scipio

> sent message after message to Masinissa explaining how the Carthaginians had violated the treaty, and urging him to mobilize as strong a force as possible and make haste to join him. Masinissa started out with his own troops reinforced by 10 cohorts of Roman infantry and cavalry together with officers provided by Scipio. His purpose was not only to recover his ancestral kingdom, but with the help of the Romans to annex that of Syphax [king of the Masaesylians in Numidia], as well, and in this aim he eventually succeeded.[12]

Polybius' account of Scipio's desperate pleading for Masinissa's support shows how truly awe-inspiring Hannibal's projection of power was to the Roman general, despite Hannibal's weaker forces. Scipio felt he needed all the support he could muster, no matter how inferior the hastily assembled Punic Army was.

Cavalry was the key to many of Hannibal's victories according to the ancient sources, and cavalry again would prove to be the ultimate combat multiplier.

Scipio's army was not as grand as that of the super army destroyed at Cannae some 14 years earlier, but his cavalry arm was to be far superior. The victorious Numidian usurper Masinissa, who had earlier fought against the Romans in Spain, seized the opportunity to rid himself of Carthaginian influence, and added an additional 6,000 foot and 6,000 horsemen, or 4,000 if we are to take Livy's numbers, to Scipio's legions.

THE CARTHAGINIAN ARMY

Hannibal left mainland Italy in 203 BC after 15 years of vigorous campaigning. He took with him a force of approximately 12,000 veterans to fight for a city he loved, but a city that did not love him back.[13] The campaign waged on the North African continent by Scipio was brutal. Towns willing to surrender were not permitted to do so but were reduced to nothing, with their citizenry sold into slavery. This was the beginning of the Phoenician holocaust which only ended in 146 BC. Hannibal must have known that he had a near impossible challenge. There was pressure from the leadership at Carthage for Hannibal to force a battle. He could certainly rely on his veterans, but the rest of the army seems to have been composed of ill-trained levy and mercenaries, and there simply was not enough time to train them.

Cavalry was also hard to come by as the internecine struggle had split apart the Numidians, as Polybius describes:

> Hannibal at this time was very poorly off for cavalry and sent to a certain Numidian called Tychaeus, who was a relative of Syphax, and was thought to have the best cavalry in Africa, begging him to help him and join in saving the situation, as he knew well that, if the Carthaginians won, he could retain his principality, but if the Romans were victors, he would risk losing his life too, owing to Massanissa's [Masinissa] greed of power. Accordingly, Tychaeus was prevailed on by this appeal and came to Hannibal with a body of two thousand horse.[14]

By the time Hannibal clashed with Scipio, the latter had the superior cavalry force, as Masinissa "brought under his rule all of Syphax's former subjects."[15] Hannibal was unable to transport his valued cavalry from Italy to North Africa and the bulk of the Numidian cavalry, so valuable on the plains, were now allies of Rome.

In general terms, the army of Carthage that Hannibal had to lead was not a cohesive one and was of variable quality. Furthermore, whereas at Cannae Hannibal had commanded some 140,000 to 150,000 soldiers, here on the North African continent near Zama-Naraggara fewer than 80,000 were available. The battle of

Zama was arguably far more important on a strategic level, but, despite what was recorded in the surviving historical Roman records, did not compare in scale to the battle of Cannae.

MARCH TO ZAMA-NARAGGARA

The Punic Army under Hannibal marched toward the town of Zama that lay five days west of Carthage. From this base of operations, Hannibal reconnoitered the surrounding area. A small reconnaissance detachment (Polybius calls them spies, since they were Carthaginians) attempted to spot the location and composition of the Roman camp and army, but it was compromised. Death was normally the reward for failed spies, but Polybius writes: "Scipio was so far from punishing them, as is the usual practice, that on the contrary he ordered a tribune to attend them and point out clearly the exact arrangement of the camp. He furnished them with provisions and an escort, and told them to report carefully to Hannibal what had happened to them."[16] The supposed kindness of Scipio may very well have been a ruse to show a much smaller army to the Carthaginian spies than the one he would ultimately field on Zama. Hannibal was so struck by Scipio's behavior that he requested a meeting to discuss the situation. It was from his fortified position at Naraggara that Scipio agreed to a meeting with Hannibal, who in turn advanced his army to within 6km from the Roman camp. The Carthaginians encamped on a hill, but it "was rather too far away from water, so that his men suffered much hardship from this disadvantage."[17] Perhaps Hannibal was aware of the hostile Numidian cavalry's range and abilities, and so decided to encamp in a safe location, rather than one where water was more accessible. Possibly he was also aware of the night-time attack by the Romano-Numidian force a year earlier.

The meeting between Hannibal and Scipio has attracted much examination by modern scholars. What could have motivated Scipio to meet Hannibal? Surely there was no interest in avoiding battle – too much was at stake for Scipio's political and military career as well as the future of Rome. Perhaps mutual respect was the sole reason for the meeting, if indeed it occurred. Polybius describes in detail how the two men met alone, apart from interpreters. Hannibal spoke first and at length, finally coming to his request:

> Consider this, I beg you, and be not overproud, but take such counsel at the present juncture as a mere man can take, and that is ever to choose the most good and the least evil. What man of sense, I ask, would rush into such danger as that which confronts you now?

> If you conquer you will add but little to the fame of your country and your own, but if you suffer defeat you will utterly efface the memory of all that was grand and glorious in your past. What then is the end I would gain by this interview? I propose that all the countries that were formerly a subject of dispute between us, that is Sicily, Sardinia, and Spain, shall belong to Rome and that Carthage shall never make war upon Rome on account of them. Likewise that the other islands lying between Italy and Africa shall belong to Rome. Such terms of peace would, I am convinced, be most secure for the Carthaginians and most honourable to you and to all the Romans.[18]

Scipio then replied, saying that if Hannibal had suggested these terms before the Romans had crossed to Africa, then perhaps they could have been agreed, but now the situation was very different, especially as the Carthaginians had violated the peace: "What remains to be done? Put yourself in my place and tell me. Shall we withdraw the most onerous of the conditions imposed? That would be to reward your countrymen for their treachery and teach them to continue to betray their benefactors."[19] Scipio concludes "Of what further use then is our interview? Either put yourselves and your country at our mercy or fight and conquer us."[20]

It all sounds so grand and so majestic – sworn enemies, each representing their culture and respective masters, meet one another and agree that Rome was in fact the victim of Carthaginian aggression. Bearing in mind the Roman origin of this account, presented as it is by Polybius and Livy, the reality of the whole exchange seems questionable, as Mosig and Belhassen argue:

> Before Zama, Hannibal and Scipio had never met directly, either in battle or in a face to face encounter. Roman historiography constructed an anecdote suggesting that Hannibal asked Scipio for a personal conference prior to the battle, and Polybius as well as Livy pretend to transcribe in detail what was said, although neither was there. The exchanges reported are probably imaginary – at least some parts are patently absurd – and the meeting itself is of doubtful historical authenticity.[21]

Whatever the reality of the meeting, on October 19, 202 BC, the fate of Carthage and Rome was to be determined.

THE ROMAN DEPLOYMENT

Data concerning the orders of battle at Zama are sketchy. What we do know from Livy is that the V and VI legions deployed to Africa with a core of survivors from the battle of Cannae. These men probably formed the lines of the older men, the principes and triarii, while the hastati must have been filled with men from the Sicilian campaign. Fourteen years is a long time for soldiering, and it seems very reasonable to assume that the front ranks, the hastati, were not participants at Cannae.

Scipio's consular army, seems to have had a total of four legions, including two allied Italian ones. In addition, one reinforced legion-sized Numidian infantry formation probably anchored the far right infantry flank. At Cannae, the Roman maniples were many times greater in depth than in front, because of their size. At Zama, by contrast, Rome fielded a far smaller army and there were no significant terrain limitations. An open plain this time favored the Romans and their superior cavalry arm. In Polybius' Book XV, which only exists in fragments, Scipio's Romano-Numidian deployment is described:

> Scipio drew up his army in the following fashion. In front he placed the hastati with certain intervals between the maniples and behind them the principes, not placing their maniples, as is the usual Roman custom, opposite to the intervals separating those of the first line, but directly behind these latter at a certain distance owing to the large number of the enemy's elephants. Last of all he placed the triarii. On his left wing he posted Gaius Laelius with the Italian horse, and on the right wing Massanissa with the whole of his Numidians. The intervals of the first maniples he filled up with the cohorts of velites, ordering them to open the action, and if they were forced back by the charge of the elephants to retire, those who had time to do so by the straight passages as far as the rear of the whole army, and those who were overtaken to right or left along the intervals between the lines.[22]

We are not told in what order the Roman and allied legions were stationed and what frontage they occupied. If the two Roman legions with their Italian counterparts formed the main battle line, they could have been arranged Roman, allied, Roman, allied. Alternatively, B. H. Liddell Hart writes that "Scipio placed his heavy Roman foot – he had probably two legions – in the centre; Laelius with the Italian cavalry on the left wing, and on the right wing Masinissa with the whole of the Numidians, horse and foot, the latter presumably prolonging the centre and the cavalry on their outer flank."[23]

At Cannae the difficulties of tightly packed maniples fighting and employing their pila, swords, and shields effectively were apparent. How then was a Roman maniple to fight under more or less normal circumstances? In his comparison of the fighting styles of the Roman soldier with the typical Macedonian phalanx, Polybius gives us a clearer understanding of the legionary's spatial requirements:

Now in the case of the Romans also each soldier with his arms occupies a space of three feet in breadth, but as in their mode of fighting each man must move separately, as he has to cover his person with his long shield, turning to meet each expected blow, and as he uses his sword both for cutting and thrusting it is obvious that a looser order is required, and each man must be at a distance of at least three feet from the man next him in the same rank and those in front of and behind him, if they are to be of proper use.[24]

Each normal-strength maniple of 120 men occupied roughly 1m per man with a 20-man front, but Polybius states that in order to be effective in combat, each legionary must be at a distance of at least 3 feet from the man next to him, and those before and behind him. This can be interpreted to give either 2m frontage per soldier, or 3m frontage per soldier. Given a 20-man front per maniple, this would mean that at Zama each maniple occupied a front of either 40m or 60m and thus each Roman legion with an equal distance between each maniple throughout required a 800m or 1,200m frontage. Four normal-sized legions would have had a front of 3,200/4,800m if they fought in open order. Many scholars argue in favor of the posterior 60-man centuria filling in the gaps left in between the maniples. In effect, they stipulate that the 120-man maniple, which has two distinct sub-units of 60 men each, centuriae, was capable of maneuvering as separate units and, hence, capable of filling in the gaps. The complete maniple is stationed in the front line, then the velites on command retreat in the gaps between the maniples throughout the battle lines. Once the velites pass the first line, the second centuria of each maniple moves to the side and to the front to fill in the gaps, forming a complete unbroken line facing the enemy. This flexibility allows the second line, the principes, also to move in similar fashion to either reinforce the front line of hastati or to allow them to withdraw and build an unbroken second line.

John Warry has an excellent schematic of the Polybian army in action. Here he describes his version of the Roman battle system:

1 The legion forms up, *hastati* and *principes* in open order, *triarii* in close order. The gap between lines might vary between 0 and 250ft (0–76m). The *velites* skirmish and distract the enemy. When all is ready the *velites* are recalled and pass through the open ranks to the rear.

2 The prior centuries of *hastati* move right and the posterior centuries advance to form a solid line. At about 150yds (137m) both sides charge. The front ranks of *hastati* throw their light *pila* at about 35yds (32m) from the enemy, quickly followed by their heavy *pila*. They draw swords and close up on the run and hit the enemy with as much impact

as possible. Succeeding ranks throw *pila* over the front ranks. The battle is a succession of furious combats with both sides drawing apart to recover. This might go on for several hours.

3   During one of these pauses the *hastati* are given the recall. The posterior centuries back away and the prior centuries slide across in front of them. Then the *maniples* of *hastati* withdraw in close order, to reform behind the *triarii*. Meanwhile the principes move up in open order and pass trough the hastati. The enemy is unable to take advantage as a continuous front is presented.

4   The posterior centuries deploy to the left of their prior centuries, the *principes* manoeuvre to within charging distance and the tired enemy is faced with a fresh foe and another fierce charge.

5   If the enemy is not broken before the *principes* too are exhausted, then their place is taken by a thin (3 deep) line of *triarii* spearmen.

6   The army can now withdraw or prepare to start again. The phrase "*Indem rem ad triarios redisse*" ("The last resource is in the *triarii*") passed into the language as a description of a desperate situation. Naturally not all battles went "by the book…"

7   Against a pike phalanx the second and third lines were used to give weight to the front ranks in an attempt to resist the push of the 16 deep phalanx. The beauty of the system was that its flexibility allowed the lines to adapt to differing situations.[25]

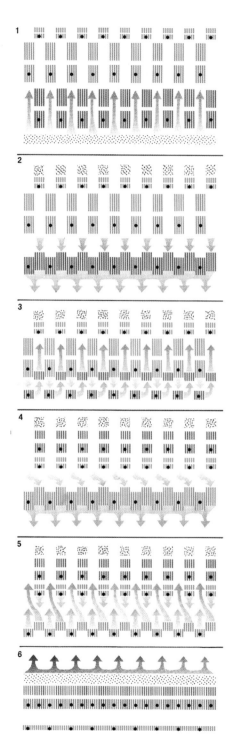

Battle order diagram from J. E Lendon's *Soldiers and Ghosts*.

	Velites
	Triarii
	Principes
	Hastati
	Posterior century
	Prior century

This system certainly looks brilliant, although nobody knows for certain how the Romans maneuvered in battle. (Polybius tells us that the front ranks were not supported by the rear ranks against the phalanx.) Yet this tactical maneuver would be a massive challenge during battle, for as we will see at Zama, the battlefield was littered with debris and dead and wounded men – the slippery surface created by their spilled blood would make any complex maneuvering nearly impossible. J. E. Lendon presents an intriguing graphic of a Roman legion, with the hastati and principes assembled in a loose formation, whereas the triarii are more in an orderly phalanx formation. It seems possible indeed that the hastati and principes fought in a more loose formation. In his book, Lendon emphasizes the individual martial tradition of Rome. He too, however, remains puzzled about the complexities of intra-legion movement in early Roman warfare: "The brevity of the surviving descriptions of the manipular legion presents notorious and ultimately insurmountable obstacles to understanding exactly how the legion operated in action."[26]

Bearing in mind the frontage figures described above, we can infer that the Roman legions may have started with 1m per legionary. Yet as the legions advanced to engage the enemy, the legionaries spread out, allowing them to discharge their pila then draw swords and engage in hand-to-hand combat. This open-order fighting system makes allowances for a tiring legionary to be immediately replaced by his comrade behind him. It would seem impossible to replace individuals or entire maniples in tighter formations. In the open order of battle, each legionary can withdraw when wounded or exhausted more easily. It would still allow his comrade behind to throw his *pilum* and then advance to replace the soldier to his front. In effect, it seems plausible to say that manipular warfare at this time may very well have been less rigid and standardized and far more loose and flexible than previous warfare, allowing for braver men to fight in the front and retreat when tired or wounded.

If, on the other hand, the Polybian Roman legions did not form solid lines, then one can argue that the average maniple with a 20-man front still required 2m/3m per man spacing, but that the gaps were not filled unless needed and then the second line maniples normally stationed behind those gaps would advance and close those spaces. The enemy was unlikely to advance into the gaps because they would become isolated on three fronts: the hastati on either side and the principes to their front.

At Zama, Scipio deployed his army in an unorthodox way. No longer did his legion present a checkerboard formation to the enemy. Instead they moved the second line of principes "at some distance directly behind" the hastati and directly in

Fantastical painting of larger-than-life elephants beginning their assault on the Roman lines at Zama. The predominance of elephants at the battle is the subject of much debate. (Author's Collection)

front of the triarii, thereby creating uninterrupted lanes in between the maniples which in turn were filled by the velites.[27] Each gap in between the maniples held approximately 40–60 of these light-armed troops.[28] The intended purpose for these gaps was to counter Hannibal's war elephants. The distance between the first line of the hastati to the second line of the principes may have been larger than normal to allow for greater maneuverability if Scipio decided to use the second rank in a flanking movement, as he had done on earlier battles.

Whatever the number of the Roman and Numidian soldiers, and whatever the actual frontage, the Italians and Numidians were veteran troops with high morale fresh from their recent victories. Also, the impact that a core of seasoned Italian troops wanting to purge themselves of the shame showered on them after Cannae could have during the battle should not be underestimated.

THE CARTHAGINIAN DEPLOYMENT

Polybius describes Hannibal's deployment very simply: more than 80 elephants to the front, behind them a line of 12,000 mercenaries, behind them Liby-Phoenicians, and the third and last line composed of his troops from Italy. The left wing was made up of loyal Numidian horsemen, while the Carthaginian horse were on the right.[29]

In contrast Delbrück argues for two lines only, possibly believing the first line to be skirmishers, but Polybius is clear enough in his line of reasoning.[30]

According to ancient sources there were supposedly over 80 elephants at Zama.[31] They were to be battering rams of the Carthaginian Army, and their intended purpose was to throw the Roman infantry into disorder. Professor F. E. Adcock summarizes the use of elephants in ancient battles:

Generals were slow to despair of elephants. They loom large through the mists of war; but they are not a talisman of victory. In fact, if all the battles in which they appear are examined, they are found more often involved in defeat than in the forefront of success. The seductive modern suggestion that they are the tanks of ancient warfare does them more than justice. And it may be appropriate to observe that when skillfully assailed

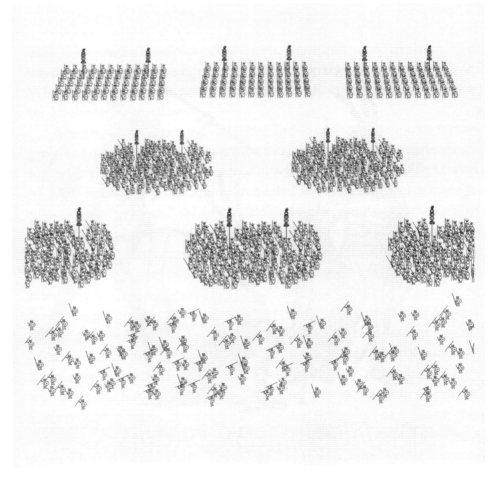

Battle formation diagram from John Warry's *Classical Warfare in the Ancient World*, "The manipular legion." Velites (front), maniples of hastati followed by maniples of principes, and maniples of triarii.

they may go into reverse, as in attack on a Roman Army in Sicily in the First Punic War. And they were prone to panic and might trample down their own men, as at Magnesia. They were, indeed, chancy combatants and needed to be very skillfully controlled by their drivers.[32]

Adcock concludes that their most striking successes in infantry battles were against troops that had never seen an elephant before.

There is some doubt over the authenticity and accuracy of the ancient sources, Livy and Polybius. Mosig and Belhassen argue that far fewer, if any, elephants were present at the battle, and they are not the only scholars to have concluded this. Delbrück as far back as 1920 argued that the "number of elephants was much smaller than the Romans stated, but at any rate it was too small for Hannibal to have based his hopes on them."[33] And again, it was the Roman historians' need to supersede the legacy of the battle of Cannae which led to the exaggeration of Scipio's victory.[34]

This is the moment at the battle of Zama where some of the elephants became frightened and ran amok, possibly crashing into their own cavalry wings on both flanks. (Author's Collection)

According to Polybius, the elephants were supported by a line of various tribes, including Ligurian, Celtic, Balearic, and Moorish mercenaries.[35] The last two were armed with slings and throwing spears. Sometimes this first line of 12,000 mercenaries is discussed as though it were a solid line of infantry, the first of three facing the Romans. Liddell Hart points out that this first line was not entirely composed of light troops.[36] They had several weapons systems in place in the form of slingers, spearmen, and line infantry, and would have made an excellent skirmish line. We have seen at Cannae a similar combination of troop types, though better trained, covering the deployment of the main army, where they were instrumental in slowing down and decimating the Roman juggernaut. At Zama, however, we must assume that this first 12,000-man line was there to support the charge of the elephants, but also to exploit any advantages gained by the elephant assault. Since recent scholarship suggests that few elephants were present at Zama, Hannibal's first line also needed to serve a similar purpose to that of the Celt-Iberian troops at Cannae, whose function was to serve as an anvil absorbing the blows of the first line of the Roman hastati.

The second line featured Libyans and Carthaginians as well as 4,000 Macedonians, mentioned in Livy's account. Perhaps the Macedonians were a formation of pikemen, or they may very well have simply been mercenaries trained to fight with swords as their primary offensive arm. Some scholars have even cast doubt on whether they were present at the battle at all.

The strength of this line has also been put at 12,000. This calculation is based on 40,000 Punic soldiers – 20,000 killed and an equal number captured by the end of the battle – with the third Carthaginian line being equal to the combined remnants of the Roman three lines. Since the combined line of hastati, principes, and triarii, may have numbered fewer than 12,000 by the time the two sides clashed, most scholars have assumed a Carthaginian triple line of 12,000 each, with the third line perhaps filled and extended with the survivors from the first and second lines and numbering up to 20,000. It would not be unreasonable to assume that the second line composed of Libyans and Carthaginians was smaller than the first line comprised of mercenaries, because Carthage did not have a standing army. Indeed Carthage was known for her employment of mercenaries. And we ought to recall that two of their armies had been previously defeated and fewer men were available to recruit. The idea of triple 12,000-men lines, then, is suspect.

It can be assumed that Hannibal, upon being recalled from Italy, took along with him 12,000 of his veteran troops based on their near-equal strength with the Italian last main battle line. Hannibal's last line is said to have equaled the entire Roman and Italian allied army, excluding Masanissa's Numidians, as Polybius does not mention them in the infantry battle, but who were positioned to the right in the traditional place of honor. Although the strength of Scipio's army is disputed, the Roman final line can have been no fewer than 10,000 excluding the velites, and could have been closer to 20,000. We are told that the Italians suffered 1,500–2,500 casualties and Masanissa's Numidians suffered more. The bulk of these casualties probably happened during the final fight with Hannibal's third line. The veteran third line was filled on its wings by the survivors from the first and second line.

The exact composition of the Punic third line is unknown, but we can assume that most were infantry and included a majority of Bruttians, southern Italians, where Hannibal had been campaigning for a number of years. Hannibal's third line was most certainly composed of his veterans. How many of his original army remained is unknown, but some of them had accompanied him over the Alps and fought at Trebbia, Trasimene, and Cannae as we know from Hannibal's pre-battle address preserved by Polybius.[37] It is reasonable to say that the cream of Hannibal's army was being saved for last.

On Hannibal's left wing he placed his best cavalry, the Numidians, to oppose Masinissa's Numidians and on the very right flank the Carthaginian cavalry was stationed opposite the entire Roman and Italian allied horse, who were commanded by Gaius Laelius. We know that Hannibal received at least 2,000 Numidians and that

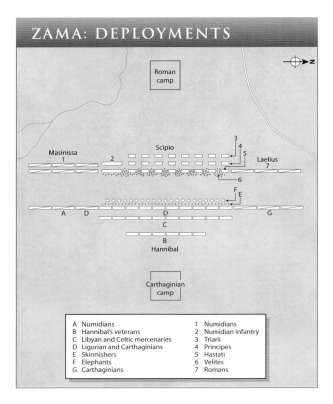

ZAMA: DEPLOYMENTS

A	Numidians
B	Hannibal's veterans
C	Libyan and Celtic mercenaries
D	Ligurian and Carthaginians
E	Skirmishers
F	Elephants
G	Carthaginians

1	Numidians
2	Numidian infantry
3	Triarii
4	Principes
5	Hastati
6	Velites
7	Romans

Scipio's army fielded up to 6,000. Furthermore, the Roman and Italian allied cavalry must have had a paper strength of 2,400, though probably less. The Carthaginian cavalry, possibly a polyglot force including Bruttians and Iberians, was smaller and part of the 12,000 men Hannibal brought from Italy, or could have been part of Mago's units as Nic Fields proposes.[38] Delbrück estimated the whole of Hannibal's cavalry to have numbered between 2,000 and 3,000.[39]

At Cannae, the cavalry had been crucial to Hannibal's victory, but at Zama, Scipio had the superior cavalry force. Scipio could count on the Numidians to fight for their lives, which were definitely at stake should they lose. Scipio could rely on his Italian allies as always – they had not deserted Rome after Cannae. The indigenous Roman troops were highly trained and professional. Scipio's army was thus one of the best that Rome had ever fielded. By contrast, Hannibal could only count on his veterans to perform to the standard that had sustained them for over 15 years. Despite Polybius' attempts to persuade his readers otherwise, the advantage was clearly not with Carthage.

THE BATTLE

The armies stood ready, having marched out of their respective camps earlier in the day, the Punic force perhaps dehydrated from lack of water. Polybius includes speeches made by both Scipio and Hannibal to their men. Scipio chose rousing words:

> Keep it before your eyes that if you overcome your enemies not only will you be unquestioned masters of Africa, but you will gain for yourselves and your country the undisputed command and sovereignty of the rest of the world. But if the result of the battle be otherwise, those of you who have fallen bravely in the fight will lie for ever shrouded in the glory of dying thus for their country, while those who save themselves by flight will spend the remainder of their lives in misery and disgrace.[40]

At Cannae Hannibal had addressed his troops altogether, but at Zama the disjointed nature of his army forced him to find another way:

> He ordered each commanding officer of the mercenaries to address his own men, bidding them be sure of victory as they could rely on his own presence and that of the forces that he had brought back with him. As for the Carthaginians, he ordered their commanders to set before their eyes all the sufferings that would befall their wives and children if the result of the battle were adverse. They did as they were ordered, and Hannibal himself went the round of his own troops, begging and imploring them to remember their comradeship of seventeen years and the number of the battles they had previously fought against the Romans.[41]

With speeches made, it was time to fight. On Scipio's right, and Hannibal's left, the cream of the world's light cavalry began skirmishing in their traditional manner – a quick charge here, a discharge of javelins, the retreat, and so on. Masinissa's 4,000–6,000 Numidians fought against the 2,000 Numidians of Tychaeus who were still loyal to Carthage. We do not know if Masinissa's 6,000 Numidian foot supported the

cavalry clash. It seems unlikely, for Scipio needed manpower on the infantry field of battle. Perhaps the legion-sized Numidian foot fought and anchored the right wing of Scipio's Roman and allied legions. Some scholars have placed the Numidian foot as a reserve behind the triarii. This positioning seems highly unlikely, as we are told that all the Numidians deployed on the far right of the Roman consular army. On the opposite wing, the 2,400 Roman cavalry under Laelius fought against a smaller cavalry force comprised of Bruttians and Iberians. Hannibal needed his cavalry to buy him as much time as possible. He knew that they would not tip the battle as at Cannae. Instead Hannibal decided that his infantry had to take the day.

The Numidian skirmish had been going on for a short while when, according to ancient sources, Hannibal unleashed the elephants. He ordered them to charge the Romans. It seems difficult not only to accept the supposed numbers of the elephants present, but also that Hannibal somehow didn't see

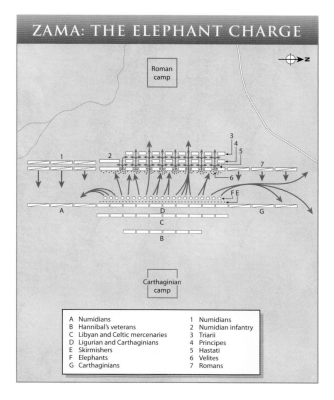

ZAMA: THE ELEPHANT CHARGE

A Numidians	1 Numidians
B Hannibal's veterans	2 Numidian infantry
C Libyan and Celtic mercenaries	3 Triarii
D Ligurian and Carthaginians	4 Principes
E Skirmishers	5 Hastati
F Elephants	6 Velites
G Carthaginians	7 Romans

the gaps between the Roman maniples which, according to Polybius, were designed as lanes for the elephants to pass through. The entire account of the charge seems simplistic and again designed to present the tactical genius of Scipio. It is highly likely that Hannibal conducted a leader's reconnaissance or had scouts reconnoiter the Roman battle formation. Hannibal, or one of his staff, must also have known if the elephants were not accustomed to war, as seems likely, for they had not been used in any previous battle. It seems haphazard to have used them, and not just because of their lack of experience, but also because the army Hannibal was facing was one composed of veterans and a significant number of Numidians who were accustomed to elephants. Perhaps Scipio ordered his maniples to create the lanes after the cavalry skirmish had begun, thus deceiving Carthaginian eyes. The entire account of the elephant charge must be viewed with a great deal of suspicion. Mosig and Belhassen correctly point out that:

> The charge of the presumed elephants supposedly opens the battle, but we are told that they were frightened by loud noises, shield clashing, trumpets, and what not. This also does not make much sense. Ancient battles typically started with loud yelling, shield banging, and other forms of intimidation, and consequently a major part of the training of animals to be used in attacking enemy positions would have consisted of accustoming them to such sounds.[42]

From Polybius' account it seems certain that most of those elephants present were not trained to participate in combat. It was said that the noise of the battle frightened some of them to such a degree that they turned and collided with their own Numidian cavalry, which had advanced forward while skirmishing. How Hannibal's Numidians advanced to support the Carthaginian attack while skirmishing remains difficult to explain. Perhaps, as was the custom, during the reconstitution of the cavalry arm Hannibal's Numidians advanced more aggressively to support the elephants and the first line of mercenaries, while, simultaneously, Masinissa's men charged again. It seems odd that two cavalry units skirmished but only one was affected by the frightened animals. The rest of the elephants

> ...falling on the Roman velites in the space between the two main armies, both inflicted and suffered much loss, until finally in their terror some of them escaped through the gaps in the Roman line which Scipio's foresight had provided, so that the Romans suffered no injury, while others fled towards the right and, received by the cavalry [Laelius' Roman and allied cavalry] with showers of javelins, at length escaped out of the field.[43]

Mosig and Belhassen write that Polybius' description of the use of these elephants "does not hold up against logical scrutiny," as "Since the animals carried mahouts on their backs, in addition to one or more armed warriors, and the animals were trained to respond to the commands or pressure of their riders, they would surely have been steered to one side or the other to trample men at the edges of any such corridors." They also note that the mahouts carried hammers and spikes to kill out-of-control elephants, so it is not credible that the elephants would have been allowed to turn against their own side.[44]

The elephants that fled toward Laelius' cavalry arm were hit by numerous javelins and "it was at this moment that Laelius, availing himself of the disturbance created by the elephants, charged the Carthaginian cavalry and forced them into flight. He pressed the pursuit closely, as likewise did Massanissa [Masinissa]."[45] It is clearly at this point that the battle turned for the worse for Hannibal.

Focusing on the infantry battle, the Roman maniples and the first two lines of the Carthaginians – the mercenaries and the Liby-Phoenicians – advanced toward each other and engaged. Hannibal's veteran line remained in place some 300 paces back.[46] How many men were engaged in the initial clash can only be estimated. Starting from the assumption that the legions were slightly enlarged on the Polybian figures, and accepting that the allied hastati were more numerous, although they may have had more light troops, gives four legions presenting a 4,800 legionary front with an unknown number of the 6,000 Numidian infantry presenting a front rank on the Roman right. The ancient sources say that the 12,000 Carthaginian mercenaries with different weapons systems were battling a smaller force composed of Roman and allied infantry, with a Numidian infantry force probably similarly equipped as the mercenaries – a mix of infantry, skirmishers, and possibly slingers. Of course, this works on the assumption that the Roman-allied Numidian infantry did not support Masinissa's cavalry and its subsequent pursuit of Hannibal's Numidians. Polybius is oddly quiet about their actual participation in the battle. Whether deliberate to aggrandize the Roman accomplishment or because the Numidian infantry were mostly held in reserve during the clashes with the Carthaginians will never be known. If they were absent from the main battle line, then the hastati presented half as large a line as the Carthaginian mercenaries from the first line. This situation would mean a two-to-one ratio favoring the Carthaginians.

According to Polybius, the clash of the first line ran as follows:

When the phalanxes were close to each other, Romans fell upon their foes, raising their war-cry and clashing their shields with their spears as is their practice, while there was a strange confusion of shouts raised by the Carthaginian mercenaries. As the whole battle

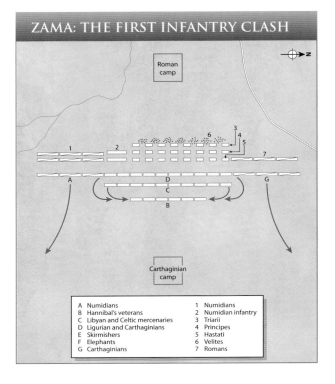

ZAMA: THE FIRST INFANTRY CLASH

Roman camp

Carthaginian camp

A	Numidians	1	Numidians
B	Hannibal's veterans	2	Numidian infantry
C	Libyan and Celtic mercenaries	3	Triarii
D	Ligurian and Carthaginians	4	Principes
E	Skirmishers	5	Hastati
F	Elephants	6	Velites
G	Carthaginians	7	Romans

was a hand-to hand affair (the men using neither spears nor swords),[47] the mercenaries at first prevailed by their courage and skill, wounding many of the Romans, but the latter still continued to advance, relying on their admirable order and on the superiority of their arms. The rear ranks of the Romans followed close on their comrades, cheering them on, but the Carthaginians behaved like cowards, never coming near their mercenaries nor attempting to back them up, so that finally the barbarians gave way, and thinking that they had evidently been left in the lurch by their own side, fell upon those they encountered in their retreat and began to kill them.[48]

The mercenary line gave a good account of itself, wounding many hastati. Yet the Carthaginian first line eventually collapsed and tried to seek shelter with the second line, which in turn became engaged and was defeated by the hastati, the principes coming to the aid of their comrades as reinforcements. Polybius gives an ambiguous compliment in his description of the clash with the second Carthaginian line:

> This actually compelled many of the Carthaginians to die like men; for as they were being butchered by their own mercenaries they were obliged against their will to fight both against these and against the Romans, and as when at bay they showed frantic and extraordinary courage, they killed a considerable number both of their mercenaries and of the enemy. In this way they even threw the cohorts of the hastati into confusion, but the officers of the principes, seeing what was happening, brought up their ranks to assist, and now the greater number of the Carthaginians and their mercenaries were cut to pieces where they stood, either by themselves or by the hastati. Hannibal did not allow the survivors in their flight to mix with his own men but, ordering the foremost ranks to level their spears against them, prevented them from

being received into his force. They were therefore obliged to retreat towards the wings and the open ground beyond.[49]

The cavalry wings were off the field of battle at this point. The clash between the hastati, principes, mercenaries, and Carthaginians must have taken some time. Mosig and Belhassen argue that Hannibal deliberately designed his tactics to draw away the superior enemy cavalry, relying on his own cavalry to engage Masinissa's and Laelius' units for as long as possible, thereby allowing the battle to be decided by the infantry.[50]

Based on this argument, Hannibal's intention may have been to draw the maniples of the hastati and principes into the quagmire of his first two lines, seeking to engulf the Roman battle line, which was shrinking as it took casualties. Hannibal's lines widened as the survivors of the first line reinforced the wings of the second line. In effect, as the Roman main battle frontage was shrinking, Hannibal's second line was extending, thereby shifting the Roman maniples into the center of his expanding second line. Any rash move by the Roman second line to force its way through the center could have spelled disaster for Scipio as Hannibal could have executed a pincer movement with his third line. If Hannibal's second line, composed of Carthaginians, had the ability to stand and fight and absorb more of the Roman second line, then Hannibal could divide his third line into halves to swing around the extended wings and roll up the flanks of the Roman Army. The key was for the cavalry to remain absent from the field and for the second line to stay intact for as long as possible. Hannibal's plan nearly bore fruit. Polybius writes that:

In this way they even threw the cohorts of the hastati into confusion, but the

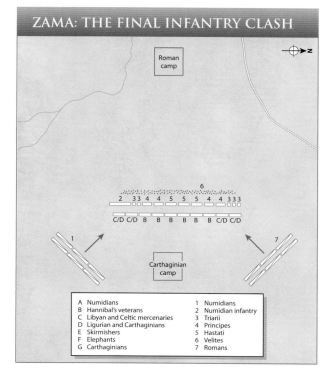

ZAMA: THE FINAL INFANTRY CLASH

A Numidians	1 Numidians
B Hannibal's veterans	2 Numidian infantry
C Libyan and Celtic mercenaries	3 Triarii
D Ligurian and Carthaginians	4 Principes
E Skirmishers	5 Hastati
F Elephants	6 Velites
G Carthaginians	7 Romans

officers of the principes, seeing what was happening, brought up their ranks to assist, and now the greater number of the Carthaginians and their mercenaries were cut to pieces where they stood, either by themselves or by the hastati.[51]

Liddell Hart writes that even the principes began to waver.[52] And Lazenby considers that "it is difficult to believe that the hastati, numbering, perhaps, about 6,500 men, actually succeeded in defeating Hannibal's first two lines, numbering, presumably, over 20,000 men, and the principes may have been involved."[53] Clearly, the central fighters, the hastati, were taking casualties and it is the presence of the officers of the Roman second line who made the correct decision to reinforce. Instead of rushing forward and adding more confusion to the already struggling hastati, the maniples of the principes restored the balance without crowding the battle space, as had been done at Cannae, and thus their actions preserved their army's integrity and survival. This decision was perhaps one of the most crucial aspects of the battle thus far.

Alternatively, the Carthaginian general was aware of Scipio's previous battles, most notably on the Iberian peninsula, where Scipio used the triarii as a maneuvering element. Hannibal wanted to make sure that by keeping his third line further back he would not become flanked, and thus retained the ability to counter-maneuver if needed. It seems reasonable to disagree with many scholars who have argued that the battle at Zama was simply a straightforward brawl.

The hastati by now must have been exhausted and depleted, although 4,800 or so principes reinforced them. We know nothing of the Numidian foot and their contribution to the infantry battle. We do know that 1,500 Romans died as well as 4,000 Numidians. Most of these casualties may have occurred during the final stages of the battle with Hannibal's third line. Nonetheless, 5,500 casualties speaks volumes about the desperate nature of the clash. The 4,000 casualties suffered by Masinissa's Numidians, not to mention the wounded, is a clear sign that they were the midst of the infantry battle even though Polybius neglects them totally in his account.

To summarize the action so far: the first 12,000-strong line of the Carthaginian Army was defeated, with some survivors joining the second line. The second line nearly broke the hastati and the timely reinforcement by the principes saved the day. Hannibal's second line of perhaps 12,000 men did not allow the retreating mercenaries through their lines and supposedly became embroiled in fighting the mercenaries, who felt betrayed or were desperate to escape. Despite Polybius' derogatory comments about the enemy, they stood firm and took on the combined power of the hastati and principes and the Numidian infantry as well as their own mercenaries. How many Italian and Numidian troops did the Carthaginian second line face? Conservatively, the hastati and principes started with 4,800 men, bringing the Roman contribution to 9,600 along with 6,000 Numidian foot. The hastati were nearly thrown into confusion and certainly must have taken the brunt of the casualties, along with the Numidians. If it is assumed that a quarter of the 5,500 died during the first clash, and reasoning that less than a third of all casualties were Roman, it can be argued that perhaps fewer than 400 Romans and more than 1,000 Numidians had been killed. These numbers are of course hypothetical and are reliant on all the Numidians being part of the fighting line. The second line of 12,000 Carthaginians battled near 14,225 Romano-Numidians, bearing in mind that the triarii and Hannibal's last line had not yet been committed.

The numbers bear out an interesting point. If Hannibal's army was larger than Scipio's, and if the bulk of the Romano-Numidian Army was engaged with Hannibal's second line, why then did Hannibal not immediately march his last line around the wings to attack the Roman Army? Certainly he had a much larger third line than anything Scipio could muster. The cavalry engagements were taking place elsewhere and Hannibal must have realized he had limited time to exploit any opportunity.

Descriptions of the battle at this stage contradict Roman propaganda, leaving us with the impression of a Carthaginian Army no larger than the Roman Army, with a third line much smaller than previously accepted. For if Hannibal truly had 10,000–12,000 men, he could have immediately advanced and outflanked his opponent. As he didn't, it seems likely that in fact his third line was significantly smaller and independently not strong enough to divide into two separate units to execute the pincer movement.

Hannibal's first and second lines, comprising 24,000 men, had been defeated, the survivors running back toward Hannibal's last line. It is possible that some joined the outer wing of the last line, thereby extending it. We turn to Polybius for his account:

> The space which separated the two armies still on the field was now covered with blood, slaughter, and dead bodies, and the Roman general was placed in great difficulty by this obstacle to his completing the rout of the enemy. For he saw that it would be very difficult to pass over the ground without breaking his ranks owing to the quantity of slippery corpses which were still soaked in blood and had fallen in heaps and the number of arms thrown away at haphazard. However, after conveying the wounded to the rear and recalling by bugle those of the hastati who were still pursuing the enemy, he stationed the latter in the fore part of the field of battle, opposite the enemy's centre, and making the principes and triarii close up on both wings ordered them to advance over the dead. When these troops had surmounted the obstacles and found themselves in a

line with the hastati the two phalanxes closed with the greatest eagerness and ardour. As they were nearly equal in numbers as well as in spirit and bravery, and were equally well armed, the contest was for long doubtful, the men falling where they stood out of determination…[54]

The account illustrates the discipline of the Scipian army. Polybius' account has the battered hastati forming the central battle line and Scipio ordering the principes and triarii onto the flanks of the hastati. It seems then that the principes were not engaged in the battle with the second line at this point, but they and the triarii now had to advance to line up with the hastati. Therefore it seems like that during the crucial fight with the Carthaginians, the principes had to stabilize battle and despite almost being broken, the Roman lines held out and the principes then withdrew. If that is correct, the argument can be made that Hannibal's second line was much smaller than 12,000, for they faced a much smaller Romano-Numidian force. Indeed one can argue that the retreating mercenaries reinforced the second line, at least some of them, and subsequently the first and second lines reinforced the last line and that their numbers exaggerated the true size of Hannibal's hodge-podge army. Perhaps the first line was 12,000, but the second much smaller as was the third, but that each time the Romans looked at the reformed Carthaginian lines they appeared sizeable.

What would have happened had Hannibal punched through the Roman center? Mosig and Belhassen suggest that

Hannibal must have also used the momentary lull in the fighting to reorganize his forces, and it seems likely that he may have displaced his veterans to the sides, to face the triarii and the principes, while the survivors of his first two lines got ready to deal with the exhausted hastati. There was nothing more that Scipio could have done at this point, and the battle resumed with increasing ferocity. In view of the rested condition of Hannibal's elite veterans, it is very likely that they were in the process of routing the principes and triarii while the center held, and defeat looked Scipio in the face.[55]

It seems that the actual central units of the Roman force were composed of the hastati and the Numidians. This composition would make more sense, as the hastati alone certainly could not have held the center against either Hannibal's veterans or a larger unit composed of survivors from the first and second lines. The hastati and the Numidians at the onset totaled over 10,000 men, and even after suffering the bulk of the army's casualties must still have presented a potent force equal, if not superior, to Hannibal's veterans. If prior to the final clash the Romans and

Numidians had suffered half their casualties, the central companies may have numbered about 8,000. However, there is no information as to how many had been wounded and were unable to fight. Nonetheless, it still provides us with an idea that the core battle line was powerful and numerous and that Hannibal's third line was probably about the same size. The principes and triarii numbered fewer than 7,000 and were positioned on the wings. In effect, 3,500 seasoned troops on each flank were facing lesser-quality troops who had survived the early stages of the clash. If, as Mosig and Belhassen argue, Hannibal shifted his line as well and pitted his veterans against the principes and triarii, we can conclude that Hannibal's veterans numbered 7,000 or so in total. The last clash then may have numbered around 15,000 Romano-Numidians against perhaps as many as 20,000, but possibly no more than 12,000, Carthaginians.

The phalanxes clashed and fought with purpose until the timely arrival of Scipio's cavalry. It is in fact their return that defeated Hannibal, as the infantry battle was certainly in the balance:

> Massanissa and Laelius, returning from the pursuit of the cavalry, arrived providentially
> at the proper moment. When they fell on Hannibal's army from the rear, most of the
> men were cut down in their ranks, while of those who took to flight only quite a few

Another interesting perspective of hand-to-hand combat during the Second Punic War. (Liebig cards printed with permission of Campbell's Soup Company) escaped, as the cavalry were close on them and the country was level. More than fifteen hundred Romans fell, the Carthaginian loss amounting to twenty thousand killed and nearly the same number of prisoners.[56]

Steven James reviews the ancient sources regarding the casualty figures:

Polybius and Livy give the Carthaginian losses as 20,000 killed, 20,000 captured (total of 40,000) and mentions "a few escaped." Appian gives 25,000 killed and 8,500 captured (total of 33,500). It is hard to reconcile Polybius' total destruction of the Carthaginian Army with the accounts given by Appian and Nepos. Appian tells us that: He (Hannibal) took refuge in a town called Thon. Here he found many Bruttians and Iberian horsemen who had fled after the defeat. (Punic Wars VIII. 47). Nepos writes: At Hadrumetum he (Hannibal) rallied the survivors of the retreat and by means of new levies mustered a large number of soldiers within a few days. (Nepos Hannibal VI).[57]

James finds an ally in Lazenby, who also believes Appian's numbers to be closest to the truth.[58] The true number of the men who participated in the last great battle of the Second Punic War and the true casualties will never be known. The outcome, however, is not disputed.

AFTERMATH

During the Second Punic War, the tactically invincible Hannibal had enjoyed successes for many years. His relatively small army, however, was entirely dependent on him and was no match for the Romans, whose singular will eventually overpowered both Hannibal and Carthage. Here lay the critical difference between the two sides. Rome raised army after army and suffered defeat after defeat, eventually winning the war of attrition by fielding armies in Spain, Italy, and finally, victoriously, on African soil. Carthage, on the other hand, did next to nothing in supporting her greatest general. Celts and Spaniards proved to be better allies than his countrymen in North Africa. Hannibal crossed magnificent mountain ranges, losing a great many men and beasts in doing so, then waged a long campaign on mainland Italy. His military success on the battlefield ended on the plains of Zama. Rome's political abilities, coupled with her military might, pried away Carthage's most prized asset, the Numidians, and it was their world-class cavalry that decided the battle of Zama in Rome's favor. Although Hannibal was able to raise another army, Carthage sued for peace. Rome's new-found ally Masinissa continued to expand his holdings at Carthage's expense, a situation that finally sparked the Third Punic War (149–146 BC), resulting not only in the destruction of Carthage and her culture, but also in the subjugation of the Numidians by Rome.

Pursued by Roman agents, Hannibal took his own life in 183 BC in what is now Turkey. His amazing feats, loyalty to Carthage and tactical acumen, however, have transcended time.

THE TEUTOBURG
FOREST, AD 9

Rome had never bitten off more than she could chew until the Senate and the people of Rome decided to conquer the vast and mysterious northern territories of the Germanic barbarians. It was these barbarians who destroyed three Roman legions and, in the end, halted Rome's imperial expansion to the northeast. Although the carnage of the Teutoburg Wald ("Teutons' castle forest") battle in AD 9 near Kalkriese, Germany, was nowhere near the scale of Cannae or Zama, its impact on both the Roman and Germanic psyches was epic.[1]

Unfortunately, ancient chroniclers of the battle are few, and none of them were witness to the battle. Dio Cassius (AD 163–229) was Roman and published a history of Rome. Marcus Velleius Paterculus (19 BC–AD 31) was a Roman officer and historian who served in northeastern Europe around the time of the battle. Florus was another Roman author of whom we know very little, other than he possibly lived during Trajan's (r.98–117) and Hadrian's (r.117–138) rule. Tacitus (56–117) was a Roman politician and author of several works.

BACKGROUND

By AD 6, most of the northern European tribes had been either brutally conquered or deemed stable, with the exception of the Marcomanni in Central Europe. The territory of the German tribes as far as the River Elbe had been declared pacified by this date, and in AD 7 Publius Quinctilius Varus was appointed governor of the new province of Germania. When, in AD 6, a rebellion flared in Pannonia and Dalmatia, in Eastern Europe, Roman legions under Tiberius (42 BC–AD 37), general and later emperor, advanced southward from the northern European area to settle the insurgency as quickly as possible. General Publius Quinctilius Varus and his legions were subsequently annihilated when he too hurried to quell a rebellion, and he is

A modern view of the Teutoburg Forest, demonstrating the thickness of the foliage and the difficulty of maneuvering through it. (Courtesy of Armenia)

often held accountable for the loss of the legions and the failure to put an end to the rebellion. However, it should be remembered that the Romans had long attracted loyalty from many German tribes, using them as auxiliary troops. Also, other Roman commanders barely avoided extermination by the barbarians east of the Rhine in previous years.[2] Nonetheless, the supposed tranquility of the Germanic tribes proved to be false. Although ancient sources blame Varus for his mishandling of the tribes, it is clear that the Romans in general, from their first meeting with the tribes, put the sword to the natives and fire to their soil, a type of warfare that rarely breeds lasting peace. Germanic tribes were semi-nomadic, and did not have a center of gravity to assault and conquer. Instead the Roman imperial war machine needed to conquer the will of the native tribes.

The Germanic tribes did not favor battles in the traditional sense. The destruction of the Roman Army under Varus took several days and was carefully planned. The strategy they adopted required a dilution of Roman forces, forcing the legionaries into unsuitable terrain and meticulously harassing the trapped force to the point of annihilation. While this planning and execution was not typical of German warfare at the time, some of Arminius' men had begun to think tactically. Based on recent archaeological finds, some scholars have proposed that the Germans may have created obstacles forcing the Romans onto a narrower passage, dug away large portions of track, exposed land to water, as well as constructed a wall of sod at the edges of the track to hamper the legionaries and provide a wall of protection for the Germans, enabling them to hurl uncontested spears at the trapped column.[3] The ancient sources mention none of these innovations.

THE ROMAN ARMY

The Roman Army that was to meet its doom in the dark of a German forest was composed of three legions (Legion XVII, Legion XVIII, and Legion XIX), six allied cohorts and three *alae* (large cavalry squadrons).[4] In the Republican era legions were composed of three distinct lines of ten maniples, each line separated according to hastati, principes, and triarii. A large number of velites and a very small cavalry contingent completed the Republican legion. Traditionally, a similar-sized legion filled with Italian allies accompanied the Roman legion into the field. The long-term wars in Numidia reinvigorated the Roman military and forced its senior leadership to reevaluate organization and equipment. General and consul Gaius Marius (157–86 BC) was the foremost reformer of the Roman legions. Under his leadership all Italians were granted Roman citizenship. He introduced a standing army filled from all classes of society, although the bulk of these new legions were formed by the poor. Marius' reforms allowed far larger armies, as extended citizenship opened up the recruiting pool throughout the territories.

Another part of the reform was to streamline the legions. No longer would the units operate with three distinctive lines composed of varying troop qualities and capabilities. Instead, the average legionary became standardized in equipment and training. The famous spears of the triarii disappeared, their numbers were raised from 60 to 120,[5] and all legionaries fought with pila, the gladius short sword, a rectangular or large oval scutum shield, and body armor made of either mail (*lorica hamata*) or of metal strips (*lorica segmentata*). The velites disappeared from the Roman organizational chart.

The legion itself was now composed of ten cohorts instead of 30 maniples. Thus one maniple each of hastati, principes, and the reinforced triarii became one cohort. Technically speaking, this would have provided about 360 legionaries. Each cohort, however, was divided into six centuries and Connolly argues that each centuria was roughly composed of 80 men.[6] The basic cohort then would have been 480 legionaries plus officers and NCOs. John Warry writes that "as a legionary unit, the cohort was 500–600 strong."[7] Ross Cowan notes that "these centuries retained the old manipular designations of hastatus, principes, and pilus (another title for the triarius), and were further distinguished by the terms *prior* (front) and *posterior* (rear)."[8]

Another change to the composition of the legion was an increase in the size of the first cohort. This now consisted of five double-sized centuries, each commanded by a senior centurion. The legion now totaled nine cohorts of 480 men and one of 800, plus supernumeraries, all together totaling about 5,200 men. Some 120 men were drawn from the ranks, and mounted as *exploratores* (scouts) and messengers. Others acted as gunners, since the legion now had one *ballista* (stone-thrower) per cohort and one *scorpio* (bolt-thrower) per century, though in practice a total of 50 or so catapults was usual. Earlier armies had siege-trains of catapults, but it was not until Julius Caesar's day that they were frequently used in the field.[9]

Since allied legions now no longer existed, units called *auxilia* were drafted from allies and were complementary in size to that of the Roman legion. The auxilia also included gunners, engineers, light-armed troops, and other support personnel, as well as cavalry. The *ala* (wing) was used to designate auxiliary cavalry units. Lawrence Keppie notes the transformation of the auxilia:

> In the Civil Wars contingents of auxiliaries varied in size; there was no set total. But by the early Empire, and perhaps already under Augustus, the numbers in each regiment were standardised. Most cohorts and *alae* contained about 480–500 men (and were consequently entitled *quingenaria* i.e. 'five hundred strong')… In addition there were mixed units of infantry and cavalry, these so-called *cohortes equitatae*. Already in Gaul Caesar had employed mixed units of Germans, which usually had cavalry and infantry in equal numbers, but it is probably wrong to envisage a direct line of descent: the proportion of infantry to cavalry in a *cohors equitata* was probably 4:1, and we have no evidence that in battle they were supposed to fight as a composite group. The cohorts were organised into centuries and *contubernia* on the legionary model; thus a normal *cohors quingenaria* contained six centuries of 80 men.[10]

Return of Germanic warriors with prisoners and booty from the battle of the Teutoburg Forest. Note the Romans at the bottom left and their captured standard. (Author's Collection)

Reconstruction of the improvised fortifications prepared by the Germanic tribes for the final phase of their battle against Varus' legionaries near Kalkriese. (Photo by Markus Scweiß)

Arminius (17 BC–AD 21), the vanquisher of Varus and his legions, had at one time been a member of the *auxilia*. He was to use his knowledge of standard Roman operating procedures to his advantage.

Few authors take into account the difficulty of supplying and transporting an army in ancient times, even despite the rightly famous Roman road system. It is usually the barbarian tribes depicted traveling by wagon, but at the time and place of this battle, it was the Romans who were encumbered by, and dependent upon, slow-moving vehicles. Mules, horses, and other animals, as well as large numbers of camp followers, completed the baggage train.

THE GERMANIC TRIBES

The Germanic tribes who formed an alliance to terminate Roman domination were composed of the Cherusci, Bructeri, Marsi, Sicambri, Chauci, and Chatti. Together, these tribes covered the northeast of the Rhine area. Tacitus describes the tribes of Germany as

...free from all taint of intermarriages with foreign nations, and that they appear as a distinct, unmixed race, like none but themselves. Hence, too, the same physical peculiarities throughout so vast a population. All have fierce blue eyes, red hair, huge frames, fit only for a sudden exertion. They are less able to bear laborious work. Heat and thirst they cannot in the least endure; to cold and hunger their climate and their soil inure them.[11]

Some of the Germans had provided manpower for the auxilia and had served earlier emperors loyally. "The elite of the Cherusci tribe emerged as special friends of Rome after Tiberius' campaign of AD 5 and Arminius of the Cherusci was one of those friends at the age of 22."[12] Earlier generations had also been recruited as mercenaries in Gaul, both as infantry and cavalry, by Caesar himself and they had brought back personal knowledge of Roman tactics and weaponry. They were "known for their loyalty and trustworthiness as well as for their equestrian skills."[13] Arminius was "one such German soldier of fortune, a 25-year-old prince. His tribal name has been lost to history. He spoke Latin and was familiar with Roman tactics, the kind of man the Romans relied on to help their armies penetrate the lands of the barbarians. For his valor on the field of battle, he had been awarded the rank of knight and the honor of Roman citizenship."[14]

These Germanic tribes were more nomadic than the Romans in nature, as they traveled with their families and were thereby more inclined to retreat completely, making them more difficult to defeat than tribes settled in villages. The tribes could simply withdraw when faced with an invasion and regroup when it was suitable to them. J. F. C. Fuller notes that it was the restlessness of the Germanic tribes and their migratory way of life that were troublesome to Rome on a strategic level.[15] The Germanic hordes were divided into clan units made up of distinct families and tribes, each capable of independent actions. "And what most stimulates their courage," wrote Tacitus, "is that their squadrons or battalions, instead of being formed by chance or by a fortuitous gathering, are composed of families and clans."[16]

Barbarian armies did not have the same organizational procedures as the Romans. Neither did they fight in the organized manner that was seen with other military units. None of this means that the Germanic tribes were disorganized or fought in an undisciplined manner, however. In many ways one can argue that their fighting techniques allowed the more aggressive warriors to lead from the front. As the historical sources are all Roman, the view of the barbarians is inherent with Roman biases. Peter S. Wells argues that the particular manner in which the Germanic tribes fought was extremely frustrating to the Romans:

Roman writers observe that barbarian warrior bands attack ferociously, but retreat quickly, often in apparent disorder. The Roman commentators attribute these behaviors to the natives' inherently inferior abilities and their lack of organization. But it is apparent that the Germanic warriors knew exactly what they were doing. Their strategy and tactics were precisely adapted to their environment and to their enemy. Although derided by the Romans as inferior fighters, they frustrated Rome's efforts to achieve decisive victories east of the Rhine.[17]

The Roman legionary had far more sophisticated equipment than his Germanic counterpart. Tacitus describes the basic tools of the trade:

> Even iron is not plentiful with them, as we infer from the character of their weapons. But few use swords or long lances. They carry a spear (*framea* is their name for it), with a narrow and short head, but so sharp and easy to wield that the same weapon serves, according to circumstances, for close or distant conflict. As for the horse-soldier, he is satisfied with a shield and spear; the foot-soldiers also scatter showers of missiles, each man having several and hurling them to an immense distance, and being naked or lightly clad with a little cloak. There is no display about their equipment: their shields alone are marked with very choice colours. A few only have corslets, and just one or two here and there a metal or leathern helmet.[18]

The individual German barbarian was therefore lightly equipped, allowing him to engage the enemy with spears at great distances before closing when it became advantageous. Furthermore, the lack of heavy armor enabled the warriors to not only attack at speed, but to also withdraw likewise. In effect, the Germanic foot soldier was a master of hit-and-run tactics, when in suitable terrain. The northern barbarians also produced fine cavalry. However, the cavalrymen's indigenous "horses are remarkable neither for beauty nor for fleetness. Nor are they taught various evolutions after our fashion, but are driven straight forward, or so as to make one wheel to the right in such a compact body that none is left behind another."[19]

The barbarian tactics were simple, but effective. The use of the combined arms of infantry and cavalry is of particular interest:

> ...their chief strength is in their infantry, which fights along with the cavalry; admirably adapted to the action of the latter is the swiftness of certain foot-soldiers, who are picked from the entire youth of their country, and stationed in front of the line. Their number is fixed – a hundred from each canton; and from this they take their name among their countrymen, so that what was originally a mere number has now become a title of distinction. Their line of battle is drawn up in a wedge-like formation. To give ground, provided you return to the attack, is considered prudence rather than cowardice. The bodies of their slain they carry off even in indecisive engagements. To abandon your

Depiction of German warriors in battle with Roman legionaires at the battle of the Teutoburg Forest. (Author's Collection)

shield is the basest of crimes; nor may a man thus disgraced be present at the sacred rites, or enter their council; many, indeed, after escaping from battle, have ended their infamy with the halter.[20]

Communication on the battlefield may have been conducted by the use of standards and trumpets and their generals led by example, not by authority. "They also carry with them into battle certain figures and images taken from their sacred groves."[21] The semi-nomadic lifestyle produced by traveling with the clans had a strong impact on the battlefield performance of its warriors, as their families were so close to the field. Tacitus tells us that:

Though fierce fighters, their military organization was of the crudest, consisting of squadrons and battalions fortuitously collected by families and clans. They hear the shrieks of women, the cries of infants. Close by them, too, are those dearest to them, so that they are to every man the most sacred witnesses of his bravery – they are his most generous applauders. The soldier brings his wounds to mother and wife, who shrink not from counting or even demanding them and who administer both food and encouragement to the combatants. Tradition says that armies already wavering and giving way have been rallied by women who, with earnest entreaties and bosoms laid bare, have vividly represented the horrors of captivity, which the Germans fear with such extreme dread on behalf of their women, that the strongest tie by which a state can be bound is the being required to give, among the number of hostages, maidens of noble birth. They even believe that the sex has a certain sanctity and prescience, and they do not despise their counsels, or make light of their answers.[22]

THE BATTLE IN THE FOREST

The Roman general Publius Quinctilius Varus had been warned by a loyal German about Arminius' betrayal, so Paterculus says in his *Roman History*, but Varus refused to believe the warning. Therefore, "after this first warning, there was no time left for a second."[23] Cassius Dio goes so far as to write that Varus "did not keep his legions together, as was proper in a hostile country, but distributed many of the soldiers to helpless communities, which asked for them for the alleged purpose of guarding various points, arresting robbers, or escorting provision trains."[24] Word reached the Romans of another rebellion at some distant area and, as was the standard operating procedure of the Romans, Varus assembled his seemingly depleted legions (near 18,000 infantry, 900 cavalry, 4,000 allied foot, 600 allied cavalry, and families) and marched off to quell it.[25] His route took him through friendly territory and his force was accompanied by Germanic allies, including Arminius. If we are to believe Cassius Dio, the Roman Army seemingly marched without taking precautions, such as rigid military formations and sending scouts to reconnoiter ahead. At some point during the march Arminius and his allies rode off, pretending to gather their troops for the expedition. Instead, they gathered their forces who were already prepared for the ambush in the midst of a forested area. At this stage Varus was unaware that the Roman detachments that had already been sent off to various areas to deal with smaller problems had been annihilated.

Once the tribes had assembled under Arminius, and after having eliminated the other Roman units, "they came upon Varus in the midst of forests by this time almost impenetrable. And there, at the very moment of revealing themselves as enemies instead of subjects, they wrought great and dire havoc."[26] Meticulous planning was yielding meticulous execution. Having killed the smaller Roman forces undoubtedly

A rare painting by Friedrich Gunkel showing more of a Roman perspective of the battle. (Author's Collection)

increased the morale of the native warriors and perhaps instilled a desire to exact vengeance on the subjugators. The Roman forces had been severely diluted, and the Roman general and his force were marching unprepared for battle through terrain that was mountainous, and whose surface was "broken by ravines and trees which grew close together and very high."[27] Fuller argues that the terrain the Romans marched upon was not as broken as Cassius Dio leads us to believe, as wagons did traverse it. Instead "we must picture the route not as a well-developed Roman military road, but as an ordinary forest trail that the Romans had improved here and there by building a bridge, throwing up a causeway, or draining off water."[28]

Although they were marching to quell a rebellion, the Roman Army traveled with many wagons and animals, as well as families and servants. These were clear signs that the Romans did not envision any hostilities during transit. Traveling with a baggage train through heavy forests and over uneven surfaces must have been extremely difficult. Whether or not the fighting men were fully armed is another uncertainty. Contrary to Fuller, the Roman scribe Dio further illustrates the Roman difficulties when he writes that "the Romans, even before the enemy assailed them, were having a hard time of it felling trees, building roads, and bridging places that required it."[29] Since they did not expect any attacks, it is likely that their security and advance guards, if any, were at best less vigilant than their hostile environment warranted. Traveling on small dirt paths through thick, dark forests, stopping frequently to manhandle wagons across unforgiving terrain must surely have caused the column to become disorganized. Hacking a suitable path through the woods was a difficult task under any condition. It was to get worse, as the ancient gods forsook their Roman children and unleashed a storm of

> ...violent rain and wind that separated them still further, while the ground, that had become slippery around the roots and logs, made walking very treacherous for them, and the tops of the trees kept breaking off and falling down, causing much confusion. While the Romans were in such difficulties, the barbarians suddenly surrounded them on all sides at once, coming through the densest thickets, as they were acquainted with the paths.[30]

Conditions could not have been better for Arminius, with the weather wreaking havoc among the Romans and obstructing their vision. The Germanic foot soldiers began hurling their numerous spears at the column and, sensing that the legionaries and their allied contingents could not defend themselves, they closed up. Seemingly the Romans were completely caught off guard. The column having become very elongated – estimated at 9–12km in length with 18,000–30,000 people – the Roman soldiers accustomed to fighting in formation on level ground were unable to mount any real resistance at first.[31] However, the attackers must have withdrawn at some point as the Romans were able to encamp "on the spot, after securing a suitable place, so far as that was possible on a wooded mountain; and afterwards they either burned or abandoned most of their wagons and everything else that was not absolutely necessary to them."[32] Perhaps the Romans were able to secure their camp at a location along the column that was under lighter attack, or the legionaries were able to form up more quickly. In either case, the exhausted men and women were able to find some comfort behind the wooden stakes carried by the legionaries as standard for just such a purpose. The Roman opportunity to build an encampment of any kind, be it with ditches, wooden stakes, or wagons, does show that the Germanic tribes may not have had the numbers required to launch and win an all-out battle. Instead, and perhaps deliberately, Arminius used what resources he had to the best advantage.

The following day, and under harassment, the Roman column entered open country. This time there could have been no doubt about their situation. The seasoned troops must have advanced in as best an order as they could with the non-fighting elements well protected within their column, the soldiers ready to face the anticipated attacks of the barbarians. Again Arminius, having planned and prepared, used the terrain to his advantage. The Germanic tribes renewed their attack with vigor from behind the protection of trees and thickets. Spears thrown at groups of beast and human must have found the easy targets, slowing down the already decimated column even further. Of this engagement Cassis Dio wrote that Varus and his force "suffered their heaviest losses… For since they had to form their lines in a narrow space, in order that the cavalry and infantry together might run down the enemy, they collided frequently with one another and with the trees."[33]

By the time the fourth day arrived and darkness yielded to light, hope of survival must have been slim for the survivors. And yet again weather added to the Romans' misery with another savage storm. In fact, the constant rain and dampness of the region rendered the arms and armor of the legionary practically useless. Their wooden, leather-covered shields were so soaked that they were too heavy to lift or too soft to withstand repeated blows. The column was unable to advance, much less stand and fight effectively. The German warriors were far less affected by the environment, as they were less encumbered by armor. Undoubtedly, many warriors retired to their homes and families to refit and prepare for the next day's skirmish.

The success of the assault thus far brought forth new warriors who had previously been less committed. These warriors may have been held in reserve, or, upon hearing of the success decided to join the fight. Cassius Dio notes bitterly that

the enemy's forces had greatly increased, as many of those who had at first wavered joined them, largely in the hope of plunder, and thus they could more easily encircle and strike down the Romans, whose ranks were now thinned, many having perished in the earlier fighting. Varus, therefore, and all the more prominent officers, fearing that they should either be captured alive or be killed by their bitterest foes (for they had already been wounded), made bold to do a thing that was terrible yet unavoidable: they took their own lives. When news of this had spread, none of the rest, even if he had any strength left, defended himself any longer. Some imitated their leader, and others, casting aside their arms, allowed anybody who pleased to slay them; for to flee was impossible, however much one might desire to do so. Every man, therefore, and every horse was cut down without fear of resistance.[34]

It was during the final spasms of the battle that

Vala Numonius, lieutenant of Varus, who, in the rest of his life, had been an inoffensive and an honourable man, also set a fearful example in that he left the infantry unprotected

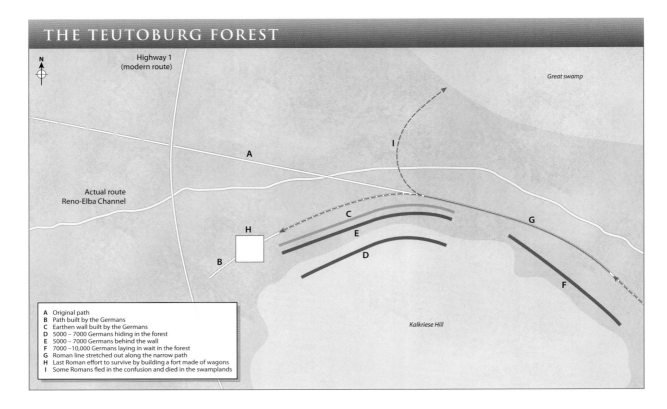

THE TEUTOBURG FOREST

N

Highway 1
(modern route)

Great swamp

Actual route
Reno-Elba Channel

A

I

C

H

E

G

B

D

F

Kalkriese Hill

A Original path
B Path built by the Germans
C Earthen wall built by the Germans
D 5000 – 7000 Germans hiding in the forest
E 5000 – 7000 Germans behind the wall
F 7000 –10,000 Germans laying in wait in the forest
G Roman line stretched out along the narrow path
H Last Roman effort to survive by building a fort made of wagons
I Some Romans fled in the confusion and died in the swamplands

by the cavalry and in flight tried to reach the Rhine with his squadrons of horse. But fortune avenged his act, for he did not survive those whom he had abandoned, but died in the act of deserting them.[35]

Clearly, then, the German alliance of Arminius did not annihilate the Roman legions under Varus in one decisive battle. Rather they maneuvered the legions onto unsuitable terrain, familiar to their own warriors, isolated the Roman Army from any reinforcements and allowed the environment and the constant barrage of spears to whittle away the legions until they were easy prey for the sword. This was the reverse of previous campaigns, in as much as there was not one clear battle, but instead the Roman column was picked apart a bit at a time and then slaughtered when trapped. As Paterculus notes: "Hemmed in by forests and marshes and ambuscades, it was exterminated almost to a man by the very enemy whom it had always slaughtered like cattle, whose life or death had depended solely upon the wrath or the pity of the Romans."[36]

Florus, in better form than most fiction writers, concludes:

Varus met his overthrow with the same fortune and spirit with which Paulus met the day of Cannae. Never was slaughter more bloody than that which was made of the Romans among the marshes and woods; never were insults more intolerable than those of the barbarians, especially such as they inflicted on the pleaders of causes. Of some they tore out the eyes, of others they cut off the hands. Of one the mouth was sewed up, after his tongue had been cut out, which one of the savages holding in his hand, cried, "At last, viper, cease to hiss." The body of the consul himself, which the affection of the soldiers had buried, was dug out of the ground. To this day the barbarians keep possession of the standards and two eagles, the third, the standard-bearer, before it fell into the hands of the enemy, wrenched off, and keeping it hid within the folds of his belt, concealed himself in the blood-stained marsh. In consequence of this massacre, it happened that the empire, which had not stopped on the shore of the Ocean, found its course checked on the banks of the Rhine.[37]

In a subsequent but ineffectual campaign, all standards were recovered but, as Florus rightly points out, the Roman Empire more or less made the Rhine its eastern border with the barbarians. The understrength legions of Varus, the XVII, the XVIII, and the XIX, six cohorts and three *alae* of cavalry were removed from Rome's imperial

A rare painting by Friedrich Gunkel, glamorizing the overwhelming rush of Germanic warriors onto the Roman legions. (Author's Collection)

The impact of this victory was so significant an event in German history that German immigrants to the United States erected a monument in honor of the victorious Arminius (also known as Hermann) in their new homeland, New Ulm, Minnesota. (Courtesy of the City of New Ulm)

war machine. While the figures are ultimately unknown, between 20,000 and 30,000 soldiers and civilians died during those stormy days in the dark forests of the Teutons.

Arminius, the former Roman mercenary, the destroyer of Varus and his Roman legions, was to become so powerful that in AD 19 he would be murdered by his own chieftains.[38]

THE IMPACT OF THE TEUTOBURG DISASTER

Emperor Augustus was said to have been so upset by the defeat that "for several months in succession he cut neither his beard nor his hair, and sometimes he would dash his head against a door, crying: 'Quintilius Varus, give me back my legions!' And he observed the day of the disaster each year as one of sorrow and mourning."[39] The effect of the defeat was so potent that Rome never seriously conducted another campaign to absorb the territories lying east of the Rhine river.

The victory of the Germanic tribes at the Teutoburg Forest left a deep psychological imprint on the German people as well. Also known as the *Varusschlacht* (Varus battle), after the vanquished Varus, or the *Hermannschlacht* (Hermann battle) after the Cherusci chieftain Arminius (also known as Hermann), this battle served as a great national symbol to the struggling German states during the 19th century. Its victor, Arminius, became a lasting symbol of the heroic soldier-leader. German immigration to the United States in the 19th century led to the creation of the impressive Hermann statue in New Ulm, Minnesota, in 1888. Even as late as the 20th century, the Teutoburg Forest victory was commemorated by the Waffen-SS of the Third Reich, who had a song named after the battle. By 2000 the Hermann Monument in New Ulm was listed on the United States National Register of Historical Places as was "Resolved by the House of Representatives (the Senate concurring), that the Hermann Monument and Hermann Heights Park in New Ulm, Minnesota are recognized by the Congress to be a national symbol for the contributions of Americans of German heritage."[40]

ADRIANOPLE, 378

In 378 Rome, fielding the greatest army of the age, was defeated by a rabble of refugee Goths at the battle of Adrianople, leaving historians to ponder this improbable event. Some assert that the battle marked the end of the dominance of ancient infantry and heralded the beginnings of the medieval knight, when in fact the battle was a typical clash between two infantries, with the cavalry mounting a successful charge at a key moment.[1] It has been also been suggested that the Goths were victorious over the Romans because of their innovation of the stirrup, but this would not be introduced until the 7th century by the Avars, a nomadic horse people originating from the steppes of Central Asia. Lastly, it has been stated that Adrianople was the battle that began the fall of the Western Roman Empire. While this is in some senses true, it must be remembered that it was actually an Eastern Roman Imperial Army that was devastated, nevertheless the Eastern Empire was able to withstand the Gothic menace and survive for more than another thousand years.

What the battle of Adrianople did herald was the end of the Roman Army as it had been traditionally known. Throughout its history, Rome had incorporated barbarians into its ranks, but always as auxiliary troops or specialists. After Adrianople, however, barbarians would operate autonomously within the Empire as mercenary armies that could upset the balance of power.[2] Never again would the Romans field an army that could be recognized by Julius Caesar.

This significant change in the history of the Roman Empire would, incredibly, come at the hands of a tribe of refugees. The Goths were a group of people fleeing from another barbarian horde, the Huns, and at first were simply seeking asylum within the Roman Empire.

THE GOTHS

According to their own traditions, the Goths were a Germanic tribe who originated in Scandinavia and migrated through what is today Poland and the Ukraine before the 2nd century AD, and finally settled on the shores of the Black Sea in the mid-2nd century. After defeating the Vandals (an East Germanic tribe that began pressing into Eastern Europe), the Goths moved westward and by the 3rd century AD came into conflict with the Roman Empire, sacking Histra on the mouth of the Danube in 238. The following decades would see more Gothic raids into Roman territory until Emperor Claudius decisively defeated them at Naissus in 269. In subsequent years, the Goths would enter into uneasy truces and alliances with the Romans: the Empire paid them an annual tribute and the Goths supplied the Romans with troops when called upon.[3] Though the Romans considered the Goths barbarians, they were a relatively civilized people, the majority of whom were Arian Christians.[4]

In the early 370s, the Huns began to press westward from Asia overrunning the Alans, a nomadic tribe of the steppes of Central Asia. Fleeing from the Huns, the Alans in turn invaded the territories of the Greuthungi, a Gothic clan living north of the Black Sea. The Greuthungi, led by Alatheus and Saphrax, then retreated to the territories of the Tervingi clan (Goths that lived in the land between the Dniester and Danube rivers) on the northeastern border of the Roman Empire. But as these two clans consolidated their power, their armies were surprised and routed by the Huns. The surviving Goths were forced to retreat to the Carpathian Mountains, where they built defensive fortifications against the Huns.

By 376, a large number of Gothic Tervingi had applied for sanctuary within the Roman Empire. Tired of scratching out an existence behind the fortifications of mountain refuges, these renegade Goths were led by a man named Fritigern. With no central organization or administration, the Goths were not a unified people. Fritigern must have been a man of great charisma, therefore, as he eventually commanded an eclectic force of that included Goths of two different tribes plus Alan, Hun, and Roman deserters. Fritigern was a prudent man whom Ammianus Marcellinus describes as "skillful in divining the future, and [fearful of] a doubtful struggle."[5] He risked battle only when he was absolutely certain of victory.

THE ROMANS

In the 4th century AD, the Roman Empire was going through an existential crisis. Little more than 50 years had passed since Constantine the Great had made Christianity the official imperial religion, and the Empire's transformation from pagan to a Christian society was far from complete. At this time, the subjects within the Empire still practiced Judaism and a broad spectrum of paganism, as well as Christianity. These various religions tended to persecute each other and it was still uncertain which faith would eventually win out. Even as recently as 361, a pagan emperor, Julian the Apostate, had occupied the throne. Julian desperately attempted to reinstate paganism as the official religion, as he felt Christianity had caused a moral decline, and only worship of the old gods could enable a return to the "golden age" of the Empire. His efforts were in vain, and cut short by his death in Sassanid Persia.[6]

Christianity within the Empire was far from unified as well. The Catholic Church was dealing with a heresy that would threaten to tear the religion apart. Arianism was a doctrine put forward by Arius, a presbyter of Alexandria, and it spread like wildfire through the Empire.[7] As virulent as the discord could be between Christians, pagans, and Jews, it was nothing compared to that between Orthodox (Catholic) Christians and the Arian Christians. Ammianus had found by experience "that no wild beasts are so hostile to men as are Christian sects in general to one another."[8]

Marble bust of Emperor Valens (AD 328–378), who was killed at the battle of Adrianople. (Photography Source Jastrow, 2006)

To add to this spiritual discord was political instability. The Roman Empire had been on the defensive for many years, with every frontier under attack. The Saxons, Picts, and Scots menaced Britain. Germanic tribes pressed against the Rhine frontier in the north, while the Goths posed a threat in the northeast on the Danube. The Moors, Blemyes, and the Arabs raided the Egyptian, African, and Syrian borders. And as always, the Empire was in a state of hostilities with the Persian Empire. Furthermore, separate Eastern and Western Emperors were currently ruling the Empire – a dissonance that usually devolved into either an unhealthy competition between the two powers or into full-blown civil war.

Flavius Valens had been ruling the Eastern portion of the Empire since 364. Valens was about 50 years old, of average height, "knock-kneed, and rather pot-bellied."[9] He had a swarthy complexion with impaired sight in one eye. Ammianus further describes Valens as "a faithful and reliable friend, [who] represent[ed] intrigues with severity… In his dealings with the provinces he showed great fairness, protecting each of them from injury… He was unwilling to endure fatigue, though he affected enormous toughness. He had a cruel streak, and was something of a boor, with little skill in the arts of either war or peace."[10] While he was not known to be an astute military leader, he had successfully campaigned against the Goths between the years of 367 and 369. He subsequently became entangled with Persia in a dispute over Armenia.

In 375, Flavius Gratianus (Gratian) became the emperor of the Western portion of the Empire after the death of his father, Valentinian. Gratian's contemporaries describe him as "a young man of remarkable talent, eloquent, controlled, warlike, and merciful, and seemed likely to rival the best of his predecessors while the down of youth was still spreading over his cheeks."[11] Gratian was exceedingly popular in the Empire, and he would win a victory against the Lentienses, a Germanic tribe, only three years into his reign.

Roman sestertius from the reign of Valens, featuring his portrait. (Courtesy of Ohtar)

THE CAMPAIGN

When Alavivus and Fritigern applied for asylum within Rome to escape the Huns, Valens was campaigning in Persia. Seeing an opportunity to receive fresh troops to use against his powerful enemy, Valens granted the request for asylum. Ammianus writes:

> Once the Emperor's permission to cross the Danube and settle in parts of Thrace had been granted, the work of transportation went on day and night. The Goths embarked by troops on boats and rafts and canoes made from hollowed tree trunks. The crowd was such that, though the river is the most dangerous in the world and was then swollen by frequent rains, a large number tried to swim and were drowned in their struggle against the force of the stream.[12]

It was the task of Lupicinus (the *comes* or count in charge of Thrace) and Maximus (the *dux* or duke of the Roman frontier troops) to deal with these new refugees. Unfortunately for the Empire, they did a less than admirable job. "Their sinister greed was the source of all our troubles," Ammianus reports. "The barbarians, after crossing the river were distressed by want of food, and these loathsome generals devised an abominable form of barter. They collected all the dogs that their insatiable greed could find and exchanged each of them for a slave." Ammianus further tells us that Lupicinus and Maximus kept the Goths in the area of their original crossing rather than move them farther south as was promised because they were making so much profit by selling them substandard food at inflated prices.[13]

While this situation was playing out, the ranks of the Tervingi Goths were bolstered by secret and undocumented crossings of the Greuthungi Goths, still being led by Alatheus and Saphrax. Though these clansmen were welcome by Fritigern, the Tervingi now had more people to feed and shelter in an already over-foraged land. Perceiving that they possessed a numerical superiority to the local Roman officials, the Goths broke away from their confinement and headed south toward Marcianople (a city south of the Danube and northeast of Adrianople, modern-day Devnya in Bulgaria), where they planned to settle. At first, the Romans did nothing to stop the advance, apparently fearing the Goths' strength of numbers. Hoping to cut the head off the snake, Lupicinus attempted to assassinate Fritigern but failed. This attempt pushed the Goths into open revolt and they began to burn and loot the surrounding villas as they approached Marcianople.

In early 377 Lupicinus hastily gathered the Roman forces in Thrace to meet the Goths outside Marcianople. The Romans lined up defensively as the Goths attacked in their traditional manner, using their shields offensively in a furious charge in hopes of breaking the Roman line. "The barbarians hurled themselves recklessly on our lines," Ammianus describes, "dashing their shields upon the bodies of their opponents and running them through with spears and swords. In this furious and bloody assault our standards were snatched from us, and our tribunes and the greater part of our men perished."[14] The Goths later equipped themselves with the arms and armor of the fallen Roman soldiers. Having defeated Lupicinus' army, they were now the masters of Thrace with no one to challenge them. Roman soldiers of Gothic origin soon joined their ranks along with some Roman prisoners. Furthermore, the Gothic slaves that had been bought and sold by Lupicinus and Maximus escaped from their masters and joined Fritigern.[15]

When Valens heard of these alarming events, he quickly made peace with the Persians and withdrew his army from the Persian front, while still leaving a force strong enough to prevent the Persians taking advantage of the situation. He also withdrew troops from Armenia and sent them to the Thracian front. Finally, he requested aid from the Western Roman Emperor. Gratian responded by sending some auxiliary troops under the command of Ricimer, his master of soldiers. But Gratian could not spare any more troops to send to Valens because of an uprising of Germanic tribes, specifically the Lentienses, along his northern border. Ultimately, Gratian planned to lead a force of reinforcements himself to aid Valens once the uprising was quelled.[16]

Valens moved his operation from Antioch (his base for the Persian campaign) to Constantinople, where he had to deal with discontent among the populace within the city. A popular vote of no confidence against the Eastern Emperor was partly due to his Arian faith, but they were mostly distressed by the recent victories of the Goths over the Roman Thracian Army and by the proximity of the Goths. Many of the local citizens of the Empire had already become the victims of their plundering, and now felt safe only behind the walls of their cities. Valens didn't stay long in the city, preferring instead to gather his forces at the imperial estate of Melanthias, roughly 20km from Constantinople.[17]

By this time, Fritigern had broken up the Gothic force into small marauding bands that roamed the countryside. These bands were vulnerable to an ambush by Roman soldiers who had been sent by Valens under the leadership of Sebastian, a Western Roman officer. Fritigern recalled his bands to reassemble in the vicinity of Cabyle "and then quickly evacuated the area, intending to keep his people in open country where they could not be surprised or suffer from lack of food."[18]

His army now assembled, Valens marched from Melanthias toward Adrianople, a city northwest of Constantinople in Thrace, modern-day Edirne in Turkey. Valens'

Carving of a Parthian cataphract (a form of heavy cavalry in which both rider and horse were covered head-to-toe in scale armor) fighting a lion. Similar units featured in the Roman armies as well. (Author's Collection)

army could have numbered anywhere from 15,000 to 20,000 troops, which Ammianus describes as a force of mixed types: "neither unwarlike nor contemptible, and had united with them many veteran bands."[19] The army was led in part by Trajan, an Eastern Roman general of the infantry, and Victor who was the master of the cavalry and of Sarmatian origin. Valens probably intended to march along the Maritsa river to Philippopolis and join up with Gratian's army. But Fritigern had directed his army toward Adrianople with the intention of cutting off Valens' supply route to Constantinople. When Valens' scouts informed him that Fritigern was marching toward Adrianople with an army of 10,000, Valens marched back to Adrianople and set up a fortified camp outside the city, awaiting the rendezvous with Gratian.

Back at the camp, Sebastian told Valens of Gratian's success against the Lentienses, "exaggerating what had taken place in pompous language."[20] Ricimer, Gratian's master of soldiers, had also arrived in the camp with a letter from Gratian imploring Valens to wait for him, so that "he [Gratian] might share in the danger."[21] Valens, however, learned that Gratian was marching to reinforce him with only a small force. Not wanting to share the glory with Gratian, whose small force he presumed would have been of little help, and hoping to bolster his popularity among his people, Valens decided to engage the Goths immediately, "being eager by some glorious exploit to equal his youthful nephew, by whose virtue he was greatly excited."[22]

Though the Roman scouts had noted that Fritigern had only 10,000 men at his disposal, they were unaware of the cavalry force of Greuthungi Goths, Alans, and Huns under the command of Alatheus and Saphrax, which were foraging along the Tundzha further north.[23] Hoping to delay the Romans for as long as possible until their arrival, Fritigern dispatched a presbyter of the Arian faith to offer peace terms to Valens. The terms were a reinstatement of the original agreements made two years earlier, namely settlement land in Thrace in return for perpetual peace. Valens distrusted the honesty of the letter; furthermore, he felt the Romans would look weak if he were to give in to the Goths' demands without any punitive action against them. He therefore rejected the offer and, "fortified by the flattery of some of the princes,"[24] decided to fight.

THE BATTLE

"When the day broke which the annals mark as the fifth before the Ides of August [August 9], the Roman standards were advanced with haste..."[25] After a forced march of 13km under the sweltering heat of the sun, Valens' army came upon the Gothic force. Fritigern had drawn up the Gothic wagons into a circular formation;

within them were all of the Gothic possessions, plus the women and children.[26] When the Romans came into sight, the Gothic "host raised a fierce and hideous yell, while the Romans generals marshaled their line of battle."[27] Valens had the right wing of his cavalry out in front, with the main core of his infantry held in reserve. The left wing of the cavalry were still arriving on the scene and moving into formation. Nevertheless, the Romans made a threateningly loud clash of arms and shields, enough to provoke the Goths to stall for time by sending an envoy to sue for peace. Predictably, Valens was offended by the lowliness of the rank of the Gothic envoy and sent them away, telling them "if they wished to make a lasting treaty, they must send him nobles of sufficient dignity."[28]

Fritigern was successfully buying more time. The cavalry led by Alatheus and Saphrax had not yet arrived and, being a careful man, Fritigern did not wish to risk battle yet. In order to wear down the Romans, he also ordered the crops of the field burned so that the smoke and heat further plagued the already over-heated Roman army. In addition, Ammianus tells us that the Romans and their beasts were already suffering from hunger and thirst.[29] Finally, Fritigern offered to negotiate in person if the Romans would in turn offer a high-ranking official as a hostage.

The Roman camp decided on Ricimer as the hostage and chose Valens' right-wing cavalry (led by Cassio and Bacurius) to accompany Ricimer as his guard. As Ricimer rode out to fulfill his diplomatic mission, the Roman envoy crossed the battlefield to the Gothic right flank. Suddenly Cassio and Bacurius made an unexpected and unauthorized attack on the right flank of the Goths. Ammianus tells us that the *scutarii* (probably elite heavy cavalry), while accompanying Ricimer on his mission, "yielded, while on their march, to an indiscreet impetuosity, and on approaching the enemy, first attacked them rashly, and then by a cowardly flight disgraced the beginning of the campaign."[30] We can only speculate as to why the scutarii attacked. Perhaps they saw these negotiations for the sham they were and, thinking that they could easily disperse the Goths, decided to take matters into their own hands. Nevertheless, they were repulsed, and it couldn't have happened at a worse time – Alatheus and Saphrax had just arrived on the scene with the Gothic cavalry and a battalion of Alans, who "descended from the mountains like a thunderbolt, spread confusion and slaughter among all whom in their rapid charge they came across."[31]

The retreating right wing cavalry (operating on the Goths' right flank) rallied briefly, but crumbled under the pressure of the combined Alan and Gothic attack.[32] At this same time, the Gothic infantry attacked all along the Roman line. "Then the two lines of battle dashed against each other, like the beaks of ships, and thrusting with all their might, were tossed to and fro, like the waves of the sea."[33]

The left flank of the Roman infantry actually advanced all the way to the wagons, but was soon left unsupported by their cavalry. Initially, the left flank cavalry had rallied in the face of the retreating right wing cavalry, but then lost heart as a number of them became transfixed with arrows and javelins, and they too fled the field.[34] The Roman infantry was now completely unsupported and was hemmed in on all sides, with the Gothic cavalry constricting the Romans on their flanks and their rear. Ammianus describes that

> the different companies became so huddled together that a soldier could hardly draw his sword, or withdraw his hand after he had once stretched it out. And by this time such clouds of dust arose that it was scarcely possible to see the sky, which resounded with horrible cries; and in consequence, the darts, which were bearing death on every side, reached their mark, and fell with deadly effect, because no one could see them beforehand so as to guard against them.[35]

Seeing the desperation of their situation, the Romans began to fight back like cornered animals. In the fog of the final battle, Ammianus vividly describes the scene:

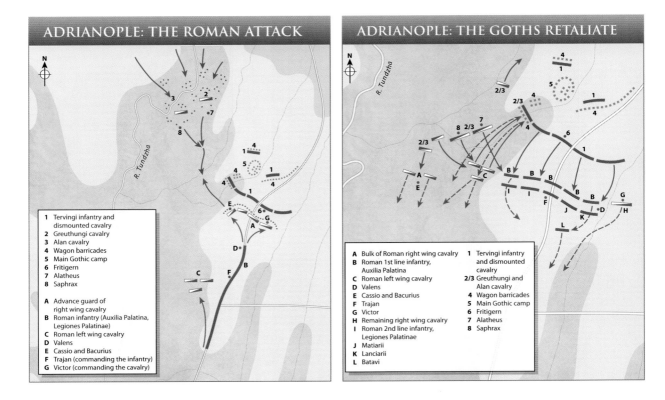

ADRIANOPLE: THE ROMAN ATTACK

1 Tervingi infantry and dismounted cavalry
2 Greuthungi cavalry
3 Alan cavalry
4 Wagon barricades
5 Main Gothic camp
6 Fritigern
7 Alatheus
8 Saphrax

A Advance guard of right wing cavalry
B Roman infantry (Auxilia Palatina, Legiones Palatinae)
C Roman left wing cavalry
D Valens
E Cassio and Bacurius
F Trajan (commanding the infantry)
G Victor (commanding the cavalry)

ADRIANOPLE: THE GOTHS RETALIATE

A Bulk of Roman right wing cavalry
B Roman 1st line infantry, Auxilia Palatina
C Roman left wing cavalry
D Valens
E Cassio and Bacurius
F Trajan
G Victor
H Remaining right wing cavalry
I Roman 2nd line infantry, Legiones Palatinae
J Matiarii
K Lanciarii
L Batavi

1 Tervingi infantry and dismounted cavalry
2/3 Greuthungi and Alan cavalry
4 Wagon barricades
5 Main Gothic camp
6 Fritigern
7 Alatheus
8 Saphrax

Then you might see the barbarian towering in his fierceness, hissing or shouting, fall with his legs pierced through, or his right hand cut off, sword and all, or his side transfixed, and still, in the last gasp of life, casting round him defiant glances. The plain was covered with carcasses, strewing the mutual ruin of the combatants; while the groans of the dying, or of men fearfully wounded, were intense, and caused great dismay all around.[36]

This aqueduct was constructed during the time of Emperor Valens. (Author's Collection)

But the Romans could not hold out forever. Their spears were broken by the frequent collisions and they had to resort to using their swords, which they thrust into the enemy lines of the Goths, searching for a route of escape but finding none.

The ground, covered with streams of blood, made their feet slip, so that all they endeavored to do was to sell their lives as dearly as possible; and with such vehemence did they resist their enemies who pressed on them, that some were even killed by their own weapons. At last one black pool of blood disfigured everything, and wherever the eye turned, it could see nothing but piled up heaps of dead, and lifeless corpses trampled on without mercy.[37]

Soon, the Romans broke, with each man fleeing for his life.

Valens was abandoned by his bodyguard and, "bewildered with terrible fear, made his way over heaps of dead," fleeing to the battalions of the Lanccarii and the Mattiarii (heavy infantry) who were still standing firm for the moment.[38] Once under the protection of the heavy infantry, Valens ordered Trajan and Victor to bring the reserves into action, but these had already left the field. Presently, even Victor and the remaining officers fled, leaving Valens alone to his fate.[39]

There are two accounts of Valens' death. One is that he was pierced by an arrow and died unrecognized among his soldiers. The other is that he escaped to a nearby farm and was subsequently burned alive by Goths who did not know he was inside.[40] Regardless of the exact nature of his death, Ammianus tells us that one thing is certain: Valens did not enjoy "that last honor of the dead – a regular funeral."[41]

The Goths pursued the remaining Romans "who were in a state of torpor, the warmth of their veins having deserted them," and slaughtered them whether or not they resisted.[42] Barely one third of the Roman Army escaped the annihilation. Among the dead were also Trajan, Sebastian, and 35 tribunes.[43]

THE AFTERMATH

After their victory, the Goths laid two unsuccessful sieges to both Adrianople and Constantinople. Theodosius, the new Eastern Roman Emperor, would continue to war against the Goths for the next four years until he finally negotiated a peace treaty that reestablished the terms of 376. More importantly, the Goths were able to maintain their own laws and the leadership of their armies under the treaty. It was this last unprecedented move that would change the Roman Empire and her armies forever, damaging the imperial structure of the Western Empire and sowing the seeds of her eventual fall.[44]

How could this remarkable turn of events come at the hands of a rabble of refugees, defeating the best organized, armed, and disciplined army in the world? First, the Goths were able to commandeer Roman arms and armor for the battle, thus negating the Roman's technological superiority. Second, the Goths maintained a unified front under the leadership of Fritigern, unlike the Romans with their competing Emperors and ideologies (with prejudices against the Arian faith of Emperor Valens perhaps playing a role). Lastly, it must not be discounted that while the Romans fought with armies that were far away from their homes, the Goths' families were directly behind them in their wagons, providing them with a palpable reminder of what was at stake if they were to fail. But ultimately, the final word may be that the battle of Adrianople "merely emphasized in dramatic fashion what students of tactics had already learned – a mobile force, which can project its combat power, has a tremendous advantage over a less mobile force, which is limited in ability to project its combat power."[45]

PLISKA, 811

The battle of Pliska reads from the sources of that period as a morality tale, with the destruction of the Byzantine Army in a rocky Bulgarian pass as an act of divine judgment. The chroniclers describe the Byzantine Emperor, Nicephorus I, as a greedy King Midas who cared nothing about the welfare of his people, but wished only to fill his own imperial coffers. He is likened to a Pharaoh with a hardened heart, refusing to listen to the pleas for peace from his barbarian adversary, Khan Krum. Instead, Nicephorus, this fanatical man obsessed with the destruction of the Bulgarian people, opted for senseless butchery and brutality. A careful reading of history shows, however, that Nicephorus had as many virtues as vices, but it was his failure at Pliska that ultimately allowed his political and religious adversaries to cast him as a villain.

BACKGROUND

The early years of the 800s represent possibly the nadir of the Byzantine Empire.[1] The reign of Empress Irene was coming to an end. By nearly all accounts, her rule was disastrous, bankrupting the Empire with tax breaks that she used to increase her popularity and weakening the imperial army by purging the ranks of its iconoclasts.[2] In the year 802, she was deposed by a coup of high-ranking Byzantine officials led by her former *Logothete* of the Treasury (or Minister of Finance), Nicephorus I.[3] The new emperor was of Arab extraction, the descendent of a Christian-Arab enclave in Syria. "He was above middle height, with broad shoulders, had a big belly, thick hair, thick lips, broad face and a very white beard, plump, very clever, sly, shrewd…" wrote an anonymous contemporary chronicler who has been dubbed by posterity as Scriptor Incertus.[4]

Nicephorus was a restless man of energy and resolve, and almost certainly was not a man of piety, as subsequent events will show. Though often described as easygoing and genial, the new emperor was to make many new enemies. As he worked quickly and decisively to effect new measures that would set the imperial treasury to rights, his radical policies made him anathema to those powers within the Church and the bureaucracy. Once Nicephorus took the reins of power, however, he was eager to show how the firm hand of a man back in the highest office could restore the Byzantine Empire to its former glory.

During the early period of his reign, through the years 802–807, Nicephorus was busy fighting the Saracens on the eastern borders of the Empire.[5] Up to this point, the Saracens had been satisfied by a yearly tribute that had been negotiated by Empress Irene. One of Nicephorus' first acts was boldly to send Caliph Harun, the leader of the Saracens, a message informing him that the days of appeasing the Arabs with tributes were over. Caliph Harun immediately sent an army to chastise the insolent new emperor. In spite of the confidence that Nicephorus must have had in his army and in his own military prowess, the Byzantines suffered many setbacks at the hands of the Saracens. On March 24, 809, however, Caliph Harun died while campaigning against rebels in Khurasan. After the Caliph's death, a protracted civil war broke out among the Arabs while Harun's sons, al-Amin and al-Ma'mun, fought over succession.

For almost another 20 years, Arab power was crippled by this internecine warfare, preventing the Arabs from carrying out an attack against the Empire. This situation allowed Nicephorus to concentrate his attention on the northern borders of his Empire, to the former imperial lands now controlled by the Bulgars.

Originally a horse people from the Central Asian steppes, the Bulgars arrived on the Danube in AD 679 and promptly defeated a Byzantine force under Constantine IV.[6] The Bulgars were to remain a problem for the

An illustration from the *Constantine Mannassas Chronicle* (a history of the world published in the 12th century) depicting the capture of Byzantine Emperor Nicephorus I at Pliska. (Author's Collection)

Byzantines for the remainder of their imperial history. Aside from the Byzantines and their own inter-tribal power struggles, however, the Bulgars were also preoccupied with the Avars in the north. Two centuries earlier, the Avars had carried large numbers of Bulgars into captivity and their descendents still lived under the dominion of the Avar Empire. But between 791 and 795, the Franks under King Charles[7] had made deep inroads into the Avar Empire and the Bulgars took advantage of this situation. By 803, a Bulgar chieftain named Krum had completed the destruction of the hated rivals and the Avars disappeared from history.[8]

The origins of Khan Krum are obscure, other than he was the leader of the Bulgars of Pannonia.[9] Khan Kardum, the leader of the Balkan Bulgars, died in the year 808, leaving them without a king. By virtue of his victory over the Avars, Krum was able to transfer himself to this superior throne, thus uniting the two kingdoms and consolidating Bulgar power. It is possible that Krum was descended from an established royal race, as he would have needed to meet the approval of the jealous Bulgar *boyars* (or nobles) if he was to rise to the throne. Regardless, the Bulgar Empire now stretched from Pesht (the modern Budapest) to the Black Sea, with its power centered in the Bulgars' capital city, Pliska.[10]

Krum seems to have been a crafty leader and, with the military strength of a combined kingdom, he was soon to put his new-found power to good use. The weakness of the Byzantine Empire in the early 800s was not lost on the Bulgars (Empress Irene, after all, had been forced to pay tribute to them), and they took pleasure in raiding the imperial territories from time to time.

THE CAMPAIGN

In 807, war broke out between the Byzantines and the Bulgars. We do not know for certain who initiated hostilities, but it appears that Emperor Nicephorus may have been the first to provoke war.[11] The campaign, however, was aborted when a mutiny was discovered among the ranks, effectively illustrating Nicephorus' shaky approval rating. The emperor successfully suppressed the mutiny, but he considered it unwise to continue further with the campaign and returned to Constantinople.

In 808, the Bulgars went on the offensive, possibly emboldened by Nicephorus' stillborn campaign of a year earlier.[12] Suspecting that Krum had ambitions for Macedonia (a region with considerable Slavic influence and population), Nicephorus mustered an army in the *theme* (adminstrative provinc) of Strymon to check their intrusions. By late winter, it appeared that Krum would not attack after all, and the Byzantines relaxed their guard. With Holy Week approaching, the *strategos* (general) of the Macedonian *theme* had his army along with its whole payroll camped at the

River Strymon. The Bulgars surprised this force, killing the general and devastating many of his army's regiments. The Bulgars also managed to capture the 500kg of gold intended as the payroll of the 12,000 Byzantine soldiers they had just destroyed. Treasure in tow, the Bulgars then melted back into the land of the Slavs.[13]

In the spring of 809, just before Easter, Krum once more went on the offensive, attacking the fortress of Sardicia, the most northerly outpost of the Byzantine Empire nearing the Danube. The Byzantines had a string of fortresses guarding their borders and protecting their trade routes, and Sardicia appears to have been a particular impediment to the Bulgars' roads to Serbia and Upper Macedonia. Krum marched his army to the fortress of Sardicia intending to take it by storm, but found its fortifications too strong. Illustrating his ingenuity, Krum was able to convince one of the defenders of the fort to allow a force commanded by him to enter. Once he gained entry into the fortress, Krum ordered the massacre of the 6,000-man garrison and, it was reported, the entire population of Sardicia.[14] He then had the fortress dismantled and the town destroyed.

Nicephorus heard this alarming news on April 3, 809, the Tuesday before Easter.[15] The mobile army of the *tagmata* (the professional standing troops of the city of Constantinople) and the army of the theme of Thrace were at Constantinople, totaling around 17,000 men, were gathered so he could depart immediately.[16] He hastily left the city with the full strength of those armies, ordering them into forced marches to make it to Pliska by Easter Sunday. Surprisingly, Nicephorus found the city undefended, as Krum's army was still in the west. Pliska was erected among low hills and had only wooden fortifications, thus it was easily subdued by the imperial armies. On April 8, Nicephorus celebrated Easter in Krum's palace, writing a triumphant letter to Constantinople speaking of his conquest and plunder of Pliska.

Nicephorus then marched to Sardicia, the site of the recent Bulgar atrocity. Frugal as ever, Nicephorus decided that he could save money by having his armies rebuild the fortress. He suspected, however, that the soldiers of the tagmata, as elite troops, would not like to be treated as mere construction workers and asked his officers to appeal to their soldiers' *esprit de corps*. But the emperor did not realize how disenfranchised his army now felt. Having been in such a hurry to leave for Pliska on April 3, Nicephorus had neglected to pay his soldiers. Additionally, the soldiers had been forced to march on Holy Week and to fight on Easter Sunday, all without pay. The officers' pleas fell on deaf ears as the soldiers staged a mutiny, tearing down the tents of their superiors and forming up in front of the emperor's pavilion to demonstrate against his avarice. Nicephorus boldly had a table set up before them and addressed their grievances. In spite of this, the mutiny continued through the night, with the aggrieved demonstrating on a nearby hill crying out, a little over-dramatically, "Lord, have mercy!"[17] The mutiny was suppressed after the emperor appeared before his soldiers the next day on the hill, making a declaration of his goodwill toward them and their families. The ringleaders, however, were punished with lashes, banishment, or were forced to join monasteries. Consequently, Sardicia was quickly rebuilt and at a low cost by the army. Victorious militarily and economically, Nicephorus returned to Constantinople without further incident.

The Byzantine emperor now intended to spend some of the political capital he had gained with his recent victory at Pliska. Still fearing the ambitions of the Bulgars, he mandated extensive relocation of the citizens of Asia Minor to Macedonia. Nicephorus believed that the loyalty of the Slavs was questionable and feared they might rebel against imperial authority and join the ranks of the Bulgars. The emperor ordered certain families, both rich and poor alike, to move from various *themes* throughout the Empire to the lands of the Balkans. These families were ordered to sell their lands to the Empire and then receive similar land grants in the new territories. This was an incredibly unpopular edict, and some of those charged opting for suicide rather than leave their ancestral homelands. Nevertheless, the move was a momentous one for the Byzantines, helping to consolidate these lands for the Empire and change the demography of the Balkans up to the present day.[18]

From among those who had resettled, Nicephorus chose those with the least landholdings to be recruited into a new army to defend the Balkans and also to receive new military landholdings there. From these recruits, the emperor created a new *tagma* (an elite battalion of soldiers) called the *Hicanati*, meaning the "Worthies" or the "Able Ones." Into this new tagma, which consisted of 4,000 cavalry, each knight with his own squire, Nicephorus recruited some of his officers' sons, aged 14 and older to add prestige and loyalty to the army.[19] Though the tagma comprised adolescents, it was intended to be a real fighting force, and by 811 it had completed a full year of training and was ready for service.[20]

In addition to this epic relocation of population, Nicephorus introduced a series of tax reforms in order to strengthen the Byzantine economy, which had suffered under years of neglect and mismanagement by Empress Irene. The emperor taxed the wealth of merchants by supervising the sale of all sorts of animals and produce, and compelled ship owners to take out loans from the state in order to stimulate the economy. Lastly, he increased the taxes on the churches and the monasteries and demanded back-taxes from his military commanders dating back to the beginning of his reign. These reforms caused a general outcry among the people. When told of this fact by his administrators, Nicephorus said, according to Theophanes, "If the Lord, who hardens hearts of men, hardened my heart as the *pharaon* [i.e. Pharaoh], what good can my subjects expect from me?"[21]

Khan Krum immortalized
in stone near the ancient
Bulgarian castle of
Missionis. (Courtesy
of Svilen Enev)

By now, Nicephorus had become obsessed with destroying Krum and the Bulgars forever and had made all the necessary arrangements in order to undertake a great expedition against them. Seeing that the Empire's borders with the Saracens continued to be at peace, Nicephorus summoned all of the themes' regiments from throughout Anatolia (Asia Minor) including their *strategoi*.

THE BYZANTINE ARMY

In May 811, Nicephorus left Constantinople with his inflated imperial army, probably the largest force assembled in the memory of the participants. Marching with Nicephorus were all the mobile tagmata and all the available troops from the themes of Thrace and Anatolia. Nicephorus also put his son, Stauracius, in charge of the "Worthies," the specialized regiment of young men. Lastly, Nicephorus was joined by a gathering of common men, who brought their own provisions and were armed with slings and clubs. The total army numbered about 70,000 men.[22]

Aside from his massive army, Nicephorus also deployed with a sparkling array of high-ranking courtiers from Constantinople, including his son-in-law Michael Rhangabe. Nicephorus was confident of victory, and so was everyone else. No one wanted to miss what they believed would be the signal event of their lifetimes. It was more like a carnival than a military campaign, with everyone attending so that they might witness or participate in the victory. The gathering was so complete, that it may be assumed that the emperor wanted to make sure that no one could plot against him while he was away. In addition, Nicephorus made sure that there were enough chroniclers to record the victory for posterity.

THE BULGAR ARMY

Reliable information on the numbers or composition of Krum's Bulgarian Army is not available. Since the Bulgars were originally nomads, we can assume that cavalry and skirmishers constituted an important part of their forces. However, as they became settled among the Slavic peoples and became influenced by the nearby Byzantines, infantry would have played an increasing role in their army.[23] Some written descriptions show that the Balkan Buglars adopted Byzantine military fashions and weapons as well.[24] Ascertaining the size of Krum's army is problematic. Scriptor Incertus claims that during the campaign Nicephorus defeated a 12,000-man regiment of Bulgars and later a 50,000-man regiment of reinforcements.[25] The latter number is clearly inflated, for if that were the case the 70,000-man army of Nicephorus would not have awed Krum as it did. Moreover, Krum's victory in Sardicia was won with cunning rather than with overwhelming force. With these considerations in mind, Krum's army could not have numbered more than 50,000 at the outset of the campaign and was soon reduced by half.

ON THE MOVE

Before entering Bulgaria, Nicephorus paused to wait for reinforcements on the frontier at Marcellae. Krum sent spies to see Nicephorus' army and was impressed by its magnitude. He desperately sent ambassadors to sue for peace. Yet Nicephorus was confident of victory and distrusted Krum's promises. He wanted to eliminate the Bulgar menace once and for all. While he idled in Marcellae, however, one of his staff disappeared from the encampment with a portion of the imperial wardrobe and 45kg of gold. It was discovered that the traitor had fled to Krum's side. Many in Nicephorus' ranks considered this a bad omen.

In July, the imperial armies pressed forward and entered Bulgaria itself, heading toward Pliska. Krum and his army ran to the safety of the mountains, while Nicephorus and the Byzantine Army entered the Bulgarian capital yet again. On July 13, the massive army of the Byzantines decisively defeated a Bulgarian regiment of 12,000 men defending the poor fortifications of Krum's palace.[26] Krum sent a relief force of 15,000 men to Pliska and the garrison arrived the following day, albeit too late. The Byzantines decimated this force as well, while suffering few casualties themselves. Once again, Nicephorus wrote back to Constantinople that he was successfully occupying Pliska, attributing his victories to the advice of his son Stauracius.

The last time Nicephorus had taken Pliska, he failed to find Krum's treasure. This time he undertook a thorough search of the palace and finally discovered it. He set aside this treasure for himself and affixed it with imperial seals. Realizing his past mistake, however, he made sure the additional plunders of the palace were doled out to his soldiers. He even opened Krum's wine cellars, letting his soldiers drink until they were sated. Nevertheless, he strived to maintain order in the ranks and threatened to cut off the noses and ears of looters.[27]

Nicephorus had become quite satisfied with his conquests, perhaps too satisfied. Scriptor Incertus writes that Nicephorus became unduly proud, as if he had achieved all this through his just deeds alone, saying, "This is what righteousness does."[28] The exultant emperor strolled around the terraces of the houses of Pliska and the walkways of Krum's palace and said, "Behold, God has given me all this, and I want to found here a city that bears my name so that I am renowned in all succeeding generations."[29]

According to Theophanes, after Nicephorus was finished plundering Pliska, he completely razed the city and massacred its civilians. This hostile source improbably reports that Nicephorus allowed the bodies of his own dead soldiers to go unburied and that he ran Bulgar babies through threshing machines.[30] As a final insult, Krum's palace was burned to the ground.

Krum, utterly demoralized, sent a message to Nicephorus saying, "Lo, thou hast conquered. Take what thou wilt and depart in peace."[31] But Nicephorus refused to bargain. He was not willing to leave a land that he considered Byzantine territory in the first place, and after his early sweeping successes he was bent on the complete annihilation of the Bulgars.

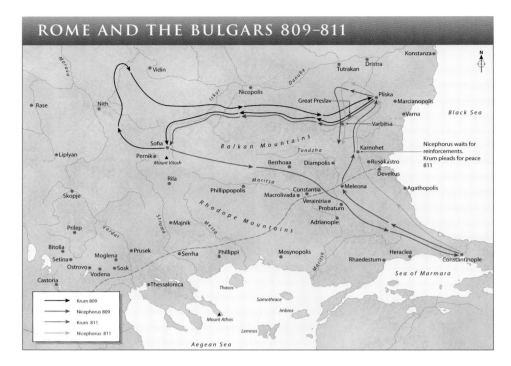

ROME AND THE BULGARS 809–811

THE BATTLE

With his army at or near its full strength of 70,000, Nicephorus pursued the Bulgars into the mountains. He intended to march through to Sardicia, confident of his total control of the Bulgarian territory. The Bulgarian Army was severely depleted and Krum was now fighting for his life, even resorting to arming the women of the nearby Slavic tribes for battle.[32]

As the imperial army chased the Bulgars, they entered into a mountain pass on Thursday, July 24.[33] The exact location of the pass and the subsequent battle is unknown, but most historians agree that it was probably the Pass of Varbitsa.[34] Nicephorus, apparently overconfident, did not order sufficient reconnaissance before leading his army into the ravine. From the cover of the forest, the Bulgars secretly watched the Byzantines' every move as the emperor's army leisurely made its way through the gorge. Krum recognized immediately that Nicephorus had made a critical mistake: the Byzantine emperor had led his army into a narrow pass, making it vulnerable to flanking attacks on each side from the cover of forests. As night fell, Krum had his engineers build wooden palisades – terrible and impassable wall-like ramparts made from large tree trunks – at either end of this narrow, rocky pass to trap them inside.[35]

On the morning of the next day, Nicephorus' scouts discovered the wooden palisades blocking the entrance and the exits of the ravine. When the emperor learned of this trap, he became paralyzed with fear as if "stricken by lightning and did not know what to do."[36] His generals implored him to take action, but Nicephorus had become resigned to his and his army's fate. Some of his officers favored attacking the palisades immediately, but Nicephorus refused. Not knowing that he had destroyed most of the Bulgarian Army, Nicephorus saw the palisades as the perfect trap. Here, within this narrow defile blocked by the wooden ramparts, a small garrison could defend against a vast army. The Byzantines' numerical superiority would therefore be neutralized, while the remaining Bulgars hiding in the forest could pick off the beleaguered army. Not willing to relent, the officers persuaded Stauracius to convince his father to assault the palisades, but Nicephorus remained steadfast in his position. "Even were we birds," he said, "we could not hope to escape."[37] It was decided that they would tell no one in the imperial army of these alarming developments.

Although the truth was successfully hidden from the rank and file, some officers who were in the know resorted to subterfuge to abscond from the ranks. The remaining soldiers, unaware of the looming catastrophe, continued to pillage the valley. Scriptor Incertus reports that during this time Emperor Nicephorus "neglected his obligations, became mad, went out of his mind, became completely insane… Inebriated by his arrogance, he did not go out of his tent, did not give any explanation, or order, and when some men reproached him and sent his son to go out of there,[38] he did not listen to him but even humiliated his son."[39] The rest of the

An illustration from the *Constantine Mannassas Chronicle* illustrating the Bulgar pursuit and wounding of Nicephorus' son and successor Stauracius. He was not killed but carried to safety by his Imperial Guard. (Author's Collection)

army, left unattended, used this opportunity to "burn unharvested fields, cut the sinews of oxen and hide their flanks to make ropes while the animals bellowed loudly and died, slaughtered sheep and pigs, and did other reprehensible deeds."[40]

Meanwhile, the Bulgars continued to work hard on their fortifications, and by Saturday, July 26, they rested, prepared to starve out the huge Byzantine Army. Each night as the work continued on the wooden palisades, the Bulgars harassed the Byzantines, clanging their swords and shields and kept them, according to Theophanes, "in a feverish restlessness and brought them to utter exhaustion."[41] But rather than wait for the Byzantine Army to starve, Krum opportunistically decided to attack the imperial encampment. By what must have been some extraordinary carelessness on behalf of the Byzantines, perhaps caused by Emperor Nicephorus' hopelessness, the emperor's camp was inadequately guarded.[42] Encouraged by this weakness, the Bulgars watched the encampment during the day and planned to target the emperor's pavilion at night, hoping to take out the Byzantine leadership.

At dawn, under the cover of darkness, they fell upon Nicephorus' tent while the Byzantines were still sleeping. The surprised Byzantines quickly armed themselves, but Nicephorus' bodyguards were able to give only a brief resistance before they and the emperor fell. No one knows exactly how Nicephorus met his doom. Some relate that his own men killed him because of his unpopularity, or that the Bulgars wounded him while the Byzantines finished him off.[43] Still, in the Bulgarian translation of the *Mannases Chronicle*,[44] it states that Krum killed Nicephorus and cut off the emperor's head himself.[45] Regardless, all of Nicephorus' generals, nobles, and high dignitaries died in the ensuing battle, many of them massacred in their own tents, including the generals of Thrace and Anatolia.[46] Theophanes reports that among those killed were

> …the patricians Aecius, Peter, Sisnius, Tryphillios, Theodosius Salivaras who offended greatly the blessed Irene and committed wicked deeds against her, the patrician Eparchos [Prefect] of the capital, and patricius Romanus, the patrician and strategos of the [theme] Anatolic, and many other protospatharios, spatharios, and archons of the tagmata, and also the domesticos of the Excubitors, the droungarios of the Imperial Watch, the strategos of the Thracian Army and many archons of themes together with innumerable soldiers. Thus perished the flower of Christianity.[47]

Since the detachments were encamped far away from each other, many of them didn't know what had happened to the emperor's pavilion at first, and therefore did not come to his aid. Had the other Byzantines become aware of the attack, it is possible that they could have repulsed the Bulgars or at least saved one of the generals and possibly turned the tide of the battle. Once it was perceived that the emperor had fallen, however, the remainder of the army took flight. The bulk of the refugees were mostly cavalry, and they rode until they reached a wide, swampy river that they were unable to ford, possibly the River Ticha or one of its tributaries. To avoid their pursuers, the Byzantines fell into the river in desperation, along with their horses. Once in the river, they could not escape and were trampled by those coming in behind them. Soon the dead bodies of horses and Byzantines in the river were enough to create a body bridge that allowed the remainder of the army to flee and, unfortunately for the Byzantines, for the enemy to pursue.

Those who were lucky enough to escape past the river, ran headlong into Krum's wooden palisades at the exit of the mountain pass. The ramparts were strong, high, and difficult to climb, though it appears that the Bulgars had too

Krum entrapped the Byzantines in the mountain passes by the use of wooden palisades. (Author's Collection)

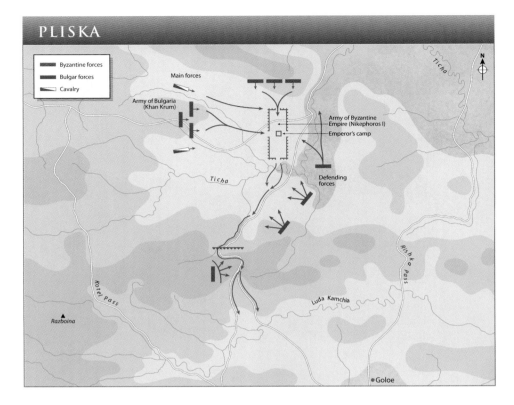

few soldiers to keep them manned.[48] After unsuccessfully attempting to create a breach in the wooden ramparts, the escaping Byzantines "dismounted and climbed with their hands and feet and hung on the other side."[49] Those who were able to climb over the ramparts found that the Bulgars had dug a deep moat on the other side. Unable to scale down the palisades, the Byzantines fell into the moat, many dying straight away from the height of the fall. Those who did survive the plummet would break their arms or legs, and then die of hunger or thirst in the wilderness. Still other escaping Byzantines burned sections of the ramparts in the hopes of freeing themselves. When the ropes that held together the palisades were burned, some of the huge tree trunks fell across the moat, creating a bridge. A portion of the Byzantine soldiers rode across the makeshift bridge eager for escape, but the beams were weakened by the fire and collapsed. The Byzantines riding across the failing timbers then fell into the depths of the moat, now filled with burning tree trunks.

Soon the moat became filled with corpses and debris, allowing a few miserable fugitives to escape. The Bulgars also created artificially induced landslides to kill the Byzantine soldiers caught between the barrier and freedom.[50] The "Worthies," the tagmata that comprised the flower of Byzantine youth, was hit particularly hard. Scriptor Incertus laments the event providing, if not the most accurate of histories, a picture of how the Byzantines perceived the disaster:

> Thus perished the commanders' sons both of the old and of the young ones who were a whole multitude, in the blossom of their youth, and they had beautiful bodies that shined with whiteness, with golden hairs and beards, with handsome faces. Some of them had

An illustration from the *Constantine Manassas Chronicle* depicting Krum's celebration of the Bulgar victory at Pliska by drinking wine out of Nicephorus' skull, thus transferring his enemy's strength to his own blood. (Author's Collection)

just been engaged to women, distinguished with nobility and beauty. All perished there: some brought down by the sword, others drowned in the river, [a] third fell from the rampart, and still others burned in the moat. Only a few of them escaped but even they, after they arrived in their homes, almost all of them died.[51]

The exact number of Byzantine dead is unknown. While most of the leaders of the Byzantine Army died in Krum's initial attack, the remainder were cut down as they fled (illustrating the virtues of an orderly retreat). It is possible that the imperial army may have suffered little more than 27,000 dead, but this is unlikely.[52] A good estimate would raise the Byzantine casualties to at least 50,000 dead, possibly more. There were some notable survivors, however. The emperor's son, Stauracius, and his brother-in-law, Michael Rhangabe, were two of the few who escaped to the safety of Adrianople. Others used the cover of darkness to steal away or hide in the shrubbery and swamps.[53] Stauracius suffered a hideous wound to the right side of his back that severed his spinal cord and paralyzed him from the thighs down. He was taken from the battlefield alive and eventually made it back to Constantinople on a litter.[54] Despite his wound, Stauracius was named emperor back in Constantinople, and managed to muster enough strength to address the troops, or what was left of them. In his speech, he was critical of his father, Nicephorus, who had refused to take his advice when he pleaded with him to break out of the valley at all costs. But his reign was to last only a few months, as he died from a grotesque rotting of his wound. Michael Rhangabe, one of the only uninjured survivors, would later be crowned emperor.

Nicephorus' severed head was impaled on a stake and exposed for all to see. After displaying the emperor's head to his warlords for several days, and to the humiliation of the captured Byzantines, Krum had the skull's flesh removed and the insides hollowed out, lining it with silver. He used it as drinking cup for the rest of his days, toasting his fellow Bulgars with the traditional Slavic blessing of "Zdravitza!"[55]

THE AFTERMATH

The news of the annihilation of the Byzantine Army and the death of Emperor Nicephorus came as a shock to Constantinople. Not since the days of Valens 400 years ago, had an emperor died on the field. It was a serious blow to Byzantine prestige and to the emperor's supposed invulnerability, which had been so carefully crafted in order to awe the barbarians. In one swift stroke, Krum had negated all of Nicephorus' gains and hard work in Macedonia and the Balkans. Now, the inviolability of Krum's kingdom could not be questioned and would not be threatened by Byzantium in the foreseeable future. As for Nicephorus, instead of being remembered as a progressive reformer who restored the glory of the Empire, he was to be immortalized by the chroniclers as a greedy Midas, an obsessive Ahab, and as a Pharaoh with a hardened heart.

HATTIN, 1187

The battle of Hattin on July 4, 1187, near the Sea of Galilee, signaled the end of the Latin kingdom that had been created by earlier Crusades. At the same time, the defeat of the Christian forces spurred the European enthusiasm for war and crusading, leading to the Third Crusade (1189–92) most commonly associated with Richard the Lionheart of England.

BACKGROUND

After the successful subjugation of Jerusalem in 1099 during the First Crusade (1095–99) and a indecisive Second Crusade (1147–49), the Middle East was once again transformed when Salāh ad-Dīn Yūsuf ibn Ayyūb (1138–1193), commonly known as Saladin, a Kurdish Sunni Muslim, unified the various Islamic tribes and their territories. By 1180 a fragile truce existed between Saladin and the Crusader states. (The Crusader states were a number of 12th- and 13th-century states created by Western European crusaders in Asia Minor, Greece, and the Holy Land.) One of the thorns that habitually pricked the peace was Reynald de Châtillon, a knight who had fought and was captured during the Second Crusade, spending almost two decades confined to Aleppo in northern Syria, before being ransomed for an extraordinary sum. Reynald raided passing caravans even during times of peace and was audacious enough to launch raids deep into enemy territories. He was recaptured near the holy city of Medina but managed to escape. "Reynald's spectacular but disastrous naval expedition into the Red Sea sent shock waves throughout the Islamic world and dented Saladin's status as Protector of the Muslim Holy Places in Mecca and Medina,"[1] as Reynald's sailors were little more than pirates who ravaged villages along their route. Saladin vowed to behead Reynald himself.

THE CRUSADERS

Guy de Lusignan, the King of Jerusalem, ordered a general mobilization of forces in May 1187 in response to the recent successes of Saladin, who had recaptured territory and managed to unify the armies against the Christians. By the end of June, Guy had assembled an impressive army comprising no fewer than 1,200 knights, including knights from the Military Orders and the Turcopoles (mounted archers). In addition to the force of heavily armed and armored knights, his army included an additional 15,000–18,000 foot soldiers, whose primary job lay in the protection of the susceptible knights – heavy Christian knights who were easy targets for the hit-and-run tactics of the Muslim light horse archers. The king's army assembled at Saforie (Saffuriya).[2] The size of the Christian army that would meet its doom at Hattin is listed by David Nicolle as having included 1,200 knights, 4,000 lighter cavalry serjeants, and Turcopoles. Its 15,000 to 18,000 infantry would have been of mixed value, ranging from professional crossbowmen to inexperienced locals.[3] Stanley Lane-Poole argues that the duty of the Franks in the Holy Land was to defend and not to attack, as the Franks in their position were more suitable for defensive work, thereby forcing Saladin to mount an offensive.[4] Following some rash offensive operations, including Hattin, the Crusaders were forced to adopt a more defensive posture in subsequent campaigns due to a loss of men.

The Crusaders were not unified. Infighting was not uncommon and, as Nicolle points out, "knights claiming French origin also looked down on knights of Italian blood, and all were despised as half-breeds by men newly come from Europe."[5] The most militant and most religiously fervent were, of course, the Military Orders

Saladin pursuing the Christians in Egypt. (Liebig cards printed with permission of Campbell's Soup Company)

119

of the Hospitallers and the Templars, but they also tended to be the most well trained. The knights were the fighting edge of the Crusader army though they were not as professional as Saladin's elite horsemen.

The Christian army was also hardly a unified voice when it came to campaigning against Saladin. There were more or less two distinct policies favored. The first was espoused by Raymond of Tripoli, Prince of Galilee, who was a veteran campaigner against the Arab armies. He realized that a military operation during the summer would be treacherous unless an ample water supply could be secured. At their current location this was not an issue, but moving further inland toward Tiberias, few springs were readily available. Raymond, who had also been a prisoner of the Arabs for many years, understood that Muslim warriors who had assembled from faraway places were more interested in immediate battles than in long campaigns. Raymond therefore argued that sooner or later Saladin's army would simply disintegrate.[6] It was just a matter of time. The second belief was championed by Gerard de Ridfort, Grand Master of the Templars, who favored battle. He was eventually able to sway King Guy's decision away from Raymond's council and should Guy "falter now, in this his first campaign as King of Jerusalem, Guy could not count on the support of the Templars in the future."[7] Stephen O'Shea describes the internal politicking:

> As a warrior, Gerard impressed upon Guy that this was not the time to shrink from the enemy; almost every able-bodied man in Outremer [Crusader States] was there, ready for combat. As his sponsor in gaining the throne, Gerard leaned on the king even harder, threatening to withdraw the support of the Templars – the backbone of the kingdom – for Guy's exalted station in Outremer. There is no record of Reynaud of Catillon [sic] being present, but his stout seconding of Gerard's arguments would have been no secret to either man. The king cracked under the pressure. The army that had gone to sleep thinking it would dig in at Zippori [Saffuriya] was awakened before dawn and told to march to Tiberias.[8]

SALADIN'S ARMY

The success of the Christians in gathering so large a force in effect led to Saladin raising an equally grand army by calling a *Jihad* (Holy War). David Nicolle explains that "Jihads became organized campaigns to recover the Holy Land, just as Crusades had been to conquer it. They were not, however, intended to convert the enemy by the sword since Islam has always frowned on forcible conversion."[9]

Units from Iraq, Syria, and Egypt answered the *Jihad* and began to assemble on the eastern banks of the Jordan.[10] Saladin, while waiting for them to gather at Tell'Ashtara, laid waste to the countryside of Frankish Transjordan and besieged, although unsuccessfully, the Crusader strongholds at Crac des Chevaliers and Montreal.[11] Saladin's military strength rested on his cavalry and of these he had about 12,000 with a "very large number of soldiers."[12] David Nicolle stipulates that 45,000 less-effective troops complemented the 12,000 horsemen.[13] These troops probably ranged from professional and paid foot soldiers to volunteers of dubious quality. The military staging areas for the Crusaders at Saforie and the Muslims at Tell'Ashtara were separated by the Sea of Galilee, with Tell'Ashtara laying almost directly east of the Crusaders' camp.

Upon receiving the news that at long last his actions had prompted the Crusaders into action, Saladin left a small force behind at Tiberias and joined the main army. Saladin had chosen to take Tiberias in order to force the Crusaders to advance onto terrain favourable to Saladin's army. His plan was successful, as the Muslims were able to attack the lumbering Crusader columns from the very start of their departure. This in itself was not enough to secure a Muslim victory, nor was the dehydration experienced by Crusader troops from the lack of essential water, as foreseen by Raymond of Tripoli. Instead it was Saladin's ability to resupply his men that proved to be the combat-multiplier and knowing where to deliver the supplies was half of winning the battle.

Saladin's army was also divided into three separate groups: the central battle group was led by Saladin, the right wing by Taqi al-Din, Saladin's nephew, and the left by Muzaffar al-Din Gökböri.[14] Both commanders had a reputation for bravery and competence. "The right wing, in traditional tactics of the Middle East," notes David Nicolle, "usually took an offensive role while the left wing acted defensively."[15] The armies of the medieval Arabs were well organized and professional and the majority of the fighting arm was composed of Kurds and Turks. Professional soldiers included *mamluks*, who were slaves trained in the arts of war. Nicolle describes the three main ethnicities of the Muslim army: the Turks, the Kurds, and the Arabs. The Turks were the largest group and had been the dominant military elements in Syria. The Kurds fought as cavalry and archers, though apparently they were not using the horse-archery tactics of their Turkish counterparts. Saladin recruited them individually or as whole units, and they generally then fought as one block in battle. The Arab bedouins' primary role as foot or cavalry troops was to disrupt enemy lines of communication.[16] Saladin's professional soldiers also drew pay and were sub-divided via a chain of command into units of varying sizes.

This painting shows the diversity of men loyal to Saladin. (Liebig cards printed with permission of Campbell's Soup Company)

Clearly, then, the Muslim armies of the time were not just filled with *Jihadis* bent on revenge but were comprised mostly of professionals, though large number of auxiliaries were recruited as well. "It was the support services, however, that really set this army apart from its Latin enemies."[17] Considerable emphasis was put on good communications, including a postal service using pigeons and couriers along with a beacon signaling system. Weapons procurement and resupply were to a very high standard. The size of the Muslim armies during this period tends to be greatly exaggerated even today, and this tendency may very well have been to belittle the Muslims' capabilities or to lessen the defeats suffered by the Christians. The manpower potential of the natives in the Middle East was far greater than that of their Christian counterparts, but the actual war-fighting capabilities were not grossly disproportionate.

> Muslim tactics were primarily conducted by the professional cavalry supported by auxiliary cavalry using Turkish tactics of rapid manoeuvre, dispersal and harassment. Saladin's cavalry tactics were far more flexible than those of the Crusaders. Saladin's horsemen would even, if the situation were suitable, stand against a full-scale charge by the enemy's knights. The primary weapon of the Muslim heavy cavalry was the spear and the sword similar to that of the Christian knights. Yet horse archery remained the cavalry's most effective tactic.[18]

It was a sophisticated and well-prepared Muslim army led ably by Saladin and his trusted commanders that was to pounce on the Christians.

THE BATTLE

Saladin sought battle. By June 26, the Arab army was assembled and reviewed by him.[19] He had laid waste to Frankish-held territory and had marched onto Christian-held Tiberias by the Sea of Galilee to force the Crusaders into action. In effect the Muslim army was going to place itself between two Christian forces: one, albeit a small one, at Tiberias and the other, substantially larger, at Saforie. Nonetheless, the Turco-Arab Army advanced to the south of the Sea of Galilee and encamped near Tiberias by Wednesday July 1.[20]

The sun that rose on July 1, 1187, saw Saladin's forces encamped near Tiberias, home of Raymond of Tripoli. Saladin "did not attack the town immediately, but took up quarters on the hills overlooking the city from the west, thus isolating it and creating a barrier between Tiberias and the Crusaders at Saforie. Protected by the Muslim forces on the hills, some picked detachments descended to the shore of the lake and besieged the city."[21] The news reached the Crusader camp the same day and by the time it did so, only the citadel stood firm. Ibn Shaddad, a close friend to Saladin, writes in *The Rare and Excellent History of Saladin*:

> He then moved and camped west of Tiberias on the top of the mountain, in battle formation and expecting that the Franks, when they heard that, would come against him. However, they did not move from their encampment. He took up this position on Wednesday 21 Rabi II [July 1], and having seen that they were not moving, he descended upon Tiberias with a light force, leaving the main divisions in position facing the direction in which the enemy were. He attacked Tiberias and took it within one hour after a direct assault. Eager hands then turned to plundering, taking captives, burning and killing. The citadel alone held out.[22]

By the early hours of July 3, 1187, the powerful Crusader army was marching to relieve Tiberias. The army was divided into three groups:

> The Latin army of Outremer gathered around the spring of Zippori [Saffuriya] and formed three separate columns. Raymond, his warnings ignored, agreed to command the vanguard of the column – it was his due as their route would pass through his fiefs. King Guy and Reynaud, accompanied by the True Cross, led the bulk of the men in the center. In the rear, the most exposed position for an army on the March, came the Templars and the Hospitallers, commanded by their respective masters and a great baron, Balian of Ibelin. The foot soldiers, archers, and crossbowmen, their body armor consisting of sturdy leather doublets, formed human walls on the sides of the marching columns, protecting the heavily armed warhorses. The latter, the tanks of medieval

warfare, had to be preserved for devastating, unstoppable charges. Lighter cavalry, many of them Turcopoles, or native Levantines forced to convert to Christianity, danced around the flanks, ready to counter any harassers with sudden sallies.[23]

One of the most interesting aspects of the Christian army on the march was their troop disposition, as it exposed the weakness of the mounted knights. The knights were grand and spectacular when they executed a cavalry charge and it was difficult to resist them. The solution for the Muslim soldiers was obvious: kill as many horses as possible. This tactic forced the marching Crusader army to safeguard the knights and their mounts. Noted Crusader scholar John Prawler describes the weakness this created in the Crusader army on the move:

> The heavy cavalry were the weakest point of the army when faced with Muslim troops far more mobile than their own. The enemy's archers could shoot from well outside the range of Crusader spears and lances and thus avoid a frontal encounter with the Frankish cavalry. Once a Frankish horse was hit, the Crusader was at the mercy of the Muslim bowmen. Against their dense rain of arrows there were only the Crusader foot-archers. Since they preceded and flanked the cavalry, they prescribed the rhythm of the march and, by slowing it down, made the Franks an easier target.[24]

The Crusaders were not under frontal attacks, which would have been better for them. Instead Saladin had planned to harass them continuously with his mounted archers and "the two armies encountered one another on the slopes of the mountain of Tiberias, to the west of the town, late on Thursday 22 Rabi II [July 2]."[25]

The Frankish army was harassed on all sides, but managed to preserve its unity. Vulnerable to the attackers' arrows, it did not break up into small units, which would have been easily destroyed by the Muslims. Many horses were hit by the enemy, who moved to within shooting distance. Time and again the same tactic was repeated. The Muslims shot and emptied their quivers from far outside the range of the Crusader weapons, then they disappeared on their light horses, only to reappear with new supplies of arrows.[26]

By midday, and after covering nearly 18km under constant harassing fire, Raymond received a message that the columns to his rear were at a standstill. James Reston believes that successful Christian campaigns had been unable to march more than 11km in a day against stiff enemy resistance.[27] "So hard pressed were the Templars and Turcopoles in the rear," writes Lane-Poole, "that they could not keep up with the king's battle centre, and were in sore danger of being cut off."[28] O'Shea's recreation of that moment is excellent, as it clearly demonstrates all the noise, confusion, and tension of the moment:

The attacks intensified, the terrifying din of cymbals and drums echoing down from the hills as wave after wave of Kurdish bowmen, and the heavily armed infantry, charged the Christian rear. The valley grew hellish, the ordeal complete, the foot soldiers with the armed monks walking backward to protect the warhorses from repeated assault. From within the rear column, the knights of the Temple and the Hospital sent riders to King Guy to call a halt to the March: they would take their mounts [and] ride out to defeat the foe. When the sun was at its zenith, the Latins stopped. Raymond of Tripoli, in the vanguard several miles ahead, cursed the folly of his countrymen.[29]

Raymond realized that the army would not reach its intended target, the Sea of Galilee, a further 17km away, which was a problem as water was now of the highest importance. Raymond made a decision to change the route of the Crusader army. He was near the junction of the Meskenah and Lubiyah roads and for the Crusaders to continue eastwards with Muslim units peppered along their route would have been almost impossible, especially given the already exhausted and dehydrated state of the Crusaders. Instead Raymond decided to move north to the abundant spring of Kafr Hattin, which was only 5km away. The terrain, however, was challenging, with a steep rise from 185m to 300m in a space of 2km.[30] It was going to be a difficult move for the army, but preferable to the longer, established route, blocked by Saladin's forces. The Arab chronicler Ibn Shaddad called the engagements of the second day, particularly around Lubiyah, "very intense."[31]

Battle scene depicting what may have transpired at Hattin, when Saladin's men overran Crusader forces. (Author's Collection)

It is at this point, when the Christian army veered north, that unit integrity was lost. Much like an accordion, the army had shrunk and expanded during its long march but now the army ceased to move together as many mounted knights abandoned their formations to reach the spring quickly. They left the foot soldiers, tired and thirsty themselves, feeling abandoned. Saladin's men, however, moved far more rapidly than the heavy Crusader knights could accomplish, and the Muslims easily barred the path to the spring at Kafr Hattin. At the same time, the rearguard under Ibelin was attacked with great vigor. The Knights Templar stationed with the rearguard were beaten back in their attempted charge against the Muslim attack. Following the army's loss of cohesion, the Templars' failed charge, and the barring of the path to the spring, King Guy sealed the fate of the Crusader army – he ordered his men to camp in place at Meskenah. Perhaps the situation was indeed so dire as to limit options dramatically, but inaction was to be of no help.

The Muslims continued their attacks until nightfall and during that time they too reorganized their formations to counter the new situation as well. Messengers were sent back and forth as Taqi al-Din's right wing units seized the entrance of the gorge leading to the spring and spread his men across the plateau approximately 4km wide. Here they guarded the two paths that led to the spring.[32] Saladin's central group, which had been in contact with Ibelin's rearguard, pitched camp at Kafr Lubiyah directly across from the enemy's camp.

Undoubtedly, the Christians were suffering from a lack of water and exhaustion, whereas Saladin's superior organization and planning had allowed for water-filled goatskins and other supplies to be distributed among his men. This was in stark contrast to the Crusaders who had to make do with what they carried. There would

After the battle of Hattin, Guy de Lusignan is spared by Saladin after executing Reynaud de Châtillon and all the other captured Knights Templar. Saladin is reputed to have said "kings do not kill other kings." (Liebig cards printed with permission of Campbell's Soup Company)

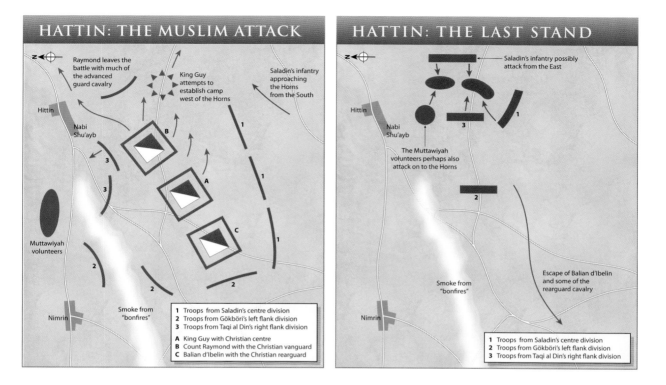

HATTIN: THE MUSLIM ATTACK

Raymond leaves the battle with much of the advanced guard cavalry

King Guy attempts to establish camp west of the Horns

Saladin's infantry approaching the Horns from the South

Hittin

Nabi Shu'ayb

Muttawiyah volunteers

Nimrin

Smoke from "bonfires"

1 Troops from Saladin's centre division
2 Troops from Gökböri's left flank division
3 Troops from Taqi al Din's right flank division

A King Guy with Christian centre
B Count Raymond with the Christian vanguard
C Balian d'Ibelin with the Christian rearguard

HATTIN: THE LAST STAND

Saladin's infantry possibly attack from the East

Hittin

Nabi Shu'ayb

The Muttawiyah volunteers perhaps also attack on to the Horns

Smoke from "bonfires"

Nimrin

Escape of Balian d'Ibelin and some of the rearguard cavalry

1 Troops from Saladin's centre division
2 Troops from Gökböri's left flank division
3 Troops from Taqi al Din's right flank division

be no resupply caravan for the Christian army. If nothing else, however, Raymond's decision to move north bought the Frankish army one more night before they were to become martyrs to their cause. One chronicler's account recalls in detail that evening for the Christians: "There was no water at all where they stood, and therefore to pitch tents on this spot was impossible; but not far from there, beyond that mountain on the left, was a village named Hattin where there was plenty of water from the springs. There it was possible to bivouac for the night, and to resume in good form the March to Tiberias the following day."[33] That was their hope and their salvation, to reach water, to re-form, to rest. The reality of the situation was best summed up by the Muslim scribe Ibn Shaddad:

> They were closely beset as in a noose, while still marching on as though being driven to a death that they could see before them, convinced of their doom and destruction and themselves aware that the following day they would be visiting their graves. The conflict continued at close quarters, each horseman clashing with his opponent, until victory [for the Muslims] and for the infidels the onset of disaster were imminent, but night and its darkness intervened. That day there occurred mighty deeds and momentous doings, such as have not been related of past generations. Each party spent the night in arms,

expecting his adversary at every moment, though too weak through tiredness to stand up and unable through fatigue to crawl, let alone run.[34]

The next morning, July 4, 1187, an exhausted and now sleep-deprived Crusader army decided to attack and break through the Muslim lines to get to the spring of Kafr Hattin. The bulk of the Crusaders moved forward toward the rising grounds between Nimrin and Hattin. The battle had not yet been decided, however. Even Ibn Shaddad, friend of the great Saladin, noted that that "both sides sought their positions and each realized that whichever was broken would be driven off and eliminated. The Muslims were well aware that behind them was the Jordan and before them enemy territory and there was nothing to save them but God Almighty."[35] The Crusaders' goal was to force the Muslim barrier at the brink of the plain leading to Kafr Hattin. The most detailed description gives the following picture: "When they were ranged and divided into columns, the foot soldiers were ordered to defend the army by shooting arrows, so that the knights could more easily resist the enemy. The knights were to be protected by foot soldiers from enemy archers, and the foot soldiers helped by the lances of the knights against the inroads of the enemy. Thus by mutual help both would be protected and saved."[36] Reality would turn out differently, of course, but the battle had been a close contest to this point. The worst had not yet come.

The initiative was not with the Frankish army and as the Muslim center and wings attacked "they let out a shout as one man, at which God cast terror into the hearts of the unbelievers."[37] Saladin with his main army struck hard at the rearguard composed of Templars, and again a counter-charge by the Military Order was broken, as they were not supported by the other troops. But the left and right wing commanders of Saladin were in fact so hard-pressed that the "whole army was routed and driven back. The soldiers then heard that the two chiefs still resisted the enemy, whereupon they returned to the charge and victory was decided in favour of the Muslims."[38] As the Crusaders attempted to reorganize and launch an assault, the foot troops, who had earlier been abandoned, scattered when attacked. The combined arms of foot soldiers and mounted knights failed miserably.[39]

The king, in despair or incompetence, yet again sought to build a camp, thereby rallying his even more disheartened troops. The attempt to rally failed miserably and everything was thrown into disorder. Simultaneous Muslim attacks coupled with absolute exhaustion and fear made for a volatile, poisonous mix. The Holy Cross, which the Crusaders believed to have been the very cross upon which Jesus Christ was crucified, served as a rallying point, but caused even more confusion as men rushed toward it with little discipline. Some time during the battle Muslim troops had started brush fires, which created an even worse scenario for the surviving Frankish soldiers and knights.[40]

Raymond and his vanguard were now cut off from the king's main battle group. Some of them surrendered to Saladin's men. There is some controversy as to whether or not Raymond was acting under orders at this stage. There is no dispute, however, that he charged down the steep slopes to Kafr Hattin. Taqi al-Din, realizing not only the difficulty of withstanding a heavy cavalry charge but more importantly recognizing that victory lay in the defeat of the king's main army, allowed Raymond's vanguard to escape.[41] Taqi al-Din, however, did have some of his men pursue the fleeing vanguard.[42]

King Guy's army was in distress. Raymond's group had disappeared, some foot soldiers and knights had started to surrender, but it was the desertion of the common foot soldier that spelled doom. Abandoned once before, these exhausted and terrified men simply fled up the steep slopes of the northern summit of the Kafr Hattin some 30m above the battlefield.[43] Lane-Poole attempts to describe the scene:

> The Frank infantry, maddened with thirst, scorched by the burning sun, and blinded by the flame and smoke of the bush which the Moslems had fired, lost their formation, neglected the combination with the knights which was the only hope of victory, and wildly struggled to push towards the lake in a desperate longing for water: but Saladin barred the way. They found themselves crowded in a heap on the top of a hill and to the king's repeated entreaty that they would come down and do their devoir for Cross and Throne, they sent word that they were dying of thirst and could not fight. Thenceforth the infantry took no part in the battle: the Saracens eventually fell upon them, cast some down the precipice, and killed or captured the rest.[44]

The remnants of the army fought against the professional Muslim cavalry, but had no protection from the showers of arrows striking them at will. Numerous attacks were repelled by the knights and the few remaining foot soldiers, but they too eventually climbed and entrenched themselves on the summit of the southern part of the hill.[45] Whatever loyal troops and knights were left at the True Cross mounted another charge for martyrdom or freedom, and attacked the Muslims twice. "It was only when the True Cross was captured and the red tent of the King of Jerusalem overthrown, that the battle was over. The Muslims who had reached the top of the hill found Frankish soldiers lying motionless on its two peaks. They had no strength left to fight."[46] Lane-Poole stipulates that the last stand around the king's tent and True Cross numbered around 150 of the bravest nobles and knights, including King Guy.[47] And David Nicolle argues that it was the division under Taqi al-Din, Saladin's nephew, who defeated the last stand and captured the Holy

Cross.[48] Ibn Shaddad's gives a vivid account of the final stages of the battle from the Muslim perspective:

> Their commanders were taken captive but the rest were either killed or taken prisoner, and among those who lived were their leader, King Guy, Prince Reynald, the brother of the king, the prince who was lord of Shawbak [Crusader castle in Jordan], the son of Humfrey, the son of the Lady of Tiberias, the Master of the Templars, the lord of Jubay [in Lebanon] and the Master of the Hospitallers. The rest of the commanders were killed, and the lowly soldiers were divided up, either to be slain or made captive. Everyone not killed was made prisoner. Some nobles amongst them willingly surrendered in fear for their lives. Someone I trust told me that in the Hawran [southwest Syria] he met a single person holding a tent-rope with which all by himself he was pulling along thirty odd prisoners because of the desperate defeat that had befallen them.[49]

THE AFTERMATH

The victory over the King of Jerusalem and the Military Orders was immense. Out of an original force of 23,200 men, only 3,000 managed to escape.[50] Casualties of the Turco-Arab Army are not known but certainly they too must have taken some heavy losses, particularly during the later stages of the battle. Nonetheless, the victory was complete, except for a vow Saladin had made years earlier. After the battle, Saladin welcomed King Guy and his surviving men into his tent. Among the men was Reynaud:

> He berated Reynaud for repeatedly breaking truces and offered to spare him if he converted to Islam. The old knight refused, truculent to the last. Saladin raised his sword and brought it down deep into Reynaud's shoulder. A bodyguard then lopped off his head. Guy fell to his knees, terrified, as the corpse was dragged out. Saladin reassured him, saying, "A king does not kill a king."[51]

Captured knights were customarily held for ransom, but the knights of the Military Orders of the Hospitallers and the Templars did not fare so well. Instead, approximately 230 of them were killed.[52] But it is the manner in which they were executed that is shocking, and the sheer misery of men defeated in battle can have no clearer picture painted than this:

> The Templars and Hospitallers ranked as the sultan's most redoubtable enemies, dedicated to permanent war against the Muslims. Past experience had shown that they

refused to be ransomed and, if sold, made rebellious slaves. Alive and in captivity, the knights of the Temple and the Hospital would have been a burden. Saladin handed over the two hundred or so monks to their Muslim counterparts, at least in religious fervor – the noncombatant volunteers of his army who had answered the call to jihad. One by one the entire contingent of Templars and Hospitallers was beheaded, in killings often gruesomely botched by the amateur swordsmen from the mosques. [53]

O'Shea goes on to describe what happened to the ordinary soldiers:

Romatic depiction of Saladin the Great raising his hands to Allah in victory. Saladin is considered one of the great commanders of his time. (Author's Collection)

131

As for the thousands of ordinary soldiers on the losing side, they too kept their heads but were henceforth condemned to a life of servitude. Shackled together, the men of Outremer were led out of Galilee in a long and sorrowful column destined for the slave markets of Damascus. Their numbers soon caused a glut in the trade, triggering a sharp fall in prices. One man, it was said, was sold for a pair of sandals.[54]

The True Cross, for Christians one of the holiest of all relics

was pinioned upside down on a spear and carried to Damascus. To the Muslims this apparent sacrilege evinced their contempt only for the story of the crucifixion, not for the Christian Savior. For Jesus Christ remained a revered prophet in Islam, but he was a great man, not a God. There was only one God, Allah. The Prophet Muhammad, with divine guidance, had clarified the mistakes and misinterpretations of Christianity. Islam rejected the tale of Christ's death as unworthy of a great religion.[55]

The defeat of the Crusader army at Hattin had far-reaching consequences. Following the destruction of the Christians, Saladin went on to take a number of Crusader-held cities, including Jerusalem, which was surrendered in early October. Saladin's victories meant that the eminent military power in the Holy Land was again Islamic. These events shook Western Europe, and plans were begun immediately for a Third Crusade to take back the Kingdom of Jerusalem.

The surrender of Jerusalem in 1187 to Saladin after his decisive victory over Crusader forces at the Horns of Hattin. (Author's Collection)

TANNENBERG, 1410

BACKGROUND

The battle fought near the village of Tannenberg, East Prussia, was one of the largest battles of its time, pitting the combined forces of the Kingdom of Poland and the Grand Duchy of Lithuania, alongside Tartars and mercenaries, against the German Military Order of the Teutonic Knights and their allies and mercenaries. The Teutonic Knights, similar to other Military Orders, were founded in the Middle East to aid Christian pilgrims and to care for the sick and injured. After Montfort and Acre fell to the Mamluks in the late 13th century, the Teutonic brothers established their new headquarters in Venice and then deployed to Transylvania, where they rendered their martial skills to the King of Hungary. Answering the call for a crusade against the pagans in northern Europe, the Teutonic Knights settled in the Baltic region of Prussia, moving their permanent headquarters from Venice to Marienburg in 1309. The Order solidified its position in the Baltic by conquest and commerce. It became a naval power and its strength in maritime operations allowed for the transport of allies and mercenaries to reinforce the land forces needed for raids and founding settlements in pagan lands. Although the Kingdom of Poland and the Grand Duchy of Lithuania converted to Christianity, the Teutonic Knights portrayed them as Saracens or infidels and continued sporadically to wage military as well as political campaigns against the two states, despite their status as fellow Christians.

The Teutonic Knights had established as ferocious an organization in Europe as their sibling rival Military Orders of the Templars and Hospitallers had in the Middle East. All of them sought to convert the pagans or infidels by the sword, while simultaneously engaging in commerce, and that dual purpose made them the most dangerous of all knights. The Teutonic Knights had become an unbearable force in the Baltic for the natives, not just because of their zeal to convert the pagans, but also because of their never-ending appetite for land and money. All of it was dictated by the need to solidify their holdings and their new headquarters in Marienburg. The Order did not wish to end as the Templars had done by 1312 – eradicated by the King of France and the Church because of their power and wealth within Europe.

The German religious knights were formidable opponents, though few in numbers. Armored and armed, the Order wore white surcoats adorned by a black cross. (Centuries on, the Prussians and Germans adopted the black cross for their military insignias and decorations.) The Teutonic Order had suffered some defeats, most notably against the Republic of Novgorod, but their warrior myth and projected power was unquestioned. Few dared to oppose the Order and those who did were punished cruelly. Most of the combat during the Northern Crusade rested on raids and not on set-piece battles.[1] (The Northern Crusade was a campaign organized by the Catholic kings of Denmark and Sweden against the pagans of northern Europe in the late 12th and 13th century.) The logistical requirements in a harsh environment made the fielding of large armies nearly impossible. And the cruelty and strength, politically as well as militarily, of the Order was truly fearsome, thus deterring opponents from giving battle.

The Order's appetite was unyielding and this led to direct clashes with the converted Poles and Lithuanians. The Poles lamented the loss of Pomerellia, western Prussia, an acquisition that gave the Teutonic Order greater control of the Vistula River and its surrounding region. The Order also saw Samogitia as vital to its interests, offering a land bridge to its more northern possessions, but in direct conflict with Lithuanian princes who sought to retain these territories.[2] Neither country could stand up to the German Order on its own and previously had even supported the Germans in exchange for aid in other areas. But at the end of the 14th century, and against the backdrop of continued expansion by the Order, former rivals Jagiello of Poland and Vytautas of Lithuania launched the Polish-Lithuanian-Teutonic War (1409–11), and encouraged the Samogitians to rebel against the Teutonic knights who controlled them. This culminated in the battle of Tannenberg on July 15, 1410.

Most of the eyewitness accounts or histories of the battle of Tannenberg are unreliable. Some sources claim that millions of soldiers were engaged in the battle.[3] Certain accounts place all the glory on the Poles, while others credit the success to the Lithuanians. German accounts describe the Polish-Lithuanian armies as Saracen or infidels or pagans, on the basis that a small number of non-Christian Tartars fought alongside the Lithuanians. Yet other accounts have blamed deliberate desertion of allies during the crucial phase of the battle as evidence of betrayal and thus the cause for the Order's defeat.[4] Nationalistic interpretations further developed during World War I (1914–18), when a decisive victory of the German Army over the Russians was renamed the battle of Tannenberg, as the village was somewhere near that particular engagement and thus was re-envisioned as revenge for a battle fought 500 years earlier. German National Socialist and Soviet propagandists have likened their struggle during World War II to that of the Military Order and those the Teutonic knights subjugated. Until the 1960s, scholarship "reflected national interest more than fact."[5]

The demands of Teutonic Grand Master Ulrich von Jungingen to cease aiding the rebellious Samogitians were not met by either the Poles or the Lithuanians, who had promised mutual support against the Teutonic Order. On August 14, 1409, the Germans declared war. Their early forays were repulsed, resulting in an armistice until June 24, 1410. During this time, and despite repeated negotiations involving third parties, all sides prepared for the continuation of war.

The strategic picture was somewhat complicated. Most of Western Europe was focused on the advances of the Turks in southeastern Europe, the wars between Burgundy and France, as well as the dissent within European Christianity, and thus little attention was paid to the conflicts in Prussia.[6] No serious coalition of Poles and Lithuanians had ever invaded the territories of the Order therefore the council of the Teutonic Knights was probably more concerned with the necessity of dealing with two distinct armies rather than one combined force of former rivals. The German forces needed to be deployed so they could deal with any incursions into their territories or deliver offensive blows, if need be on several fronts. Another consideration for the Grand Master was that in previous centuries the Order was able to rely on crusading allies to rally to them in times of war. Fighting newly converted Christians, however, was not viewed favorably and his allies were not going to be as numerous or dedicated as in previous campaigns. Considering all of the known factors, Von Jungingen and his council were more inclined for defensive actions, seeking to repulse any raids or attacks, and then ending the war quickly by defeating the invaders and then seeking a truce, as experience had taught them. The Poles, on the other hand, had to keep an eye on the Hungarians, who could use the Prussian diversion to invade Poland from the south, while the Grand Duchy of Lithuania had to be aware of potential raids or attacks from the eastern Tartars.[7] The Kingdom of Poland under Wladyslaw II Jagiello and the Grand Duchy of Lithuania under Vytautas both realized that their salvation lay in striking at the very heart of the Order in Prussia, the capital Marienburg. It was an audacious plan. The Poles and Lithuanians raided the frontier at various locations, thereby reinforcing Von Jungingen's belief that the enemy would attack in separate columns. These operations screening the true objective of the Polish-Lithuanian coalition, Marienburg.

THE ARMIES

The force composition of the opposing armies is nearly impossible to reconstruct, as histories of the battle are tainted with patriotic zeal and propaganda. Nonetheless, William Urban argues for more than "30,000 cavalry and infantry (18,000 Polish knights and squires, with a few thousand foot soldiers; some Bohemians and Morovian mercenaries; 11,000 Lithuanians, Russians, and Tartar

Monument commemorating the victory at Tannenberg (known in Poland as Grünwald) in Krakow. (Author's Collection)

cavalry, a formidable contingent from Moldovia led by its prince, Alexander the Good, and some Samogitians."[8]) The Grand Master was able to raise around 20,000, perhaps 10,000 were cavalry while "the rest of his warriors were pilgrims and mercenaries."[9] Hans Delbrück, citing other sources, stipulates 11,000 men for the Teutonic Order, of which 3,850 were heavily armed, 3,000 were squires, and 4,000 were marksmen. In addition, he argues there were a few foot soldiers who were stationed with the wagon laager of the Order and that they did not go in the battle proper. The Poles and Lithuanians numbered 16,000 in cavalry.[10] Given the fact that about 200 Teutonic Knights were killed or executed, one must draw the conclusion that perhaps even these numbers are greater and probably included the thousands of camp followers that traditionally accompanied armies. No matter what numbers are real or imagined, one common thread is the proportion between the combatants with "three to two in favour of the Polish king and Lithuanian grand prince."[11]

Examples of Polish knights and soldiers from around 1333–1434. (Author's Collection)

The Polish Army was organized in "banners." Each "banner" comprised between 50 and 120 "lances," each of which was an armored knight and his escort, a group of between two and five men. Vytautas' Lithuanian Army was organized into banners only after it united with the Polish Army on July 1, 1410. Stephen Turnbull explains that "He also gave orders that in battle the poorer armed and mounted men were to be positioned in the centre of each Banner. While companies were to fight in compact formation with little space between the ranks, there was to be ample distance between Banners."[12]

The Teutonic Knights had a similar military organization, with banners made up of lances. In the Teutonic Order, a lance usually consisted of a knight and up to seven other men, usually mostly crossbowmen.[13] Turnbull notes that "only a small percentage of the Order's army at Tannenberg consisted of heavily armoured and mounted 'Teutonic Knights' clad in the white mantle with black cross. During the battle 203 were killed and few fled or were captured; their total number cannot have been much more than 250. The bulk of the Prussian knights who fought at Tannenberg lived on the Order's lands but were not actually members of the Order."[14]

THE BATTLE

The Polish Army crossed the Vistula river by the city of Czerwinsk, where it joined forces with the Lithuanian formations and advanced northwards, en route to Marienburg. Polish Army units were also deployed out of Bomberg further west to further confuse the Germans, who were stationed within 50km of Bomberg at Schwetz. Although long-range raids and troop deployments helped the unified armies screen their intended purpose for a while, soon enough the Teutonic Order realized the true intentions of the assault. The Polish-Lithuanian Army marched toward Kauernick, where they had intended to cross a tributary of the Vistula, the Drewenz River. Various villages and the countryside as a whole were pillaged and devastated, although there were also times when punishment was handed down on several individuals by the Lithuanian command after the sacking of Lautenburg en route to Kauernick.[15] But near the fords at Kauernick they encountered the Teutonic army, which had driven "stakes into the river and fortified the western bank with crude artillery and archery emplacement."[16] The decision was taken to move east, reduce several castles that may have been seen as a threat to their rear, then swing back north near Gilgenburg, reduce it, and thus open the route toward the Order's center at Marienburg. Sometime during the march, Hungarian emissaries assured the Polish-Lithuanian command that they would not launch an attack on Poland, as sufficient bribes had been offered by both sides to ensure neutrality. On July 13, less than ten days after having crossed the Vistula, Gilgenburg was sacked and the combined army stopped the next day to rest and refit. On July 15, they reached the small town of Faulen, where the Poles encamped to the southwest of a small lake and the Lithuanians further north.

The Grand Master of the Order, in the interim, had marched north and crossed the Drewenz, then paralleled the movement of the invaders, seeking to cut them off just northeast of Gilgenburg. Ulrich von Jungingen must have been outraged at the audacity of the enemy and their seemingly unrestrained destruction of Prussian territories. Yet he realized the prudence of reinforcing Marienburg and thus ordered the 3,000 soldiers still stationed at Schwetz to move with haste toward their headquarters to bolster its defenses. This command was to save the Teutonic Order's

A 16th-century engraving depicting the battle of Tannenberg. (Author's Collection)

existence for the next 100 years. The extra manpower he lost, however, may have made a big difference on the battlefield.

On July 15, after having already marched 24km, the advance scouts of the Teutonic Knights spotted the camps of the Polish-Lithuanian forces. Ulrich von Jungingen arrayed his army between the villages of Tannenberg to the northeast and Grünfelde to the southwest. Some historians and scholars have argued that the advantage the smaller German Army achieved with its surprise arrival was lost when the Grand Master chose not to attack, but instead sought to issue an official challenge to fight, sending messengers with two swords in hand to the overall Polish-Lithuanian commander, Jagiello. Perhaps this is so, but we should also bear in mind that the Order had been on the march for many hours already. Like all armies on the move, it was perhaps stretched out over a long distance and therefore the council of the knights decided to wait in place until the entire army, or perhaps only the fighting men, had an opportunity to catch up and prepare for the battle. Delbrück argues that the rearguard of the Prussians did not even arrive until the battle was almost over.[17] Typically, histories are unkind toward the losing commander of a battle, campaign, or war. In this case some historians ascribe Von Jungingen's actions to a poor temperament or rage. Perhaps this was true, for no commander would remain unmoved when his territories and people are destroyed by an invader. Yet Von Jungingen had shown exemplary tactical acumen when he checked the intended Polish-Lithuanian river crossing, and by his sound decision to reinforce Marienburg with 3,000 men. It is possible that the troops he sent to the Teutonic headquarters would have changed the outcome of the battle, but no one knows for certain.

There is not single accurate assessment on a reliable number of actual participants in the battle. As already noted, armies on campaign, either marching or camping, are spread out over a great distance. It seems likely that the German rearguard was not present at the battle until its end. A number of soldiers were also absent from the Polish-Lithuanian Army, as they camped separately. Two hundred Teutonic Knights were definitely either killed in combat or executed immediately after the battle and it seems likely that numbers cited by sources are inaccurate. Historical data reveals that most casualties of ancient and medieval battles occurred when one side had been broken. Furthermore, few Military Order knights flee a battle. It stands to reason, then, that the actual number of combatants was far fewer than our sources suggest and thus the casualty figures were smaller. In order to present this as a great and decisive battle the numbers may have been exaggerated.

As the combined armies of Poland and Lithuania prepared for battle, the Grand Master, so William Urban writes had his men dig camouflaged pits to trap the charging Polish cavalry, then ordered a withdrawal from that line so that the royal forces in the woods could have room to deploy in two lines in the open field against him. As a result, not only were his pits now part of the Polish defensive line, but his powerful artillery was now stationed at a place where it was ineffective, moreover, his infantry was standing where it was difficult to provide proper support for the massed bodies of knights.[18]

Turnbull suggests that the pits were dug in the center of the defensive line, but pits are defensive weapons systems intended to give the defenders an advantage over the attacker. We must conclude, therefore, that Von Jungingen and his council sought a defensive stratagem considering their smaller numbers, and as such also explains why they did not charge immediately upon sighting the enemy. Seemingly, the Germans deployed on a line from the northeast to the southwest with their left wing nearest Tannenberg and their wagons laagered near Grünfelde and its forest. It is probable that the wagons did not form part of the main battle line. The Teutonic and allied knights probably deployed in front of their artillery as a screen, with the infantry and archer and crossbowmen units just behind the cannons or alongside them. The artillery was probably, along with the pits, positioned in the center of the main battle line. The allied knights seemed to have been deployed on the left flank, while the Teutonic Order held the center and the right flank, so argues Urban, but Turnbull, citing Polish sources, assumes the bulk of the German left flank to have been composed of the Order's elite troops.[19]

The Poles under Jagiello formed the left wing of their main battle line and the right flank was composed of the Lithuanians under Vytautas, along with Tartars and

Painting by Jan Matejko, which is thought to illustrate the moment at which Ulrich von Jungingen (Grand Master of the Teutonic Order) is killed, with Vytautas the Great shown in his moment of triumph. (Author's Collection)

other lighter cavalry units. It seems that the heavier cavalry was on the left wing and the lighter cavalry on the far right flank, divided by several contingents of Czech mercenaries in the center. The invaders may have been aware of the pits and massed artillery in the enemy center, and that if they were to attack they would do so from their wings, thereby either avoiding the canon and crossbowmen. If they were to advance along the whole line, the brunt of the carnage would be then inflicted on the mercenaries in the center.

Around 0900hrs, the Teutonic Knights repositioned themselves, doing so probably either to show their true disposition or to indeed allow for the artillery to fire with greater effect, facing the center of Jagiello's army. But the impact of the cannon fire was negligible, as an early morning shower had dampened the powder – they were only able to fire twice. The redeployment, however, triggered an audacious charge by the Lithuanians and allies from the right wing, where they met devastating volleys from the German archers and crossbowmen. And shortly thereafter, the Polish and mercenary units advanced toward the center and right wing of the Germans, where they clashed in brutal combat. The pits in the center proved seemingly ineffective or were never crossed. Perhaps only the Polish left wing was able to engage the German knights, while the center simply advanced. Yet after approximately an hour, the Lithuanians, following a bitter hand-to-hand struggle, turned and fled, pursued for many miles by the victorious Germans. A dangerous gap had opened along the main battle line, one that the Grand Master of the Teutonic Knights sought to exploit. Other Teutonic units charged the exposed Polish flank as the Lithuanian right wing disintegrated. Ulrich von Jungingen, realizing the shift in the battle, rode around the center with his 16-banner force at his disposal, veered off to the space on the left vacated by the rout and charged headlong into the now-exposed Polish flank. It was an audacious offensive maneuver, seeking to end the battle by killing the Polish king in one ferocious charge with an inferior number of knights. At the same time, he exposed his left wing. A calculated risk no doubt, as the Lithuanians had been swept from the field and pursued by some of the victorious Germans. The melee was intense and the Poles were near panic, but they continued to fight.

At this crucial stage of the battle, the Grand Duke of Lithuania, who had been everywhere on the battlefield, rallied his cavalry and returned to the battle, smashing into the right flank, however, as he did this his rear and left flank were charged by the returning Lithuanians. It was a devastating counter-charge.

There are arguments that the initial Lithuanian retreat was a carefully constructed ruse to pull enemy troops away from the battlefield. Such is certainly possible, as Eastern European and Asian horsemen routinely employed this tactic. It seems unlikely in this case, however, as the event took place after hours of combat. Instead it seems more reasonable to propose that the German cavalry pursuing the Lithuanian light cavalry simply ran out of steam, and did not engage in a serious pursuit. After all, the Germans had marched more than 25km that day already, sat on their horses for three hours, then engaged in combat operations, which also lasted a few hours. After all this an attempt to pursue the less exhausted and less heavily armored Lithuanian and allied horsemen would be a daunting, if not impossible task. Instead a more reasonable explanation would seem that the right wing of the invading army was indeed defeated, but that the pursuit ended almost immediately as the victors then started to loot the dead and wounded and possibly plundered the Lithuanian camp. The lack of a real pursuit would explain the ability of the Lithuanians to reorganize and then to return to the battlefield.

The fact that remains undisputed is that the return of the light horsemen changed the dynamics at Tannenberg almost immediately. The Germans were hit hard from the rear and the flank. Ulrich von Jungingen, aged approximately 50 years old, died fighting on his horse. Repeatedly wounded, he was finally killed by a lance thrust to his neck. Other Teutonic Knights died in combat unable to meet the repeated charges by the faster-moving enemy forces.

The death of the Grand Master led to a withdrawal of the German troops, who were pursued, harried, and killed by the now victorious Poles and Lithuanians. Survivors of the battle, along with the rearguard and camp followers, built a wagon laager where they were destroyed. The majority of the German casualties occurred near the village of Grünfelde. Others who fled were cut down in a pursuit that stretched for miles on end, and some surely perished in the wilderness. The total death toll is unknown, but was certainly in its thousands, and thousands were also captured. Many of the highest-ranking Teutonic Knights were killed in battle, and the ones who were captured were executed.

THE AFTERMATH

Three days later the combined Polish and Lithuanian army advanced to Marienburg and besieged it for many weeks. The defense was organized by the commander of the 3,000 soldiers sent to reinforce the headquarters, the future Grand Master Heinrich von Plauen. The siege proved unsuccessful, particularly after disease ran rampant in the Lithuanian camp. On February 1, 1411, the Peace of Thorn ended the Polish-Lithuanian-Teutonic War. The Kingdom of Poland and the Grand Duchy, nevertheless, were on the rise as one of the most powerful Military Orders was on the decline.

The victorious Polish
Lithuanians preside over
the carnage in this painting
by Alfonse Mucha.
(Author's Collection)

The battle of Tannenberg is of relatively minor significance in the overall context of history. It was, however, one of the largest battles of its time and it ended with the annihilation of one side. It has often been hailed as the decisive battle that destroyed the Teutonic Order, but the reality is that the Order not only retained its castles but also most of its territories for another century. The significance of the battle does not lie in the defeat or annihilation of the 200 Teutonic knights, but rather in its foreshadowing of the rise of national identities. As William Urban points out, it is not as though the balance of power changed dramatically because of the battle; the transformation and rise of the Kingdom of Poland was already well on its way. In fact, he argues that the days of the Military Orders had long passed and it is unlikely that the Teutonic Knights could have maintained "political and military equality with a nation as populous, creative, wealthy, and energetic as Poland."[20]

NÖRDLINGEN, 1634

BACKGROUND

The battle of Nördlingen in Bavaria was fought on August 27 (Julian calendar) or September 6 (Gregorian calendar), 1634, during the Thirty Years' War (1618–48) or perhaps better phrased by Hans Delbrück as part of the "The Period of the Wars of Religion."[1] On one side were the forces of the Catholic Imperial Army, alongside 19,000 Italian and Spanish soldiers. On the other were coalition forces of the Protestant armies of various German allies, plus the Swedes who had hurried to relieve the siege of the city of Nördlingen. The Thirty Years' War was generally a religious war between the Protestants and Catholics, although many other facets were involved, including the realignment of political power and territorial disputes.

The official beginning of the Thirty Years' War was on May 23, 1618, when a Protestant assembly in Prague tried two Catholic governors for violating the right to religious freedom and, upon finding them guilty, threw them out of an upper-story window to their deaths. This event is commonly known as the Second Defenestration of Prague, the first having occurred in 1419, triggering the Hussite Wars that ended in 1436. The war quickly engulfed many nations and was one of the greatest, costliest, and deadliest wars in European history. Entire regions and populations were obliterated by marauding armies. Disease was rampant and devastated vast areas of the German States as well as the Low Countries and portions of Italy.

OPPOSING ARMIES

The art of war during that time may have included some genuine tactical innovations, but in general terms "seventeenth century battles," argues historian John Childs "were crude slogging matches, fought at hideously close quarters amidst

An example of an Austrian foot soldier/pikeman from around 1580. (Anne S.K. Brown Military Collection, Brown University Library)

fogs of powder-smoke. Victors usually lost as many men as the vanquished and were too disorganized, understrength and exhausted to pursue. Manoeuvers and sieges, both of which produced more predictable and tangible results, were much preferred to the hazard of battle. Full-scale battles or sieges were infrequent."[2] Soldiers from the rear ranks of the combat formations would often disappear during battle, only to make an appearance after the event was settled. Units rarely broke from the front; instead, "armies nearly always disintegrated from the rear to the front."[3] Most campaigning involved ambushing convoys delivering either military or civilian goods, while opponents attempted to prevent such raids from happening. The Swedish forces had gained remarkable victories over Catholic forces at Breitenfeld in 1631 and at Lützen in 1632, but failed to exploit their advantage because of the untimely death of their king, Gustav II Adolph (Gustavus Adolphus), who had led a cavalry charge during the battle.[4] Gustav's art of war was reliant on mobility and speed. He developed a more rapid, fast-moving army capable of combined arms operations. Cavalry, which traditionally operated as its own arm and usually on its own, was now able to integrate with infantry and artillery units and was able to retreat to the relative safety of those formations. His infantry formations were no longer as cumbersome and unwieldy as, for example, the contemporary Spanish equivalents, which were large phalanx-type units susceptible to artillery fire and infantry long-range weapons. The Swedish Army, including the artillery component, could move rapidly because their formations were far smaller but still packed the punch of black powder weaponry, coupled with their interlocking fields of fire. This new type of combat operation required trained professionals who were capable of multi-tasking on the battlefield and executing orders with precision and speed.

By contrast, the *tercio* ("one third") was an infantry formation founded and developed by the Spanish and based on the Swiss pike formations of earlier centuries. It was comprised of an integrated infantry block, square in shape, of 3,000 pikemen and swordsmen as well as arquebusiers. It had its strengths and weaknesses, but during the Thirty Years' War it suffered some setbacks as the predominant formation on the battlefield:

> Spanish infantry forces of the seventeenth century often are viewed as conservative in their organization and dependent upon deep squares of pikemen supported by wings of musketeers and cavalry. While it is correct that the *tercios* possessed grand traditions that extended back for well over a century, they did evolve smaller more flexible formations to employ arquebuses and muskets that earlier had been regarded as secondary to the heavy squares or rectangles of pikemen. Seventeenth-century Spanish pikemen now deployed in looser formations that permitted the musketeers to fall back through their ranks for protection. With technological improvements in muskets and firepower, all army commanders had to reorganize their forces to take into account improved rates of fire, accuracy, and the striking power of bullets. Nevertheless, older organizational deployments of forces on some occasions defeated more modern systems.[5]

ADVANCE AND BATTLE

In 1634 the Swedes and German allies launched a two-pronged attack. One army composed of Saxons was directed against Silesia, Bohemia, and Prague, while the

Coin from the year 1649, during the reign of Ferdinand III (1608–1657), Holy Roman Emperor and commander of the victorious Catholic forces at Nördlingen. (Author's Collection)

Swedish and German allied armies, respectively commanded by Swedish field marshal Gustav Horn and German noble Bernhard von Sachsen-Weimar (Bernard of Saxe-Weimar), advanced on Bavaria.[6] The Imperial-Bavarian Army under command of Crown Prince Ferdinand, future King of Hungary, and General Count Gallas moved toward Bavaria to lay waste to Protestant territories, thereby forcing the enemy away from their respective assault into Bohemia. The Imperial Army began to lay siege to the large town of Regensburg on July 30, 1634. This in turn led to the decision by the Protestants to counter the threat and move toward the beleaguered town, but Regensburg fell before they were able to close with the imperial forces. Ferdinand's cousin, Cardinal-Infante Ferdinand of Austria, who was the governor of the Spanish Netherlands, was marching toward the victorious Catholic army with 19,000 Spanish and Italian soldiers from northern Italy. The Protestant leadership was aware of the pending arrival of another large force and sought to prevent it from joining. Nevertheless, before the combined armies of Horn and Sachsen-Weimar were able to close with Ferdinand, who was now besieging Nördlingen in Bavaria, his Imperial Army was joined by the 19,000 Italo-Iberian soldiers on September 2.

The combined Imperial Army, now numbering 33,000–40,000 battle-hardened troops, constructed fortifications on the hills to the south of Nördlingen.[7]

The Swedish-German Army, many of whom were raw recruits, concentrated its forces approximately 10km to the west of Nördlingen at Bopfingen, where they consolidated the units and awaited whatever reinforcements could be mustered quickly. Their strength had been depleted to about 22,000–26,000, as some of their troops had been ordered to Poland. Nevertheless, Bernhard von Sachsen-Weimar pressed for an attack, probably conscious of the previous failure to help the citizens of Regensburg. Bernhard was an ardent Protestant who certainly had shown his courage in previous engagements. Yet Gustav Horn did not support an outright attack. Their soldiers were outnumbered. By how much they may not have known, but both commanders were aware of the Spanish reinforcements Ferdinand had received. Sieges and large standing battles were not as eagerly sought out during the Thirty Years' War, and the decision was taken to advance closer to the southwestern supply route of the Imperial Army, thereby threatening its logistical lifeline

Bernhard of Sachsen-Weimar (1604–1639). Commander of the German forces at Nördlingen. (Author's Collection)

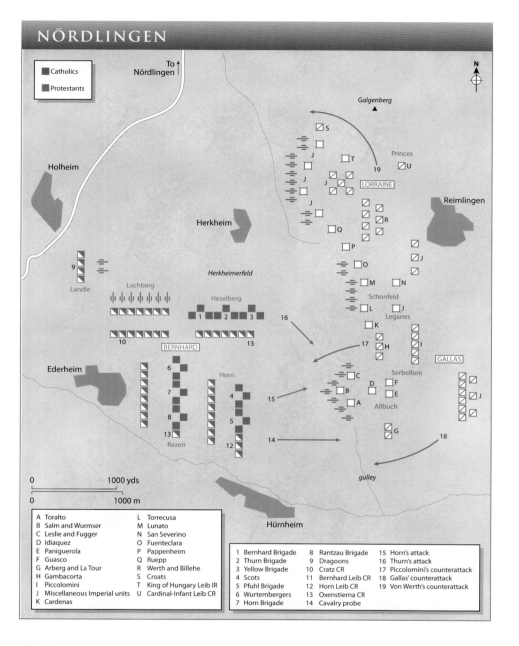

NÖRDLINGEN

■ Catholics
■ Protestants

To Nördlingen

N

Galgenberg

Holheim

Herkheim

Herkheimerfeld

Landle
9

Lachberg

Heselberg

1 2 3

16

BERNHARD

10

13

Ederheim

6

7

Horn

4

8

5

13

Rezen

12

15

14

Princes

LORRAINE

19

S

T

U

J

J

J

J

J

Q

P

O

M

N

L

Schonfeld

J

K

17

H

C

B

A

D

E

F

Serbelloni

Allbuch

G

Leganes

GALLAS

I

J

18

gulley

Reimlingen

Hürnheim

0   1000 yds

0   1000 m

A	Toralto	L	Torrecusa
B	Salm and Wurmser	M	Lunato
C	Leslie and Fugger	N	San Severino
D	Idiaquez	O	Fuenteclara
E	Paniguerola	P	Pappenheim
F	Guasco	Q	Ruepp
G	Arberg and La Tour	R	Werth and Billehe
H	Gambacorta	S	Croats
I	Piccolomini	T	King of Hungary Leib IR
J	Miscellaneous Imperial units	U	Cardinal-Infant Leib CR
K	Cardenas		

1	Bernhard Brigade	8	Rantzau Brigade	15	Horn's attack
2	Thurn Brigade	9	Dragoons	16	Thurn's attack
3	Yellow Brigade	10	Cratz CR	17	Piccolomini's counterattack
4	Scots	11	Bernhard Leib CR	18	Gallas' counterattack
5	Pfuhl Brigade	12	Horn Leib CR	19	Von Werth's counterattack
6	Wurtembergers	13	Oxenstierna CR		
7	Horn Brigade	14	Cavalry probe		

while keeping the Protestants' supplies flowing. The objective was to force the Catholics to lift the siege and maneuver away from Nördlingen.

The Protestant Army was delayed in its departure and the commanders realized that any surprise would be lost unless they took a different approach toward their objective. In essence, they marched south to create a ruse. The U-shaped route took the combined armies of Horn and Bernhard south from Bopfingen to Neresheim, west to Kösingen, back north, and then onto the main supply route to Nördlingen in an eastern direction, where they hoped to seize high ground which would give them an advantage. In total, the Protestants had to travel 16km with Bernhard's troops leading the way. Bernhard's mission was to seize the heights just north and past the road leading to Nördlingen, Gustav Horn's men were to take the Allbuch heights just northeast of the road leading to the town of Schmämingen in the east. Their army was to deploy on a north–west to south–east axis. Their route of march, however, took them through "difficult defile and forest."[8]

Croat pickets of the Imperial Army spotted the approach of the Swedish-German forces and engaged them as other Catholics joined the fray, and by the time Bernhard's men had organized their ranks and Horn's men were spilling out of the woods they discovered that the Allbuch heights were already teeming with Catholic troops and artillery. Thus the battle began in a piecemeal fashion and so, after a cavalry clash that ultimately involved some 6,000 troopers, Bernhard's assault fizzled out by 0600hrs.[9] The Protestants' right wing was not able to extend the main battle line as was intended. Instead, they repeatedly attempted to seize the heights against a numerically superior, prepared and equally determined enemy. As Bernhard and his men on the left wing maintained holding operations, Horn was in the fight of his life. A cavalry charge proved useless, as did one general assault onto the hill as more and more Imperial *tercios* reinforced the hastily built fortifications along their lines. Night brought the first day of fighting to close.

The Catholic forces on the Allbuch had three bastions or redoubts, along with 14 canons. Approximately six regiments were deployed between the cloverleaf-shaped redoubts in defensive works on the hill, and there were a further three regiments in reserve. The Spanish cavalry was posted on both sides.[10] "The Catholic right flank stretched from a point opposite the Lachberg to the village of Herkheim. It was composed of the bulk of the Imperial-Leaguist infantry, surplus Spanish musketry and, on its outer margin, of Bavaro-Habsburg cuirassiers and Croats."[11] The combined Swedish-German armies deployed in the following manner:

> Bernhard had charge of the left which extended from the western edge of the Heselberg across the Lachberg to the solid pillar of the Ländle. The cannon were set up at an appropriate, high vantage, the cavalry stationed as a matter of course on the far left. The Württemberg peasants also seem to have been put under ducal command, but were probably kept in the rear. Horn's right wing lay somewhat constricted in a corner angle running from the Heselberg down into the Retzenbach hollow. It could fully unfold only as the storming of the Allbuch progressed. Since the Swedish general was short of

infantry, he was given all of Cratz' corps plus a portion of Bernhard's foot. The position of the right wing was potentially precarious: should the hill be taken and the advance pressed too far, the connection with Bernhard's flank would become tenuous and subject to rupture by the enemy.[12]

On the second day, September 6, around 0500hrs, the preparatory bombardment on both sides began as Field Marshal Horn unleashed his brigades. Horn's foot regiments were able to punch through the Catholic lines and capture the hills. The lack of discipline and exuberance of the Protestants was to cost them dear, however, as the pursuing two regiments bumped into one another and thus became too disorganized to withstand a timely and well-executed counter-charge supported by Spanish cavalry.[13] It was vital at this stage for the Protestants to seize the advantageous terrain, and Horn's Swedish regiments were sent in one after the other in 13 separate assaults. More troops were fed into the cauldron, desperately attempting to dislodge the Imperial troops again.

A German illustration of the manual of arms, as well as tactical formations from the Thirty Years' War. (Anne S.K. Brown Military Collection, Brown University Library)

During this brutal fight, at about 0800hrs, Bernhard dispatched units from his command under Count Johann von Thurn to support Horn's attacks against the redoubts in the center, while Bernhard and his cavalry squadrons charged three times against the Imperial right wing. The formidable numbers of the Catholic units proved to be too much for the smaller relief detachment, as Thurn in the center was beginning to give way under renewed pressure from the Imperial formations. Thurn had to retire into the woods. As the Protestant center was about to fold, and thus was going to separate the two armies, Thurn's command was the linchpin holding them together. Horn and Bernhard decided on a disciplined withdrawal. Bernhard's regiments provided covering attacks while Horn used his cavalry to aid his disengaging infantry units. The withdrawal of Horn's army behind the protection of Bernhard's units was going well until two or three well-timed Imperial counterattacks by the Bavarian cuirassiers and Croats broke Bernhard's lines, forcing them back onto Horn's retreating masses.

The German infantry had to stand and fight off the Catholic cavalry charges. Finally the Imperial reserves advanced and drove Bernhard's weakened and exhausted men back while simultaneously, on the Catholic left, the remaining Protestant cavalry was driven off.[14] "With this, the only other route leading to the rear was cut off. The whole flank was turned and pushed in the direction of Ederheim where Horn had intended to station a forlorn hope of musketeers in order to make good his escape. The columns of the two [Protestant] wings collided head-on."[15] The ensuing chaos resulted in a near collapse of the entire combined Protestant Army, with 8,000 killed, thousands wounded, 4,000 captured including Gustav Horn, as well as the seizure of 300 battle standards and all 68 cannons.[16] The Imperial Catholic Army suffered 1,500 killed and 2,000 wounded. Nördlingen surrendered the next day.

THE AFTERMATH

The battle near Nördlingen was one of the most devastating defeats suffered by the Protestant forces, and its tangible outcome was the diminished prestige and influence of Protestantism in Germany. The Catholic forces were, for a brief moment, in control of the majority of Europe, until France began to enter the war in earnest and continued the bloodshed until 1648. Many German Protestant rulers, however, sought a separate peace with the Holy Roman Emperor, which was accomplished with the Treaty of Prague in 1635.[17] Bernhard's fate was not a bad one, though:

> Bernard realised that no further help was to be expected from the German Protestant princes, virtually all of whom had joined the Peace of Prague, and began to negotiate with France. On 19 November he agreed that, in return for annual subsidies of a million *livres*, he would maintain an army of 12,000 infantry and 6,000 cavalry. Saxe-Weimar was promised the Landgravate of Alsace, and rights over all lands conquered by him. The Swedes were irate that their French allies had "debauched" an army sworn to Swedish service but were powerless to do anything about it.[18]

The battle of Nördlingen established France as the pre-eminent power on the continent, as Sweden's political prestige and power waned. The battle also demonstrated that numbers can off-set technological innovation, although in this case one must remember that the Swedish-German armies were hardly filled with the professional soldier seen under the command of Gustav Adolph.

JENA-AUERSTÄDT, 1806

BACKGROUND

On August 7, 1806, the Prussian court secretly elected to engage in war with France and its master-soldier, Napoleon. So began the period later referred to as the War of the Fourth Coalition (1806–7). The Prussians would soon find willing allies in the Russians, who were gathering an army of their own to check the growing French Empire. Shortly thereafter, the Prussian general staff met to decide how to execute the upcoming war. Napoleon scoffed at the idea of Frederick William III, the King of Prussia, taking action against France. He would ignore the warnings of his own advisers until it became impossible to deny that Prussia would take to the field. This miscalculation benefited Prussia immensely because it would take the Prussian command the better part of a month to come up with a plan to prosecute the war.

We can gauge the level of strategic knowledge represented in Berlin by taking note of the only point that the Prussians could agree on: Napoleon "would take up a defensive position and await attack behind the Upper or Franconian Saale, or indeed upon the Main."[1] Starting from this strategic analysis, the Prussians went about drawing up a plan. Colonel Gerhard Johann von Scharnhorst, the latter-day Prussian reformer, would come up with the first, and perhaps the most sensible, plan: fight a series of delaying actions along the Thuringerwald, the Elbe, or the Oder with the final goal of meeting up with the Russian Army. The Prussian Army, combined with the 120,000 men being raised by the Tsar, would be more than able to meet whatever force Napoleon could muster. This plan was rejected outright. It wouldn't do for the Prussian Army to run from battle; honor was at stake. Prince Friedrich Ludwig von Hohenlohe, providing a taste of the tactical plan he would deploy at Jena, suggested waiting on Napoleon in the environs of Erfurt and Hof. They would wait here for Napoleon to advance, and then the Prussian Army would outflank the Grande Armée and win the day. This plan was vetoed as too defensive.

Charles William Ferdinand, Duke of Brunswick, a veteran of the Seven Years' War, suggested sending the entire army toward Stuttgart, where it might catch the French still in camp, or at least threaten the French line of communications. Hohenlohe, who was not about to accede to an older rival, advocated a move further east, but this would stretch the Prussian Army too thin. Rudolf Massenbach, another of the three chiefs of staff, suggested what amounted to marching in a gigantic circle. At this point, the king himself made an executive decision and mashed together Brunswick's and Hohenlohe's plans. Orders were issued.[2]

While the Prussians underestimated Napoleon and dithered about the proper course of action, the Tsar tipped his hand to the French when he refused to sign the 1805 peace treaty that was negotiated in the wake of Austria's surrender. Napoleon went to work immediately on the task of waging war on the Prussians before the Russians could mobilize. Napoleon quickly identified three possible plans for invasion. The first two were discarded as they might alert the Prussians to his true intentions too early as well as taking too long to develop. The plan Napoleon settled upon was an advance through the difficult Thuringerwald toward Gera, a town a few kilometers away from Jena. He would issue no fewer than 120 separate orders

Napoleon watches his troops engage in battle at Jena. (Library of Congress)

over the course of two days and set out immediately upon his adventure. Napoleon's orders went out to the various commands on September 17; the Prussians were still debating the best course of action as late as the 27th. In the end, Napoleon would end up determining the strategic plan for both himself and the Prussians: the Prussian Army would be forced into a variant of Hohenlohe's plan: wait for the French advance around the Salle river near Jena.

NAPOLEON'S MOVE

Napoleon split the Grande Armée into three columns. V Corps under the command of Marshal Jean Lannes and VII Corps led by Marshal Charles Pierre Francois Augereau made up the left column. The two corps fielded 41,000 men between them. This column moved along the Saalfeld river on a course for Jena. The right column consisted of the IV and VI Corps, commanded by Marshal Nicolas Jean-de-Dieu Soult and Marshal Michel Ney respectively, and was bolstered by the Bavarian Corps. This force of 50,000 skirted the Elster river, moving toward Gera. In the center, Marshal Jean-Baptiste Bernadotte's I Corps and Marshal Louis-Nicolas Davout's III Corps were paired, accompanied by Napoleon himself and the Imperial Guard, making up a total of 70,000 men. Each column would make for a separate pass through the Thuringerwald. There was some risk of the Prussians disrupting this movement due to the narrow transit, but Napoleon was certain that at worst one of the three columns would make it through and come to the aid of the others, should the Prussians dispatch one or even two armies to defend the passes. The Prussians, of course, did no such thing.[3]

For their part, the Prussians had been spread around the vicinity of Jena, content to wait on Napoleon to show his hand. The main army, under the command of Brunswick, was deployed as far forward as Erfurt. To his left, Hohenlohe's divisions were spread out around the environs of Jena, where they would eventually encounter the bulk of Napoleon's army. An advance guard under Prince Louis Ferdinand was thrown out to Saalfeld. It was this advance guard that would give the Prussians first warning of the Grand Armée's advance. The prince himself would perish in the initial skirmish with Bernadotte's advancing corps.[4]

Upon learning that the French were through the Thuringerwald and in the vicinity of Saalfeld, Brunswick ordered a general retreat. Hohenlohe was ordered to concentrate his forces near Jena to cover the flank of the Prussian Army, while the main army would withdraw by way of Auerstädt. In this way, the Prussians would determine the course of battle while actively trying to avoid it. When Lannes reported that the Prussians were in front of him, at least 20,000 strong, Napoleon

issued orders to give battle at Jena, unaware that the bulk of the enemy army was streaming north. It wasn't a preferred field of battle, with the River Salle at his back cutting off his only path of retreat, but he was determined to seize the initiative; Napoleon hated to let an enemy determine the time and place of battle.

Orders were dispatched on the night of October 13, starting around 2230hrs. Bernadotte had originally been dispatched to Dornberg, a town to the rear of the Prussians that would be their best line of retreat, but he hadn't actually reached the town by the 14th. Napoleon hoped to push the Prussians back with the bulk of his forces right into a full corps of his own, which would mop up the survivors and put the finishing touches on the upcoming victory. Napoleon added a postscript to his orders for Davout. If Bernadotte wasn't in Dornberg, he was to change course and coordinate with Davout on the morrow. This order and Bernadotte's peculiar interpretation of it would nearly result in Bernadotte's court martial.[5]

With I and III Corps deployed to the north, in the flank of what Napoleon supposed to be the main Prussian Army, the remaining corps of Napoleon's Grande Armée were ordered to converge on Jena. Lannes' V Corps, already in camp outside of Jena on the night of October 13, would lead the attack the next morning.

This corps would be the centerpiece of the French assault. Soult was ordered to bring IV Corps across the Salle toward the north, aiming for the town of Rödigen. The divison under General Louis Vincent Joseph le Blond Sainte-Hilaire took the lead, moving to cover Lannes' right flank. Augereau's VII Corps was ordered to move up through the Schenke Pass and advance on Lützeroda, where it would anchor Lannes' left flank. Marshal Ney, who was considerably further away, rode overnight with a fraction of his men and the reserve cavalry brigade under Prince Joachim Murat. He hoped to arrive in time for battle the next morning at dawn. The rest of Ney's men would arrive later to act as a reserve force. Napoleon would begin the day with roughly 40,000 men to throw against the Prussians. These new dispositions would bring another 50,000 men to Jena by noon the next day.[6]

THE PRUSSIANS

As noted, the Prussian force near Jena was under the command of Hohenlohe. He had some 38,000 men at his disposal, so the odds would have been fairly matched in the early morning had he concentrated his forces. Unfortunately, Hohenlohe was laboring under the impression that the French forces gathering around Jena were a picket, sent to harass the Prussian flank. The Prussian Army under Brunswick was already moving north and Hohenlohe was to cover the rear; his forces were spread thinly around the towns north and west of Jena.[7] He had placed only a single division, that of Generalmajor Bolesas Friedrich von Tauentzien, close to Jena and right in the path of where the French attack would develop the next morning. These 8,000 men would be the whole of the Prussian force called upon to check the advance of V Corps (18,000 men). The majority of Hohenlohe's men were concentrated around the towns of Isserstedt, Kötschau, Kapellendorf, and Gröss Romstedt, well to the rear. These 22,000 men were held back to be thrown against whatever French forces would appear along the Salle.[8] Hohenlohe would spend the better part of the 14th holding forces in reserve, unwilling to believe that he was facing Napoleon and the Grande Armée itself.

THE BATTLE OF JENA

For his part, Napoleon spent a good part of the night of the 13th ranging the field, scribbling orders, and adjusting his plans for the next day. He even oversaw the construction of an artillery road at the front. He would finally make it to bed at 0300hrs, with orders to be woken in a few hours when Lannes was to launch his attack.[9]

The next morning, a thick fog covered the entire battlefield. Even though the sun was up, men could barely find comrades in the same battalion, much less coordinate with other brigades. Both divisions of Lannes' V Corps somehow managed to deploy and waited for the fog to lift. For his part, Napoleon wasn't willing to leave the outcome of the battle to Mother Nature or, worse still, the Prussian commander. At 0630hrs, he ordered the divisions of General Louis Gabriel Suchet and General Honoré Théodore Gazan forward. The fog was so thick that Suchet's division was quickly off-course; rather than advancing directly to the village of Closewitz, its intended destination, the force veered left and ended up striking the Prussians along the road between Closewitz and Lützeroda. Gazan's men managed to stay with Suchet, so no gaps developed in this little force, but Napoleon's plan was already being tweaked by the elements.

Of course, the fog was just as effective at isolating the Prussian forces. Hohenlohe thought he was being probed by a small French force the day before, so none of his divisions had been ordered to prepare for an all-out assault. The men of Tauentzien's division were still gathered around campfires, preparing for another day of what they believed would be picket duty. As the first French skirmishers happened upon the regiments of Generalmajors Rechten and Zweiffel, the Prussians were rallied by the sound of gunfire and the unexpected roar of a cannon booming out of the fog. It could have turned into a mad scramble, but the Prussian officers took to their mounts and quickly formed lines to meet Suchet's push.

The battle was announced when 28 French guns opened fire on the Prussian lines, answered by the Prussian batteries. The next couple of hours would see Suchet in a tough battle, but one that would eventually be his. His men would break through the Prussian lines and take Closewitz by 0930hrs. Napoleon's plan may have been delayed, but there would still be plenty of time to fight this day. Gazan's force ended up in Cospeda to the west. He was resisted by Generalmajor von Cerrini's Regiment, a Saxon unit fighting on familiar territory. They repulsed Gazan's first push into the city, but were unable to exploit this success. When Cerrini moved to press his advantage, Gazan's men held and forced the Prussians to retreat in turn. About this time, the fog finally lifted from the field and Gazan was able to see the disposition of the Prussians. He reformed in order to secure the French flank.[10]

As the fog lifted, Marshal Soult's IV Corps was only now fully engaged with the enemy. He started the morning further away than Lannes, and Saint Hillaire's division had a hard time during the march through Löbstedt and Zwatzen. Soult had brought these men to a halt in the early morning in order to re-form lines and give his artillery a chance to catch up. It was 0815hrs before Sainte-Hilaire's tirailleurs moved through and cleared out the village of Closewitz and the Prussians there that threatened Lannes' right flank. The Prussians were thrown back toward the northeast and Sainte-Hilaire's men, with Soult himself leading, pursued them toward the town of Rödigen.[11]

If Hohenlohe had been closer to the front, he would have seen quite clearly that the French were present in force; this was no feint. Instead, he stayed at Klein Romstedt, a good three miles away from where his men were engaged. In fact, when Gazan was getting a good look at the Prussian left wing and making a detailed reconnaissance for the French, Tauentzien was already falling back toward Vierzehnheiligen. Hohenlohe still believed that he was facing a small contingent of French soldiers. The only man who could have known what was happening at the front was now retreating.

A member of Tauentzien's staff had finally been able to brief Hohenlohe on the withdrawal around 0930hrs. Hohenlohe then sent orders to General Ernst Philip von Rüchel's reserve army that was encamped at Weimar, instructing it to join his forces near Jena. It should be noted that Hohenlohe still didn't believe that he faced the main French army; Rüchel wasn't induced to hurry his men. Three brigades of Saxons were sent to safeguard the road Rüchel would need to take, however. Rüchel broke camp, formed his men, and marched toward Jena.[12] This was a critical juncture in the battle. If Hohenlohe had taken greater pains to focus the men at his disposal on the advancing French, the outcome might have been radically changed.[13]

Back at the front, Lannes was pushing his men hard. They swept through Vierzehnheiligen and then forced the Prussians to abandon the Dornberg heights beyond. Tauentzien's men were moving back to re-form and the Prussian cavalry were called on to check this French advance. The Prussian horsemen were able to push Lannes back again, forcing him even to abandon Vierzehnheiligen. It was at this point that Marshal Michel Ney finally made his appearance on the battlefield. Ney was desperate to play a part in the coming battle. Marshal Louis Alexander Berthier, Napoleon's Chief of Staff, ordered Ney up to the front to support Lannes' right flank and he marched toward Vierzehnheiligen to deploy eastward. But as he arrived at the front, he witnessed this latest French repulse. Ney quickly surveyed the scene and seeing an opportunity to grasp glory, he threw caution, as well as his orders, to the wind. With only two squadrons of cavalry and two battalions of infantry at his disposal, Ney made a beeline directly for Vierzehnheiligen and the advancing Prussians.[14]

It appeared to be a brilliant maneuver at first. The Prussians had just thrown back Suchet's men and hardly expected to engage fresh troops in Vierzehnheiligen. Ney immediately captured a horse artillery battery and pushed back its cavalry guard. His men then forced two Prussian cavalry regiments to fall back and the French were, for

Panoramic view of the
battle of Jena depicting the
classic linear formations of
the time. (Anne S.K. Brown
Military Collection, Brown
University Library)

Panoramic view of the battle of Jena depicting the classic linear formations of the time. (Anne S.K. Brown Military Collection, Brown University Library)

the second time that morning, masters of Vierzehnheiligen. Flush with success, Ney kept pushing. He followed in Lannes' footsteps and retook the Dornberg heights. Unfortunately, he was now on his own; he had lost contact with Lannes' corps. Plus, the Prussians were sending more cavalry into the center in order to buy time for Tauentzien to reset. This effort was well supported by Prussian artillery. Ney was forced to form his infantry into squares, his cavalry tucked away inside, and watched as the entire Prussian cavalry detachment bore down upon him. It seems that Hohenlohe was finally taking the French seriously and had ordered a combined assault on the central village behind Ney. A sum total of 45 squadrons of cavalry and 11 infantry squadrons were moving forward. Ney's men suffered under the fire of 35 guns, unsupported in the open, and his ammunition was fast depleting.[15]

It was this moment on the battlefield that best illustrates the difference between Hohenlohe and Napoleon. Hohenlohe was still back in Klein Romstedt trying to build a coherent picture of what was going on from the reports streaming in. He would send out messengers with his orders, often responding to events that had occurred some time before. Someone closer to the front might have taken note of Ney's perilous position and the gap it had created on Lannes' right, for to the north Marshal Soult's forces had encountered stiff resistance from a force under Generalleutnant von Holzëndorf around Rödigen, which had delayed his advance. While Holzëndorf's men would not prevail against Sainte-Hilaire, they detained the French force and this increased the distance between the French right wing and center. Ney was supposed to have held the French center, but he had left it center dangerously exposed, as well as leaving himself stranded in the open. Had the Prussian commander been able to see this, those cavalry squadrons might have been better used to split the French Army in two, upsetting Napoleon's plan.

To his credit, Napoleon was at the front. He had ridden out with his cavalry guard so he could observe the battle for himself and issue further orders. He was none too pleased to see the results of Ney's insubordination. Comparing Ney's tactical acumen to that of "the last-joined drummer boy," he quickly assessed the situation and dispatched orders to address it.[16] Augereau's VII Corps was to hasten its advance to Isserstedt and then to cover Ney's left flank. Lannes was ordered to attack through Vierzehnheiligen once more and make contact with Ney. In essence, Napoleon reshuffled his forward lines so that Ney and Lannes would switch places. In order to shore up the suddenly weak French center, he moved up the only available forces, two squadrons of cavalry and the Guard artillery, to close the gap. His quick thinking would save the French from disaster.[17]

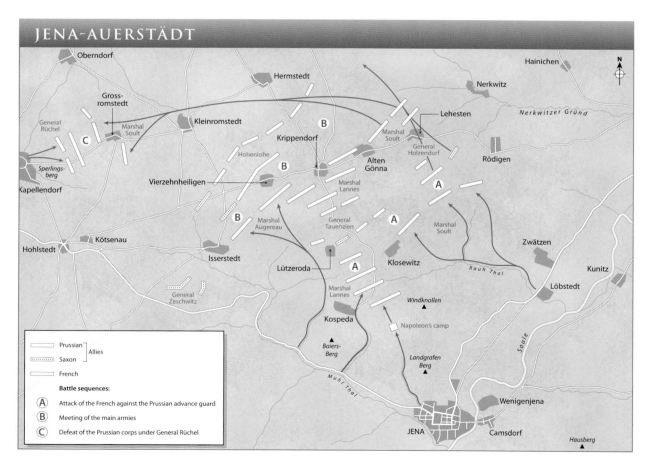

While this transpired, Saint-Hilaire was breaking down Holzëndorf's men near Nerkwitz. Holzëndorf had pulled part of his men back toward Nerkwitz, leaving the bulk of his troops in the woods of the Dornberg to wait for the French to pass and launch a flank attack. At 1000hrs, half of his infantry, supported by cavalry and light troops, marched out of the woods in perfect Prussian order. Thirty years earlier, it would have been a devastating blow to an enemy. Saint-Hilaire kept his cool, though; at the last possible moment, he unleashed his own light infantry into Holzëndorf's flank. The precision fire of French sharpshooters was too much to bear and the Prussian commander gave the order to retreat. Soult sent his light cavalry in to finish the work and captured six guns and about 400 men. Saint-Hilaire kept up the pressure, pushing against Holzëndorf's forces at Nerkwitz. Again, the French light infantry were too much for the Prussians to handle. They streamed around the Prussian infantry regiments to harass them while the light cavalry pressed the center and Holzëndorf's command broke, rushing toward Apolda in the rear. Holzëndorf would lose most of his guns, but he did manage to rally a single battery and a remnant of cavalry, who were dispatched to Klein Romstedt. Sainte-Hilaire might have done far worse to Holzëndorf and his troops, but he received Napoleon's latest orders and quickly set course for Krippendorf.[18]

While Saint-Hilaire was mangling Hohenlohe's left flank, Augereau's VII Corps was having its way with the Prussian right. General Jacques Desjardin's division of VII Corps made a hard push against the Saxons in Isserstedt and moved toward Vierzehnheiligen. The remaining division was left to hold this position while Desjardin moved to Ney's rescue. Gazan's division of the V Corps moved into Vierzehnheiligen itself and came into contact with Prussian *Jäger* (militia). They were forced into a hard scrabble to take the town. The two sides fought house to house, but despite fighting on home territory, the Prussians were again forced back. Gazan then managed to throw his men forward toward Ney's position. The rest of Lannes' Corps was working its way around the city and this force met the brunt of the Prussian cavalry advance. Lannes was halted, but so were the Prussians and the appearance of Desjardin's division in the nick of time allowed Ney and his battered survivors to retreat toward Isserstedt.[19]

As the French were extricating Ney, Hohenlohe was only just learning of Lannes' earlier repulse. He had massed forces of the French front in order to attack, but this news adjusted his plans. He elected to hold back his own offensive in order to give Rüchel time to make his appearance. Rüchel himself received word around 1030hrs that things were going well at Jena, and he pointed his columns toward Kapellendorf to take up a reserve position.[20] Hohenlohe was also counting on Holzëndorf, descending from the Salle above the Dornberg to join up on his left flank. It's clear that Hohenlohe was finally hearing enough evidence to convince him of the threat the French attack represented, but he still had no idea how badly things were going for his men at the front. At this moment, Holzëndorf's men were falling apart, leaving his left flank completely open, and his right flank would soon fall under the weight of VII Corps, a movement that was only delayed by the need for Desjardin to reroute and provide cover for Ney's withdrawal. While Hohenlohe's infantry regiments weren't a match for the better-trained French units, Ney's massive blunder had presented a choice opportunity to disrupt the entire French line and buy more time; Hohenlohe had no idea, though, and never took advantage of the situation.

As Hohenlohe's orders reached the men at Vierzehnheiligen, they found themselves in the same position that Ney had occupied only minutes before. The French batteries were well served and the massed Prussian infantry, held in place before the French Army, fell in clumps. The men tried to volley with the French, but muskets are little counter to artillery. Hohenlohe's center was quickly being reduced while he pored over reports and waited for the best moment to strike. Lannes elected to take the initiative and sallied out of Vierzehnheiligen to strike the immobile Prussians. The Prussians were forced back a little, but were still remarkably well served despite the rough treatment by artillery. The Saxon cavalry were able to rush in and push Lannes back into the town. Word of the Saxon success was sent to Hohenlohe, but it arrived at the same time as news of Holzëndorf's abandonment of Nerkwitz in the north and the loss of Isserstedt in the south. All Hohenlohe could see was light infantry and cavalry on his left and right; the center-right would have to be reinforced to withstand a French advance.[21]

Now that Ney was safely back in the French fold, Napoleon sent out his orders for the afternoon. It was close to noon and with fresh troops streaming across the Salle, Napoleon was ready to make a fresh push against the Prussian force. IV Corps under Soult, with Sainte-Hilaire in the lead and the freshly arrived divisions of generals Jean François Leval and Claude Juste Legrand supporting, were to move against what remained of Holzëndorf and the Prussian left flank. The VII Corps was to march out against the Prussian force defending the Weimar–Jena road. Once these two corps were engaged, the V and VI Corps were to strike the Prussian center in concert. Murat's cavalry would be positioned behind Lannes and Ney, ready to exploit any breach.

The onslaught began at 1230hrs. Augereau's men, who had been held back for an hour on the left flank, quickly overran the isolated Saxon regiments along the Weimar road. The only thing that saved these Saxon units from complete destruction was the inability of the French to stay together and exploit the breakthrough. To the north, there was little left to stand in Soult's way; the Prussian

Prussian light troops skirmishing during a fighting withdrawal, covering the remnants of the Prussian Army, after its defeat at Jena. (Author's Collection)

left flank was gone in a stroke. As Lannes and Ney engaged the Prussian center, these poor men began to give ground. Hohenlohe, mindful of his duty to protect the Prussian flank, ordered a withdrawal toward Gröss and Klein Romstedt. His army would finally be joining him. As the Prussians began to retreat, Napoleon released Murat's light cavalry, which had remained unengaged throughout the morning. The Prussian withdrawal had started in good order, but the fresh dragoons disrupted the Prussian lines and these men, hard-pressed all day and having suffered from the ministrations of the French artillery for close to an hour, broke and ran for Weimar. After hours of Prussian mismanagement, Napoleon completed one of his greatest masterpieces of battle. There were still actions of great valor on the part of the Prussians; a regiment of grenadiers led by Colonel Winkel helped staunch the French cavalry advance and the tattered remnants of Tauentzien's division bought time for the Prusian right wing under Generalleutnant Grawert to reform before retreating to Apolda. In the end, though, these acts would only alleviate the losses suffered in this catastrophic defeat.[22]

Rüchel arrived on the field to be told that Hohenlohe was defeated and that Rüchel's men were to retake the offensive. Hohenlohe himself assumed command and immediately ordered these troops to advance. This would be Hohenlohe's final mistake of the day. Rüchel's forces were splayed out in an open plain between Kotschau and Gröss Romstedt. Lannes made contact with this force near the latter town and was halted, but Saint-Hilaire had pushed his men hard all day and was quickly upon Rüchel's open left flank. Rather than anchoring himself in the towns and covering the retreat, Hohenlohe's rash decision to seize the initiative resulted in another disastrous retreat. The French artillery would make Hohenlohe pay once more for mishandling his troops. When the dust settled, Napoleon would count roughly 5,000 French casualties in the day's exertions. Even more remarkable was the final tally of Prussian casualties: 10,000 men killed and 15,000 taken prisoner. In addition, the Prussians had lost 120 guns to the French forces. It was a good day for the Grande Armée. Napoleon was certainly pleased with the work he did on October 14. He had exacted a terrible price from his Prussian enemies.[23] But an even more remarkable feat took place alongside Napoleon's great victory. The single French corps under Davout would engage the Prussian Army commanded by Brunswick and defeat it at the town of Auerstädt.

Neither side started the day with a complete tactical reading on the other. Napoleon was convinced that he was facing the better part of the Prussian Army outside of Jena. In reality, this was only the rearguard. For the night before, Brunswick himself had given orders to move away from Jena and meet up with Prussian forces gathered in Halle. He believed that Napoleon was nearby and his orders were to avoid contact with Napoleon on this day. His decision to move north took the Prussian Army out of Napoleon's path, but would set him on a collision course with Marshal Davout and III Corps.[24]

THE BATTLE OF AUERSTÄDT

If Jena was the triumph of Napoleon's tactical flexibility on the battlefield, Auerstädt was the vindication of his skill at military structural design. When Napoleon reorganized the French Army and introduced the corps system, it was a revolution. Every corps was designed to function as a separate miniature army when deployed on its own. Each corps contained infantry, cavalry, and artillery units, balanced in such a way that a single corps could withstand an enemy army for a period of 24 hours, giving Napoleon enough time to bring the supporting corps to the field of battle in relief. This construct was to be tested and proved in action on this part of the field. Davout's single corps would face off against the bulk of the Prussian Army.

Davout ended up all alone because of Marshal Bernadotte's insubordination the night before. Bernadotte and I Corps were nowhere near Dornburg on the evening of the 13th, but Bernadotte was determined he wouldn't subordinate himself to Davout. He disobeyed Napoleon's direct order to march with Davout and instead continued to push toward Dornburg. It was an act that would not only leave Davout in danger, but would also prevent him from reaching Apolda in time to cut off the retreat of the Prussian Army, which Napoleon assumed would be fleeing in disarray by the afternoon of the 14th.

Davout was furious at Bernadotte, but to his credit he carried out orders with his usual élan. He awoke early on the 14th and arrayed himself in his full uniform. By 0530hrs, he had joined the division of General Etienne Gudin in person at the frontline. Around 0700hrs, Gudin's division entered the town of Hassenhaussen and his cavalry screen made contact with their Prussian counterparts just outside of the city. Gudin formed his infantry into squares and marched out under the fog that covered the entire area. As the fog cleared for a moment, Gudin saw the Prussian cavalry and opened fire. The opening barrage wiped out the Prussian guns and the Prussian cavalry fell back. Gudin occupied the village of Hassenhaussen in force and sent light infantry out to patrol the River Lissbach beyond. Here he would wait for the divisions of generals Friant and Morand to reinforce him. The bulk of the day's fighting would be centered upon this point.[25]

At this time, the French were horribly outnumbered on the field. General Gebhard Lebrecht von Blücher, who incidentally had been kicked out of the army by Frederick the Great himself 33 years prior because of his wild behavior, commanded 12 squadrons of Prussian cavalry near Spielberg, while nine battalions of infantry under General Schmettau were approaching Hassenhaussen, accompanied by General Brunswick and King Frederick. Unfortunately, the Prussian baggage lines had become entangled with the two divisions that were to reinforce the Prussian line, so Schmettau was ordered to hold his men and wait to attack. Blücher, unable to contain himself, struck the French flank with his cavalry around 0830hrs, long before Schmettau would move forward. Gudin quickly formed square and easily beat off the Prussian cavalry. Since there was no infantry to coordinate with Blücher, Gudin was able to reform line after the engagement in safety. The Prussian division under General von Wartensleben took the better part of an hour to reach Schmettau and deploy. This gave the French division under Friant time to deploy on Gudin's right, where Blücher had struck earlier. A battery of 12lb artillery was part of this reinforcement. By now, Davout discerned that the Prussian goal was to strike his right flank again, in order to keep a road open to Freiburg, the direction in which the Prussian Army was rallying. With this in mind, he stripped the area just south of Hassenhausen down to a single regiment and redeployed the units to the north.[26]

It was close to 1000hrs, more than an hour after Blücher's charge, when the infantry divisions of Schmettau and Wartensleben finally advanced on Hassenhausen. Schmettau's division was caught between two French divisions and the crossfire decimated him; his men were thrown back. On his right, Wartensleben only faced a single regiment. He, in turn, was able to rout the French defenders. It was only Davout's quick thinking that prevented a further disaster. He pulled two regiments from Gudin's second line and led them in a counter-charge to reestablish the French left flank. The Prussians under Wartenslaben retreated from this engagement. Unfortunately, Davout had now committed every soldier at his disposal to the frontline; there would be no more reserves to call upon if the Prussians overran another position.[27]

The Prussians, however, seemed to have no idea how close the fighting to the south of Hassenhausen had been. General Brunswick elected to force the village itself and ordered four frontal assaults into the teeth of Gudin's division. Each of these assaults was turned back. Even worse, Brunswick himself took a mortal wound, shot through both eyes while leading a regiment of grenadiers. To add insult to injury, Schmettau himself was struck down during the assault. In a matter of moments, two critical generals were removed from the battle.[28]

Brunswick should be lauded for his bravery; he can also be faulted for a lack of prudence. He put himself in the thick of the action, but he seemed to fare no better than his counterpart to the south in determining the situation before him. He took up a course of action that involved attacking the enemy at his strongest point, rather than taking advantage of the weakness in the French left flank. His men were surely in high spirits to have him at the front of their columns, leading on the charges, but when he fell on the battlefield it was an unmitigated disaster for the army. The poor command structure of the Prussian Army doomed the enterprise to failure. When Brunswick went down, he took the entire Prussian Army with him.

After Brunswick fell, command devolved upon King Frederick William III. The only thing he shared in common with his famous ancestor was the name. Frederick William was overmatched this day. He neglected to appoint a new commander for the army or Schmettau's division and the Prussian division at the front was left to fend for itself. Prussian squadrons moved without regard to other squadrons and a logjam developed while pushing through the narrow terrain in front of the town. Units in the front struck without support or coordination and were quickly turned back by the French. Davout was taking losses from these fruitless attempts and feared that an all-out Prussian assault would finally break his corps. Fortunately for the French, the Prussian Army remained headless for close to an hour and Davout was able to bear these uncoordinated strikes until his own reinforcements arrived.

Napoleon and his staff in the foreground watch Lannes' advance with V Corps and part of Murat's cavalry. (Anne S.K. Brown Military Collection, Brown University Library)

In addition, King William could only remember the orders of Brunswick to avoid a fight with Napoleon. He spent the afternoon trying to avoid a fight with someone who wasn't even on the battlefield.[29]

At 1100hrs, William Frederick, the Prince of Orange, later William I of the Netherlands, arrived at the front with the right wing of the Prussian Army. On the other side, the French division under Morand finally made an appearance after marching from Kosen. In another example of superior French tactics and Prussian bungling, all of Morand's troops were immediately deployed on the weakened French left flank. On the other side of the field, Frederick William halted his own right wing and split it in half. One brigade was sent to the left, another brigade to the right. Morand's division, deployed in columns, moved to the south of Hassenhausen just in time to break a Prussian infantry charge. The French quickly redeployed in firing lines and engaged the Prussians in volley. The Prussians couldn't hold up and fell back. As the infantry was retreating, the Prussian cavalry moved forward and Morand quickly redeployed his units into squares. Another unsupported Prussian cavalry charge crashed into the French units; once more, the Prussian cavalry were forced to withdraw in disarray. The cavalry charged five times to no avail before withdrawing, leaving Wartensleben's infantry to fend alone. As the horses galloped away, Morand quickly deployed into column and moved forward to strike the Prussian right flank. It was a remarkable display of French tactical control in the face of an enemy. Morand quickly surrounded Wartensleben and only a single brigade of Prince Orange's division was available for support. The Prussian right flank was quickly overwhelmed and Wartensleben's men streamed back toward Auerstädt.[30]

Frederick William still had the advantage of numbers, with 14 battalions in reserve, but he had lost any nerve he might have had. He was firmly convinced from the events of the morning that he faced Napoleon. Seemingly haunted by Brunswick's orders to avoid a fight with Napoleon, Frederick William did absolutely nothing.[316]

Davout, on the other hand, had no fear of the fight. At noon, he sent his three divisions forward on the offensive. Morand's division forced its way into the massed Prussians, who had been trapped in a gulley, and he did great damage to them, albeit taking considerable casualties of his own from the massed Prussian artillery here. Davout described it thus: "We were within pistol range, and the cannonade tore gaps in their ranks which immediately closed up. Each move of the 61st Regiment was indicated on the ground by the brave men they left there."[32] Morand wouldn't let up the pressure, artillery or no. He pushed the Prussian infantry and artillery back remorselessly. When the Prussian cavalry tried once more to staunch the advance, he calmly formed his well-trained troops into square and threw back another unsupported charge. He quickly took the forward position at Sonnenkuppe Hill, where Morand placed his artillery and trained it on the flank and rear of what remained of Wartensleben's division. The Prussian right flank disintegrated under the resulting barrage. On the French right flank, Friant moved forward as ordered with haste. The Prussian defenders in the village of Pöppel gave great resistance to the French and it took some time to clear the village, but the result was another French victory and 1,000 Prussian soldiers taken prisoner. At 1230hrs, when Morand's guns opened fire, both flanks of the Prussian Army were untenable.[33]

Napoleon, in all his glory, in front of his old guard. Painted by Jean-Louis Ernest Meissonier (1815–1891). (Author's Collection)

The peculiar lack of coordination between the Prussian armies and even between the units within each force exacerbated the tactical situation. Frederick William thought Napoleon had to be in his front, that the whole of the Grande Armée would come rushing forward at any moment. The absence of intelligence from Jena and lack of forward reconnaissance from his own cavalry caused him to hold his entire reserve back through the course of the battle. He kept waiting for the "real" French attack that had to be coming. By the time the outnumbered men of the single French corps he faced turned his flanks, it was too late for that reserve to help matters. The morale of the Prussian men, already hard-tested by seeing Brunswick fall on the field and then forced to fend for themselves in the resulting command vacuum, ebbed from the field. One would be hard-pressed to find another commander on the field who did as little with so much as Frederick William III. If Napoleon still feared that Frederick the Great lived on, he would sleep well after learning that one of his lieutenants had crushed the heir to the great man's throne.

The force under Davout did its best to hound the retreating Prussians, but only so much could be expected of men who had fought so long and so hard this day. By 1630hrs, he had to bring his infantry to a halt; only a few cavalry units would continue to harass the Prussians. Still, the Prussians suffered some 13,000 casualties at the hands of Davout's little army. The odds at Auerstädt were flipped from Jena, though; Davout had been outnumbered two-to-one and the hard fighting cost him nearly 8,000 men and officers. Gudin's division, which had seen the hardest fighting at Hassenhausen, was down to 60 percent effectiveness.[34] Still, when Davout sent word of his victory to Napoleon, the Emperor would act incredulous. "Your marshal must be seeing double," Napoleon replied to Davout's messenger bearing news of the battle.[35] There was no way that Davout had defeated the main Prussian Army; the same army that Napoleon thought he had been assailing all day at Jena.

The final reports would bear out the massive accomplishment at Auerstädt. Between them, Napoleon and Davout wrecked the whole of the Prussian Army in the field. Over the next few months, the Grande Armée would chase and destroy the remnants of what had once been feared as the greatest army on the continent.

THE AFTERMATH

Three famous Prussian military figures were present at the battle of Jena: Gerhard Johann David von Scharnhorst, August von Gneisenau, and Carl von Clausewitz. As Brunswick's chief of staff, Scharnhorst had front-row seats, so to speak, for the disaster at Auerstädt. Gneisenau served on Hohenlohe's staff and was privy to the dreadful decision-making that produced the outcome at Jena. Clausewitz would draw on lessons from this battle in his later work *On War*. These three men would go on to craft a new Prussian military that would one day be the envy of others.

The Prussian Army of 1806 was horribly outdated. The tactics employed were straight out of Frederick the Great's army of 30 years prior. No provision had been made for military advances in the years since. Most importantly, the Prussian command-and-control was a bickering cabal of septuagenarian generals with no direct line to the units actually fighting at the front.

The outcome of the battle would go a long way toward overhauling the Prussian command, as none of the Prussians who stood at the pinnacle of command on these two battlefields would serve in that capacity again. There followed a complete revamp of the Prussian command structure and its training regimen. This also afforded Scharnhorst and others the opportunity to change the training and recruitment of Prussian soldiers, in particular the training of the milita units.

The crowning moment for this newly reconstituted army would come at the battle of Ligny (June 16, 1815). Yes, the Prussian Army would once again fall to a French Army, but the outcome would be considerably different. The superior command-and-control exhibited by the Prussians allowed them to leave the battlefield in an orderly fashion, fighting a successful rearguard action. The same army would then be able to maneuver to meet up with the forces of Wellington on the famous battlefield of Waterloo. Here, the Prussian's unexpected march into the fray would shatter the French right flank and provide the Prussian Army the distinction of helping to put an end to the reign of Napoleon.

Just as a crushing defeat can ultimately be the best thing for an army in need of reform, overwhelming victory can be a bane to the army that carries the field. Jena was a brilliant victory for Napoleon, another example of how his mastery of strategic maneuver and the superior organization of the Grande Armée could put overwhelming force at the point of greatest effect in the shortest amount of time. The results also allowed that same army to gloss over some serious deficiencies that would one day come back to haunt the French. Napoleon let personal feeling get in the way of proper military discipline in his treatment of Bernadotte, hoping that the near disaster he had avoided would keep him in check. Similarly, Napoleon had only harsh words for Ney following his impetuous actions that could have seens Napoleon's army split in two.

Seeing how Napoleon loved to seize the initiative himself in all circumstances, Ney's failing was one that Napoleon could forgive more easily. Unfortunately, Ney couldn't always count on Napoleon to arrive and save him from his own mistakes.

Finally, the results at Jena reinforced Napoleon's belief that he was above mortal men. Napoleon had been forced to engage an enemy on ground that he hadn't

View of modern-day Auerstädt, headquarters of the Prussian Army during the twin battles of Jena and Auerstädt against Napoleon. (Courtesy of Andreas Toeri)

chosen, with scant reconnaissance that had nearly led him to disaster. Not only had he decimated the force before him, a single corps of his glorious army had beaten back the whole of the Prussian Army all by itself. Napoleon believed, and the evidence seemed to indicate, that he was unbeatable.

THE ALAMO, 1836

BACKGROUND

After nearly three centuries of colonial subjugation by the Spanish Empire, Mexico threw off the yoke and celebrated independence on August 24, 1821, with the Treaty of Córdoba. Yet it took a few more years for Spain to finally relinquish any hopes of reinvigorating their colonial empire in Mexico. Spanish land grants given to foreigners, most notably to Americans, were upheld by the newly founded Mexican government. Following the country's independence, civil war erupted in Mexico, pitting the liberal *federalistas* against the conservative *centralistas* and its military dictator Antonio López de Santa Anna Pérez de Lebrón, who dismissed the existing government in 1834. American colonists known as "Texians" joined the ranks of the federalistas, who were supportive of the colonists and the economic growth they represented.[1] After having mercilessly crushed a rebellion in the state of Zacatecas, Santa Anna aimed to reduce the Texian rebellion as well. But first he had to suffer several setbacks; the rebellious Texians defeated a small Mexican force at the battle of Concepción on October 28, 1835, and on December 10 Santa Anna saw the defeat of a centralist force in San Antonio de Béxar, Texas, which was immediately occupied by the victors. By 1836, the time had come for the Mexican dictator to deal with the insurgents north of the River Rio Grande in Texas, and to reassert his authority both politically as well as militarily.

THE MEXICAN ARMY

The Mexican Army, which was called the Army of Operations, was well organized in theory, and at the outset of the campaign numbered around 6,000 soldiers. The table of organization for a Mexican battalion called for eight companies of 80 men, bringing the total to 640 soldiers. The company breakdown included six central

An example of a Mexican Regular Dragoon. The Mexican cavalry formed a line around the Alamo to intercept anyone attempting to escape the siege. (Anne S.K. Brown Military Collection, Brown University Library)

fusilier companies with one company of veteran soldiers, the grenadiers, and one fielded light troops for skirmishing and flank protection. The reality, however, was very different from the paper record. "Many companies fielded fewer than 40 *soldados*," writes Professor Stephen Hardin.[2] The battalions in turn were sub-divided into two basic types: the *permanentes* (regulars) and the *activos* (militias).

The regular battalions derived their names from heros of the revolution against Spain, while the militias took to their local regional affiliation. Santa Anna's army also fielded highly regarded *zapadores* (sapper units). The Mexican cavalry could draw on local friendly *rancheros* or *vaqueros* (cowboys) in certain areas of operations. Distant Mexican forts were garrisoned by competent cavalry troopers, who acted as scouts, and Indian-fighters called *presidiales*. The core of the cavalry arm of Santa Anna's Army of Operations was drawn from the permanentes and activos units, just the same as his infantry forces. (The cavalry regiments took the names of famous revolutionary engagements.) Traditional cavalry weaponry included sabers, lances, and carbines.

The artillery arm of the army was in shambles. Technical skills required to operate the guns were taught haphazardly, if at all, and by the time the Mexican forces crossed the Rio Grande only 21 pieces of ordnance were available and in various stages of maintenance. Professor Hardin notes that

of the 17 field pieces at his [Santa Anna's] disposal, he had seven 4-pdrs, four 6-pdrs, four 8-pdrs, and two 12-pdrs. For siege work, four 7-in. Howitzers rounded out the total. Regulations authorized each artillery company a complement of 91 *soldados* and officers. In ideal conditions, a company could split into six squads to man six guns.[3]

The Army of Operations totaled nearly 6,000 soldiers at the beginning of the campaign, but the artillery component had just 182 crew.[4]

Similar to other armies of the world, the Mexican centralistas were accompanied by a throng of *soldaderas* (female soldiers), including camp followers, wives, prostitutes, and children. The soldaderas were in effect the support structure needed for the army to function, as well as make life somewhat more bearable for the soldiers. Often these women would be the only medical help available to the wounded or injured men. Feeding the camp followers in a system that was not only corrupt but also incompetent, added to the strain of logistics. The leadership was a mix of professionalism and rank amateurism based on connections and social standing very similar to many other armies of the era.

An example of Mexican light cavalry, who were often used as scouts by General Santa Anna. (Anne S.K. Brown Military Collection, Brown University Library)

THE TEXIANS

The Texian volunteers were a mess in all aspects, except of course fighting, where they proved to be excellent shots. The organization of the Texan Army was brilliant on paper, however, the fighting was done by volunteers who disappeared once the battle had been fought, something of a militia. Civilians were as afraid of some of the volunteers as they were of marauding bandits or Indians. Uniforms, equipment, and formations were as varied as the men themselves and the army never exceeded 3,700 troops during the seven-month war.[5] The defense of San Antonio de Béxar (the site of the Mexican defeat in 1835), and the Alamo, a former Roman Catholic mission and fortress compound in Béxar) was assigned to Lieutenant-Colonel James Clinton Neill with a force of 150 men. Factionalism also wreaked havoc within the provisional political leadership of Texas under Governor Henry Smith, as some supported the original Mexican government that had been abolished by Santa Anna, while others desired to found a new independent state of Texas. A third faction sought a republic aligned neither to Texas nor Mexico.[6] By the time Santa Anna's dysfunctional Army of Operations crossed the Rio Grande on February 16, 1836, the commander of the Provisional Texas Regular Army Sam Houston "was a general without a government, without an army, and without a clue"[7] due to the volunteer nature of the army.

THE CAMPAIGN

The Mexican Army, stretched over nearly 500km, suffered much during their trek toward Béxar.[8] A lack of water and food during the march through the desert caused great hardships and eventually disease struck down camp followers and soldiers alike. The terrain and weather, including a severe two-day snow storm, punished them mercilessly, as did the marauding Comanches and Apaches. At long last on February 21, the decimated and elongated army reached the Medina river just south of Béxar. Santa Anna would soon have his revenge for the earlier defeat inflicted upon his forces at the town. But even the Medina was against him, as it was too swollen to cross immediately. This obstruction not only prevented the Mexican cavalry from seizing the town, it also prevented the defenders from fleeing to within the walls of the Alamo.[9] Two days later Santa Anna's troops seized the town and flew "a red flag atop the bell tower of San Fernando church," making their intentions clear that there would be no prisoners taken. Yet Santa Anna gave the defenders of the Alamo the opportunity for an unconditional surrender, which was rejected by its commander Lieutenant Colonel William Barret Travis with a discharge from one of the Alamo's cannons. The Mexican artillery was deployed – even without serious heavy siege artillery it was just a matter of time before the walls of the Alamo were reduced to rubble. One survivor of the Alamo, Susanna Dickinson Hanning, recalls the beginning of the battle:

Antonio López de Santa Anna Pérez de Lebrón (1794–1876), victor of the battle of the Alamo. (Library of Congress)

> On February 23rd, 1836, Santa Anna, having captured the pickets sent out by Col. Travis to guard the post from surprise, charged into San Antonio [San Antonio de Béxar] with his troops, variously estimated at from six to ten thousand, only a few moments after the bells of the city rang the alarm. Capt. Dickinson galloped up to our dwelling and hurriedly exclaimed: "The Mexicans are upon us, give me the babe, and jump up behind me." I did so, and as the Mexicans already occupied Commerce street, we galloped across the river at the ford south of it, and entered the fort at the southern gate, when the enemy commenced firing shot and shell into the fort, but with little or no effect, only wounding one horse.[10]

The commander of the Alamo, holding a regular army commission, had been Lieutenant-Colonel James Clinton Neill, but after much work to reinforce and prepare the Alamo's defenses, including the disposition of its 18 cannons, he was forced to depart to visit his ailing family as the invasion began. Command passed on the next regular army officer, Lieutenant-Colonel Travis. Travis had been sent to reinforce Béxar with 30 cavalrymen just after the arrival of another small group of volunteers under legendary frontiersman Colonel James Bowie, and another group under equally respected David Crockett. The situation was of course dire, the Texians were few and the chances of a relief column, organized by a provisional government and army that only existed on paper, were slim. Travis wrote a letter which is now with the Texas State Library and Archives Commission:

Send this to San Felipe by Express
night & day

To
The People of Texas
and
All Americans

Commandancy of the Alamo –
Bejar, Fby 24th 1836 –

To the People of Texas &
all Americans in the world –

Fellow citizens & compatriots –
I am besieged, by a thousand
or more of the Mexicans under
Santa Anna – I have sustained
a continual Bombardment &
cannonade for 24 hours & have
not lost a man – The enemy
has demanded a surrender at
discretion, otherwise, the garrison
are to be put to the sword, if
the fort is taken – I have answered
the demand with a cannon
shot, & our flag still waves

proudly from the walls – I
shall never surrender or retreat.
Then, I call on you in the
name of Liberty, of patriotism &
everything dear to the American
character, to come to our aid…

Since the above was written I heard a very heavy
Cannonade during the whole day think there must
have been an attack made upon the alamo We were
short of ammunition when I left Hurry on all
the men you can in haste
When I left there was Albert Martin
but 150 determined to
do or die tomorrow I leave
for Bejar with what men I can
raise [copy here illegible]
at all events –
Col. Almonte is there the troops are
under the Command of Gen. Seisma

[printed sideways]
Nb I hope that Every
One will Rondevu at
gonzales as soon poseble
as the Brave Solders are
suffering do not neglect this
powder is very scarce
and should not be delad
one moment
L. Smither[11]

Santa Anna's army, though heavily depleted by disease, desertion, and distance, still managed to create a formidable force and although its artillery arm was not the best, it was certainly effective during its bombardment of the Alamo. The artillery needed to be closer to its target while avoiding the Texian sharpshooters on the walls. To defeat the murderous crossfire, the Mexican sappers dug trenches during the siege, which enabled them to get closer and closer to the fort. During

the siege another 32 men cut their way through the Mexican lines and reinforced the garrison.[12]

By now perhaps some 250 Texians along with civilians were fighting for their lives against an estimated 2,000 soldaderos. The battered walls were reinforced by the defenders to the best of their ability, but the defenders knew that any breach would be exploited and that the superiority of their sharpshooting was going to make no difference against the overwhelming force of the Mexican troops.

On March 4, the tenth day of the siege and bombardment of the Alamo, Santa Anna sensed that the time was ripe for a glorious bayonet charge to take possession of the Alamo. There was no apparent reason to rush the final assault, an action that was surely going to cause unnecessary casualties on his side. Certainly, his scouts had not indicated the presence of any relief column heading for the Alamo. Nonetheless, glory was to be had at the tip of the bayonet. And even a last-minute offer by the Alamo's commander Travis was rejected by Santa Anna. So in the late evening of March 5, the bombardment ceased, lulling the exhausted defenders into sleep as the Mexican Army prepared for its final and bloody assault.

In the very early morning, at approximately 0530hrs, on March 6, 1836, a total of 1,700 veteran soldaderos advanced in a multi-pronged surprise attack.[13] A ring of Mexican cavalry was positioned to cut down any escapees from the Alamo. The Army of Operations deployed into four assault groups. General Martín Perfecto de Cos' group, 300 strong, advanced toward the northwest side of the Alamo. Colonel

Painting by Percy Moran depicting the last moments of the battle inside the walls of the Alamo. (Library of Congress)

Francisco Duque's 400 men moved against the northern wall. Colonel José María Romero's force totaling 300 men assaulted the fort from the east, while Colonel Juan Morales and his detachment of 100 light infantry advanced on the southside against the church and the abatis. The veteran troops marched silently toward their target but the tension led several and then many more men into yelling war cries, which alerted the garrison.[14]

The Texians' excellent shooting abilities, coupled with the proximity of the enemy, enabled them to unleash a hail of steel and death onto the soldaderos. Each advancing column was battered severely, forcing the Mexican soldiers to alter their approach. Colonel Duque was wounded as his men were pounded by cannon and small-arms fire. Colonel Cos' men fared no better, as they also took heavy casualties and began to waver and disperse. Colonel Morales and his light infantrymen were picked to bits and forced to move toward the southwest corner of the fort, away from their intended target, the church and the *abatis*. His men sought cover behind several small huts. Colonel Romero's column was forced to veer as well, as his men were hit by heavy fire from the east wall. It was during these early stages of the final fight that the Alamo's courageous commander, William Barret Travis, was shot in the head and died. Mexican Army officer Lieutenant Colonel José Enrique de la Peña witnessed his death:

Travis was seen to hesitate, but not about the death he would choose. He would take a few steps and stop, turning his proud face toward us to discharge his shots; he fought like a true soldier. Finally he died, but he died after having traded his life very dearly. None of his men died with greater heroism, and they all died. Travis behaved as a hero; one must do him justice, for with a handful of men without discipline, he resolved to face men used to war and much superior in numbers, without supplies, with scarce munitions, and against the will of his subordinates. He was a handsome blond, with a physique as robust as his spirit was strong.[15]

The combined firepower of the Mexican Army, which also encountered some lethal friendly fire onto their positions from Santa Anna's reserve forces, finally managed to force access into the compound. After this point, the battle had only limited time left to run. The Texian perspective of those momentous days and hours were well

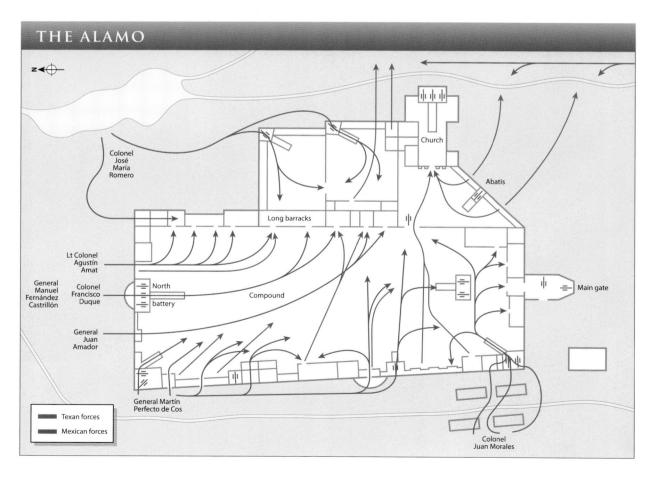

THE ALAMO

presented by several survivors. Susanna Dickinson Hanning, who lost her husband during the fighting, recalled simply:

> There were eighteen guns mounted on the fortifications, and these, with our riflemen, repulsed with great slaughter two assaults upon them before the final one. Under the cover of darkness they approached the fortifications, and planting their scaling ladders against our walls just as light was approaching, they climbed up to the tops of our walls and jumped down within, many of them to their immediate death. As fast as the front ranks were slain, they were filled up again by fresh troops. The Mexicans numbered several thousands while there were only one hundred and eighty-two Texans. The struggle lasted more than two hours when my husband rushed into the church where I was with my child, and exclaimed: "Great God, Sue, the Mexicans are inside our walls! All is lost! If they spare you, save my child." Then, with a parting kiss, he drew his sword and plunged into the strife, then raging in different portions of the fortifications.[16]

William Barret Travis (1809–1836) became the commander of the Alamo and was subsequently killed during the Mexican assault. (Author's Collection)

The battle for the Alamo ended rapidly once the walls had been stormed and subsequently a number of the defenders were killed during close-quarters fighting around the fortress. The entire garrison did not perish, although most if not all of the men who attempted to escape were either lanced or shot to death by the Mexican cavalry, who had formed an impenetrable ring around the Alamo. Some of the defenders did survive, but the vast majority died in combat. The garrison may have lost 250 (including civilians) while the Mexican Army's casualties may have been near 600, with a great number wounded. Santa Anna spared several Texians found at the Alamo, he hoped his mercy towards slaves would convince other Texian slaves to support the Mexican government. Upon meeting Susanna Dickinson he offered to adopt her daughter and educate her in Mexico. Dickinson refused the offer.

Others were not so lucky. David Crockett was captured and executed, while James

David Stern Crockett (1786–836), legendary American frontiersman, was killed in the interior courtyard of the Alamo, although there is some speculation that he was among those who surrendered and were executed after the fighting had ceased. (Library of Congress)

James Fannin attempted to relieve the siege at the Alamo, however not only did his column depart late, it didn't even make it past the San Antonio river. Their wagons broke down, the oxen wandered off, there was little food, and some men had no shoes. (Author's Collection)

Bowie, wracked with disease, was killed in his cot. De La Peña was witness to this and also to the cruelty of Santa Anna, who ordered the execution of a number of prisoners:

Some seven men survived the general carnage and, under the protection of General Castrillón, they were brought before Santa Anna. Among them was one of great stature, well proportioned, with regular features, in whose face there was the imprint of adversity, but in whom one also noticed a degree of resignation and nobility that did him honor. He was the naturalist David Crockett, well known in North America for his unusual adventures, who had undertaken to explore the country and who, finding himself in Béjar at the very moment of surprise, had taken refuge in the Alamo, fearing that his status as a foreigner might not be respected. Santa Anna answered Castrillón's intervention on Crockett's behalf with a gesture of indignation and, addressing himself to the sappers, the troops closest to him, ordered his execution. The commanders and officers were outraged at this action and did not support the order, hoping that once the fury of the moment had blown over these men would be spared; but several officers who were around the president and who, perhaps, had not been present during the danger, became noteworthy by an infamous deed, surpassing the solders in cruelty. They thrust themselves forward, in order to flatter their commander, and with swords in hand, fell upon these unfortunate, defenseless men just as a tiger leaps upon his prey. Though tortured before they were killed, these unfortunates died without complaining and without humiliating themselves before their torturers.[7]

The Alamo served as a rallying cry for the Texians and on April 21, 1836 the newly formed Texian Volunteer Army attacked Santa Anna's army and won a resounding victory at the battle of San Jacinto. During the fighting, many of the Texian soldiers repeatedly cried "Remember the Alamo."[18]

JUGDULLUCK, 1842

BACKGROUND

At the start of the 19th century, Britain feared Napoleonic French influence in Persia and its potential to threaten British India. Yet with the Treaty of Turkmenchay in 1828, by which Persia ceded tracts of its northern territory to the Russian Empire, the focus of British fear in the region shifted to Russia.[1] There it would remain, inexorably focused as "The Great Game" played out between the two rival empires over the next century.

In the aftermath of Turkmenchay, Russia encouraged Persia to attack western Afghanistan in general and the semi-autonomous state of Herat in particular. From the west all routes to India wound via Herat, and through it ran the only road that could be used by an army laden down with heavy artillery. In 1834 the Persians tried for Herat but failed, drawing an official warning from Lord Palmerston, the British Foreign Secretary, against ever again attacking Afghanistan at the behest of the Russians.[2] The British fear was that if Herat were taken it would put the Afghan city of Kandahar within reach and if Kandahar were taken it could place Russian armies within striking distance of British India. In the summer of 1837, the Persian Shah dispatched another army to Herat, which finally arrived at the gates of the city on December 1. Their ranks included a Russian general, an unofficial "observer," who, as the siege dragged on, would take personal command of all the besieging Persian forces.[3]

Meanwhile, in Kabul, Captain Alexander Burnes, the recently arrived representative of the British East India Company, had another troubling development to report to Lord Auckland, the Governor-General of India. On Christmas Eve, 1837, Viktorovich Vitkevich, a captain of Cossacks, arrived in Kabul bearing a letter of goodwill from the Tsar, which he delivered into the hands of Amir Dost Muhammad Khan.[4] At that point Dost Muhammad had ruled over

Kabul and the surrounding provinces for more than a decade. Throughout his reign, "the Dost" had faced two major problems: the ongoing efforts of Shah Sujah-ul-Mulk – the dethroned prince of the previous Sadozai dynasty – to regain the throne; and the expansionist ambitions of his neighbor to the southeast – Maharajah Ranjit Singh.

Ranjit Singh's Sikh Empire stretched from the border of Afghanistan in the west to Tibet in the east and from Kashmir in the North to Sindh in the south. In the 1830s its well-armed, formidably modern army – the *Khalsa* – consisted of nearly 90,000 men, largely trained and led by European mercenaries.[5] In the late 1830s, Singh and his empire were arguably the strongest of British allies on the Indian sub-continent. In 1834 Dost Muhammad had faced coordinated attacks by his two enemies. While the Afghan pretender Shujah tried and failed to take Kandahar, Singh succeeded in taking Peshawar.[6]

From that point on, Dost Muhammad persistently tried to enlist British support for a future effort to retake Peshawar from the Sikhs.[7] But Ranjit Singh was an older and better trusted ally of the British than Dost Muhammad. By constantly pushing the British to help him against the Sikhs, Dost Muhammad unwittingly encouraged them to join *with* the Sikhs and Shah Sujah in an effort to overthrow the Dost himself. Whether Dost Muhammad met with the Russian emissary because he was looking for a new super-power benefactor, or because he was attempting to encourage his current benefactor to do better by him, will never be known. What is known is that the British quickly decided they would implement a regime change in Kabul. To accomplish the overthrow of Dost Muhammad, the British would enlist the aid of Afghan and Sikh forces. Together with an army from British India, the Sikhs and Afghan exiles would depose Dost Muhammad and install Shah Sujah in his place.[8]

Once set upon this course of action, Lord Auckland justified it to the world at large with the publication on October 1, 1838, of a document entitled "Declaration on the Part of the Right Honourable the Governor-General of India." To history the document has forever been known as the Simla Manifesto, in reference to its place of original publication. The manifesto went into great – though largely inaccurate – detail on recent developments in Afghanistan and on its borders and stated how "The Governor-General felt the importance of taking immediate measures for arresting the rapid progress of foreign intrigue and aggression towards our own territories." It then went on to champion "the position and claims of Shah Sujah-ol-Mulk." Auckland concluded with noting how happy he was that "in the discharge of his duty, he will be enabled to assist in restoring the union and prosperity of the Afghan people."[9] The Manifesto paid special attention to the ongoing siege of Herat by Russian-backed Persian forces as a key reason for entering Afghanistan.

But soon after it was published, the siege was lifted. Yet siege or no siege, the invasion of Afghanistan would be going forward.[10] Before it did, however, Ranjit Singh had a change of heart. Although still an enthusiastic supporter of the coming British action in Afghanistan, he thought better of the plan and chose to sit this one out.[11]

At first things went well for the British. In November 1838, the 21,000-man army of the Indus set off. On May 4, 1839, they took the major city of Kandahar. Between Kandahar and Kabul lay the fortress city of Ghazni, which commanded the trade routes and roads to the capital. For Kabul to be effectively captured, Ghazni had to be taken first. It was the most powerful fortress in all of Afghanistan and the Afghans were convinced it was impregnable. Heavy losses to their draft horses had forced the British to leave all the heavy siege equipment behind in Kandahar. But that did not stop the British, under General Sir John Keane, from taking it anyway.[12]

After the fall of Ghazni, Dost Muhammad sent an emissary to General Keane and offered his surrender and submission, in exchange for the office of Vizier, a hereditary title long held by his clan. But this was not part of the British plan. The British countered with the offer of honorable asylum down in India. The Dost rejected this and chose to fight on.[13] As Keane's triumphant army advanced from Ghazni to Kabul, Dost Muhammad attempted to make a heroic last stand in front of his city. His Persian-descended Kizilbash mercenaries, however, refused to accompany him on one last cavalry charge, so he released them from their allegiance and, with a handful of his most devoted followers, rode north, toward the towering mountains of the Hindu Kush. On August 6, 1839, Shah Sujah reentered his capital. It was remarked by several British officers at the time that no one in the local population seemed to notice or care, one way or another.[14]

The British Army at first occupied the natural citadel and strongest point in the city of Kabul, the Bala Hissar – a medieval fortress that commanded the entire city. But Shah Sujah wanted the Bala Hissar to himself, so the British Army was relocated to hastily built cantonments, which were especially ill-suited for defense, being sited on low, marshy ground and surrounded by hills and orchards on all sides. The British camp was enclosed by a mud-brick wall, only waist high in places, which would offer little protection.[15] In fact the British high command in Kabul didn't think it possible that they would ever find themselves actually having to fend off an attack. They had already defeated the Afghans, so that would not be a problem.

In October 1840, General Sir John Keane handed command of Anglo-Indian forces in Afghanistan to Sir Willoughby Cotton. These forces included a division of infantry, a regiment of cavalry, artillery, and ancillary units.[16] Despite having achieved a signal victory at Ghazni and to all appearances succeeded in pacifying the country, Keane was not bullish on the future of British fortunes in Afghanistan. As he left

An example of Bengal Native Infantry. (Anne S.K. Brown Military Collection, Brown University Library)

Kabul behind, the general remarked gloomily to a young lieutenant accompanying him back to India: "I cannot but congratulate you on quitting the country; for, mark my words, it will not be long before there is here some signal catastrophe!"[17]

Only a month after taking the reigns of command from Keane, General Cotton presided over the surrender of Dost Muhammad. By then, the Dost had spent 15 months on the run throughout Afghanistan. In November 1840, after leading his men in a victorious skirmish with a British-led Indian cavalry troop, Dost Muhammad decided that enough was enough. The British accepted his surrender and sent him to exile in Ludhiana.[18]

As the British settled down to occupy Kabul and various cities, towns, and fortresses throughout the land, the Afghans found new reasons to resent their presence. First, they were offended by the attention certain British officers paid to Afghan women. Then the arrival in Kabul of British wives and children, sent from India to join their husbands, led the Afghan population to suspect the possibility of a permanent British occupation, which caused new levels of alarm and resentment.[19]

In April 1841, Cotton handed over command of the British army of occupation to Major General William Elphinstone. The force had been somewhat reduced since Cotton took command from Keane. It now consisted of the 5th Bengal Light Cavalry; one troop of Horse Artillery; the Queen's 13th Foot; the 35th Bengal Native Infantry; the 37th Bengal Native Infantry; the Queen's 44th Foot; the 5th Bengal Native Infantry; and the 54th Bengal Native Infantry. In addition, there were Shah Sujah's native units, including at least two regiments of cavalry and one of infantry.

General Cotton assured his successor: "You will have nothing to do here, all is peace."[20] But to his credit, even the old and ever more infirm Elphinstone saw immediately the vulnerability of British position in the cantonments at Kabul. In response, he had plans drawn up to construct a "citadel." The first steps for enacting this plan were begun – but when the Company's government in Calcutta learned that the plan would cost £2,400, it was immediately vetoed and the work was shut down.[21] Still, in the spring of 1841 Sir William Hay Macnaghten, the envoy and the senior British representative in all of Afghanistan, was certain that – with the possible exception of Herat – the pacification of all Afghanistan was at hand: "The whole country is as quiet as one of our Indian chiefships – and more so."[22] Macnaghten convinced himself that there was no longer a need to keep such a large and expensive garrison on hand. It was his opinion that Shah Sujah's own Afghan forces required

An example of a Bengal Horse Artillery Officer around 1845. (Anne S.K. Brown Military Collection, Brown University Library)

the supplement of only one British regiment at Kabul and another at Kandahar "to keep the entire country in order."[23]

Not everyone agreed. A year earlier, in 1840, Captain Colin McKenzie (who would conduct himself with characteristic intelligence, energy and courage throughout the ill-fated Afghan campaign and go on to greater glories thereafter) had written: "Our gallant fellows in Afghanistan must be reinforced or they will all perish." But Macnaghten disagreed. In September 1841, he informed his superiors in Calcutta that in addition to the drawdowns in military costs, "I am, too, making great reductions in our political expenditure."[24]

For centuries, the Gilzai tribe of southeastern Afghanistan had controlled the mountain passes along which ran all the major trade routes connecting India to Afghanistan. They had levied fees one way or another upon anyone passing through, either at the tip of their *tulwar* swords and muzzles of their *jezail* rifled muskets or in the form of an annual subsidy from whatever government happened to hold sway at the time. When the British had successfully returned Shah Sujah to the throne in Kabul, they had intelligently maintained his predecessor's policy in this area by paying the equivalent of £8,000 to the eastern Gilzais in exchange for the safety of the road through the Kyber Pass, over which they held sway. In exchange, Major Henry Havelock (who would go on to serve as a general in the Great Mutiny, winning multiple victories, fame and fortune) reported, the Gilzai tribe "has prevented even a finger from being raised against our posts, couriers and weak detachments. Convoys of all descriptions had passed through these terrific defiles, the strongest barrier of mountains in the world, with little or no interruption from these predatory tribes."[25]

But all that was about to change. At the start of October 1841, the Gilzai chiefs were called to Kabul and informed that their payment was at an end. They received the news with surprisingly calm indifference – then returned to their tribal land, 16km east of Kabul, and blocked all the passes to the south. From that point on every caravan coming from India with supplies for the British was mercilessly plundered and the army of occupation was effectively cut off from reinforcement and resupply.

In the face of these disturbing developments, Macnaghten was not fazed. He was more focused on preparing for his next post as Governor of the Bombay Presidency, the second most powerful – and profitable – position in the entire Company. This was to be his reward for successfully overseeing the political side of British conquest and regime change in Afghanistan over the prior two years. He was scheduled to leave Kabul for India before the end of October and nothing would convince him that anything was seriously wrong. He wrote: "The country, I trust, will be left in a state of tranquility, with the exception of the Gilzais … and I hope to settle their hash on the road down, if not before."[26]

One brigade of the Kabul garrison, under the command of Brigadier Sir Robert Sale, was scheduled to return to India and was ordered to clear the Gilzais from the nearby Khoord-Kabul Pass, less than 9.5km from Kabul itself. The plan was for this to be accomplished by the brigade's advance guard, composed of the 35th Bengal Native Infantry. However, the 35th were attacked while encamped on the first night of their march. In due course the entire brigade – including the British Army's 13th Foot, the 37th Bengal Native Infantry, a squadron of the 5th Bengal Light Cavalry, one battery of horse artillery, one of mountain artillery, 200 of Shah Sujah's Afghan irregulars, as well as Sujah's sappers and miners – was committed to the fight.[27] Sale's brigade succeeded in pushing its way through the pass and continuing on to Jalalabad, but it would be hard for anyone to claim they had settled the issue of the Gilzais.

Anyone that is but Macnaghten himself, who remained confident the Gilzais could be put down with ease, thanks to their being incapable of teaming up with any of the various other Afghan tribes. Some other British officers were not so sure. Lieutenant Eldred Pottinger was already a hero for his service at the siege of Herat; he had then been assigned as the political officer to the province of Kohistan. Pottinger was convinced that the Gilzais, Kohistanis, and Duranis had been plotting together as allies since September, but when the Gilzais fought the British in October, their fellow tribes remained on the sidelines. This, in turn, convinced Macnaghten that Pottinger was an overly cautious alarmist.[28] This despite the fact that Pottinger was already a certified hero of the empire for his exemplary service in leading the successful defense of the city of Herat.

By now the tribal leadership in and around Kabul had made the decision to rise en masse against what remained of the British army of occupation.[29] Two prominent chiefs in particular – Abdoolah Khan and Amenoolah Khan – set a two-part propaganda campaign in motion to add more fuel to the anti-British fire already smoldering just below the surface throughout Afghanistan in general and Kabul in particular. First they sent word to the chiefs of the Kabul region that Macnaghten was planning to take them all into custody and ship them to London to be held as hostages. Then they drew up a document calling for all good Afghans to rise up and slay every foreigner in Afghanistan, forging Shah Sujah's signature on the document.[30] At the top of the list of *ferenghi* (foreigners) to be killed was the British resident, Alexander Burnes. By this time Burnes was eagerly waiting to hear whether or not he would be chosen to succeed Macnaghten as envoy in Kabul. He himself had said, "We shall never settle Afghanistan at the point of the bayonet."[31] Yet he had turned a blind eye to developments when they did not fit into the picture of Afghanistan that he, his political superior Macnaghten, and the highest ranks of leadership in

This painting displays some of the obstacles associated with moving an army across rugged terrain. (Anne S.K. Brown Military Collection, Brown University Library)

British India wanted to see. And for that he would pay the highest possible price.

Burnes made his home in the British Residency, set apart from the cantonments that housed the British forces. On the morning of November 2, 1841, an angry mob of Kabulis sacked and torched the residence, plundered the British paymaster who resided next door – making off with no less than £17,000 – and slit the throat of every Englishman and Indian and Afghan in British employ they could get their hands on, including women and children. Burnes himself was hacked to pieces.[32]

Why didn't the British take decisive action of any kind in response to the murder of Burnes? The answer is leadership. Or, more precisely, the lack of it. "Unfit for it, done up body and mind." This was the judgment rendered by Elphinstone upon himself and his readiness to command the garrison at Kabul. He went on, in a letter to his relative Lord Elphinstone: "I shall apply to Lord Auckland to be relieved. My stay would be useless to the public and distressing to myself."[33] Unfortunately for the British, by the time Lord Auckland assented to the pleadings of the feeble Elphinstone and sent word he could be replaced, it was too late. Burnes was dead and Kabul was in rebellion, with the rest of Afghanistan to follow. Later, after the garrison had ceased to exist, Captain George Broadfoot would write, "if we had had a single General fit to command, no disaster would have happened at Kabul."[34]

But the crisis in British leadership was not confined to General Elphinstone. His second-in-command, Brigadier John Shelton, held him in contempt, and made no attempt to hide the fact. Elphinstone, a combat veteran of the Peninsular War and a regimental commander at the battle of Waterloo (the last time he had seen combat), was known above else for his gentle courtesy and kindly nature.[35] Shelton, who had lost his right arm during the storming of St Sebastian in the Peninsular War, was an embittered, morose, and stubbornly unlikable man.[36] Elphinstone and Shelton and the dysfunction that characterized their command relationship, sealed the doom of the army of occupation in Kabul.

THE BEHMARU

Several hundred meters to the northwest of the ill-sited British cantonments was a range of low hills called the Behmaru. At the foot of these hills lay a village by the same name. After the siege began, the inhabitants of the village sold supplies of fresh food to the British – until the insurgents found out they were doing so and razed the village to the ground. They then occupied the spot and installed a pair of small guns, which kept up a continuous fire upon the camp's inhabitants. The British made two attempts to dislodge the enemy from atop the Behmaru. The first attempt on November 13, under the command of Brigadier Shelton, carried the heights. The Afghans withdrew and abandoned their guns, one of which the British spiked, taking the other with them. A few days later the Afghans returned to Behmaru and began another incessant barrage on the inhabitants of the cantonments. Shelton, over his strong objections, was ordered to try again. Under cover of darkness early on November 23, Shelton led another force of 17 infantry companies, two cavalry squadrons, and 100 sappers out to silence the guns once and for all and perhaps take possession of the surrounding hills as well. However this time Shelton only brought a single gun as artillery support.

When the sun rose on the 23rd Shelton and his force had crowned one hill. From it the one British gun opened fire on the Afghans below, leaving the Behmaru village open to assault. But Shelton hesitated before sending a storming party to take the village itself, and when he finally did, its leader, Major Swayne, bungled the job. He and his men found themselves helplessly pinned down, under constant fire from Afghan snipers for half an hour – until Shelton issued the order for them to withdraw. By now the sun was up and the entire population of Kabul could see there was a battle being fought just outside their city. Before long thousands of Afghan horsemen and infantry were pouring out of the city toward the Behmaru hills.

Shelton held his ground. He did not advance to occupy any of the other nearby hilltops nor dispatch a stronger storming party again to attempt to take the village itself. He simply remained in place, with his entire force atop one single hilltop.

Reaching Behmaru, the Afghans swarmed onto the hill closest to that which the British were occupying. Only a narrow gorge now separated them from Shelton and his men. The Afghans opened up a telling fire with their jezails upon the British.

In reply to this development, Shelton made the very worst tactical move possible; he ordered all 17 companies of his infantry to form two squares.[37] Perhaps he was concerned that still more Afghans would come pouring out of Kabul and attempt to charge into the melee with his force. Forming square would be the proper thing to do in such circumstances. But at the time, the only threat they were currently facing was incessant small-arms fire from troops who, separated from his own men by a gorge, were physically incapable of closing into hand-to-hand combat with them any time soon. By packing his men even tighter together than before, Shelton turned them into even better targets.

In the opinion of most British officers of the time, the Afghans' jezails were acknowledged to outrange British muskets and the Afghans were far better marksmen. The British squares began to take heavy casualties. The only thing holding the Afghans at bay was the one British gun – until it overheated and was forced to cease firing. This failed gun was to be expected and was the main reason why standing orders for British forces in India were never to take the field with fewer than two guns. Shelton, however, had brought only one gun. With nothing to fear but one-quarter of the generally ineffective British musket fire (the other three-quarters wasted facing in other directions, due to the square formations) the Afghans advanced so close to Shelton's force that a number of British officers began to throw rocks at them, the rocks apparently proving more effective than their muskets.

The Afghans poured more and more fire onto the mass formations of British and Indian infantry, now at close range, inflicting escalating casualties. Yet Shelton would not order a retreat back to the cantonments, nor an advance to clear the hillside. With so many Afghans so close he couldn't risk trying to bring the other three-quarters of his muskets to bear on the foe, since that same foe would likely take advantage of the opportunity to rush in with their swords and shield and fall upon his men as they were in the midst of adjusting formation from square back to line.

Shelton was hit five times by spent rounds while marching around the hilltop, but did not suffer one serious wound. At one point Shelton left the square nearest the Afghans to go and bring back reinforcements from the second square. The troops of the frontline square, observing this, came to the instant conclusion that their commanding officer was retreating and instantly broke and ran. Moments later the entire British force was running down the hill and back to the cantonments. Afghan cavalry gave chase and more British and Indian troops were cut down in the pursuit. Shelton's effort to silence the Afghan guns on the Behmaru Heights had turned into a complete British defeat. It had shredded whatever was left of morale on the British side and destroyed whatever confidence the troops might have had in Shelton's combat leadership.

TREATIES AND CHOICES

In the simplest terms, there were now three routes open for the British to take. The first was a fighting retreat to Jalalabad, which lay about 145km to the southwest. This was dismissed by General Elphinstone himself as being "most disastrous." It would mean abandoning a great deal of valuable government property as well as the fall of Shah Sujah from the throne. It would also mean fighting their way through defiles and passes filled with tribesmen and *ghazis* (fanatic religious warriors) along the way. It was assumed by Macnaghten as well as others that "in such a retreat very few of our camp followers would survive."

The second option was a fighting movement to take the Bala Hissar. Once there, the British would have to hold it until spring, by which time relief forces from British India would surely arrive. This objective was less than 3km away, but would involve moving through narrow streets, and the abandonment of all heavy artillery. There was uncertainty regarding what supplies were in the fortress.

When both of these choices were vetoed, the only remaining option was to continue occupying their present position. To quote Macnaghten once again: "…I would on no account leave the cantonment."

Had there been decisive or effective leadership at the top, either of the first two choices would almost definitely have led to a better outcome. For the remainder of their time in the city, the British force would sit, wait, and do little else. The only exception to this rule was the British high command, who were busy doing two things: arguing among themselves and negotiating at painful length with the enemy.

As the British garrison at Kabul withered under the orders of men who had no place to command, the one force which might have come to its rescue chose not to do so. This was Sir Robert Sale's brigade, at the time occupying Gandamak, some 129km to the southwest. Elphinstone had sent a message to Sale that explained the desperate circumstances in Kabul and ordered him to march to the city at once, "provided the sick and wounded could be placed in security with the irregulars at Gandamak." Sale had more than 300 sick and wounded soldiers with him and was certain that leaving them at Gandamak in the charge of his local Afghan irregulars would be sealing their doom.

Sale was right, for when his brigade marched off to Jalalabad those same Afghan irregulars rose along with the local Ghilzai tribesmen and attacked him for two days straight, fighting three major battles with the British between Gandamak and Jalalabad.

Yet it wasn't just concern over the sick and wounded that led Sale to go south, rather than north to Kabul. He was worried about what in fact was ailing Elphinstone and his army in Kabul. After all, they were nearly 5,000 regular soldiers well armed, well supplied, and with a large number of guns. If they were in such terrible straits it wasn't because they didn't have enough manpower or ammunition, it was because of a loss of courage by those in command. Despite the fact that his own wife and daughter were trapped with the Kabul garrison, Sale decided he was not going to risk the last able British force in Afghanistan to save a garrison that should have been able to save itself. So he fought his way to Jalalabad instead and once there, strengthened the fortifications, cleared fields of fire in all directions, and collected a month's worth of supplies from the countryside. He and his brigade accomplished all this while constantly fighting actions against heavy numbers of local tribesmen, each of which the British won with little or no loss to themselves. Back in Kabul, Elphinstone had at least three times as many troops as Sale did and was occupying established positions the British had been holding for more than a year. It was eminently reasonable for him to wonder how bad things in Kabul could really be.

Back in Kabul, word from Sale arrived by secret courier on November 17 saying it was impossible for his brigade to fight their way back through the mountains to Kabul. Sale saw his most important duty as maintaining a strong British hold on Jalalabad until a relief force arrived from India. Meanwhile, if Elphinstone chose to abandon the cantonments and fight his way south, he would only have to march about 145km to Jalalabad in order to reach safe haven.

The day after Brigadier Shelton's debacle on the Behmaru Heights, the Afghans had offered terms to the British. They promised safe conduct if they would quit the country and leave hostages behind to be exchanged for their rightful ruler, Dost Muhammad, after he was returned to them from his position as a prisoner in British India. The details of this first offer included demands that the British surrender all their arms and abandon Shah Sujah to his fate. Macnaghten did not accept these terms but he did continue negotiations, under the insistent urging of Elphinstone, his military superior.

Macnaghten did as instructed. He treated with the insurgent leaders and the various tribal chiefs. On December 11, he rode out of the cantonments, met with a dozen of them and came away with an agreement. In exchange for allowing the British forces in Kabul to leave Afghanistan unmolested, the British garrisons at Ghazni, Kandahar, and Jalalabad would all take their lead and withdraw back to

India. When they safely reached Peshawar, right across the border, they would see that Dost Muhammad – the once and rightful ruler – was released by the British authorities there and safely returned to his throne in Kabul. Shah Sujah would be free to choose between leaving with the British or remaining behind, safely, in his native land. The moment the treaty was signed, the Afghans would provide as many fresh provisions to the British as they were willing and able to pay for. It was agreed the British would depart before three days were out.

A small amount of supplies were brought up to the cantonments, but all of them were looted by bandits and ghazis before the British could reach them. The Afghan leaders claimed they had no control over these men and refused to interfere.

The schedule for departure dragged on. In desperate straits, Macnaghten began discussions with various Afghan factions, in particular with some Durani chiefs who seemed to have no love for Dost Muhammad.

On December 22 a proposal was brought to Macnaghten from Akbar Khan, son of Dost Muhammad and a senior leader of the Afghan insurgents. In exchange for a good deal of money, Akbar and the eastern Gilzais were ready to switch sides and join with the British. Shah Sujah would remain on the throne in Kabul and the British would save face by remaining in Afghanistan for another eight months, at which time they would withdraw back to India, apparently of their own volition. In exchange Akbar asked that the British turn their backs on those tribal chiefs with whom they had earlier allied themselves. Akbar also offered up Amenoolah Khan, the last of the two ringleaders guilty of Burnes' murder (Abdoolah Khan having fallen mortally wounded at the battle of Behmaru Heights). After seven weeks of fruitlessly negotiating to play one Afghan party off against another on the one hand, and failure and inactivity from the British military leadership on the other, it was too good an offer for Macnaghten to refuse. The next morning he informed Elphinstone and asked the general to have two regiments and two guns ready to play their part in the coming plot. Elphinstone, as usual, said it would be impossible, but Macnaghten would not be deterred. He believed he knew better than the doddering old general, told him so, then rode off with an escort of several British officers to meet with Akbar and his fellow plotters.[38]

Only 300m from the cantonments, in virtual full view of the British garrison, Macnaghten was hacked to pieces.[39] The plot had been an entrapment. By signing his name, Macnaghten had sealed his own doom. His trunk was hung in the Kabul bazaar, his head and limbs paraded in triumph around the city. Incredibly enough, reports to this effect did not deter Elphinstone from continuing to pursue negotiations with the Afghans, whose leaders now placed blame for Macnaghten's unfortunate demise on fanatical ghazis whom they had unfortunately again been unable to control.

Even now there remained two ways forward for the British, neither of which need have ended in complete disaster. They could either fight their way up to the Bala Hissar and hold it until the spring, by which time relief forces from British India would surely arrive. Or abandon the camp and all its encumbering baggage and march straight down to India. With 4,500 soldiers it could have be done – had there been determined and effective leadership at their front. Unfortunately for the British, there simply was none. And so, the army of occupation again did absolutely nothing.

On New Year's Day 1842, a treaty was signed by no fewer than 18 Afghan chiefs. The British side was represented on the document by the reluctant signature of Major Eldred Pottinger.

The final form of the agreement stated that all British forces throughout the country would leave Afghanistan. They would be escorted out by "trustworthy persons … so that none shall offer molestations on the road." The sick and wounded could remain where they were and would be free to return to India on recovery. The force in the Kabul cantonments would be allowed to take with them six horse artillery guns and three mule guns. All the other guns and all the muskets and ammunition stores in the British magazine were to be given up to the Afghans. The treaty noted this would be done "as a token of friendship." But the British knew that the surrender of an army's guns was the telltale sign of a defeated force, a permanent indignity and disgrace.[40]

The most direct route from Kabul to Jalalabad was about 145km. It was the dead of the Afghan Winter. Two things would matter above all else to the safety of the Anglo-Indian force about to embark: moving quickly through the ferociously cruel environment and being well enough organized to defend themselves against the constant attacks that had to be expected.

THE RETREAT

On January 6, 1842, 4,500 soldiers and close to 12,000 camp followers – largely women and children – finally departed from the Kabul cantonments and began the final chapter of the story of the British army of occupation. On the part of the British leadership, the chapters leading up to this point were filled with near-criminal ignorance, arrogance, and incompetence; with unforced errors and missed opportunities. But this final chapter would be filled with death.

"Dreary indeed was the scene over which, with drooping spirits and dismal forebodings, we had to bend our unwilling steps. Deep snow covered every inch of mountain and plain with one unspotted sheet of dazzling white, and so intensely bitter was the cold as to penetrate and defy the defences of the warmest clothing," wrote Lieutenant Vincent Eyre. The troops had been restricted to a near-starvation diet for several days and the camp followers had even less to subsist on. But the high command was still eating rather well. If the British had managed to move off before sunrise they could have reached the Khoord-Kabul Pass and possibly fought their way through it on that first day. That choice, however, would have required a great deal of careful preparation. By this time the relationship between Elphinstone and Shelton had deteriorated to the point where Shelton was not aware the entire garrison would be marching out in the morning until he read the published order the night before. He strenuously argued for preparing the baggage and whatever transport remained while it was still dark, but his arguments fell on deaf ears. Early the next morning, he went to see Elphinstone to again argue the need for speed, but Elphinstone was enjoying a "leisurely breakfast" and Shelton "got offended for my trouble."[41] The army, if it could still be so called, did not begin to leave the

This artwork depicts the retreat of the British columns during its famous retreat from Kabul. (Author's Collection)

cantonments until the morning was half over. It consisted of 600 men of the 44th Foot; 100 men, one troop, of British Horse Artillery; 300 men from the Bengal Army cavalry; 500 men from the Afghan levy cavalry; approximately 2,500 men in three battalions of Bengal Native Infantry; approximately 800 men in one battalion of Afghan levy infantry; and approximately 200 sappers and miners; an approximate total of 4,500 men.[42] The camp followers and their families were almost three times as many – nearly 12,000. The vast majority of them were Indian Hindus and it was they who would suffer worst of all on the ensuing retreat.

The advance guard consisted of the 44th Regiment, the sappers, and miners, one squadron of Sujah's Afghan cavalry, and three mountain guns; it was led by Brigadier Thomas Anquetil, the commander of Shah Sujah's forces. This was followed by the main body, consisting of two battalions of Bengal Native Infantry and the remainder of the Afghan levy cavalry, commanded by Shelton. The 54th Bengal Native Infantry, the Afghan levy infantry battalion, the 5th Light Cavalry, and four Horse Artillery guns made up the rearguard, led by Colonel Robert Chambers, Elphinstone's senior cavalry officer.

When Shelton had led the first half of the column out of the walls, Elphinstone had a change of heart and sent orders for him to halt and return to cantonments. He passed the order to Captain Charles Mackenzie, who decided on his own that delivering it to Shelton at such a tactically inopportune moment would lead to the entire force being "ignominiously butchered by the enemy."[43] When he reached the brigadier, instead of passing on the order to about-face, he told him to keep marching.

Before the British had left their cantonments, a mixture of ghazis, tribesmen, and riotous Kabul residents descended on the camp, looting what was left and picking off British stragglers, members of the rearguard and camp followers. No retaliatory action of any kind was organized, making it clear to the Afghans that the British force was now so demoralized it was nearly incapable of taking any determined action. Emboldened with this knowledge, the Afghans stepped up their harassing attacks on the column as it wound its way toward the Khoord-Kabul pass, lining the road with bodies staining the snow with blood. Even at this early stage of the retreat, many of the camp followers realized it was pointless to go on. They simply dropped to the side of the road and waited to have their throats cut. Captain Mackenzie would later write about seeing an Indian child alone and naked in the snow, he wanted "to take up this poor little native of a foreign climate and cuddle it in his arms," but he did not. She was not the only innocent child to die at the roadside. There were far too many for him to save from the Afghan children he saw "stabbing with their knives at wounded."[44]

The confusion of the column's departure from the cantonments finally worked itself out and they marched toward Kabul in order to reach the Jalalabad road. Doing so brought it closer and closer to the Bala Hissar. Some of the British officers, Pottinger among them, hoped that at the very last moment Elphinstone would change his plan and order the army to assault the ancient fortress that loomed so close, before the Afghans might be able to organize its defense.[45] But the column reached the crossroads and turned left, heading south toward Jalalabad. The Bala Hissar faded into the winter sky behind them, while a great fire blazed where the cantonments had stood. The force halted for their first night on the road and watched in the distance as the place where they had been trapped for the past six weeks went up in flames.

If it were not so tragic it would funny to note that on that first day, virtually every single piece of baggage and all stocks of ammunition, the preservation of which had been one of the main objects of Elphinstone's policy of command, had been lost in the general chaos of the departure from the cantonments. Lady Sale would later note that the entire force had with it "no tents, save two or three small palls. All scraped away the snow as best they could, to make a place to lie down on. The evening and night were intensely cold. No food for man or beast procurable."[46] When they settled in for this first terrible night the column had advanced only 10km. They had more than 129km to go.

At 0200hrs the rearguard reached the bivouac. They had fought most of the way, passing through what Captain George Lawrence described as "a continuous lane of poor wretches, men, women and children, dead or dying from the cold and wounds, who, unable to move, entreated their comrades to kill them and put an end to their misery." So ended the first day of the retreat from Kabul.[47]

When the sun rose on January 7, it shone on many bodies, dead from exposure over the course of that first night. The advance guard and rearguard were detailed to exchange places in the order of march and the new advance guard set off at 0730hrs. They soon caught up with large numbers of camp followers and Bengal Army sepoys, who had set off earlier on their own. By now most of the Afghan levy infantry and cavalry had deserted and returned to Kabul, preferring captivity to almost certain death.

As the column advanced on the Jalalabad road, "the very air we breathed froze in its passage out of the mouth and nostrils, forming a coating of small icicles on our moustaches and beards."[48] Chunks of snow were so thickly frozen to horses hooves that they had to be carved out with hammer and chisel. On the road the snow was a foot deep, off the road several feet.

Afghan horsemen were soon spotted on both sides of the road, moving alongside the column. There was hope at first that these were the "trustworthy persons" assigned by the chiefs to ensure the safety of the British forces. Needless to say, this was not the case. The Afghan irregular cavalry charged the rearguard, which broke and fled, leaving behind their three 3pdr mountain guns. Brigadier Anquetil courageously rallied some men, counter-charged, and recaptured the guns. But as Lady Sale later recorded, most of the rearguard, made up of the 44th Foot, "precipitately made themselves scarce," requiring all three of the guns to be spiked in order to keep them from falling into enemy hands.[49]

At this point, even the British high command could not help but see that in all likelihood the Afghan promises of safe conduct to the Indian border were not worth the paper they were written on. The Afghan chiefs sent word advising the British to halt so that they could send up food and firewood and disperse the brigands who had attacked earlier. In exchange for this they now demanded six hostages, to be held until the Afghans received confirmation that Sale had abandoned Jalalabad. At this point, the column had covered six more kilometers, with two-fifths of their rations having been consumed. Elphinstone ordered his troops to halt and remain in place. During the second night, soldiers began burning their hats and personal equipment in a desperate effort to keep from freezing. Eyre called the night of January 7 "a night of starvation, cold, exhaustion, death."[50]

The next day, January 8, brought the British to the near end of the Khoord–Kabul Pass. Again, the Afghans demanded hostages. This time Pottinger, Lawrence, and Mackenzie agreed to be taken. The rest of the column pressed on, crossing and re-crossing the icy stream that wound through the pass no fewer than 28 times. This, combined with sniping and sudden attacks by Gilzai tribesmen, left no fewer than 500 soldiers and 2,500 camp followers dead before the remnants of the army emerged from the far side of the pass and settled down for the night in the highest and coldest location yet. Snow started to fall and continued throughout the night. Lieutenant Eyre recorded that, "an immense number of poor wounded wretches wandered about the camp destitute of shelter, and perished during the night. Groans of misery and distress assailed the ears from all quarters."

On the morning of January 9, the column set off once again, but Elphinstone ordered a halt after advancing less than 1.5km. In addition to hunger and exposure, much of the force was now suffering the debilitating effects of snow-blindness.[51] The halt was called to parlay with Akbar Khan. Akbar said he wanted to ensure the protection of the refugees and make arrangements for their resupply. Shelton went to Elphinstone and pleaded with him to dismiss the Afghan overture as the lie it obviously was and keep marching toward Jalalabad as fast as possible. But Elphinstone would not listen. The column would remain in place until provisions arrived and Akbar Khan managed to rein in his less diplomatically minded fellow chiefs. So the rest of the day was wasted in place. By now the roster had been reduced to 200 men of the 44th, approximately 85 troopers of the 5th Light Cavalry, 85 troopers of Indian cavalry, and approximately 120 sepoys in each of the four battalions of Bengal Native Infantry – a total of roughly 850 men in some semblance of uniform.[52]

This sketch portrays two Afghan warriors awaiting battle in the Khyber Pass in 1841. (Anne S.K. Brown Military Collection, Brown University Library)

Now Akbar made a new proposal to the three hostages he had taken the day before. He told Pottinger, Lawrence, and Mackenzie that he would take protective custody of all the British wives and children and bring them down to India safely, one day behind the rest of the column. The message was relayed to Elphinstone. Most officers believed it to be the best chance the women and children had to survive. Elphinstone agreed to hand the families over, but either via misunderstanding (or perhaps in some final effort to save more of the lives for which he was responsible) he took Akbar's offer of protection for "all the widowed ladies and married families" to include the husbands. So, together with the women and children, a number of British officers departed the lines for a nearby fort that Akbar had turned into his command post. Needless to say, no one – either Afghan or British – ever gave a moment over to debating or negotiating the fate of the wives and children of the Indian Army soldiers of the column.

On January 10, the advance guard, now comprised of the 44th Foot, 50 troopers of the 5th Light Cavalry, and the very last Horse Artillery gun, valiantly fought their way through the single-file wide gorge at Tunghee Taraeekee. But when the main body of the column reached the narrowest section of the gorge, they were massacred. The Afghans had occupied the heights on both sides and poured volley after volley down into the packed mass of desperate refugees, then realizing the troops below were too exhausted to fight back, chose to save their ammunition and descended with sword in hand. As Lady Sale later reported, when they were done, "there was not a single Sepoy left of the whole Kabul force."[53]

The advance guard continued on through the snow for several miles, then halted to let the main body catch up. But there was no main body left, only a handful of stragglers. All the baggage was gone, as were nine-tenths of the 4,500 soldiers Elphinstone had led out of the Kabul cantonments. He now commanded 250 men of the 44th Foot; 150 cavalrymen; and 50 horse artillerymen – a total of 450. The Indian camp followers had been dropping like flies, but the Afghans hadn't been able to kill them all yet. Of the more than 10,000 who had set off with the column four days earlier, 3,000 remained, clogging and blocking the movements of Elphinstone's last 450 men.

The column struggled on, under the watchful eye of Akbar and his cavalrymen. Akbar sent another offer to Elphinstone: if the remaining several hundred British troops would lay down their arms and surrender, Akbar himself would deliver them safely to Jalalabad. As for the 3,000 or more Indian camp followers who remained, he could do nothing. Elphinstone refused the offer and the column continued its march south. They left the snow behind as they descended from the high ground, but found at the foot of the hill something even worse. A mass of camp followers had rushed ahead through a narrow defile and run into an Afghan ambush. The defile was choked with corpses of men, women, and children, none of whom could have put up any sort of fight. As the British picked their way through the sea of bodies, the ambushers appeared again, determined to wipe them out as well. Shelton, with the men of his own 44th Foot, held annihilation at bay – for the moment – by leading a desperate rearguard action. Elphinstone, Shelton, and what remained of their command marched on through the night, heading for the next challenging terrain feature: the pass at Jugdulluck, which was 3km long and extremely narrow, with very steep hills on both sides. By marching through the night they hoped to get through the pass early the next day, before the Afghans had a chance to line the hillsides on both flanks with sharpshooters.

In the early morning of January 11, the advance guard – 16km short of reaching the little village of Jugdulluck – paused to allow what little remained of the rearguard to catch up before attempting to fight their way through the pass. Between this delay and an earlier one caused by the remaining thousands of camp followers refusing to clear the road and allow the troops through unhindered, too much time had been wasted. By the time the British were ready to advance on the pass, the heights on both sides were covered with Afghans. It took until the middle of the day for the entire British force to reach the small village of Jugdulluck, where they took cover behind some broken stone walls. The Afghans kept up a steady and accurate fire, keeping the British, who were desperate for food and fresh water, pinned down all through the night. At one point a party of Afghans advanced close to the village walls, inciting Captain Bulstrode Bygrave to lead a band of the 44th Foot in a bayonet charge. The Afghans turned and ran – not off the field but back to the high ground, from which they resumed their deadly sniper fire.

As the night wore on, one more entreaty for parlay from Akbar was delivered to the village. The Afghan chieftain invited the two senior British commanders, Elphinstone and Shelton, along with the former paymaster of Shah Sujah's army, Captain Johnson, to a conference. Out of desperation or for whatever other reason they agreed and rode off to the conference in the dead of night. Eyre would later write that the remaining British officers and men watched their commanders depart, "with a feeling of despair, having seen enough of Afghan treachery to convince them that these repeated negotiations were mere hollow artifices, designed to engender confidence in their victims, preparatory to a fresh sacrifice of blood."[54]

On the morning of January 12, several local Gilzai chiefs arrived at Akbar's camp to settle the fate of the high-ranking "guests" and the remaining British troops holed up in the village below. Captain Johnson, who understood their language, listened as a debate raged between the chiefs and Dost Muhammad's son. The Dost's son

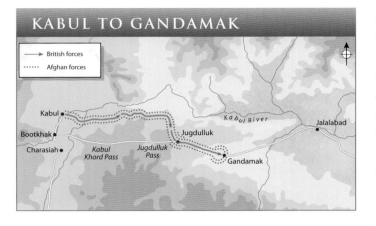

KABUL TO GANDAMAK

→ British forces
······ Afghan forces

Kabul
Bootkhak
Charasiah
Kabul Khord Pass
Jugdulluk Khord Pass
Jugdulluk
Kabul River
Jalalabad
Gandamak

offered the chiefs 60,000 rupees in return for allowing what was left of the British force to escape back to India. He was concerned that if the Afghans wiped out the entire British Army his father in India would never be seen again. But the chiefs were less concerned and argued "Let us, now that we have the opportunity, take advantage of it and kill these infidel dogs."[55] The debate raged on. Elphinstone – who had come to Akbar's camp as an invited guest to parlay, not a volunteer hostage – grew impatient and demanded to be allowed to return to his men. The old general was adamant not to be seen to have deserted his men at their final hour. But then it was reported that the Gilzais had finally agreed to accept Akbar's gold in exchange for allowing what remained of the army to slip through the Jugdulluck Pass and back to India. Whether or not this was true will never be known. For the moment after the news was communicated to Elphinstone, the sound of renewed gunfire resounded from the British lines at Jugdulluck…

Down in the village, the British had been left without their commander or his deputy for an entire day. Before leaving, Elphinstone had passed command on to Anquetil, who had struggled over how to proceed as first the night of the 11th and then the day of the 12th had dragged on. The final deciding factor was when Captain Skinner – the chief liaison officer who had ridden back and forth between Afghan and British camps to facilitate the negotiations – was shot in the face. After that Brigadier Anquetil decided the time had come to act. By this time the British forces had been reduced to 150 men of the 44th Foot, 25 cavalrymen, and 16 dismounted Horse Artillerymen – a total of 191. Huddling for protection as close as they could get to the remaining soldiers were a "teeming rabble" of camp followers.

Anquetil led his men through the entrance of the Jugdulluck gorge, but when they reached the narrow summit of the pass, they discovered "two barriers had been thrown across the road, constructed of bushes and branches of trees." The road itself was a mass of ice surrounded by very deep snow. Here, in this grim defile, the penultimate chapter of the story played out. Under Anquetil's leadership the men fought desperately to clear the spiky branches off the road with their bare hands, while the Afghans on all sides poured deadly fire into their midst and then rushed in among them with sword and knife. Anquetil was killed, along with a number of other British officers. Finally the infantry did manage to tear a gap in the barricades

– but then they were ridden over by officers and men of their own side, desperate to escape the fatal confines of the narrow pass. In blind rage the infantrymen who were being ridden over fought back by firing at their own side. Six days earlier Elphinstone and Shelton had led 4,500 men out of Kabul. When the last British survivors cleared that terrible place, their ranks consisted of 20 British officers and 45 British soldiers, a total of 65 all ranks.

Having fought through Jugdulluck, the country became more open and clear, much easier to travel through. The Afghans were too busy plundering the hundreds of dead to pay close attention to a few scattered bands of men as they pushed desperately on toward Jalalabad. They reached the Sourkab river, found the bridge in enemy hands and fought their way across, dragging their wounded comrades with them.[56]

LAST STAND AT GANDAMAK

At dawn on January 13, 1842, the remaining British followed the road toward the village of Gandamak. Constant jezail fire, however, drove them off the road and the senior surviving British officer, Major Charles Griffiths of the 37th Bengal Native Infantry, led the pitifully small command to a stronger defensive position atop a small, dome-shaped hill. Three hundred or so Indian camp followers followed in the soldiers' wake, hoping against hope to survive the last 48km to Jalalabad.[57]

The tribesmen ceased firing and a party of Afghan horsemen approached and was waved on by Major Griffiths. They invited him to a parlay. As he was escorted by a handful of the horsemen to meet with their chieftain, the remaining Afghans approached the British lines under cover of friendly conversation. The next thing the British knew, the Afghans were trying to wrest their muskets from their hands and swords out of their scabbards. The remaining British rose to the challenge and drove the tribesmen away. The tribesmen then opened up with their jezails. The remaining British returned what fire they could. Several times the tribesmen rushed the hill and several times they were beaten back by point-blank musket fire and bayonet. But the British ran out of ammunition long before the Afghans ran out of tribesmen. The Afghans made a final rush for the hill and after one last desperate melee, slaughtered every man on it, except for Captain Thomas Souter of the 44th Foot and seven or eight British enlisted men. Captain Souter would later explain how he believed his life had been spared because of his attempt to save the tattered remains of the Regimental Colors of the 44th, which he had tied around his waist, beneath his sheepskin overcoat. During the last desperate round of hand-to-hand fighting, the coat had come undone and the colorful flag made visible to his enemies, whom he believed chose to take him prisoner rather than kill him in expectation of the large ransom.[58]

Major H. Bycalle, officer of the 14th Bengal Native Infantry. This portrait was painted around 1840. (Anne S.K. Brown Military Collection, Brown University Library)

Earlier, when the British had made it through the pass at Jugdulluck, about a dozen men had ridden ahead on horseback, in advance of the main body. At one point or another between Jugdulluck and Jalalabad, each of them was overtaken and slaughtered by Afghans – except for one…

In British-occupied Jalalabad, on January 13:

One of us espied a single horseman riding towards our walls. As he got nearer, it was distinctly seen that he wore European clothes and was mounted on a travel-hacked yaboo, which he was urging on with all the speed of which it yet remained master. A signal was made to him by someone of the walls, which he answered by waving a private soldier's forage cap over his head. The Kabul gate was then thrown open and several officers, rushing out, received and recognized in the traveler the first, and it is to be feared the last, fugitive of the ill-fated force at Kabul in Dr. Brydon.[59]

So recorded Major Henry Havelock. After listening to Brydon's story, Brigadier Sale ordered that for the next three nights a huge signal fire be lit atop the Kabul gate accompanied every half-hour by the call of four buglers sounding the advance. Although no more survivors appeared for several days, a handful of Bengal Army sepoys and camp followers did manage to reach Jalalabad before the fires were doused and the bugles silenced. But Doctor William Brydon, an assistant surgeon serving in the employ of the Bombay Presidency of the British East India Company, was the sole European to make it out alive.

THE AFTERMATH

Elphinstone died in captivity, while Major Eldred Pottinger, Lady Sale, Captain Griffiths, and the rest of the British officers, their wives, and children taken hostage during the retreat were freed by the victorious British "Army of Retribution," which was dispatched to balance the scales of international justice and British public opinion. Shah Sujah remained holed up in the Bala Hissar, until he was convinced to emerge and lead his countrymen against the advancing British. At the end of March 1842, he was carried out in a chair of state to review

This gives a good idea of the type of terrain on which some of the fighting at Gandamak took place. (Anne S.K. Brown Military Collection, Brown University Library)

the assembled troops – and shot in the head by his godson. His body was tossed into a ditch.[60] Brigadier Shelton survived his captivity alongside the other British prisoners, returned to England and laid all the blame for the disaster at the feet of the dead Elphinstone. He was acquitted by a court martial on three out of four counts and given no punishment.[61]

If Shah Sujah had lived to lead an Afghan army against the British in 1842, he would have had no chance of victory. The "Army of Retribution," under better generals than Elphinstone and better brigadiers than Shelton, defeated each and every Afghan force that stood in its way. But no matter how many victories British arms won in the spring and summer of 1842, they could not erase the memory of what British hubris and incompetence had lost in the fall and winter of 1841. The annihilation of the British army of occupation in Afghanistan on the road from Kabul to Gandamak was an extremely important story in its time. The forces of the British Empire in the East had been decisively defeated by native armies, made to quit what should have been an impregnable position. In revenge, the British would destroy the legendary Kabul bazaar and paint the entire city red with the blood of Kabulis, but this would not change the fact that they had been beaten and everyone knew it. The lessons the British learned from that defeat were less important than those the officers and men of their Indian Army learned:

that their heretofore invincible colonial masters could be defeated. They would put that lesson to use 17 years later in the Great Mutiny. Dost Muhammed was released by the British and restored to his Kabul throne in 1843 and remained there until his death in 1863. Ironically enough, the man whose conversation with a Russian officer set in motion events which led to the annihilation of the British forces, proved himself to be the most loyal and steadfast ally in the history of the Raj, most notably standing by the British during the Great Mutiny of 1857 itself.

CAMERONE, 1863

BACKGROUND

Benito Pablo Juárez García (1806–72) was reelected as President of Mexico in 1861, shortly after the opening shots were fired in the American Civil War (1861–65). The election of the much-beloved Juárez signaled an end to conservative rule in Mexico. Although the conservatives lost the Presidency, certain lobbying groups were able to exploit France's desire for a return to its status as a great Empire, which it had lost several decades earlier. They found a sympathetic and self-glorifying audience with French Emperor Napoleon III (r.1852–70) and Empress Eugénie, who were both easily persuaded to aid the conservative movement in Mexico and together create a Catholic Latin Empire south of the border of the United States. This new Empire was to be governed by Austria's Archduke Maximilian and as such would be allied to France, opening new and favorable trade routes, returning power to the conservatives, while also reinvigorating the glory and power of France.

Benito Juárez had taken the bold step of voiding all foreign debt and confiscating the Church's Mexican holdings, aiming to reduce poverty, bolster the economy, and demonstrate Mexico's rise from a country destroyed by a vicious civil war to a sovereign state. By the end of 1861, and in direct response to the moratorium on repayment of foreign debt, France, Great Britain, and Spain dispatched troops to the troubled country of Mexico. In April 1862 France was the only power that had troops left in Mexico, as once Britain and Spain realized the French ambition to conquer Mexico they withdrew.

In a grand failure of military intelligence, the French had neglected to realize that the Vera Cruz area, their debarkation point, was one of the most liberal regions and loyal to Benito Juárez.[1] France, with a force of 6,000 soldiers, marched toward Mexico City, but first needed to reduce the city of Puebla, which stood in its way. Mexico celebrated a great victory over the French at Puebla under their General Ignacio

Zaragoza on May 5, 1862, and the triumph is celebrated to this day as *Cinco de Mayo*. Yet the Mexicans were unable to drive the invaders and conservative allies out. France, unwilling to yield, reinforced the troops in Mexico and subsequently marched toward the interior with a much larger army from Vera Cruz to yet again lay siege at Puebla.

It was imperative that the French maintain the supply artery that ran some 177km from Vera Cruz to the French lines around Puebla.[2] Guerrillas roamed the Mexican countryside, ambushing convoys and harassing troops and were creating serious havoc along the main line of communication. A nasty counter-guerrilla operation was conducted by the French as a direct response. The humid and tropical conditions of the province caused the French much distress as well.

It is against this backdrop that perhaps the most memorable battle ever fought, or at least recalled, by the French Foreign Legion happened near a small town called Camerone (Camarón) along the convoy road between Vera Cruz and Puebla. The battle of Camerone created a myth for the Foreign Legion far beyond its tangible real-world impact. It was fought on April 30, 1863 between the 3rd Company, 1st Battalion, of the Foreign Legion and elements of the Mexican Republican National Guard under the command of Colonel Francesco de Paula Milan, plus local militias and guerrillas loyal to Benito Juárez. The Foreign Legion company was led in the action by Captain Jean Danjou (many other officers had been struck down sick by yellow fever), and Second Lieutenants Clément Maudet and Jean Vilain, who also volunteered. Under command were 62 legionnaires, along with two supply-carrying mules under the care of Mexican Jose Dominquez.

Benito Pablo Juárez García (1806–1872), arguably one of Mexico's most beloved presidents. (Library of Congress)

THE FRENCH FOREIGN LEGION

The Foreign Legion was made up of foreign volunteers, many of whom were seen as troublemakers. As such, the Legion was not given the best postings, instead they were used throughout the French empire. The invasion of Mexico was thought to be a glorious adventure and so did not involve the Legion. The Legion stood to suffer from future manpower cutbacks, so some Foreign Legion officers believed a good showing in Mexico would polish their tarnished mercenary image and permit their continued existence as a fighting force, and so undertook to petition Emperor Napoleon III. At long last the Emperor permitted the much-maligned battalions of legionnaires to reinforce the French Army in Mexico.

By March 28, 1863, two battalions of the Legion had disembarked at Vera Cruz and were almost immediately tasked with safeguarding the resupply route to Puebla. Guarding the convoy route was considered beneath the regular French Army and thus it was immediately handed over to the legionnaires and the notorious *contre-guerrillas* serving their French paymasters. Nevertheless, the Legion took its task seriously and spread its disease-ridden companies throughout strategic locations along the convoy route from Vera Cruz to Cordoba en route to Puebla. "The Battalion's position and logistical requirements called for a Company to be based as Headquarters at Chiquihuite, one at Paso del Macho, another to guard the bridge over the River Gallego, a third on post at Atoyac, and two to be available for convoy protection."[3]

The French Army under the command of General de Lorencez did not charge the twin forts safeguarding Puebla, as the French had previously done on *Cinco de Mayo* of the previous year. Instead, the French were besieging the well-defended and well-supplied Mexican city. As was typical for all sieges, vast amounts of supplies were required by the besiegers and to that end in April 1863 a convoy was dispatched to carry war *matériel*, including ordnance for the siege artillery, as well as 3 million francs in gold, to Puebla. "It was of a size, scope and content such as had never been seen before ... it comprised two to three hundred heavy wagons, each pulled by 12 mules, supply wagons, ammunition wagons, five or six hundred mules carrying all sorts of provisions ... extending some five kilometers."[4] As the convoy route fell under the Foreign Legion's

Maximilian I (1832–1867), was proclaimed Emperor of Mexico in 1864, though many foreign governments did not recognize his sovereignty, which allowed Juaréz to garner support and reclaim power. (Library of Congress)

François Achille Bazaine (1811–1888), Commander of the French forces in Mexico. (Author's Collection)

operational control, the Legion was tasked with protecting the convoy and ensuring its safe arrival to the regular French forces. In particular, the task fell to the understrength companies of the 1st Battalion of the Foreign Regiment. The 3rd Company under Danjou was dispatched from Legion headquarters at Chiquihuite to reinforce them en route, once intelligence had indicated that the *Juaristas* were aware of the convoy and had made plans to ambush it somewhere along the convoy route over the next two weeks (that was the expected travel time required by the giant resupply convoy traveling west).

Late on April 29, 1863, the 3rd Company of the 1st Battalion of the Foreign Legion mustered its contingent of able legionnaires; Sergeant Major Tonel, four sergeants, six corporals, a drummer, and 48 fusiliers (infantry), one unknown legionnaire called Holler, and Captain Danjou's orderly who belonged to the 5th Company. Additionally, two mules under the aforementioned Mexican muleteer Jose Dominguez completed the force destined for Legion lore.[5]

THE BATTLE

Danjou's men departed the Legion headquarters at 0100hrs and reached the French post at Paso del Macho, where Danjou refused additional troops, rather asking for them as a quick-reaction force should they encounter the enemy. In the early morning hours, they marched past a local Indian village just shy of the Hacienda de la Trinidad and within another 30 minutes, traveling in two columns on each side of the road, they reached Palo Verde. Here the company took a well-deserved rest and began to brew coffee, only to be alerted to the presence of an enemy advance cavalry scout in the distance. Raising the alarm, and without even replenishing their water, the legionnaires formed up. The cavalry scouts disappeared as the 3rd Company hacked its way through the woods and the column emerged some 300m east of Camarone, one of the legionnaires was struck by a shot from the Hacienda de la Trinidad.[6] A quick search of the local village revealed nothing and the company, in two sections on either side of the road with a small rearguard with Danjou and the mules in the middle, moved forward again on the road leading back to Chiquihuite. The heat of the day started to dissipate what cool air may have been present during the early hours of the morning.

On a hillside to the north and overlooking the road stood the lancers of the Orizaba Squadron, 250 Mexican cavalry drawn from Cotaxtla and Cueva-Pentada of the Vera Cruz region.[7] Captain Danjou formed his company into a square, but during the movement the two mules became a danger to the men. They were so agitated that they bucked and kicked their way out of the square, taking vital supplies with them. The legionnaires repelled the first Mexican charge by volley and subsequent individual firing. Danjou, seizing the moment, advanced over a cactus-filled ditch just below and to the south of the road, hoping that it presented enough of an obstacle to the Mexican lancers, thus allowing the foreign legionnaires to make it to a nearby wood some 500m away.[8]

An example of a Mexican Irregular Cavalryman. The Mexicans were excellent horsemen. (Anne S.K. Brown Military Collection, Brown University Library)

Once in the woods and free from the danger of further mounted attacks, Danjou had hoped for a safe return to Paso del Macho. Instead, they had to form another square to repel another attack, which they executed successfully. Yet during the movement to contact the 3rd Company had become split, with the larger part under Captain Danjou to the front, while slightly to the rear, with the previously wounded legionnaire and a now wounded Mexican muleteer, a group of 16 fusiliers.

The Orizaba Squadron had taken casualties, but had not lost their fighting spirit. Some of them charged the smaller group, while others rode around the cactus-filled ditch to rejoin their comrades. The rest of the 3rd Company fixed bayonets on Danjou's order and advanced quickly toward the Hacienda de la Trinidad, seeking the protection of its walls against further cavalry charges. Three officers and the remaining 46 legionnaires with bayonets leveled charged toward the enemy shouting "Vive l'Empereur," dispersing the lancers. The second group of 16 legionnaires including Dominquez was attacked and was forced to surrender. No officers or NCOs were with this section of the 3rd Company.

Inside the Hacienda de la Trinidad the legionnaires immediately prepared the defense by using anything they could find to barricade the two main gateways, which no longer had any wooden doors attached. The legionnaires were positioned along the interior walls by their experienced commander. The Mexicans, however, had managed to enter the hacienda through an outside door leading to the interior house. They too immediately positioned men on the second floor and several rooms below, although only one of those rooms had access to the courtyard and that room was occupied by the French.[9] The Mexicans now fired from the top floor into the courtyard. Exposing themselves, of course, led to some well-aimed shots by the legionnaires in return.

The hacienda was situated on the southern side alongside the convoy road. "It was a large square enclosure, measuring about 50 meters along each wall," recalls Corporal Phillipe Maine of the 3rd Company, 1st Battalion.[10] The northern wall was occupied by legionnaires, who only had access to the bottom floor, where Captain Danjou fought. This had access to the courtyard. The Mexican dismounted cavalry troopers occupied and fired from the second story into the courtyard. The other rooms of the hacienda on the ground floor were also occupied by the horsemen, but these did not grant them such targets of opportunity. On the western side of the Hacienda de la Trinidad stood two main gates, which had now been temporarily been blocked with large planks and other debris scattered throughout the buildings. Each barricade was manned by squads of about eight legionnaires each, under Second Lieutenant Vilain. The southern end housed a dilapidated stable with another squad officered by Maudet and on the southeastern corner there was a breach in the wall structure "large enough for a man to pass through on a horse."[11] The western wall housed several sheds with another squad.[12] One sergeant acted as a lookout on top of the roof. Legion corporal Maine recalled how "Danjou inspected everywhere where it appeared that danger was likely to be most pressing. These dispositions made, we waited patiently for the attack. It was about half past nine o'clock."[13]

At this point of the battle, the 3rd Company of the Foreign Legion had fought off two cavalry charges, lost a quarter of its strength, and lost all of its supplies after the two mules who carried them had raced off in terror. So far they had been battling lancers who with their carbines, lances, and bayonets could not effectively get involved in house-to-house or more precisely room-to-room close-quarters battle.

Furthermore, the Juaristas lacked the artillery necessary to punch holes into the walls. Sporadic gunfire rippled across the hacienda. And as if the bullets and sabers and lances of the Mexicans were not enough, the sun was starting to take its toll on the men, especially the men who had no water left in their canteens. It is around this time that Captain Danjou shared his bottle of wine with the men, who so far had acquitted themselves well. Perhaps a relief column would appear, as surely someone must have heard the gunfire. Danjou, who had lost his left hand in Algeria when his gun exploded, moved from legionnaire to legionnaire with his loyal orderly. Maine recollected that Danjou gave "each one of us a few drops, which we drank from our cupped hands."[14]

The respite was short-lived as Colonel Milan with his 400 cavalry composed of Mexican Republican regulars as well as guerrillas, arrived in advance of his slower-moving infantry of the Central Brigade composed of National Guard battalions and companies from Jalap, Cordoba, Zamora, and Vera Cruz, as well as a the Independence battalion.[15] Milan's infantry numbered more than 1,000. An offer to surrender was refused by Captain Danjou, who must have realized that these troops were intending to ambush the supply convoy. Clearly a surrender was out of the question at this point. His lookout must have informed him of the number and troop types assembled around the hacienda, and there was not a single French artillery piece present.

Bullets started to fly across the hacienda as Mexicans and Foreign Legion men tried to cut loopholes or break down walls to get at one another. Dark and acrid smoke created by gunpowder parched the lips of the dehydrated men, now fighting for their lives. Their shooting skills exacted casualties given their limited amount of cartridges – by now far fewer than the 60 each legionnaire carried as standard. Danjou demonstrated his leadership as he went from post to post exhorting his men. Back at his command post in the northwest section of the hacienda, Danjou raised his hand and "'swore to fight to the death' – *jusqu'a la mort* – and had his men give their word too."[16] Returning to the squads manning the main gates, Danjou made other legionnaires swear the same oath. At 1100hrs Danjou, the interim commander of the 3rd Company, was struck by a bullet which hit him in the "middle of his back and came out below the left nipple… For the next five minutes his wild looking eyes rolled in their sockets. He gave two or three convulsions … and suffered for an hour and then expired in the arms of Mr. Vilain and Mr. Maudet."[17]

Second Lieutenant Vilain took command. Shortly thereafter the Mexicans had punched a hole through the room-dividing walls. The Mexicans were now exchanging point-blank fire with the French, killing and wounding the majority of the legionnaires, who nevertheless managed to move five men to other sections of the

This rider represents the units that were founded to combat the swift-moving Mexican guerrillas, dubbed Contra Guerrillas, who waged a ruthless campaign. (Anne S.K. Brown Military Collection, Brown University Library)

hacienda. Sergeant Major Tonel was killed and the Mexicans took control of the hacienda building.

By midday the French thought they heard the sound of a bugle, which lifted their spirits. The steady drum beat that soon followed conveyed with it devastating news. The Mexican infantry had arrived – 1,000 men and along with them came more guerrillas as well. Milan's command had swelled to between 1,700 and 2,000. Legionnaire Morzicki returned to his previous observation post on top of the roof and vividly described the arrival of the Mexican Army. "We looked at each other without saying a word," recalls Corporal Maine years later. "In that moment we understood that all of us were lost and that we would be here until we were all dead."[18]

Once again, Colonel Milan offered surrender to the trapped 3rd Company of the Foreign Legion, and once more they refused in a most undiplomatic manner – it has been assumed Legionnaire Morzicki muttered *merde!* (shit!) as a response.[19] Commander Vilan reminded his men one more time of the oath they had taken. The fighting was intense. Desperate charges came in waves, to be met by equally desperate defending. One charge was repulsed, only to have the brave Mexican soldiers consolidate and charge again. Other Mexican soldiers worked feverishly in the heat to open more breaches along the walls to allow their comrades to flood the inner courtyard. According to various sources, Vilan was killed at 1430hrs when a "bullet fired from the building hit him square in the forehead."[20] The death hit the legionnaires hard, as they lost another well-liked commander. Corporal Maine described that Vilan "fell as if struck by lightning. In that moment, it is fair to say, a feeling of terrible sadness came over us, penetrating to the foundation of the soul."[21]

Lieutenant Maudet immediately redeployed what was left of the company to the shed in the southwestern corner of the hacienda. The "partly demolished shed was nothing more than a low wall of bricks, on which rested various pieces of wood, intended to support a thatched roof."[22] The company had taken many casualties and most of the survivors had some type of wound or injury. Although the legionnaires had fought well throughout the day, there can be very little doubt that they realized the hopelessness of their situation. The sheer reality of the brutal fight is best described by Corporal Maine:

The heat was overpowering. The sun, at its zenith, fell directly on our heads, a pitiless sun, devouring us as it can in the tropics. Under its direct rays the walls of the courtyard were a brilliant white, which hurt our eyes. When we opened our mouths to breathe, it was as if we were swallowing fire. The air was heavy as lead, and with the shimmering I had seen on plains and deserts at midday in the Summer. The dust kicked up by the spent bullets hitting the ground in the courtyard rose slowly in heavy spirals. At the same time, overheating because of the sun's rays and the rapidity of our shooting, the barrels of our rifles burned our hands like red hot iron. So intense was the heat that the redoubt was transformed into a furnace. We could see the decomposing bodies of the dead. In the space of an hour, the flesh began to smell and took on a strange palour.[23]

Maine went on to point out it was hardly any better for the Mexican soldiers, who so valiantly had thrown themselves into the withering and deadly accurate fire of the French Foreign Legion's rifles.

Jumbled up among the dead, because there was no means of helping them, our wounded lay where [they] fell. We could hear the Mexican wounded on the other side of the wall moaning and crying out in their anguish. They invoked the Virgin or cursed God and the Saints. Our men, by a supreme effort, despite their suffering, remained silent. They were fearful, the poor fellows, of revealing our losses and giving encouragement to the enemy.[24]

Guerrilla fighting during the Mexican campaign often involved swift-moving horsemen raiding towns, villages and convoys.
(Anne S.K. Brown Military Collection, Brown University Library)

219

The suffering and needless deaths of many more men was yet to come. Surrender was not an option anymore. Oaths had been given, people killed and wounded, many would lose their limbs given the primitive medical conditions of the time. The extreme physical duress is often forgotten when heroic deeds are ascribed to an action, but 3rd Company's Corporal Maine remembers it clearly:

> The thirst dried the throat and we knew again the horrors of our situation. A white froth formed in the corners of our mouths and coagulated there. Our lips were dry like leather, our tongues swelled up and every breath was painful. Our chests heaved, our temples pounded as if to burst and our poor heads were spinning. Suffering to this degree was intolerable. Only those who have lived in such a deadly climate, and who know from experience the value of a drop of water, will understand. I saw wounded men dragging themselves on their stomachs, heads thrust forward, and to appease the fever which consumed them, lick the pools of congealing blood which covered the ground. I saw others, mad with pain from their wounds, greedily drink the blood which flowed from their own bodies. Even though it was repugnant, disgusting, the thirst was so acute that we drank our own urine.[25]

The firefight continued. Legionnaires were emptying the pockets of their fallen comrades in a search for more cartridges. The Mexicans kept coming despite their casualties, but certainly their commander did not demand that all his men had to fight to the death. Instead, he decided to burn or smoke the entrenched legionnaires out. To that end the Mexican soldiers burned straw and wood and anything else they could find on the northeast corner, the flames assisted by the north-to-south wind that was blowing. One legionnaire described the smoke as a veil coming down on the men.[26] Maine paints a hellish picture: "We were literally blinded and the acrid smoke from the burning straw caught in our throats, making far worse the already terrible thirst which gnawed at our guts. Finally, after about an hour and a half, the fire burned itself out. This incident could have been deadly, as, using the swirling smoke to mask their movements, the Mexicans had been able to come quite close. We fired more accurately."[27]

By 1700hrs the battle slackened and the legionnaires could hear Milan and his officers haranguing their troops. For the third and final time, Colonel Milan asked for a surrender. The legionnaires did not even bother to reply, according to Maine's account.[28] The Mexican drums and bugles sounded for the last attack as the Mexican forces piled into the courtyard to finish off the last 12 legionnaires. The Mexicans overwhelmed several legionnaires who were defending the gates and after a hot exchange, with his men running low on ammunition, Lieutenant Maudet ordered his remaining five men to load, fire, and charge with their bayonets. Legion lore was born at that very moment. As the last of the men charged forth from the shed they were met by a volley that cut down several of the remnants of the 3rd Company. A wall of bayonets and lances and sabers then ended the battle, only two survived.

At long last the Mexicans had triumphed but at what cost? The battle lasted 11 hours, and the 3rd Company lost in total three officers (Maudet was to die of his wounds despite excellent care), 28 dead men and 14 wounded, out of an understrength company of 65.[29] The remaining 15 were captured. The Mexican casualties are less clear, but seem to have been approximately 300 dead and wounded.

THE AFTERMATH

A column of legionnaires arrived at Camerone the next day to discover one young legionnaire drummer near death, who had survived with severe injuries and had managed to escape a mass grave site undetected. He was soon revived with refreshments and mounted on a mule as the column made its way to the hacienda, where they witnessed the destruction for themselves. The column rushed back to safeguard the convoy and to report the destruction of 3rd Company. A few days later, they returned to conduct a proper burial for the legionnaires and separately buried the Mexicans in open trenches. One legionnaire present at the aftermath of the battle of Camerone would never forget:

> the sight which met my view filled me with horror. Owing to the great heat, decomposition had set in, and their bodies were swollen to an enormous size. Already those horrid birds, the *zopilotes*, [had] commenced to prey on their naked bodies. The recollection of his [Sergeant Major Tonel's] bloated, distorted features, clenched hands, vividly distended eyes, with the flesh torn from the bones by the *zopilotes*, has left upon my mind a picture I cannot contemplate without a shudder.[30]

Despite having lost their battle, the French Foreign Legion were still instrumental in the wider war; the supply convoy safely reached Puebla on May 3 and the city fell shortly thereafter. The war ravaged Mexico for another four years, but at long last the American Civil War concluded – the Americans had favored the Juaristas from the beginning. Diplomatic as well as military pressure aided the Mexicans in gaining their independence from France. Maximilian of Austria was executed on June 19, 1867.

John Robert Young's magnificent photographic history of the Foreign Legion sums up the mythos of Camerone well:

Painting by Edouard Manet of the execution of Maximilian after his capture by Mexican forces loyal to Juaréz. (Yorke Project)

At the request of Colonel Jeaningros [Commander of the Foreign Legion] the Emperor Napoleon III decreed that the name of Camerone be inscribed on the regimental colours and standards of the Foreign Legion. In 1892, a monument was raised on the site of the battle; and its dignified Latin inscription sums up admirably not only the final action of the 3rd Company, but also the essential spirit of the Legionnaire: "Here stood fewer than sixty men against an entire army. Its weight overwhelmed them. Life, sooner than courage, forsook these soldiers of France." Each year, in every unit of the Foreign Legion, the anniversary of the battle of Camerone is celebrated with pomp and a sense of rededication. At Aubagne, the wooden false hand of Capitaine Danjou, recovered from the battlefield, is paraded before the troops as a sacred relic.[31]

The battle of Camerone demonstrated the difficulties in taking fortified positions without artillery. If the Mexican forces even had just one artillery piece they could have breached the hacienda's walls in several places and then launched an assault. To be fair however, one must remember that the Mexicans were under pressure to remove the French threat so that they then could ambush the French convoy. Nonetheless, Camerone is interesting in the sense that an under strength infantry company was able to fight off several cavalry charges, then advance through the enemy into a fortified position and subsequently repel numerous attacks by larger forces.

LITTLE BIG HORN, 1876

Arguably the most famous battle in America's military history is that of the annihilation of the 7th Cavalry Regiment, under Lieutenant Colonel George Armstrong Custer, by the combined Sioux and Cheyenne tribes, under the religious leadership of Sitting Bull and the military leadership of Crazy Horse, at the Little Big Horn in Montana on June 25, 1876. The battle by itself is not worthy of the scholarship dedicated to it. The death of a couple of hundred American troopers in the wilderness does not compare to the carnage of an average American Civil War battle or the slaughterhouse of the trenches in France during the Great War. And yet it could very well be argued that this single battle, so glorious a victory for the Plains Indians, served only to hasten their demise as the US government in effect launched a total war against the Native Americans. Effective resistance to the ever-growing white population in the United States more or less ceased after the annihilation of Custer's regiment, and in that sense it is important. However, for many years the tendency has been to glorify and perpetuate the myth of a last stand of a glamorous Civil War hero and his troopers. The facts, now revealed by modern archeological excavations, have painted a different scenario. In truth, the Indian warriors did win a decisive victory, but the magical last stand did not occur. Instead, the evidence suggests an organized murder both cowardly and courageous, with a number of US troopers fleeing in sheer panic when all seemed lost, similar to most battles throughout time.

BACKGROUND

By 1876, America's appetite for expansion and the gold discovered within the stronghold of the Plains Indians' reservations led to a military expedition. The intention was to crush whichever tribes had abandoned the reservations – and thereby threatened the immigrants' westward expansion – and resettle them under the watchful but corrupt eyes of the Indian Affairs Office on the reservations set aside as virtual prisons for the Native Americans. The rebellious enemy numbered between 400 and 800 warriors and their families and was composed of Hunkpapa Sioux, Ogala Sioux, and Northern Cheyenne. They were thought to have congregated in the Big Horn Valley of Montana.[1] The plans of generals George Crook and Alfred Terry called for a three-pronged assault, seeking to converge into the Big Horn Valley. The official order to launch an offensive against hostile tribes was ordered on February 8, 1875, by Geneal William T. Sherman.[2] In the end, only the southern column under Crook departed on the operation during the winter. Crook's command encountered not only bad weather, but also stiff resistance in the Powder River Valley on March 17, 1876, ending his winter drive. The combined multi-pronged assault was going to have to wait a few months.

The operation was in full effect again by May, this time with three columns. To the south was General Crook's column with 1,000 troops, including infantry. Colonel John Gibbon with 450 men was maneuvering from the north of the Little Big Horn toward General Alfred Terry's column, which was advancing with well over 900 men from the east toward the Big Horn Valley.

The Indian insurgents under the spiritual leadership of Sitting Bull grew in numbers, and by June

> the scattered bands had begun to come together in a single village that formed one of the largest in the history of the Great Plains. All the Teton Sioux were represented – Hunkpapas under Sitting Bull, Gall, Crow King, and Black Moon; Oglalas under Crazy Horse, Low Dog, and Big Road; the Miniconjou followers of Hump; Sans Arc, Blackfoot, and Brule Sioux. There were also Northern Cheyennes under Two Moon, Lame White Man, and Dirty Moccasins, and a handful of warriors from tribes of Eastern Sioux. They clustered around six separate tribal circles, and altogether they numbered perhaps 10,000 to 12,000 people, mustering a fighting force of between 2,500 and 4,000 men.[3]

Other scholars have placed the Indian numbers at about 7,000 natives in 1,000 lodges, including perhaps up to 2,000 fighters.[4] The Indians were obviously spread out over a large area, forcing the American Army to engage them in a multi-pronged attack, more so than the original plans of Crook and Terry had allowed for.

George Crook's column ran into large numbers of Sioux and Cheyenne warriors on June 17 at the Rosebud Creek, east of the Big Horn mountains, and the battle was salvaged only by his Shoshone and Crow allies, who numbered around 260.

He decided to turn back despite having suffered only a handful of casualties. The multi-pronged attack ended ingloriously, but the campaign continued as Terry and Gibbon unified their troops, with Colonel Gibbon retiring from command due to an illness. General Terry now commanded all the American forces, except Custer and his men, who had an independent command. Terry thus became the commander-in-chief of a one-column operation against a foe who was numerically their equal. It would take the demise of the 7th Cavalry for the Americans to realize the size of the enemy they faced.

On June 21, General Terry ordered his understrength 7th Cavalry to act as a mobile force preventing the Indians from escaping to the south, but not to approach the Little Big Horn directly, while his slower-moving columns of infantry acted as a blocking force to the north. This was a "hammer and anvil" operation, with Custer's fast-moving troops being the hammer. The key was, of course, to allow Terry's command enough time to reach its position and to avoid engaging the insurgents until the trap was in place. Terry suggested that the 7th take Gibbon's battalion of the 2nd Cavalry as well as the Gatling gun

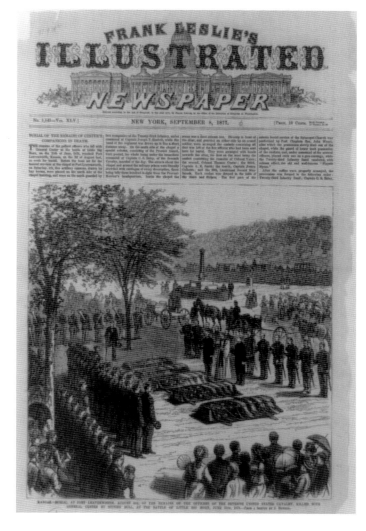

Newspaper illustration of the funeral at Fort Leavenworth for the 7th US Cavalrymen who died at Little Big Horn. (Library of Congress)

battery along for support, but Custer declined the offer. The column included all 12 companies of the regiment numbering 31 officers, about 585 enlisted men, 40 Arikara and Crowe Indian scouts, and nearly 20 packers, guides, and other civilian employees, including Custer's youngest brother Boston Custer. Each trooper carried 100 cartridges for his carbine and 24 for his pistol. A pack train of 175 mules transported another 50 rounds of carbine ammunition per man together with rations and forage for 15 days.[5]

From June 22 to 24, fresh trails were discovered along with a few abandoned tepees, and instead of moving south as had been planned by General Terry, Custer's 7th followed the spoors, preparing for combat. A night movement toward the Little

George Armstrong Custer (1839–1876). Controversial commanding officer of the 7th US Cavalry, who divided his forces in the face of opposition at Little Big Horn. (Library of Congress)

Big Horn further exhausted his column, but by the early morning hours of June 25 the troopers were allowed a little rest before the anticipated discovery of and attack on the insurgents' camp. Custer received intelligence reports from his scouts indicating a sizable camp, but had doubts about the reports, and didn't believe his scouts. He knew somewhere he would find the enemy, however. Yet during this time his column was compromised, as a party of warriors discovered troopers of the 7th Cavalry. Undaunted, Custer decided to advance and to seek out the camp even though the element of surprise had now been lost. He opted for combat operations against an enemy of perhaps 800 warriors with a force of fewer than 700 men. His orders had called for an advance south, then to await the arrival of Terry's army on the following day. But Custer had a different plan, or perhaps he sought to close with the enemy before he could slip away.

The order of battle for the advance just after midday included three maneuvering elements, with a fourth comprised of the pack mules: Major Marcus Reno took command of one element, consisting of 175 troopers from A, G, and M Companies, although straggling later reduced the number somewhat. Captain Frederick W. Benteen headed the second, consisting of H, D, and K Companies, of 120 men. Custer himself retained five companies divided into two wings – one under Captain George Yates of E and F Companies, while Captain Miles Keogh commanded C, I, and L – 221 men. Captain Thomas McDougal was assigned with B Company to guard the pack train and seven men detached from each company to keep the mules moving.[6] The whole operation was movement-to-contact, as the precise location and number of enemy forces was not known. Custer probably sought flexibility in his command, perhaps aiming to pin down insurgent forces while the other elements under his command maneuvered into position to counter the Indians' defense. The Native Americans were not tied to permanent towns or villages; indeed, once engaged the entire tribe could very well be packed and on the move while the warriors kept the enemy at bay. Experience had taught the senior cavalry commanders that speed and closing with the enemy or pinning him down was crucial lest he slipped away. Benteen was on the far left wing, Reno in the center and Custer with his unit covered the right side, while the baggage train was to the rear. Splitting his command into smaller groups was not to everyone's liking but Custer dismissed the criticism proffered by Captain Benteen.[7]

At the start of the battle, the right wing of the 7th spotted Indians in the distance and Custer pursued. He ordered Reno, the center component, to advance and engage the enemy when encountered – Custer would support the action with his own wing when needed. Benteen had fallen behind as he had stopped to water his horses, in order to keep his animals fresh and avoid stragglers. The center formation at long last spotted some tepees in the distance and commenced its attack with three companies in line as Custer continued forward, ready to charge the camp. But the enemy did not flee as had been anticipated. Instead the warriors flooded forward to the edge of the camp. The camp was just one of a handful and this particular one belonged to Sitting Bull and his Hunkpapa Sioux. Reno was forced to dismount into a skirmishing line and exchanged gunfire with the ever-growing number of insurgent fighters. Some of the mounted natives rode toward Reno's left flank and threatened to cut his force off completely from the rest of Custer's command. The center column of Custer's command moved into a copse to its right flank, which had served as its anchor point. Men and horse alike sought shelter while more Indians joined the fight from throughout the massive camps. Other warriors from different tribes hurried to the sounds of gunfire.

Custer's group advanced north, paralleling the ridge, and finally spotted a different part of the huge camp. Quickly he sent a messenger to Benteen ordering him to bring his command and mule train to his aid. By 1600hrs Custer was fully aware that he had indeed stumbled onto a sizable enemy concentration, that his central command was in a tough fight and somewhere Benteen's companies were moving forward. Instead of consolidating the command and immediately aiding Reno's by now trapped force, George Custer decided to swing onto the village to engage and defeat the enemy.

Major Reno was in trouble and he knew it. Men and animals alike were under intense pressure from an enemy that was stronger than anticipated and one that was not choosing to melt away to fight another day. Instead the warriors of the various tribes wanted to destroy the hated invaders. During the fight, as Reno was issuing commands, his scout named Bloody Knife was shot in the head and his brain mass and other fragments slammed into Reno, who at that point panicked, screamed orders unheard by the majority of troopers, and charged out of the woods toward the ridge. There he was probably hoping to find friendly troops from either Benteen or McDougal's units. Or perhaps he simply fled. The result was a rout and his command took many casualties and abandoned dozens of men, some of whom managed to retreat safely later in the afternoon. His panicked and disorganized

The commonly held ideal of Custer's last stand at the Little Big Horn, included Native American warriors on horseback riding circles around the remnants of Custer's command. The reality was that the warriors fought as individuals both on foot and horseback and advanced in short rushes, isolating the American troopers, and then killing them through superior firepower or hand-to-hand combat. (Library of Congress)

companies fled up the 30m ravine to the top of the ridge. All told, Major Reno had 140 troopers and 35 scouts when he started his advance and by 1600hrs 40 had been killed, including three officers with 37 missing and a number wounded.[8] In the distance, gunfire indicated another fight was underway. The majority of the native Americans turned back toward their village to deal with the next attack, although some must have also seen Benteen's column in the distance.

Captain Benteen, without the mule train, had hurried along the ridge after he had been informed by his scout of a large enemy presence to the west and as the gunfire in the distance increased. He arrived to see the battered remnants of Reno's troops. Captain Thomas Wier arranged a hasty defensive perimeter while engaging the remaining warriors below the ridge. Major Reno plunged back into the woods looking for a fellow officer, whom he did not find.[9] In the meantime, the perimeter was set up and ammunition redistributed and forces consolidated. Returning from his fruitless but brave task, Major Reno took charge and ordered the advance of the mule train under McDougal. Ammunition and supplies were needed. He had wounded personnel to deal with as well. Captain Wier with D Company moved forward following Custer's order to advance. Some 30 minutes or more later, Captain Benteen with his unscathed companies, and finally Reno with the baggage train and wounded, arrived as well. But matters did not get any better:

Topping the high pinnacle now known as Wier Point, Wier saw the Custer battlefield 3 miles in the distance, but smoke and dust obscured all details of the activity taking place there. Hundreds of warriors ascending the north slope of Wier Point halted the advance. After a brief skirmish, the soldiers fell back to Reno Hill. Mounting numbers of Sioux pressed from behind, swiftly surrounded the 350 or more troopers and packers, and at once brought them under a deadly fire that did not subside until twilight, 3 hours later.[10]

The left and central wings and the mule train of the 7th Cavalry under Captain Benteen, Major Reno, and Captain McDougal respectively were united and surrounded by 1830hrs. The fight around the remnants of the 7th Cavalry was ferocious and the beleaguered troops charged out of their perimeter to collect water during the fight. George Herendon was a civilian scout attached to Major Reno's command:

Benteen led the charge and was upon the Indians before they knew what they were about and killed a great many. They were evidently much surprised at this offensive movement, and I think in desperate fighting Benteen is one of the bravest men I ever saw in a fight. All the time he was going about through the bullets, encouraging the soldiers to stand up to their work and not let the Indians whip them; he went among the horses and pack mules and drove out the men who were skulking there, compelling them to go into the line and do their duty. He never sheltered his own person once during the battle, and I do not see how he escaped being killed. The desperate charging and fighting was over at about one o'clock, but firing was kept up on both sides until late in the afternoon.[11]

By 1730 General Custer and all his companies were dead, but this was still not known to the rest of the command. What happened to Custer and his men is only known to the Indian warriors who battled them, for nobody of Custer's command survived:

Whether part or all of them reached the river at the mouth of Medicine Tail Coulee is not known. If Custer intended to cross the river, here was a likely place one in fact that would have placed him right in the center of the Indian camp. But hordes of Sioux warriors under Chief Gall poured across the stream at this ford and, either near the mouth of Medicine Tail Coulee or farther back on the slope dividing it from Deep Coulee, collided with the troops. Deflected to the right, the battalion fought successive rearguard actions toward a long ridge to the north. More warriors forded the river

Frederic Remington's version of a last stand of cavalry troopers caught in the open. (Library of Congress)

behind Gall. Others crossed still farther down. And Crazy Horse started down the valley with another large force, crossed the river, and swept round in a great arc that brought him ultimately to the battle ridge from the north. Caught in rough terrain unsuited to mounted action and surrounded by overwhelming numbers of Sioux and Cheyenne warriors, the battalion swiftly disintegrated. The fight probably opened shortly after 4 p.m., just as Reno reached the refuge of the bluffs. Probably by 5p.m. not a man of Custer's battalion remained alive.[12]

The supposed last stand of Lieutenant-Colonel Custer and his remnants seems to have been just a myth. Recent archeological and forensic research revealed that the slaughter of Custer's men, who were caught by a enemy superior in numbers and firepower, was more akin to a buffalo hunt:

"The myth is the gallant, heroic last stand – that the Indians drove him to the killing field, where he fought to the last man and last bullet against overwhelming odds," says Richard Fox, a professor of anthropology at the University of South Dakota. "My research says the outcome was a function of panic and fear, a very common thing in battle. There was no last stand in the gallant, heroic sense." By analyzing the distribution of cartridges (which have unique firing-pin patterns) unearthed on the battlefield, Fox's team was able to trace the movement of individual guns, and the soldiers who carried them, during the course of the fight. "A study of the distribution of certain artifact types indicates that ... the soldiers resisted but little."[13]

One account by Sioux Lakota Chief Red Cloud recalls the attacks by Major Reno and Custer's command:

> The soldiers charged the Sioux camp about noon. The soldiers were divided, one party charging right into the camp. After driving these soldiers across the river, the Sioux charged the different soldiers [i.e. Custer's] below, and drive them in confusion; these soldiers became foolish, many throwing away their guns and raising their hands, saying, "Sioux, pity us; take us prisoners." The Sioux did not take a single soldier prisoner, but killed all of them; none were left alive for even a few minutes. These different soldiers discharged their guns but little. I took a gun and two belts off two dead soldiers; out of one belt two cartridges were gone, out of the other five.[14]

The fight was not about Indian horsemen riding circles around a beleaguered group of soldiers under Custer's command. Instead the Indians decimated not only the separate columns but also the individual companies when they started to take casualties and panicked. On foot and on horseback, young and middle-aged warriors decimated the smaller American groups, most of whom seemed to have fired their weapons wildly into the air and tried to run for their lives. Nearly 40 percent of the troopers were foreign-born, averaged 22 years of age, and tended to be in somewhat poor health given the nature of their work and the difficult living conditions of the time. The Sioux and Cheyenne were well equipped, with over 40 different caliber types found by Richard Fox on the battlefield. Their firepower and will to destroy the enemy was boundless. The battle eventually ended as the Native Americans slowly departed the area. Scores of cavalry troopers were mutilated once dead, including limb removal and castration. The 7th Cavalry and its allies lost 268 men, of which 210 died under Custer. Only about 56 or so dead soldiers were positively identified. The insurgent Indians lost more than 50 killed with an unknown number of wounded.

THE AFTERMATH

The Battle at the Greasy Grass, as it became known to the native Americans, was Sitting Bull's "Last Stand," not Custer's, for never again would his power have so

The memorial at Little Big Horn. A plaque at the base of the memorial reads: THE MEMORIAL. The remains of about 220 soldiers, scouts, and civilians are buried around the base of this memorial. The white marble headstones scattered over the battlefield denote where the slain troopers were found and originally buried. In 1881 they were reinterred in a single grave on this site. The officers' remains were removed in 1877 to various cemeteries throughout the country. General Custer was buried at West Point. (Courtesy of Durwood Brandon)

profound an impact on the history of the West. Within a few years, resistance to the United States yielded and the once proud and free-roaming Native Americans died their deaths on reservations dependent on the US government for hand-outs.

ISANDLWANA, 1879

BACKGROUND

Parts of southern Africa were settled in the 17th century by Dutch settlers, and on the back of a rise of European nationalism and colonialism in the 19th century, more territories were explored and conquered by industrial powers. The southern tip of Africa saw an influx of British settlers. Indigenous tribes not only fought one another, but also became more entangled with the new colonists. The discovery of gold and diamonds only served to hasten the power shift, and toward the end of the 19th century Britain was the dominant force in southern Africa.

The strongest native resistance to British rule came from the kingdom of the Zulus, who had unified by sword and diplomacy a large part of the region. Great Britain decided to bring all "the disparate British colonies, Boer republics and beleaguered African kingdoms under one central infrastructure" into an entity known as the Confederation.[1] To that end the Zulus needed to be defeated militarily and brought under the rule of the British. So, on January 11, 1879, a relatively small British army, allied with thousands of natives hostile to the Zulus, crossed into Zululand, determined to strike at the capital of the kingdom at oNdini (Ulundi).

THE BRITISH FORCES

The British Army and its allies was arranged in a multi-pronged offensive that included five columns, but a poor logistical infrastructure forced two of the columns to act more as a defensive shield while the three remaining ones stumbled forward with a massive wagon train. The commander of the British troops was Lord Chelmsford, and he took command of two of the columns, unifying them into one central attacking force. The tactical reason for the multi-pronged attack was to pin down the fast-moving Zulus and force them into combat. One ponderous slow-moving column was not going to accomplish the goal of destroying the Zulus if the Zulus chose to avoid a confrontation. Lord Chelmsford threw out to the far left wing Column No. 5 under Colonel H. Rowlands, not to guard his extended flank, but to defend the border and also pose an attacking threat from Swaziland in the north onto Zululand. This column comprised a number of units, including the 80th Foot, the Border Horse, and the Transvaal Rangers. It numbered over 2,000 combatants, and was accompanied by six 7pdr guns and two rockets troughs.[2] The No. 1 Column, under Colonel Pearson, was sent to the coast on the far right flank, also acting in a more defensive posture. It included the 99th Foot and a battalion of the 3rd Foot, four units of Mounted Rifles, two 7pdr guns of the Royal Artillery, a company of Royal Engineers, and several native units. Total strength was around 4,750, comprising 2,000 British Army regulars and more than 2,000 native troops.[3]

Wood's No. 4 Column was to advance north of the central column with the intended purpose of guarding the center's left flank, as well as check any local Zulu advances. No. 4 Column totaled 1,565 officers and men from the 90th Foot, the 1st Battalion, 13th Foot, the Frontier Light Horse, and Wood's irregulars, and the Royal Artillery accompanied by several guns. The central columns were composed of No. 2 and No. 3 Columns under Chelmsford's direct control. No. 2 Column numbered nearly 4,000 officers and men under Lieutenant Colonel Durnford. He led three

Sir Garnet Wolseley is pictured here presenting the Victoria Cross to Major Chard. Chard was the commander of the Rorke's Drift station, which was attacked by several Zulu regiments that were stationed in reserve at Islandlwana. The small British garrison fought off thousands of Zulu warriors. (Anne S.K. Brown Military Collection, Brown University Library)

battalions of the 1st Regiment Natal Native Contingent (NNC), five troops of the Natal Native Horse, one company of the Natal Native Pioneer Corps and a Rocket Battery. No. 3 Column was commanded by Brevet Colonel R. Glynn. His officers and men totaled 4,709 from a large number of regiments, including two battalions from the 24th Foot, the Natal Mounted Police, two battalions of the NNC and a battery of the Royal Artillery. The column had six 7pdrs and two rocket troughs.[4]

The five columns together numbered around 17,000 officers and men, accompanied by hundreds of wagons and carts, thousands of oxen, horses, and mules driven by over a thousand conductors, and drivers. The near-Herculean effort to supply a European army in the field meant that a relatively fast campaign, especially when operating in hostile terrain, was by far the preferred option.

THE ZULU ARMY

The Zulu command council realized that the initiative lay with the British, and to combat them they called in all their regiments from young to old and waited to see where to send their troops. In total King Cetshwayo, the Zulu leader, was able to muster an impressive army of 22,000–25,000 warriors of all ages at oNdini. Strategically the Zulus looked for a defensive, reactive operation.

The Zulu Army was organized on the *amabutho* (singular *ibutho*) system, where the companies and regiments are age based. All young men across the kingdom, regardless of their local allegiances, were bound to serve the king. Every three or four years a call up would be held, and all men who had come of age since the previous call up would be formed in an ibutho. They would remain within this ibutho throughout their lives, though they would only be required to fight until they married, except in cases of national emergency. The British referred to amabutho who were based at the same ikhanda (barracks) as a "corps," hence "uNdi Corps."

It is difficult to get a very clear picture of the numbers of Zulus fighting in each unit, as the Zulus calculated strength in the number of companies of a regiment present on a given occasion, rather than in complete regiments. As the size of companies varied greatly, estimates of numbers are only rough. Strengths given here are estimates based on official British Intelligence counts before the war, and during the Isandlwana and Khambula campaigns:

The main Zulu army, was under the command of Ntshingwayo kaMahole Khoza. The uNdi Corps, under Prince Dabulamanzi kaMpande, comprised around 3,400 warriors from the uThulwana (1500), iNdlondlo (900), and iNdluyengwe (1000) amabutho. The uNodwengu Corps included the uDududu (1500), iMbube (500), and

A painting of the Zulu war by John Dunns, 1879. If the British had better protected their weapons using their wagons, they may have been able to repulse the Zulu warriors at Isandlwana. However, the British underestimated the Zulu determination to close into battle. (Anne S.K. Brown Military Collection, Brown University Library)

isAngqu (1500) amabutho, totaling around 3,500 men. There were also a number of unattached amabutho: Khandempemvu (umCijo) (2500), iNgobamakhosi (4000), uMbonambi (2000), uNokhenke (2000), uDloko (2500), and uVe (2000).[5]

ISANDLWANA

The British central columns, which had divided into two by January 19, advanced past Rorke's Drift station into Zululand unopposed, except for a short action against local Zulus, and moved toward the massive Isandlwana mountain. There they established a camp, and unloaded the wagons that were to return to Rorke's Drift. The British raised their tents and lined up the massive wagons, but failed to set up a laager or erect any defensive earthworks. The ground was rocky and would have taken a long time to build upon and the army was going to be moving along soon. Thus far no concentration of Zulus were to be found anywhere. Lord Chelmsford ordered several reconnaissance missions by his some of his native units. Mounted as well as foot patrols scoured the areas south and east.[6] Overall command of the massive reconnaissance force was given to Major J. G. Dartnell. His mounted unit encountered hundreds of Zulus, who charged but then retreated. Dartnell decided to send a messenger back to Chelmsford alerting him of the enemy sighting, but instead of retreating Dartnell, fearing a night-time rear attack should he withdraw, opted to stay in place overnight.

Chelmsford in turn decided to move out as quickly and quietly as possible, with the intention of surprising the enemy in the early hours of the morning and thus preventing them from escaping. The British commander sent for Colonel Durnford's No. 2 Column, mostly comprising natives, who were encamped at Rorke's Drift on the Zulu side with the Rorke's Drift station acting as a resupply point. Lord Chelmsford divided his army in the face of the enemy in order to pin the Zulus down and kill them. But he did order additional reinforcements under Durnford to come to his temporary camp at Isandlwana. The camp was left under the control of Lieutenant Colonel Henry Pulleine, with orders to defend and to serve as a reserve if they were needed.

The Battle of Isandlwana 1879 painted by C. E. Fripp. This famous painting captures the final moments of the 24th, although the colors were not unfurled during combat. (Author's Collection)

By the time Colonel Durnford arrived at the camp around 1030hrs, the situation had changed, as hundreds of Zulus had been spotted in the distance. The Zulus spotted may very well have threatened the rear of Chelmsford's columns and Durnford decided to scout the area in force, while Pulleine had also sent one company to the north of the actual camp and stationed it there as a picket. Durnford's column split and reconnoitered to the north and east, while Durnford himself and a rocket battery advanced east together, then slightly northeast. One of the mounted auxiliary units located the massive Zulu Army under Ntshingwayo kaMahole Khoza in the valley below. The Zulus charged without having been ordered, and the native auxiliary horse formed skirmish lines and began a fighting retreat.[7] The native infantry broke and fled as the mounted units kept up their discipline during their withdrawal.

The horns and chest of the Zulu formation numbered around 19,000 warriors, while the reserve included about 4,500 men. The Zulu army at Isandlwana under inkhosi Ntshingwayo kaMahole Khoza and inkhosi Mavumengwana kaNdlela Ntuli was arranged in three sections. The right horn comprised approximately 4,000 men from the uDududu, iMbube, and iSangqu amabutho. The chest was formed of men from the uNokhenke, uKhandempemvu (also known as the uMcijo), and uMbonambi amabutho, and numbered around 9,000. The left horn was made up of the uVe and iNgobamakhosi amabutho, and totaled around 6,000 warriors.[8]

This rendition gives an idea of the insurmountable odds faced by the British. Note that the Zulu warriors fill the horizon. (Author's Collection)

There were a few other amabutho present, including some small detachments from amabutho from elderly age grades. There was also an unknown number of men present who had joined the army from chiefdoms through which the army had marched. While all troop numbers for the Zulu Army must remain just estimates, it seems that the total number of warriors engaged in the battle of Isandlwana numbered around 19,000, with another 4,500 men remaining in reserve. Most of the reserve had no significant role in the battle, but some elements broke away to join the left horn. The men of the reserve who did not participate in the battle went on to attack Rorke's Drift later that day.

Captain George Shepstone, Dunford's staff officer, who earlier had witnessed the collapse of the NNC, arrived at Isandlwana, as temporary camp commander Pulleine received orders from Chelmsford, who had not encountered the Zulu Army, to break camp and advance the rest of the column.[9] However, at the urging of Shepstone, the camp commander decided to ignore the order. Shepstone seemed to have understood the gravity of the situation. Transport officer of the Royal Artillery Horace Smith-Dorrien, one of only five officers to escape the subsequent massacre, recalls that others, in essence the command staff, had not taken in the seriousness of the circumstances they now faced:

> Forty-five empty wagons stood in the camp with the oxen in. It was a convoy which I was to have taken to Rorke's Drift for supplies early in the morning, but which was stopped until the enemy should be driven off. These wagons might have at any time been formed into a laager, but no one appeared to appreciate the gravity of the situation, so much so that no steps were taken until too late to issue extra ammunition from the large reserves we had in camp.[10]

The Zulu regiments swarmed toward the British camp at Isandlwana. The numerically inferior British deployed roughly in this manner: The left flank, northeast of the camp, was composed of A and F Companies, 1st Battalion, 24th Foot (1/24th); the two native horse units under Robert and Raw and the two NNCs were retreating to the east of the British companies. Thrown forward and in front of the actual camp was the mounted detachment of Bradstreet, a two-gun section of N Company, 5th Battalion along with E Company 1/24th. Behind them were two companies of 1/24th and one company of 2/24th. To the battery's right, was another NNC under Lonsdale. Off to the right and more than a kilometer away was the gun battery with escort under Russell and Nourse, while on the extreme flank, perhaps some 4–5km away, was Colonel Durnford's mounted force. And one ought to remember the hundreds of support personnel, including

Cavalry verses light infantry. In general terms the advantage lay with the mounted troops who would charge through or evade the Zulus. (Author's Collection)

engineers, transport and hospital personnel, along with civilian contractors who were within the camp. Officially the British and native forces at Isandlwana numbered 1,768.

The Zulu regiments, in their respective formations, assaulted the spread-out combined British/native columns with rapid speed. The tactical maneuver and assault elements of the Zulus from the right horn to the left one was lined up as follows: iMbube, uDududu & iSangqu; uNokhenke; uKhandempemvu; uMbonambi; iNgobamakhosi; uVe and detachments of oNdini regiments. The fighting was at times very intense, and on several occasions the various Zulu regiments retreated while at other times they sought cover, only to charge forward sporadically. The British rifle fire was constant and lethal, slinging lead into the open-order formations of the Zulus. Panic, however, did creep in on several British-allied units. The NNCs, mostly armed in similar fashion to the Zulus, gave way. Horse-mounted units armed with rifles gave a good account of themselves, but the British line was fragmented and spread out over many kilometers. Finally, the far right flank under Colonel Durnford and the battery detachment were either overwhelmed or retreated toward the camp.

At the camp, the heavily armed line companies of the 24th fought off the Zulus as best they could, but their numbers as well as ammunition were dwindling and the Zulus moved rapidly, exploiting gaps and flanking the various formations they encountered. Pulleine, the commander of the understrength column, ordered the retreat into the camp. The remaining British/native companies formed fighting squares. Not all made it back to the camp as another company waged a fighting retreat toward the slopes of Isandlwana where it was overwhelmed once it exhausted its ammunition supply. The other companies, now disorganized by the tents and wagon and the chaos at the camp, were quickly overcome. Captain W. Penn Symons, who arrived at the battlefield after the event with Lord Chelmsford's column, reported his version of the fight a while after the battle:

> Soldiers were surrounded before they could fix their bayonets, and used the butts of their rifles to fend off the exultant Zulus. In ones and twos they were quickly overwhelmed, shot, stabbed, or bludgeoned with knobkerries. Some bigger groups kept together and worked their way back to the tents and ammunition, beneath the cliff of Isandhlwana [*sic*]. They rallied and fought to the last, their desperate resistance being revealed later by heaps of 50 and 60 dead soldiers. Outnumbered by twenty to one, laden with equipment, they stood no chance against their quicker, deadly enemy. By a coincidence that might come from the novels of Rider Haggard, just before noon there was a total eclipse of the sun. A Zulu warrior of the uNokenke regiment, who broke into the rear of the British position, tells how "the sun turned black in the middle of the battle. Then we got into the camp, and there was a great deal of smoke and firing. Afterwards the sun came out bright again"… In ten minutes' time there was not a white man left alive in

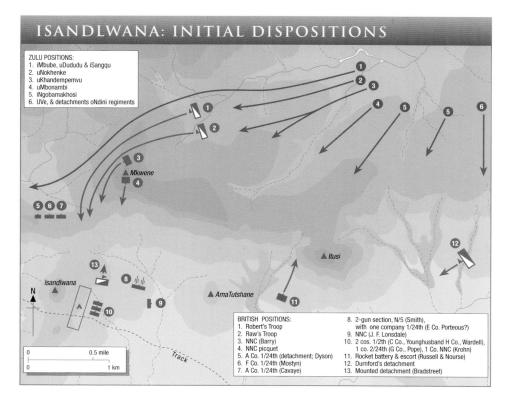

ISANDLWANA: INITIAL DISPOSITIONS

ZULU POSITIONS:
1. iMbube, uDududu & iSangqu
2. uNokhenke
3. uKhandempemvu
4. uMbonambi
5. iNgobamakhosi
6. UVe, & detachments oNdini regiments

Mkwene

Itusi

AmaTutshane

Isandlwana

Track

0   0.5 mile
0   1 km

BRITISH POSITIONS:
1. Robert's Troop
2. Raw's Troop
3. NNC (Barry)
4. NNC picquet
5. A Co. 1/24th (detachment; Dyson)
6. F Co. 1/24th (Mostyn)
7. A Co. 1/24th (Cavaye)
8. 2-gun section, N/5 (Smith), with one company 1/24th (E Co. Porteous?)
9. NNC (J. F. Lonsdale)
10. 2 cos. 1/2th (C Co., Younghusband H Co., Wardell), 1 co. 2/24th (G Co., Pope), 1 Co. NNC (Krohn)
11. Rocket battery & escort (Russell & Nourse)
12. Durnford's detachment
13. Mounted detachment (Bradstreet)

All of the surviving British officers were mounted and they barely managed to escape the swift moving Zulu warriors. (Author's Collection)

camp, no one was spared, not a prisoner taken. As soon as a man fell, he was thrown on his back, ripped open by the stabbing assegai and otherwise mutilated. It is the Zulu custom to thus treat a slain enemy, as superstition preserved and inculcated by their witch doctors, who tell them that if they neglect this precaution they themselves will die of a swollen belly. Many of the bodies were found tied with *riems* or strips of raw hide by the hands and feet, but it is doubtful if this was done for the purpose of torture. We believe that all mutilation was done in sheer glut of blood, after death. Most of the bodies were more or less stripped; one little band-boy of the 2/24th Regiment, a mere child, was hung up by his heels to the tail of a wagon and his throat cut. Even the dogs and goats about the camp, and the horses and mules tied to the picket ropes, were butchered. Further details would be too sickening.[11]

Horace Smith-Dorrien, who was a transport officer with the Royal Artillery at Isandlwana, survived and wrote a stirring account of those final, frightful moments.

Our right flank had become enveloped by the horn of the Zulus and the levies were flying before them. All the transport drivers, panic-stricken, were jostling each other with their teams and wagons, shouting and yelling at their cattle, and striving to get over the neck on to the Rorke's Drift road; and the red line of the 24th, having fixed bayonets, appeared to have but one idea, and that was to defeat the enemy.

When this final charge took place, the transport which was in-spanned had mostly cleared the neck, and I jumped on my broken-kneed pony, which had had no rest for thirty hours, and followed it, to find on topping the neck a scene of confusion I shall never forget, for some 4,000 Zulus had come in behind and were busy with shield and assegai. Into this mass I rode, revolver in hand, right through the Zulus, but they completely ignored me. I heard afterwards that they had been told by their King Cetywayo that black coats were civilians and were not worth killing. I had a blue patrol jacket on, and it is noticeable that the only five officers who escaped – Essex [Captain Edward Essex], Cochrane [Lieutenant William Cochrane], Gardner [Captain Alan Gardner], Curling [Lieutenant Henry Curling], and myself – had blue coats. The Zulus throughout my escape seemed to be set on killing natives who had sided with us, either as fighting levies or transport drivers.[12]

Smith-Dorrien rode to Fugitives' Drift, over several miles of bad ground. When he got there, he stopped to help an injured comrade, but the Zulus caught up with him, and he had to thrown himself down the steep descent of the Drift to the river, leaving his horse, and the injured man to the assegais of the Zulus. He managed to cross the river, and found himself among friendly natives, however Zulu warriors were still trying to cut him off, they continued to pursue him for another three miles, as he held them off with his revolver. Smith-Dorrien survived, and became a general ranked officer in the Great War.

The disaster for the British/native forces was complete. More than 1,300 men, black and white, died on the British side, with probably thousands of Zulus dead and wounded. Most of the survivors were auxiliaries; scarcely 60 whites survived. The Zulu victory not only destroyed British morale, but ruined any chance of immediate reprisal, as the army had lost all their spare ammunition, their tents, transport, and food supplies. The victory was one of three attacks made by the Zulus that day, one on each of the invading columns. The other two actions had been won by the British, but the annihilation of the center columns left the flank columns unsupported. The Zulu Army's attack was magnificent in its conception and execution.

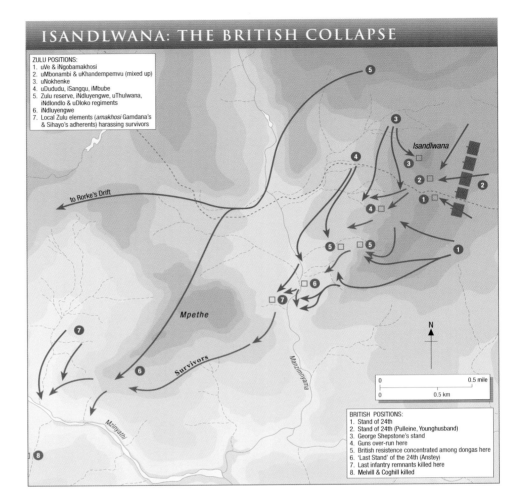

ISANDLWANA: THE BRITISH COLLAPSE

ZULU POSITIONS:
1. uVe & iNgobamakhosi
2. uMbonambi & uKhandempemvu (mixed up)
3. uNokhenke
4. uDududu, iSangqu, iMbube
5. Zulu reserve, iNdluyengwe, uThulwana,
   iNdlondlo & uDloko regiments
6. iNdluyengwe
7. Local Zulu elements (*amakhosi* Gamdana's
   & Sihayo's adherents) harassing survivors

Isandlwana

to Rorke's Drift

Mpethe

N

Manzimnyana

Survivors

Mzinyathi

0   0.5 mile
0   0.5 km

BRITISH POSITIONS:
1. Stand of 24th
2. Stand of 24th (Pulleine, Younghusband)
3. George Shepstone's stand
4. Guns over-run here
5. British resistence concentrated among dongas here
6. 'Last Stand' of the 24th (Anstey)
7. Last infantry remnants killed here
8. Melvill & Coghill killed

THE AFTERMATH

The Zulus retreated as Lord Chelmsford's column slowly made its way back to
Isandlwana. The British Army had to camp overnight on the blood-soaked soil of
the battlefield, surrounded by the bodies of their fallen comrades. Shortly thereafter,
Lord Chelmsford retreated to refit and reorganize, and to restore morale. The
response to the call for reinforcements, encouraged by news of the slaughter, was
swift, and by March Chelmsford resumed the offensive, setting out on a campaign
that saw the reduction of the Zulu kingdom. In fact, the slaughter at Isandlwana
hastened the demise of the Zulus, and by July 4 of the same year the Zulus lost their
final battle at their capital of oNdini (Ulundi).

OPERATION *DINGO*, 1977

BACKGROUND

The violent struggle for racial and political equality in Rhodesia did not exist in a vacuum. In fact, insurgency campaigns pitting indigenous people against colonial powers or minorities had been an ongoing struggle worldwide since the conclusion of World War II, although it had its roots in the arbitrary land grab of the victorious allies after the Great War. The ideals of nationalism and communism swept up many previously oppressed tribes and clans from Algeria to Zimbabwe (Rhodesia). Persecuted European Jews settled into the former Ottoman Empire, then British holdings in Palestine. Some Zionists resorted to what currently would be called terrorist tactics, assassinating Jews, Arabs, and Europeans alike. The creation of the Jewish nation-state of Israel in turn fomented additional terrorist activities after the Palestinian diaspora. Indo-China saw the rise of communist nationalists seeking in many ways to duplicate the American revolutionary ideals of the 18th century, ironically leading to a bloody war with the United States of America. North Africans sought to throw off the shackles of European powers just as fervently as black Africans sought their independence. All such peoples were pawns during the great struggle, the misnamed Cold War between the two newly created superpowers – the United States and the Union of Soviet Socialist Republics (USSR). One way or another, each superpower or its satellites had an interest and an active participation in the international conflicts. Cubans, Soviets, Chinese, and other communist military advisers dotted the globe, while the United States and its allies served in the same capacity, further inflaming worldwide uprisings.

Against this background Rhodesia sought its independence from Britain, whose government were attempting to press the white-controlled regional Rhodesian government into "expanding suffrage to include the majority native African population in the political process."[1] The European minority Rhodesian Front government declared independence on November 11, 1965. As a result of this declaration, the United Nations placed Rhodesia under sanctions. These events signaled the beginning of a more serious armed insurgency by the military wings of the main insurgency groups: the Zimbabwe African People's Union (ZAPU) headed by Joshua Nkomo, and the Zimbabwe African National Union (ZANU) eventually led by Robert Mugabe, currently President of the ruined country. The war became known as the Bush War or the Second *Chimurenga* (Liberation Struggle). Beginning in bordering Zambia, the early phases of the war ended badly for the insurgency and because of their lack of discipline the fighters were forced out of Zambia and were welcomed into Mozambique, where insurgent group Frente de Libertacao de Mocambique (Liberation Front of Mozambique; FRELIMO) was fighting a successful campaign against the Portuguese colonial military.[2] The insurgents struck with quick hit-and-run strikes into Rhodesia, killing not only whites but blacks as well, each time retreating to the relative safety of their host country. These raiding units tended to be relatively small with just a handful of men crossing the borders, but it became common to see units of up to 100 conducting quick strikes.[3] However, the majority of the attacks involved targeting civilians of all races.

THE INSURGENTS

The military operational unit of ZANU was the Zimbabwe African National Liberation Army (ZANLA) and the Zimbabwe People's Revolutionary Army (ZIPRA) was the fighting arm of ZAPU. ZAPU and ZANU received material and training support from the Soviet Union and the People's Republic of China respectively. Black leaders of the nearby nations, Zambia, Angola, Tanzania, Botswana, and Mozambique, also supported the guerrillas and furnished training areas and base camps.[4] The main difference between the insurgent groups was that Mugabe's ZANLA force was steeped in a Chinese-adviser-taught guerrilla campaign, while ZIRPA followed the more conventional mechanized tactics taught and supplied by their Soviet advisers. The black insurgents did not form a cohesive military strategy against the Rhodesians. In general terms, numerous insurgents trained not only with communist advisers, but many also traveled to those countries for additional military training.

Although the actual numbers of fighters was never fully documented, estimates placed them in the tens of thousands along with families. Charles Lohman states: "The largest tactical unit of ZANLA was normally the company, consisting of 90 to 100 men. The company was subdivided into three platoons of equal size, which were further organized into two 15-man sticks. For infiltration from Mozambique

The assault elements of the SAS and Rhodesian Light Infantry during Operation *Dingo* were composed of men like these. Note the camouflaged faces. (Courtesy of Craig Fourie)

into eastern Rhodesia, the company would be broken into these smaller units which would reassemble at a designated time and place across the border to receive final instructions."[5]

THE RHODESIAN ARMY

Although many blacks served exceedingly well with the Rhodesian Army, the brunt of the fighting was to take its toll on the 80,000 white Rhodesians and its foreign fighters, the Americans, Australians, and British. The Rhodesian Light Infantry and Rhodesian Special Air Service (SAS) were the only two units not racially integrated.[6] Any casualty or loss of equipment was a massive blow, as they couldn't source more due to trading sanctions imposed on Rhodesia by the United Nations. The black population numbered well above two million and the insurgents well into the tens of thousands, and could more easily replace their losses. Nonetheless, the Rhodesian military and political commands realized that only pro-active measures could potentially force some type of resolution, mainly through the deaths of insurgents, thereby forcing insurgent groups into retreat or causing enough casualties to bring them to the negotiating table for a more palatable peace.

In order to combat the hit-and-run tactics, the Rhodesian forces, who were small in numbers and struggling with worldwide sanctions, utilized several techniques to trap and kill the insurgents. The primary concept was that of the "Fire Force," where aerial assets were used in conjunction with ground troops, creating a kill box surrounding the enemy unit on all sides. One of the finest memoirs to have emerged from that war is Chris Cocks' *Fire Force: One Man's War in the Rhodesian Light Infantry*.[7] The author, though not present at Operation *Dingo*, recounts his experience from training to combat, including the techniques used to annihilate the insurgents, such as Fire Force and the "box." What sets this book apart from most is that Cocks paints the human canvas with plain, simple, and yet vibrant strokes, thereby creating a modern masterpiece of war literature.

OPERATION *DINGO*

The insurgents organized, recruited, trained, and staged combat patrols out of Mozambique. This situation was very similar to the American experience in the Vietnam War, as the insurgency was able to use neighboring Cambodia as a resupply and staging area for combat operations into Vietnam. After nearly one year of planning and preparing, the Rhodesian government authorized two deep strikes into the neighboring country to destroy the training centers where Robert Mugabe's ZANLA launched their cross-border raids. Operation *Dingo*, the codename for the deep strike against the ZANLA camp near Chimoio and Tembue, Mozambique in 1977, included air assets and 200 soldiers from the Rhodesian SAS and the

A stick of Rhodesian paratroopers preparing for parachute operations. (Courtesy of Tom Argle)

Rhodesian Light Infantry. By 1977, the Rhodesian Army intelligence estimated the forces at Mugabe's training facility to number between 9,000 and 11,000, with well over 4,000 believed to be actual trigger-pulling fighters who in recent months had killed over 200 civilians, many blacks, in Rhodesia.[8]

The previous year, the SAS commander, whose unit numbered no more than 150 men, had received reliable information about the training centers in Mozambique and had authorized high-altitude aerial reconnaissance missions. The Chimoio training camp was approximately 90km inside Mozambique and 17km north of the actual town of Chimoio.[9] The facility covered 5km[2] with 13 separate training areas and intelligence analyst noted approximately 700 insurgents on a rifle range.[10] The site itself, being the largest of its kind, was well defended with trenches, anti-aircraft positions, and towers throughout. Large numbers of family members and their civilian huts dotted the camp as well.

Combat experience had taught the Rhodesian planners that the enemy forces simply scattered in whichever direction they faced, instead of following planned escape routes. Thus the Rhodesians developed the tactic of the "box," in which the entire area would be surrounded by infantry and available aerial assets to kill and capture as many of the enemy as possible. SAS A Troop Commander Robert MacKenzie, an American mercenary and Vietnam veteran later killed in Sierra Leone in 1995, describes the box as "using slow sticks of paratroopers jumping at the rate of one per second [thereby creating roughly a 20m gap between each soldier] from C-47 ParaDaks flying carefully coordinated runs, landed troops all around a target, hopefully making a complete, if rather thin, perimeter surrounding most of the enemy."[11]

Because helicopters are limited in their range, especially in increased humidity or temperature, plans for the assault on Chimoio called for an administration base for re-arming and refueling point inside Mozambique.

On external operations the Rhodesians would para-drop fuel into temporary administrative bases set up in remote areas of Zambia and Mozambique along the

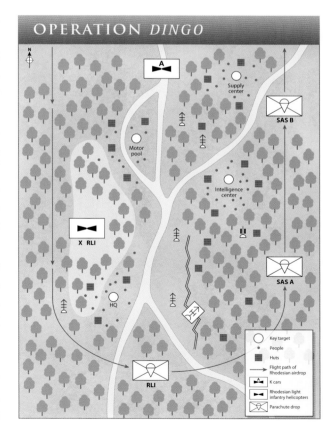

OPERATION *DINGO*

Rhodesian SAS Captain Robert Callen MacKenzie (1948–1995) was an American Vietnam veteran who fought in several African Wars. Here he is being presented with the Silver Cross of Rhodesia for "conspicuous gallantry and leadership in action." He was also awarded the Bronze Cross of Rhodesia for "gallantry and determination in action." He was killed in action in Sierra Leone. (Rhodesian Ministry of Defence)

flight path of helicopters flying in troops and attacking external camps. In the case of the second phase of Operation *Dingo* in October 1977, two administrative bases were needed to allow the helicopters to reach Tembue camp in central Mozambique near the Malawi border. The personnel at these administrative bases had no easy task because the areas were full of trees and rocks among which the drums would land. There would be little time before the attacking helicopters would be returning to refuel and helicopters could not land near drums on pallets to which parachutes were still attached because of the danger of fatal entanglement.[12]

The use of admin invited disaster, for any attack on these positions could spell doom not only on the assault but the withdrawal as well, and fewer than 200 infantry were to be used to protect these bases given the lack of Rhodesian air assets.

Rhodesian Light Infantry (RLI) commando Mike McDonald recalls Operation *Dingo*'s briefing:

The 48 3 Cdo soldiers along with [97] SAS soldiers had the mission briefing by a General in a hangar with a big model of the ZANLA Chimoio base complex 80 km inside Mozambique. Complex contained sub camps, one being for urban guerrilla warfare etc. Each camp had a card with the number of terrorist within. I added up all the cards and came to roughly 5000! I looked around the room at all us tough professional veteran soldiers, we seemed a very small force for a big camp but we also had 40 2 Cdo guys and the whole Rhodesian Air Force. This raid started the joke for all big externals taken from the book/movie "A Bridge Too Far" to us joking "A Gomo [hill or mountain] Too Far." Hopefully we would rescue some Rhodesian prisoners held in the base. We even fancied catching Robert Mugabe there.[13]

Operation *Dingo* was a two-phase attack: the first phase against Mugabe's largest camp at Chimoio (ZULU ONE) and the other at Tembue (ZULU TWO), totaling approximately 13,000 enemy personnel including women and children.

The Rhodesian forces were limited to the air assets they could muster to accomplish the mission. "Ultimately a force of some 35 Alouette III G-cars (troop carriers) and K-cars (gunships mounting a 20mm canon from a side door) was assembled, along with virtually all of Rhodesia's ground attack fighters and bombers. Six C-47 Dakotas were required for the parachute assault, with several more being used to establish an admin base nearby."[14] Nonetheless, the operation called for the SAS and the paratroopers of the RLI to parachute on two sides of the camp after an initial air strike, while a heliborne unit made of the RLI was to act as a blocking force on a third side of the camp. The fourth side of Chimoio was to be turned into another killing zone by ten armed helicopters, the K-cars, who were to be on battle station eight minutes later.[15]

Ten South African G-cars ferried supplies back and forth from an admin camp to Chimoio.[16] Command-and-control elements would be in the air over the camp as well, in a modified helicopter and a Dakota. The camp was very large, however, and subsequently the five most vital areas were to be assaulted.[17] The entire operation was preceded by one civilian aircraft, a DC-8 jet, making a fake run over the training camp as a distraction. The idea was that once Mugabe's men realized they were not being bombed, they would form back up into their formations for the day's training, allowing for the Rhodesian Air Force to catch them unaware.

In the very early hours of November 23, 1977, the Rhodesian veterans suited up for their deep raid into Mozambique. Commando McDonald recalls that in the "morning we kitted up, put on parachutes, I had 16 50-round belts for my MAG [machine gun], some were carried by the rest of my stick [squad made up of paratroopers]. It was an unforgettable awesome sight 6 long lines of paratroopers marching to the 6 waiting Dakota transport planes for this historic raid."[18] Robert MacKenzie, captain and commander of A Troop, told his men:

> to bring a minimum of 600 rounds per rifleman, 1,500 per RPD (Soviet 7.62mm) machine gun, and four frag [fragmentary] grenades each, in addition to their normal load of RPG-7 rockets, flares, white phosphorous and smoke grenades, medical equipment, rations, radios and batteries and survival gear. FN FAL rifles were chosen over AK-47s due to their extra-hitting power and rifle-grenade capability (two phosphorous and two frag each for this attack). My men would fix bayonets once on the ground, both for psychological advantage and the more practical one of saving ammunition at very close quarters.[19]

At 0800hrs, H-Hour, on November 23, 1977, the Rhodesian Air Force bombed the Chimoio training camp. Eight Hawker Hunter fighter-bombers, followed closely by four B-57 Canberra bombers at low altitude, six aging Vampire jets from higher altitude, and 12 Cessna 337s (called Lynx by the Rhodesians) carrying bombs, rockets, and machine guns would begin the attack.[20] "The bomb aimers in the

Canberras saw a sea of faces looking up at them from the parade square… Huge columns of black smoke and dust were enveloping the camp."[21] Multi-colored green and red anti-aircraft fire was littering the sky. Every airplane on the mission was hit, and although many of the paratroopers had previously conducted combat parachute assaults, none of them had been involved in anything this massive before.

MacKenzie "stood in the door of my Dakota while red and green tracer rounds zipped by, signaling the beginning of the battle for Chimoio 500 feet below."[22] Rhodesian paratrooper Mike McDonald's experiences of this daring combat jump revealed that although the Rhodesians achieved surprise in their attack, it was going to be hardly unopposed:

> As I jumped out I noticed a huge fireball over the main camp and the sound of constant gunfire. I quickly checked my canopy then the paratrooper on each side of me then studied the ground for running terrorists. Of 12 combat jumps I have this damn parachute has to land all over me on my hottest LZ ever. I fight this entanglement and even use my knife to slash paracords with bullets cracking all around. My fellow stick mates help pull the chute off. Both chutes off [including the reserve] I take cover 10 yards away behind the right side of a large tree with another soldier on the left side. Part of my chute is hooked on the branches of a young tree this draws lots of fire from several terrorists in a bushy river line about 70 yards away.[23]

During Operation *Dingo*, the paratroopers staggered their jumps to maintain a 20-yard distance between each man as they hit the ground. (Courtesy of Tom Argle)

MacKenzie describes the immediate actions on the ground:

> The 25 men in my stick closed to 10-meter intervals [from their original 20-meter distance between each man] in thick bush and mopani forest, forming a sweep line some 250 meters in length. The other half of A Troop, under command of Captain Colin Willis, was in similar formation on my left flank, with B Troop's 48 men on line at least a kilometer off to my right. On command from [the SAS Commander] Robinson, the SAS sticks started advancing toward the camp, while the RLI troopers held their positions and shot any terrorists fleeing the sweep lines. As every fourth trooper on the sweep line was carrying an RPD light machine gun, a heavy volume of fire could be, and was, delivered even while moving, and the sweeps continued to inexorably close on the terrorists' perimeter.[24]

Overall coordination suffered a serious loss when the command-and-control air element – the helicopter carrying the commanding officer – was so seriously shot up that it had to retire to the refueling area. The close air support so crucial for ground troops in combat had lost its most valuable asset – overall proper communications and coordination. The command-and-control element monitored "64 individual army radio stations alone and scores of air force ones and the two commanders had to handle all requests for casevac, ammunition re-supply and air strikes."[25]

A sketch of the Rhodesian SAS sweeping through the guerrilla camps as they engage an anti-aircraft position. (Author's Collection)

The ground assault consequently slowed down. Everywhere Rhodesian soldiers were engaged with Mugabe's men, some of whom simply tried to flee in all directions. Operation *Dingo*, however, had its box more or less in place. The RLI and SAS paratroopers had jumped in and fought ZANLA soldiers while consolidating with their sticks and relying on close air support runs to clear out stiff pockets of resistance. Meanwhile, other troopers with the RLI were dropped off by helicopters on a third side to act as a blocking force, while the K-cars were on station pummeling the fleeing enemy and other assets continuously. Within 30–60 minutes the command-and-control element returned to station, coordinating the lethal and efficient use of combined arms. In the meantime "officers and men waited in the heat, fuming at the delay, knowing the enemy must be slipping away through the inevitable gaps in their lines and through the side of the box that was supposed to be closed by K-Cars wasn't completely cut off... Also because of the diminished number of helicopter gunships on re-arming and re-fueling missions."[26] The Rhodesians who had been slowed down, however, now renewed their sweeps of their areas, by this time only encountering token resistance throughout. Many of the anti-aircraft positions lay abandoned though not destroyed. At other locations Rhodesian troopers cleared slit trenches but found only dead "gooks" in them.

Throughout the rest of the day, the RLI and SAS cleared the five main areas that had been targeted. As members of the SAS advanced toward the ZANLA garage; one of the Rhodesians was killed by a single shot between the eyes.[27] An armed helicopter, the K-Car, subsequently strafed the area to flush out the enemy. During the day, Mozambique FRELIMO insurgents engaged a Vampire and the pilot was killed during a crash-landing in Rhodesia.[28] MacKenzie's SAS troopers were "sweeping through another 150 meters of woods, during which 15 to 20 more terrorists were flushed and killed, my patrol reached ZANLA's intelligence center. It comprised 18 grass huts which served as offices, classrooms and storerooms, and although surrounded by more trenches, had been abandoned."[29] In the headquarters area of the camp, more than 600 dead guerrillas were counted, killed by aerial bombardments and strafing runs as well as by small-arms fire.

Night was now falling, and the RLI and SAS formed two separate defensive positions and experienced some contacts throughout the night as guerrillas, thinking the camp abandoned, returned. In the morning hours of November 24, the Rhodesian forces swept through the camp again, destroying anything that had not been previously annihilated. The SAS advanced to the camp's transport area where they destroyed the workshop, fuel storage tank, and vehicles. One truck was used to collect seven 12.7mm guns to be recycled in future campaigns against the Mugabe's guerrillas. Shortly thereafter, the Rhodesians withdrew from the destroyed Chimoio base to the refueling area, back to Rhodesia whereupon they executed part two of Operation *Dingo* with great success at the training camp of Tembue. Figures for the attack on Tembue vary wildly, from around 90, to 1,000 killed.[30] At Chimoio, 2,000 enemy including families had been killed and thousands more wounded. Both ZANLA camps were destroyed and valuable intelligence gathered for the Rhodesian Army. Two Rhodesians were killed in action with another eight wounded.[31]

Three years later the white Rhodesian government was replaced by Robert Mugabe, who became Prime Minister in 1980.

GROZNY, 1994–95

BACKGROUND

The battle of Grozny pitted Chechens against Russians at the end of the 20th century, but the conflict has its roots buried deep in history. In the international media, Chechens often only hit the headlines as terrorists who murder innocent Russians, or fight in foreign wars as mercenaries on a *jihad*. Repulsive attacks on civilian targets are sometimes wrongly blamed on the Chechens, while other times they indeed committed the crimes. But it is easier to label them universally as terrorists and blame them for all misdeeds. We read about Chechens fighting in Afghanistan and Iraq and we hear of a few Chechens involved with various al-Qaeda groups. To most Westerners, the Chechens are a mysterious people. Few people understand the deep-rooted warrior tradition of the Chechens and even fewer people have heard of their centuries-long oppression by the Russians, culminating in a Chechen diaspora during World War II, under order of Stalin. Jeffrey Burds explains the strategic importance of Chechnya to the Russians:

> Located at a strategic crossroads of Caspian, Azerbaijani and Georgian oil and gas reserves, the Northern Caucasus was a vital Soviet strategic zone held together by Soviet military control of a vulnerable network of bridges, roads and mountain passes. The narrow, mountainous isthmus that separated northern Iran from southern European Russia provided 93.5 percent of all Soviet oil and fuel reserves, concentrated at three key points: 58.5 percent passed through Baku and Batum in the south and another 27.5 percent passed through Grozny, the capital city of Chechnya, in the Northern Caucasus. Likewise 91 percent of all Soviet fuel was refined at these three sites. There were also strategic oil reserves located in Malgobek, Maikop and Kievskoe in the Northern Caucasus.[1]

The Chechen people took advantage of internal uncertainty in Russia throughout the early twentieth century to rise up against Soviet oppression. In particular, they rebelled during World War II. The Russians retaliated by implemented a plan to deport the entire population of the Northern Caucasus to Siberia and modern Kazakhstan, transporting nearly half a million Chechens and Ingushi, and leaving thousands dead across the region. They also destroyed Chechen books and manuscripts, and "There are reliable reports of ... the poisoning of food and water supplies to liquidate any guerrillas who remained behind ... more than 100,000 more died in the first three years after deportation."[2] During the de-Stalinization period of the mid-1950s under Nikita Khrushchev, the scattered Chechens were allowed to return to their native lands. "By the end of the 1980s unemployment in Chechnya was widespread, levels of medical care and education were among the very lowest in the USSR, mortality from infectious diseases and parasites was very high, and most of its important offices were held by Russians"[3] And with the collapse and break-up of the Soviet Union in 1991, Chechen leaders seized the opportunity for independence by November of the same year. A half-hearted attempt by the Russians to quell the secession proved unsuccessful and for ever so brief a moment, Chechnya, the Chechen Republic of Ichkeria, was independent under its President, former Soviet Air Force general and son of a deported family, Dzhokhar Dudayev, who was assassinated in 1996.

Having her territorial integrity challenged and with Chechnya unwilling to sign any treaty, Russia decided to support Dudayev's opponents in their coup attempts in October and November of 1994, both of which failed.[4] When Russia's involvement became public knowledge it forced President Boris Yeltsin into action. Similar to the post-Vietnam debacle for the Americans, the Russian government of the post-Afghanistan debacle had to act. Russia could not allow further erosion of her territorial integrity or more challenges to her now-tenuous superpower status,

A Russian BMP-1 (Boyevaya Mashina Pekhoty or Infantry Fighting Vehicle). Numerous vehicles like this one were destroyed by small hunter-killer teams of Chechen guerrillas. (DOD)

especially since the United States had waged a number of wars to regain its own status as a military superpower, which included support for the Mujahideen warriors in Afghanistan who were on a jihad against the Soviet invaders. The Russian planning staff had two weeks to get the entire operation in place and deploy their troops into Grozny. They would, however, pay the price for their hurried response.

THE CHECHENS

The Chechen fighters were not professionals by any standard, though a number of them had served in the Soviet Army and most spoke Russian. This obviously gave the Chechens a distinct advantage, both through listening to Russian communications and through their familiarity with Russian tactics. Their armed forces were mostly militia or local district paramilitary forces, inter-sprinkled with a few regular components. What really set them apart from traditional modern fighting units, however, is that their society was based on families and clans, similar to the tribes in Afghanistan and Somalia. Dr Theodore Karasik notes that:

> Chechen clans, called *taip*, identify member descent from a common ancestor twelve generations removed. A particular *taip* might consist of two to three villages of 400 to 600 people each and supply 600 fighters. For combat purposes, these groups are broken down into units of 150 and further subdivided into squads of about 20 for combat operations that work one-week shifts, one after the other. Islam influences the Chechen clan system and also strongly influences Chechen military culture. The Chechens' tribal/clan structure provides an ideal organizational structure for the war the Chechens are fighting. Their basic combat group consists of fifteen to twenty personnel, subdivided into three or four-man fighting cells. These cells are deployed as anti-armor hunter-killer teams consisting of an antitank gunner, a machine or sub-machine gunner, and a sniper. The sniper and machine gunner pin down Russian supporting infantry, while the antitank gunner engage the armored target. Normally, five or six hunter-killer teams attack an armored vehicle in unison and can force serious delays in Russian actions.[5]

The familial pressure to do well in combat is another by-product of the *taip*. Its close-knit nature also makes it very difficult for foreign intelligence to infiltrate it, a decided advantage in any conflict.

For weapons and equipment, the Chechens depended solely on whatever the Russians had left behind or sold to them individually. Their combined forces ranged between 1,000 and 3,000 fighters. "By one account the Chechens had 40–50 T-62 and T-72 tanks, 620–650 grenade launchers, 20–25 "Grad" multiple rocket launchers, 30–

35 armored personnel carriers and scout vehicles, 30 122mm howitzers, 40–50 BMP infantry fighting vehicles, some 200,000 hand grenades, and an assortment of various types of ammunition."[6] In terms of reliable manpower, the Chechens may have had the following: President Dudayev's National Guard consisting of about 120 men; Shamil Basaev's [Basayev] so-called Abkhasian Battalion of around 350 men; a tank unit (called regiment) with between 12 and 15 working tanks (T-54, T-62); an artillery unit of approximately 80 men and 30 light, medium, and heavy artillery pieces; a motorized "Commando Battalion" of approximately 250 men and led by Ruslan Galaev (Gelayev); finally, the Chechen MVD [Ministry for Internal Affairs] force of maybe 200 men. The Chechen Air Force consisted of about 15 L-29 or L-39 trainers, all of which were destroyed on the ground during the first hours of the war.[7] Of course, there were also other paramilitary forces whose numbers are hard to estimate, although some Russian sources have claimed 15,000 enemy combatants.

THE RUSSIAN ARMY

The post-Afghanistan Russian military was in shambles. Ten years of blood-letting in Afghanistan, combined with the internal political turmoil leading to the disintegration of the Soviet Union, added to severe defense budget cutbacks, crippled the armed forces. Officers as well as enlisted personnel frequently went unpaid and had other jobs to meet their personal financial needs. Troop abuse by senior enlisted personnel was common. Beatings, murder, and sexual assaults were not unheard of. "The brutality the Russians were about to display in Chechnya reflected the brutality inside the Soviet and Russian army," writes Anthony James Joes.[8] Units that did deploy to combat were woefully undermanned and inadequately prepared, with some soldiers entering combat without rifles.[9] Logistical support during the battle for Grozny was almost non-existent, forcing desperate behavior. Some soldiers ate dogs they killed on the streets.[10] Life in the Russian service was horrific in general and in Grozny it became particularly cruel. Many officers and enlisted soldiers were often drunk during the invasion and assault on Grozny.

Expert Timothy Thomas paints a bleak picture of the training the troops received: "In the 81st Motorized Regiment of the 90th Tank Division, out of 56 platoon commanders, 49 were yesterday's [civilian college] students. More than 50 percent of the men sent to war had never fired live shells with their tank cannons, and had no idea of how to do so. Military cooks, signalers, and mechanics were appointed to shoot antitank guns and missiles as well as machine guns."[11] Certainly, the Russian Army was not the one that had defeated the Germans in World War II, or the one that had entered Afghanistan in 1979.

Chechen fighter at the
Presidential Palace surveys
the damage to the city
of Grozny. (Courtesy
of Mikhail Evstafiev)

Chechen fighter at the Presidential Palace surveys the damage to the city of Grozny. (Courtesy of Mikhail Evstafiev)

PLANS FOR THE CAMPAIGN

The Russian plan for the Chechen campaign was divided into four distinct phases and was intended to last less than three weeks.[12] In Phase I, Chechnya was to be surrounded while the Russian Air Force secured air superiority. At the same time three military ground groups would converge on Grozny from the northwest, west, and east. The intended purpose was to surround the city, but to allow the southern part of Grozny to be left open for the Chechens as an escape avenue. The Russians believed the Chechens would not stand and fight, but flee when given the opportunity to retreat. At this point the city was not to be taken by force, but persuade the Chechens to reconsider their political and military positions. Phase II, and after the majority of rebel Chechens had fled, would secure key points in the city such as government buildings and radio and television stations. Phase III envisioned a Russian drive, pushing the rebels in a southerly direction while establishing local friendly governing bodies throughout the regions. The last operation, Phase IV, planned for the Russian forces clearing out small pockets of resistance in the southern mountain ranges. The only phase of the operation that was considered a pure combat action was the last phase. Certainly the Russians did not fully grasp the hatred the Chechens had for them, and that they would fight despite the odds.

The Chechen plan was rather simple; slow down the Russian juggernaut to allow the defenders of the city enough time to prepare for battle. This action would be accomplished by "pin-point and ambush attacks in forests and hilly terrain primarily against the Russian rear and MVD troops. A first set battle was planned to take place a few kilometers outside Grozny. However, this should not be a drawn-out battle either. The purpose was to delay the Russian advance in order to gain time for preparing the defence of Grozny, where the Chechens planned for the decisive confrontation."[13] The Chechens knew that the Russians could not sustain a long and bloody campaign, which had been the cause of their demise in Afghanistan. All they had to do was to make the Russians suffer and eventually, they would achieve their political objective of winning permanent independence. Chechnya, a small republic with about 800,000 inhabitants was taking on Russia, a country with more than 140 million people.

THE BATTLE

On December 11, 1994, the Russian operation commenced with approximately

38,000 soldiers manning 230 tanks, 353 Infantry Fighting Vehicles, and 388 tube and rocket artillery pieces. Attack helicopters and fixed wing close air support from the NCMD's [North Caucasus Military District] 4th Air Army would support the ground assault force. This force was further augmented with two heliborne Spetsnaz [Special Forces] groups for landing in southern Grozny. Their task was to disrupt the Chechen rear areas.[14]

A bread ration station during the assault of Grozny by Russian forces. (Courtesy of Mikhail Evstafiev)

261

Of course, not all of the troops were used in a full-scale attack; after all, the Russian military command expected the insurgents to flee southward. By the end of the year Grozny, as planned, had been surrounded on three sides and the air force had secured complete air superiority and was bombing the city. The problem was that the Chechens did not retreat to the south as the Russians had expected, but instead used the southern opening to bring in reinforcements and supplies. Boris Yeltsin had had enough and ordered an outright attack, despite his commanders' desire for more time. The poorly trained, ill-equipped, and badly led Russian soldiers drove into a hell. Their mechanized columns were not supported by infantry as they rolled into the city after a ten-day bombing campaign. Initially they penetrated the city rather easily. The Chechens allowed them to enter, and drive into the streets that would essentially become shooting galleries.

> Two units, the 131st Maikop Brigade and the 81st Motor Rifle Regiment, launched mounted attacks into the city. The 131st Maikop Brigade first seized the airport on the outskirts of the city unopposed, then it was ordered to continue the attack to seize the downtown railway station, its lead units arriving by early afternoon. The 81st Motor Rifle Regiment was ordered to thrust into the city from the North, down Pervomaiskaya Street, also toward the downtown area. The Russians' initial success proved illusory; soon, both Russian units would be engaged and fighting for their lives against skilled swarms of Chechen infantry, armed with automatic weapons and rocket propelled grenades (RPGs). Over the next three days, the 131st Maikop Brigade would be totally destroyed, with only a handful of survivors among its 1,000 troops, and the 81st Motor Rifle Regiment would suffer 50 percent casualties.[15]

The first unit to enter Grozny was the 1st battalion of the 131st "Maikop" brigade numbering some 1,000 soldiers. In under a month the brigade had lost 800 men, 80 percent of their original strength, "20 of 26 tanks, and 102 of 120 armored vehicles."[16] The *Spetsnaz* units, ill-informed and without supplies, surrendered to the guerrillas after several days of chaotic fighting.

The Chief of Staff for the Chechens, Aslan Maskhadov, who would be killed in combat a decade later in 2005, describes the early parts of the battle:

> The Russians did not wage war properly, they were just prepared to take enormous losses and destroy everything that got in their way. While they did not value their soldiers, we counted every man. Our first problem was to avoid retreat and engage the Russians in combat. The first "battle" was literally fought on the doorstep of the Presidential Palace in Grozny; my headquarters (HQ) was in the basement. The 131st Motorized Brigade,

the 31st Samara Tank Regiment and other units were able to enter Grozny without opposition. We had no regular army to speak of to oppose the Russians, only some small units defending various points within the city. The Russians were able to ride into Grozny on their armored personnel carriers (APCs) and tanks, without dismounted infantry support as if they were on parade. After my HQ was surrounded by Russian tanks (they filled the city) I decided that we must engage in battle. I gave the command to all our small units to immediately descend on the Palace. They did not know that I was surrounded but knew that once they did arrive, they would be engaging the enemy.

As the Chechens arrived they saw the Russian positions and immediately began the fight. The Russians did not know what hit them. They were sitting ducks; again, all lined up as if on parade around the Palace and on the square opposite the railway station.[17]

The perspective of the Russian mechanized soldiers who were being targeted by the small Chechen hunter-killer teams vividly shows the confusion and chaos that ensued when the battle proper began. This is a partial text from a Russian video, subtitled in English, of a survivor from Alpha Company, 1st Battalion, 131st Maikop Brigade:

We entered the city and didn't know even the street, we didn't know absolutely nothing. Very first time…[in the city] No notes, maps are just shit. We could not orient with them [the Chechens deliberate changed street signs as well]. We went just in random directions. Company was destroyed, at the railway station. It was just hell. Everyone tried to escape from railway as he could.[18]

Sergei Bochkarev, of Beta Company, a gunlayer for the BMP-2 Infantry Combat Vehicle, explains how he survived the fight:

We were surrounded for 24 hours. My APC was destroyed when we tried to retreat from the town. I was there for a day. I had to hide. We went on the APC with [soldiers] wounded in action. Then APC was destroyed on enemy territory. The whole A Company died there. I didn't have gun. Sniper gave me his secondary AK. I crawled near Sadovoe [Grozny district] looked around. I thought to find our control point but found only Chechen points and saw a Chechen with AK. I was frightened and pretended to be killed. I had very dirty face. He crossed nearby and didn't stop. Then I saw that he had gone. I run away from that place. But then they started to look through that [another] area and found me. I went to Sadovoe and saw our APCs. Then I was told it was Alpha company who completely died there. Chechens found me again but I managed to run from them again. And only then I found our troops. Company commander was already killed.[19]

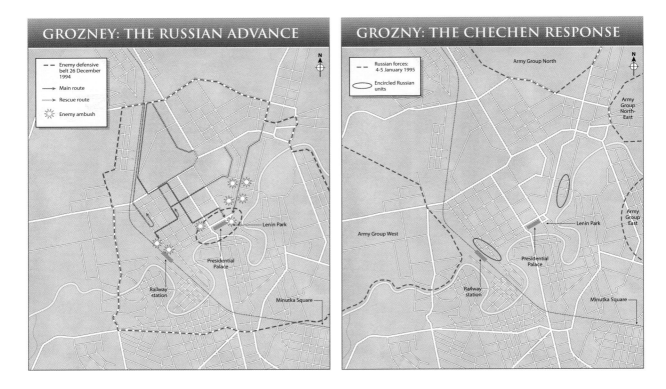

The Chechens operated in small teams or groups of 8–10 men, according to district. "Chechens knew the city and were very mobile – moving through passages, back alleys and even sewers."[20] Some had military training and were at least competent enough to learn how to handle any infantryman's portable weapons systems. They understood their own limitations, were highly dedicated to their cause, hated the enemy, and worked in loose formations capable of making independent decisions within larger tactical parameters. They easily blended in with the civilian population. The Chechens intercepted radio communication signals and used portable, low-level tactical signal devices such as cell-phones and or hand-held radios.

The Chechens also exploited the weaknesses of the Russians, who failed to coordinate their combat arms effectively. Thus the rigidity of the Russian military hierarchy and its top-heavy command structure interfered with timely on-the-ground decision-making. Instead of being properly integrated, where all assets can be brought to bear on one target or many targets if needed, the Russian structure with its compartmentalized branches and departments acted individually, or incompetently, due to lack of real-time information. Thus motorized columns went into built-up areas without infantry or close-air support.

The small 3–4-man Chechen teams, who were made up of RPG [rocket-propelled grenade] gunners, machine-gunners, and snipers, hunted like

> wolf packs searching out an isolated member of a family of deers, frequently attacked a single armoured vehicle simultaneously from several different directions, peppering it with rockets, grenades and Molotov cocktails. Areas that might be targeted included the crew hatches, the engine transmission compartment, decking and the area behind the turret. Because of the absence of significant numbers of dismounted Russian infantry, the Chechen fighters turned the streets of Grozny into death traps for Russian armoured vehicles.[21]

A favorite tactic was to allow armored columns to enter a killing zone the Chechens had prepared based on their superior knowledge of the city. The columns would enter a street and at a pre-arranged point multiple hunter-killer teams destroyed the first and the last vehicle in the advancing column. Unable to move in any direction the mechanized units were destroyed piecemeal. The antitank gunners using RPGs and Molotov cocktails would deal with the armor, while the machine-gunners and snipers attacked any personnel in the open. Russian tanks were unable to elevate their cannons high enough to engage their attackers, who would use the middle floors of a building for their attacks. As the Russian soldiers tried to disperse they often found the lower, street-level, floors sealed off – unable to hide or seek cover, they were easily killed. Hundreds of vehicles were destroyed in this manner. Lester Grau, a leading expert on Afghanistan and Chechnya, describes some of the techniques utilized by these small teams:

> [The Chechens] use multiple hunter-killer teams to engage armored vehicles from basements, ground level and from second- or third-floor positions. A problem with the RPG-7 and RPG-18 antitank weapons are the backblast, signature and time lapse between shots. The Chechens solved the time lapse problem by engaging each target simultaneously with five or six anti-tank weapons. [They] engage armored targets from the top, rear and sides.[22]

The Chechens developed another interesting new tactic. Although the city center had been more or less captured by the Russians, and the Chechens were unsure about their continued role of defense, they decided to try a new approach. Aslan Maskhadov explains this first in on-the-spot tactical development:

> It was then that we decided, against all military logic, to counter-attack. It was a first in terms of military tactics and we forced tank units to retreat. How was it done? Our soldiers did not know how to dig trenches, they considered it humiliating, but there was

A ZSU (zenitnaya samokhodnaya ustanovka or anti-aircraft self-propelled mount). Russian forces used this weapons system against Chechen hunter-killer teams, as it was able to elevate its guns up and down a multi-storied building. (DOD)

no choice – the houses were too small and fragile, they could not withstand a tank attack. So we made a line between the Sunzha and Minutka, dug trenches, and with approximately 40–50 men facing the tanks we advanced meter by meter, digging more trenches as we crawled forward until we reached the tanks and burned them. We pressed them until the tanks retreated, then we build more trenches and advanced further. It was highly unconventional trench warfare![23]

The early assault had failed miserably with many Russian units annihilated. Moscow rushed reinforcements to Grozny, including marine troops from the Pacific, Northern and Baltic Fleets, as well as more *Spetsnaz* (the other two units having previously been captured), and MDV troops. The reinforcements were sent in to shore up the demoralized units in Chechnya and reduce the possibility of open revolt, as parts of the officers' corps were on the verge of disobeying orders from the Kremlin.[24] For the next 20 days and nights, Russian artillery rounds rained down on the city, sometimes at the rate of 4,000 an hour.[25] The Russian military went back to reducing Grozny in the same way as they had previously destroyed German cities in World War II. Many Russian civilians who had not fled were victims of these assaults as well. "Russian soldiers committed random atrocities upon persons, property, and animal; looting, beatings, rape, arson, even murder – against Chechen and Russian alike – went on openly."[26] By February 1995, the sheer size of the Russian military machine pushed the Chechen guerrillas out of Grozny. The Chechens, however, would continue a guerrilla war for years to come, even recapturing Grozny in 1996. "The estimated Russian casualty count between January and May of 1995 totaled 2,805 killed, 10,319 wounded, 393 missing, and another 133 captured."[27] "Sergej

Kovalev, the Russian Duma's commissioner for human rights and President Yeltsin's adviser on human rights, who had been in Grozny during part of the fighting, estimated the number of civilian dead to 27,000. At the same time the Federal Migration Service put the number of displaced persons at 268,000. The Chechen losses are not known."[28]

THE AFTERMATH

Chechnya's first President, Dudayev, would be killed in 1996 after his location was detected by a Russian reconnaissance aircraft, which had intercepted his satellite telephone call. Some suspect the NSA (National Security Agency of the United States) was involved in the assassination by providing one of their SIGINT (Signal Intelligence) satellites to assist in the triangulation.[29] On May 12, 1997, a peace treaty was signed between the Chechens and Russians, but in 1999 the Russians again invaded the republic, under the pretext that the country had violated its agreement by supporting an insurgency in neighboring Dagestan. Russia was successful in installing a pro-Moscow government and has since engaged in assassinations of numerous Chechen insurgency leaders, including the defenders of Grozny, Shamil Basayev and Aslan Maskhadov, the third President of Chechnya.

QALA-I-JANGI, 2001

BACKGROUND

Afghanistan is a complex country, creating varied responses in the foreign troops sent there to fight since 2001. By some, the country is viewed as poverty stricken, dirty, and inhabited by a people who in many ways seem to live in the Stone Age rather than the 21st century. Yet there are many others who cannot forget Afghanistan's majestic beauty. "Trees, grass, green pastures not to mention the amazing skies and the horse-shoe shaped mountains with banks of haze on the top," is how Navy SEAL Marcus Luttrell describes his memory of the country.

There is not a single ethnicity known as "Afghan." The population is diverse, made-up of 42 percent Pashtuns; 27 percent Tajik; 9 percent Hazara; 9 percent Uzbeck; 4 percent Aimak; 3 percent Turkmen; 2 percent Baloch; and the remaining 4 percent are categorized as "Other." The overwhelming majority (80 percent) of the country are Sunni Muslims and 19 percent Shia. Half the population speaks Afghan Persian or Dari (official); Pashto (official) – 35 percent; Turkic languages (primarily Uzbek and Turkmen) – 11 percent; 30 minor languages (primarily Balochi and Pashai) – 4 percent.[1] All the peoples, however, have a shared tradition of military resistance. Because of this tradition, enemy soldiers' bones have lain strewn and bleached across its landscape since ancient times, from Alexander the Great's multi-ethnic armies, to the Mongols, Persians, Mughals, British, and the Soviets.[2] Today soldiers from the US-led coalition are fighting a guerrilla war similar to the one that destroyed the Soviet forces during their ten-year-long campaign in Afghanistan (1979–89), beginning with an ill-advised Soviet invasion in 1979.

Afghanistan was founded in 1747 under the leadership of the Ahmad Shah Durrani, a Pashtun. The country had the unfortunate strategic purpose of acting as a buffer between the imperial ambitions of the British and Russian Empires, but was finally granted independence in 1919 after World War I. A bloodless coup in 1973 was soon followed by a bloody one in 1978, which established a communist government. By 1979, the Soviet Union entered Afghanistan with 80,000–100,000 troops to bolster the less-than-popular secular regime, and to retain a buffer state between the Soviet Union and the American sphere of influence, the latter most notably in Iran, although the Iranian royal government had just been overthrown. A peace treaty between former Soviet client Egypt and Israel further added to the Soviets' sense of loss. Over a decade, the Soviet Union engaged in an unsuccessful war of attrition against Mujahideen ("the strugglers"), warriors supported by the American Central Intelligence Agency (CIA) and large numbers of foreign fighters.

Afghanistan, long a troubled country, was in even greater anarchy following the withdrawal of Soviet troops in 1989. Mujahideen warlords, tribal leaders, and the Taliban were at war with one another, each attempting to fill the vacuum created by the Soviet Union's withdrawal. By the end of the 20th century, the Taliban controlled the majority of the country and had ended corruption, opium growth, and lawlessness. Their rule, however, was draconian at best and rooted in the extreme interpretations of Sunni Islam. A loose alliance of warlords and tribes commonly known as the Northern Alliance who opposed the new Afghan Taliban government controlled less than 15 percent of northern Afghanistan by 2001. The United States, as part of her anti-drug campaign, contributed $43 million to the Taliban government for its effort in destroying the opium crop.[3] This contribution, along with negotiations by American oil companies with the new Afghan leaders, did not prevent the United States from planning their overthrow. In an effort to stabilize

US Special Forces operating with Northern Alliance fighters in northeast Afghanistan in 2001. (DOD)

US Special Forces and their Afghan allies pose for a picture during the opening stages of Operation *Enduring Freedom* in 2001. (DOD)

the country, from the American perspective that is, and to open it up for oil exploitation, the United States sought to replace the hostile Sunni Muslim Taliban with a more pro-American government comprised of factions of the Northern Alliance, who had been on the losing end of the bitter internecine struggle. By 2001, perhaps as many as two million Afghans had been killed since the invasion by the Soviets and near five million had been displaced.

On October 7, 2001, the United States launched a military offensive against Taliban-controlled Afghanistan. The official reason for the invasion was the Taliban's refusal to hand over Saudi national Osama bin Laden, the leader of a group of radicals known as al-Qaeda ("The Base"), who were training and operating out of Afghanistan. Al-Qaeda was held responsible for the commercial aircraft hijackings and subsequent suicide attacks on New York City and the Pentagon on September 11, 2001, which resulted in the deaths of 3,000 people. US-led military operations were primarily conducted by special operations soldiers and aircraft in support of Northern Alliance forces. The main goals were to topple the Taliban, capture or kill bin Laden as well as other Tier 1 (highest ranking) personnel, and to eliminate the fighting strengths of the al-Qaeda and Taliban/Afghan army militias.[4]

The US-led coalition, most notably its special forces and CIA paramilitary wings, coupled with a bombing campaign, saw the Afghan Army defeated rather quickly by the Northern Alliance confederation. The first two weeks in November 2001 witnessed the collapse of Taliban control in Mazar-e-Sharif and Konduz. Many surviving Taliban fled east and south to resume a guerrilla campaign later, but thousands surrendered to the American-led Northern Alliance and "300 were spirited away by Pakistani Intelligence services, the ISI."[5] Captured Chechen Taliban were sold to the Russians, and Uzbeck Taliban to the Uzbeck Secret Service.[6]

QALA-I-JANGI

On November 24, 2001, a group of between 300 and 600 heavily armed foreign Taliban fighters known as *Ansar* (a class of warrior famed for mobility and speed), among them Arabs, Pakistanis, Chechens, as well as other foreigners, surrendered near Mazar-e-Sharif to Afghan-Uzbek warlord and accused mass-murderer Abdul Rashid Dostum, who proclaimed their surrender a great victory.[7] The Taliban had negotiated a surrender agreement with Dostum and the foreign fighters were promised repatriation to Pakistan.[8] The actual surrender was tense, as Dostum was well known for his cruelty and barbarity toward his enemies, his treatments including castration, rape, and torture. Some time after the prison riot at Qala-i-Jangi (House of War), Dostum and the Northern Alliance were accused of having murdered over 4,000 Taliban out of more than 7,000 Taliban forces who had surrendered.[9] Sadly, the very same American forces who had supported the attacks so effectively were also accused of the same war crimes involving Dostum and the 4,000 Taliban dead at Sheberghan (Dasht-e-Leili desert) and Qala-i-Jangi by the end of 2001.[10]

Mazar-e-Sharif had recently fallen and was touted as a major victory by the coalition forces. It now housed various special forces elements, including the US

F-18 Hornet used to drop smart bombs on Qala-i-Jangi. (DOD)

Army's Combat Applications Group (CAG), commonly known as Delta Force or 1st Special Forces Operational Detachment-Delta (1st SFOD-D), plus the elite Army Rangers of the 75th Ranger Regiment, Green Berets from the 5th Special Forces Group, members of the CIA, soldiers of the 10th Mountain Division, and a handful of soldiers from the British SAS and Special Boat Service (SBS), along with seconded US Navy SEAL Stephen Bass from SEAL Team 1.[11]

The SBS/SAS team was tasked with observing the surrender of the Taliban at Mazar-e-Sharif, but were ordered to remain out of sight of the surrendering *Ansar* as their presence might disturb them.[12] Clearly this order shows the precarious situation at the surrender. The Northern Alliance even had five tanks present. Video footage shot by Arnim Stauth of German television station ARD shows American special operations personnel at the surrender. The British special operations men noted a stand-off between the heavily armed parties, but after several hours the Taliban handed over their weapons.

Damien Lewis, in his book about the British special operations forces (SOF) at Qala-i-Jangi, *Bloody Heroes*, writes that the prisoners expected to be jailed in Mazar. However, after its fall it had become a US base and so was no longer deemed suitable to imprison the foreign fighters.[13] Another speculation has it that the Taliban were to hand over their arms and then leave the area unmolested, but instead they were jailed by the Northern Alliance, so that the CIA could interrogate their possible links with al-Qaeda.[14] Alex Perry of *Time* magazine, who was present during the Taliban uprising, wrote that "Dostum wanted to make a gesture of reconciliation to help unite Afghanistan's warring tribes. Afghan members of the

Taliban would be free to return to their homes, while foreigners would be detained before being handed over to the UN."[15] But for several months the CIA and Dostum had been negotiating over what exactly to do with the foreign Taliban fighters, as the Americans were interested in gathering as much intelligence as possible, even if that meant Dostum broke his word to the foreign volunteers. It seems certain that the *Ansar* never agreed to a formal surrender, but rather to a surrender of their arms and immediate release. The British *Guardian* newspaper quotes Pashtun commander Ami Jan: "The foreigners thought that after surrendering to the Northern Alliance they would be free. They didn't think they would be put in jail."[16] Most, if not all, of the *Ansar* knew of the killing of a hundred foreign Taliban trapped at Mazar-e-Sharif by the Northern Alliance, killings that had also involved an American airstrike.[17] Many of the foreign Taliban had been on the run for several days and by the time they were told of the surrender were in poor physical shape and many of them were wounded.[18] Many felt betrayed, as they had not been immediately released upon relinquishing their arms, while others worried about Dostum's intentions – as a precaution, a few of the *Ansar* kept grenades hidden in their cloaks.

The upshot was that the Taliban fighters were certainly ill at ease during the surrender and their arrival at the 19th-century fortress of Qala-i-Jangi, with its 30m-tall and 20m-thick walls and a circumference of more than half a kilometer. The fort was divided into two halves, the northern part housing Dostum's headquarters while the southern half housed several buildings, including a makeshift prison, classroom, and armory. The main gate was on the eastern side. The fortress, once under Taliban control, now housed Dostum's prized horses plus a 500-man garrison with tanks and APCs. The British special operations personnel who had earlier witnessed the surrender had returned to their base at Mazar-e-Sharif.

AC-130 Spectre Gunship with 105mm artillery and 45mm grenade launchers, as well as other heavy small arms, used to suppress rioting Taliban prisoners. (DOD)

Upon arrival at the castle, the Taliban fighters were quartered in the southern portion of the fort. None had been throughly searched, as that would have violated the long-standing agreement of an honorable surrender, but also because it was getting dark and the prisoners needed to be transported.[19] Once inside the Qala, however, they were asked to empty their pockets for any weapons they might still have. Things did not turn out to well that first day, as the Taliban fighters were being searched:

A prisoner, waiting until Alliance commander Nadir Ali was near, suddenly produced a grenade and pulled the pin, killing himself and the commander. In a similar attack the same night, another prisoner killed himself and senior Hazara [Persian-speaking Shia Muslims in Afghanistan] commander Saeed Asad. The remaining men were led into underground cells to join scores of other captured Taliban fighters. Despite the grenade attacks, the Alliance guards were not reinforced.[20]

Hundreds of bound Taliban were herded into the makeshift prisons – the cellars of a pink classroom building – for the evening. One of Dostum's men threw a grenade into the basement, "killing and injuring several detained soldiers."[21] That night word spread among the *Ansar* that the suicide grenade attacks had been resolved and the next day "all would be released to continue their journey to Herat" for repatriation.[22]

The next day, November, 25, 2001, two CIA operatives, Mike Spann and Dave Tyson, from the clandestine Special Activities Division (SAD), arrived to interrogate the foreign Taliban prisoners. The interrogation and uprising are well documented by several television news crews, most notably by Arnim Stauth and by Dodge Billingsley of Combat Films and Research. General Dostum's soldiers manhandled the bound Taliban into an open courtyard, where they were made to sit in rows. Spann and Tyson questioned a number of the *Ansar* fighters, but received little if any information. The Americans videotaped the prisoners using a small hand-held camera. The Taliban, when in power, destroyed television sets and videos, and certainly some of them must have resented this affront to their interpretation of the Koran. Spann and Tyson are also overheard indicating that only so many cooperative Taliban would be helped, that some may die here at the fort unless they answered their questions. One of the Northern Alliance commanders said that the video crew was rude to the prisoners – clearly he meant the CIA operatives. All the insults and fear the Taliban fighters had experienced came to a head as some of them, with their arms bound behind their backs, charged the two Americans and Northern Alliance guards. In a short and furious fight, Mike Spann was overwhelmed and probably killed immediately as the guards on the parapet, dividing the northern and southern parts of the fort, sprayed the hundreds of Taliban prisoners in the courtyard with gunfire. Mike Spann was the first American killed during the invasion of Afghanistan. Dave Tyson managed to reach Dostum's headquarters 150m away from the open courtyard holding the rioting prisoners.

Having seized guns from Northern Alliance soldiers, the Taliban now engaged the Northern Alliance in a heated firefight, as Tyson stumbled upon Arnim Stauth. Fearing for his life, Stauth allowed Tyson to use his satellite telephone to contact the US Embassy in Tashkent. There was a great deal of confusion at Qala-i-Jangi at this time, but Tyson was clear and concise in his situation report. It was a relatively short conversation, but the essence is that although possibly hundreds of Taliban were dead, they controlled the southern part of the fort and the Northern Alliance the northern part. He referenced the possible death of Mike Spann, though he did not mention him by name. Finally, he reiterated that there should no aerial attacks on the fort because of the proximity of Dostum's guards.

As Tyson and the German news crew, along with wounded guards, beat a hasty retreat across an open area and down one of the walls, the constant hail of bullets forced the Taliban to hunker down and around the buildings, where they discovered the armory. Here the foreign Taliban manage to re-arm themselves with assault rifles, RPG launchers, and even a mortar. Dostum's men reinforced the parapet and eventually drove a T-55 tank up onto it to pound the Taliban positions with heavy gun rounds.

Meanwhile, back at the special operations headquarters in Mazar, word came down that there had been some kind of fight at Qala-i-Jangi and that an American was missing. According to Damien Lewis, quoting a SBS soldier, the American special forces "were charging around the base like headless chickens," whereas the SBS took their time to make sure they had everything they needed for the impending relief mission.[23] The briefing at Mazar was conducted by a CIA agent.

By 1400hrs, Lewis continues, a mixed special operations team composed of 8 SBS, 10 US 5th Group Green Berets, as well as 50–100 Northern Alliance soldiers were fighting 600 battle-hardened insurgents.[24] Certainly this was not the case. There can be little doubt that ultimately a small number of special operations soldiers, reinforced by a squad of infantrymen from the 10th Mountain Division, and Northern Alliance soldiers were involved in a firefight, but clearly they were not battling 600 insurgents as most accounts mention only 300 prisoners. By the time the SBS/special forces team reached Qala-i-Jangi, their only function was to prevent the Taliban from escaping the fortress. Furthermore, the *Ansar* were mostly exhausted and wounded from having been on the run for days. Many, while still bound and seated on the courtyard ground, had been killed by the guards immediately following the uprising that killed Spann and a number of Dostum's men. Others were still bound and underground in the makeshift prison. CIA operative Tyson mentioned hundreds dead during his report, and even if that number was a guess, we can safely assume that only several dozen Taliban were fighting in the early part of the prison riot. An investigation revealed that "the prisoners inside were armed only with thirty guns, two anti-tank guns, and two grenade launchers."[25] How many managed to escape is unknown, but certainly some did as Irish filmmaker Jamie Doran in *The Convoy of Death* documents Dostum threatening local village elders with looting, rape, and death if they did not reveal information about the escaped *Ansar*.

Steven Perry describes the dramatic arrival of the SOF team:

> At 2 p.m. two minivans and a pair of open-sided white Land Rovers mounted with machine guns pulled up outside the fortress gates. From the minivans jumped nine American special-operations men wearing wraparound sunglasses and baseball caps and carrying snub-nosed M-4 automatic rifles. The Land Rovers disgorged six British SAS soldiers armed with M-16s and dressed in jeans, sweaters, Afghan scarves and pakuls, the distinctive woolen hats of the Afghan mujahedin. The Americans and British quickly convened a conference with the Alliance leaders. "I want satcom [satellite communications] and JDAMS [guided munitions]," said the American commander. "Tell them there will be six or seven buildings in a line in the southwest half. If they can hit that, then that would kill a whole lot of these motherf******."[26]

The firefight in the early stages must have been intense and the coalition forces called in eight or nine airstrikes by F-18 Hornets to achieve tactical superiority. The majority of the JDAM (Joint Direct Attack Munition) smart bombs missed their targets, though the concussion of the ordnance must have been shocking for anyone near the explosion. And the bombing did achieve the coalition forces' aim, as it drove the Taliban into the building and underground. Some time during the bomb runs, Dave Tyson, along with the German news crew escaped, Qala-i-Jangi.[27]

The special operations soldiers still had no idea as to the whereabouts of CIA agent Spann. The SBS thought both Spann and Tyson had been captured, although Tyson had managed to escape earlier. As night was fast approaching, Navy SEAL Bass who was on secondment to the SBS, made a daring raid into the southern courtyard to locate his missing American comrades. He was subsequently awarded the Navy Cross for his actions during that evening:

> He was forced to walk through an active anti-personnel minefield in order to gain entry to the fortress. After establishing the possible location of both American citizens, under heavy fire and without concern for his own safety, he made two

Major Mark Mitchell and unidentified Green Beret during a firefight, observing enemy positions. (DOD)

attempts to rescue the uninjured citizen by crawling toward the fortress interior to reach him. Forced to withdraw due to large volumes of fire falling on his position, he was undeterred. After reporting his efforts to the remaining members of the rescue team, they left and attempted to locate the missing citizen on the outside of the fortress. As darkness began to fall, no attempt was made to locate the other injured American citizen. Chief Petty Officer Bass then took matters into his own hands. Without regard for his own personal safety, he moved forward another 300–400 meters into the heart of the fortress by himself under constant enemy fire in an attempt to locate the injured citizen. Running low on ammunition, he utilized weapons from deceased Afghans to continue his rescue attempt.[28]

Upon locating Spann and realizing he was dead, Bass finally withdrew from the fortress.

That night the special forces personnel drove back to their headquarters. On the second day they were joined by another dozen men, including a squad of eight from the 10th Mountain Division. The first day was by far the most difficult and pressing, and the coalition forces had done well. The Taliban were held in place, except for a few who had managed to escape, and they had mostly been forced underground. The second day was going to be about rooting out entrenched enemy positions. And to accomplish this they needed to break the will of the prisoners. Another airstrike was called in by the American Close Air Support (CAS) team in the form of a 2,000lb JDAM. The previous day's CAS missions had all dropped the much smaller 500lb smart bombs. The idea behind this new bomb run was to simply to obliterate the pink building. Human error, however, led to a disaster. The American bomb landed directly on the Northern Alliance and SOF command post. Dust, dirt, debris, and shrapnel rose hundreds of feet into the air. The T-55 tank was flipped on its back, killing the crew and injuring virtually everyone in the vicinity. Dozens of Alliance and SOF soldiers staggered out of the fort, leaving behind a destroyed tower and a hole in the wall the size of a large "swimming pool."[29] Five American and four British troops were injured. Dostum's men suffered several killed and dozens wounded. Their precise number of casualties is not known. The Taliban, nevertheless, must have been shaken to the core by the explosion.

Later on that evening, two slow-moving AC-130 gunships designated GRIM 11 and GRIM 14 reigned death and destruction on the southern portion of Qala-i-Jangi. During that time, an ammunition dump was hit, followed by an explosion so powerful that the doors to a house where English journalist Steven Perry was staying blew open. He was 11km away. One cannot imagine the pounding the Taliban took during those first days of their uprising.

The early morning hours of November 27 revealed some of the destruction, but not to the extent one would have expected given the preceding bombardments. Taliban resistance had receded, but the survivors, starved and shell-shocked, were still in no mood for surrender. Slowly and surely, the individual fighters of General Dostum regained possession of the southern area of the fort. One incident detailing the brutality of what should be considered urban warfare was described by Perry:

> In a basement under one pock-marked house, five Taliban fighters were trapped alive. Grenades were thrown in the tiny windows and AK-47s fired after them. With Alliance soldiers too afraid to enter the stables, a tank was brought in, crushing bodies under its tracks before firing five rounds into the block. In a ditch on the main parade ground, a young Taliban fighter, lying sprawled on his side, was still breathing. An Alliance soldier dropped a rock on his head. A few yards away lay a bloodied prayer book.[30]

During these actions, supposedly mopping-up operations, a handful of Taliban laid down suppressive fire and charged at the Alliance soldiers, driving them out of the fort momentarily. Eventually, though, they too were killed. Mike Spann's body was recovered by coalition special operations personnel and was found beneath the body of a dead Taliban fighter, who was supposedly booby-trapped with a grenade.

On Wednesday November 28, General Dostum arrived at Qala-i-Jangi and was "in a pissed off mood,"[31] due to the loss of his men, the outbreak at Qala, and the destruction of his headquarters. Last-minute attempts to achieve a truce were made, perhaps because of the large media presence, but they resulted in a continued stalemate. Over the next two days, sporadic gunfire echoed around the fort. Dostum's men used small arms, grenades, and RPGs in various attempts to dislodge the remaining foreign Taliban. The *Ansar* fought back with whatever weapons they had left. Dostum's troops responded by pouring oil into the basement of the pink building, then throwing grenades in to ignite it. Smoke rose to the skies, but to no avail – the Taliban did not surrender, even though Dostum's men fired RPGs down into the main basement, killing many of those who were trying to escape the fire and smoke.[32] Finally, underground irrigation systems were redirected and filled the basement of the pink building with freezing cold water, killing most of the remaining prisoners.

Nearly 20 hours later, on December 1, 2001 at 1100hrs, 86 *Ansar* surrendered out of a force of 300–600, the exact figures remain unknown. One of them was the white American John Paul Walker Lindh, who had joined the Taliban a week before September 11, 2001, in Afghanistan, joining them on their crusade to rid the world of the Northern Alliance. Many of the foreign Taliban of the Afghan Army were sent to America's Camp X-Ray at Guantanamo Bay, Cuba. Walker Lindh, after being stripped naked, blindfolded, taped to a gurney, and photographed, received a 20-year prison sentence, which he is currently serving in the United States. The other American, Yaser Esam Hamdi, born in the United States to Saudi parents, was shipped to Guantanamo, then a federal prison, and ultimately stripped of his citizenship and released into the custody of Saudi Arabia.[33] General Dostum lost approximately 45 soldiers killed and 205 wounded.[34] One of the survivors of the foreign volunteers, an Uzbeck called Jabar, of the Taliban Afghan Army, when interviewed in a *New York Times* article

Major Mark Mitchell is shown receiving a Distinguished Service Cross for his leadership US and British Special Forces during the early stages of the riot of foreign Taliban fighters at Qala-i-Jangi. (DOD)

said that the fighters had survived the bombings by hiding in ditches and trenches out in the open, and then moved into the deep basement of the classroom building to take cover from the Northern Alliance gun and tank fire. But two days ago the Northern Alliance poured diesel fuel into the underground rooms and set fire to it. "The smoke was so bad, you could not breath," he said. "And the rocket explosions were really bad. We survived that but then it turned cold and they poured the water in, and none of our weapons worked."[35]

American special force major Mark Mitchell, who was in overall command of the coalition forces, was awarded the Distinguished Service Cross (DSC) the first issued since the Vietnam War.[36] The US Army Public Affairs Office released the following statement along with the citation:

Mitchell, a Special Forces officer, was awarded [the DSC] for leading a team of 16 American and British soldiers into combat operations against about 500 Taliban and al Qaeda trained fighters who had taken over a fortress near Mazar-e-Sharif, Afghanistan, where they had been imprisoned. Mitchell's actions freed an American held in Qala-I-Jangi Fortress by the rioting prisoners and ensured the posthumous repatriation of another American.[37]

CONCLUSION

War has evolved in a great many aspects over the millennia of human conflict but ultimately it still depends on basic age-old tangible elements such as holding onto terrain, killing people, and forcing one's will onto another. Most annihilations have occurred after one side lost its will or its firepower. Panic often leads up to the collapse. The constant, and changing, elements of warfare can be traced through the battles of annihilation gathered in this book. Comparing the battles collected in this book brings up many similarities through history: the role of unfamiliar terrain, technology, inadequate planning, political will, and communications are all evident across many of the battles, but the most crucial theme that runs through almost all the battles is the importance of leadership.

There are leaders who put in a great deal of planning before the battle to ensure victory, going as far as manipulating the landscape to aid their men, for example Arminius' obstacles in the Teutoburg Forest, although conversely, the preparations made by the Teutonic Knights at Tannenburg, digging pits in front of his army, failed to make any difference to the outcome. Saladin used his knowledge of the terrain to his advantage, making his army wait for their fight, allowing them to harass the enemy but not close battle until the desert terrain and stifling heat had done the hard work for him. He then demoralized his enemy further using fire to exacerbate their thirst – as the Goths did at Adrianople, and the Mexicans at Camerone – before finally picking off the desperate and scattered crusaders.

Equally, several of the battles can be framed as having been lost due to the decisions and battle actions of the vanquished leader. Nicephorus' vanity and his wish to prove himself took his army into a battle they never needed to fight, as they had already taken the capital of the Bulgars. Whether due to an overly trusting nature, or blindness to spot the obvious, Varus' failure to consider that the German tribes might again be acting nefariously towards the Romans despite specific warnings meant that he took a small army, encumbered with wagons and camp followers through a dense, unfamiliar forest, making themselves easy prey to the German warriors. Jugdulluck was another completely avoidable battle, Elphinstone himself realized his inability to lead. He had been advised many times to take one of several other options open to him, but had failed to act. Even the tragic march to Jalalabad could have been less disastrous if he had at any point stepped up to the challenge. Little Big Horn is famous mainly due to the personality of Custer, and without his personality the battle would not have taken place as it did, or may indeed never had happened.

Given the prominence of leadership in these battles of annihilation, it is understandable that the most significant change in the waging of these, and all battles, through time leadership, not, as one might predict, technology, although most often the army equipped with superior technology will defeat that with outdated technology, though the battle of Isandlwana is an obvious exemption to this rule. The greatest difference between the battles of Cannae or Hattin and those of the 21st century is the removal of leadership from the battlefield – no longer does the senior combat leader feel the sweat, stench, fear, exhilaration, exhaustion or a myriad of other things. No longer can they judge whether their men will stand or run, and watch the enemy make their moves. Instead, cool, air-conditioned buildings house senior leaders making incomplete decisions. In almost all the earlier battles covered in the book, commanders were either killed or captured. The modern battles included here, in which the commanders were not killed or captured, illustrate the trend in modern times to direct and wage war from a distance, even a few earlier ones, like the battle of Jena-Auerstädt, illustrate the problems caused by a commander like Hohenlohe, out of touch with events on the battlefield. Prior to the age of industrialization, military, and political leaders often led or were in close proximity to battles. At Cannae, for example, a multitude of high-ranking Roman politicians and military leaders were killed. At Pliska, the death of Nicephorus caused the total disintegration of the army, leading to their annihilation. At Jena, the death of good combat officers left units under dubious leadership, thereby almost guaranteeing their defeat.

The trend for senior leaders on the battlefield began to disappear in the late 19th and early 20th century, when larger forces were used and with them larger headquarters, which in turn required more officers and soldiers to staff. Those in a position of power can now participate in all the profit and glory without risking life or limb.

In modern America, the military has bred an officer corps unwilling and unable to share the burden of daily combat operations, preferring the pen to the sword. Few senior officers are ever in genuine combat situations. Statistics show that very few

Count Alfred Graf von Schlieffen (1833–1913). He was one of the principal men responsible in the reexamination of the battle of Cannae, in order to help formulate military strategic operations. (Author's Collection)

men of the rank of lieutenant colonel or higher have been killed or wounded in action since World War II, and most of those were not participating in actual combat operations. The actual delivery of combat operations is left to the junior ranks. Today's officer corps does not fear failure as Hannibal or Scipio did, nor does its senior leadership see the campaigns through to their conclusion, often rotating after their stint of commanding for a year. Today's military and political leadership are not held accountable, but retire in the grand manner befitting top executives who are equally unaccountable for their actions.[1] However, the US Defense Secretary's request for the resignation of the top commander in Afghanistan only 11 months into his post may perhaps signal a return to more accountability for military leaders.[2] Still, it seems that too often military officers are more comfortable sitting behind their desks or standing in front of cameras than crouching behind walls leading their men in combat operations.

Modern military thinkers and reformists have enacted certain rules to combat inaccurate decision-making from the rear, and thus the commander on the ground in the actual fight has precedence in decision-making. But reported incidents in Afghanistan, in which desperate pleading by fighting men for reinforcements have been ignored, show that this is still a flawed system, because requests from the commander on the ground do not necessarily get approved nor is their evaluation of the situation necessarily respected.

This change in leadership style may well contribute to the infrequency of modern battles of annihilation. Yet even the modern battles of annihilation included in this book were not conclusive in terms of ending the overall conflict. Grozny's Chechens were able to withdraw into the welcoming arms of her mountainous regions, while the white Rhodesians' victory during Operation *Dingo* was marred by the number of civilians involved and a hostile media. These examples show how modern war, particularly those involving irregular or guerrilla forces does not create opportunities for decisive encounters or conclusive battles: conventional forces and guerrillas in

Iraq and Afghanistan can simply strip off their uniforms, blend in with local citizens and hide in cities. This isn't just a modern phenomenon; much of the planning for the battles of Little Big Horn and Isandlwana was to try and ensure that the enemy could be brought to battle and forced to fight, but it is perhaps now more pronounced given the speed of modern transport and communications. The battle of Qala-i-Jangi only happened because the Taliban forces involved could not disperse to fight another day, but were instead cornered, left with limited options. Also, in modern warfare the smaller but extremely mobile armies move at such speeds that they outpace enemy forces and don't have enough men on the ground to kill or capture enemy combatants.

Though the aftermath of these battles varies immensely, the reaction is almost always decisive, and extreme. This is not to say that other battles do not also have a decisive outcome, but that perhaps battles of annihilation have particularly marked results. However, as noted in the introduction, the result is not always what might be expected when reading an account of the battle out of context. There are times when vanquishing the enemy does completely defeat the enemy's will and win the war, Zama falls into this category. However, other battles don't have that effect, starting with Cannae, which didn't win the war for Hannibal. Perhaps this is because the annihilation of an army is such a shocking event that it cannot fail to stir powerful emotions, even when the people of a country are jaded through years of exposure to warfare and death. There are several examples of the vanquished winning the war, or where battles might end one round of hostilities quite conclusively, but the vanquished country then came back for revenge in a new round of battles and killing.

In the midst of the bloodshed and hatred of the Crusades, the wiping out of the Crusader army at Hattin was said to be so shocking the Pope died of grief. In fact he died before news of the event could have reached him, but it says something about the reaction of Christian Europe, as does the speed with which a new crusade was planned and funded, even though it was delayed some years in actually setting out. After brokering a deal with the Afghans in Kabul in 1841, which later turned out to be meaningless, the British envoy to Afghanistan wrote: "The terms I secured were the best obtainable, and the destruction of fifteen thousand human beings would little have benefited our country, whilst our government would have been almost compelled to avenge our fate at whatever cost."[3] On this, if not on any other point, Sir William Hay Macnaghten was spot on. After the awful events of the retreat from Kabul became known, the British raised a huge "Army of Retribution," which defeated every Afghan army it met the following year. The destruction of forces at Little Big Horn and Isandlwana also prompted retribution on a massive scale. After Little Big Horn, the US government's treatment of Native American tribes moved to a whole new level, and the Zulu victory at Isandlwana only hastened the end of the Zulu kingdom as the British government rushed seven regiments of reinforcements to Natal to aid the re-invasion later the same year.

Apart from prompting immediate, or near immediate action against the victor, battles of annihilation have often had longer-term effects on both participants, but mainly on the vanquished army. As Professor Herwig argues, "defeat drives reform," and many battles have caused a military force to stop and examine what they were doing.[4] In undertaking reform, many military commanders and strategists have then turned back to previous decisive battles, many of them battles of annihilation, and the king of all battles of annihilation, Cannae, for inspiration. Cannae became an archetype for subsequent commanders, the definitive battle, that if its tactics were duplicated, might win an entire war. From Frederick the Great in the 18th century, to Norman Scharwzkopf, the commander of the coalition forces in the Gulf War, Cannae has been the battle to emulate.

Probably the best example of a battle that caused huge reform in an army is the battle of Jena-Auerstädt. On the surface, the battle of Jena-Auerstädt was a disaster for the Prussian Army, their tactics were out of date, their generals were older than the tactics, and training was also behind the times. When viewed as part of the Napoleonic Wars as a whole, it was exactly what the Prussians needed. Had the Prussian Army not been exposed as a military museum piece, it could never have been reformed into one of the most feared military machines of the later 19th and early 20th centuries. Conversely, it bolstered Napoleon's arrogance even further, planting the seeds for his eventual downfall.

As mentioned, three famous Prussian military figures were present at Jena, and over the next few years, Scharnhorst, Gneisenau and Clausewitz were at the forefront of change in Prussia, as Prussian military infrastructure was reinvented. Rigorous analysis and discipline led the wave of successive victories against the French beginning with the Wars of Liberation from 1813–14.

The unification of Germany in 1871 under the partnership of Chancellor Otto von Bismarck and Chief of Staff Helmuth Graf von Moltke came about due to a string of superlative Prussian victories over Denmark, Austria, and France, possibly due to the work of Prussian generals and military theorists, notably Carl von Clausewitz. As the 19th century ended, Prussian arms were heralded worldwide, but the position of Germany in the center of Europe meant that the country had to prepare for a war on two fronts. The German officer corps realized that in such a situation their armies would be outnumbered, and would have to fight a lightning campaign or die Vernichtungsschlacht ("battle of annihilation") against France before the vast hordes of the Russian armies could be unleashed against them.

Romanticized depictions
of comrades facing
imminent death have
created societies that
worship the cult of
militarism and war.
(Anne S.K. Brown Military
Collection, Brown
University Library)

Count Alfred von Schlieffen, chief of the German General Staff, believed that
the key to such a victory could be found in the strategies of Cannae, as had been
written by notable German historian Hans Delbrück.[5] The historical section of the
General Staff was tasked with producing "a set of 'Cannae Studies' that would
demonstrate that the principle of double envelopment practiced by Hannibal at
Cannae was the master key to victory in battle."[6]

When World War I erupted in 1914, the Schlieffen Plan, as it was known, based on the envelopment principle of the battle of Cannae, deteriorated rapidly into a quagmire of static trench warfare. The introduction by German general Baron Hugo von Freytag-Loringhaven in an interwar edition of Schlieffen's Cannae explains:

> Before the war we all could only surmise their actions on the ground and in the air. Reconnaissance, Victory, and Pursuit, the paving of the way for a Cannae, as well as the penetration, all evinced more than ever before, and in a much higher degree, that they depended on the effect of the weapons of the enemy. This explains partly why, except for Tannenberg [1914, with nearly 160,000 Russians killed out of 400,000], a real Cannae did not occur in the World War. That one did not occur in the west at the beginning of the war is the fault, in the first instance, of the Supreme Command. Indeed it was the Schlieffen plan on which our operations were based, yet in their actual execution it was departed from. His constant exhortation to make the right army flank as strong as possible was not heeded.[7]

Although the Germans were able to defeat the Russians, the stalemate on the Western Front proved to be their eventual undoing, at the cost of nearly 38 million casualties for all combatant countries.[8]

In the aftermath of World War I, military professionals began to understand more completely the impact of the expanded battlefield where, as Matheny explains, "armies were so large it was impossible for tactics alone to crush the enemy and achieve strategic aims. On the field of Waterloo (1815) some 140,000 men faced each other. By 1914 a combined total of 3.3 million men struggled in the Battle of the Frontiers in France."[9] Matheny goes on to note that "The Germans were among the first to grasp the need for a new concept to link national strategy with tactics." Freytag-Loringhaven stated:

> The annihilation doctrine has not died in the German Army. Count Schlieffen was the one best fitted to further Moltke's art of war. He drew the most pertinent deductions from the constant growth of armies and the enlarged conditions of the present. The fear of mass armies we have overcome, thanks to him, and in the handling of the weapons we have shown ourselves to the last superior to our opponents.[10]

The German Army did carry out reforms between the wars, and in the opening stages of World War II, they did, with incredible speed, outflank and destroy their opposition.[11] But, as Carl von Clausewitz argued, "in war the result is never final."[12] Thus it was that the army that introduced the world to the concept of Blitzkrieg (lightning war), nevertheless lost the war.

As is aptly demonstrated by the effort put into learning the lessons of Cannae, the historian or scholar can easily fall into the trap of looking for systems in battles – attempting to find a mechanism, a scientific approach, or a formula to win battles decisively. Nothing like that exists. It defies the very essence, the intrinsic nature of warfare – human interaction. As Steven Perry sums up when discussing the experience of 21st-century combat:

> …a lot of war eventually has to be dirty hand-to-hand combat. You can't just press a button looking at a radar and think it's problem over. You've got to get down there and kill people. You've got to get down there and look them in the eye as you are killing them. [War is] still as base and as brutal as it's ever been. Nothing is clean. It's coordinated and courageous murder.[13]

Wars are not waged by machines; even in today's high-technology leveraged warfighting, people make decisions, not machines. A pilot may drop a smart bomb, as at Qala-i-Janghi, but human error or even technical glitches caused friendly casualties. War brings out all human emotions and that range, which defines a human being, is not quantifiable. One cannot predict reactions. There are of course certain similarities. Soldiers tire, are hungry, are frightened, are courageous, are murderous, are kind, are ruthless, are honest, are liars … but the range of human emotions and physical restrictions prevents predictability. The greatest of all philosophers of war, Carl von Clausewitz, realized that intangible element in warfare and articulated the "friction" in war, the difference between absolute or total and real war, the special unique quality of an individual and the will of people to achieve certain goals. Systems, simulations, science, and studies are of course all very valuable, but not defining in and by themselves. War is uncontrollable once unleashed.

NOTES

INTRODUCTION

1. Chris Cocks, *Fireforce: One Man's War in the Rhodesian Light Infantry* (Boulder, Paladin Press, 2007), p.112.
2. Yozan D. Mosig and Imene Belhassen, "Revision and Reconstruction in the Punic Wars: Cannae Revisited," *The International Journal of the Humanities*, Vol. 4, No. 2 (2006), pp.4–5.

CANNAE

1. Nigel Bagnall, *The Punic Wars 264–146 BC* (Oxford, Osprey Publishing, 2002), p.48.
2. Polybius, *The Rise of the Roman Empire*, trans. Ian Scott-Kilvert (New York, Penguin Books, 1979), 3.107.5.
3. Mark Healy, *Cannae 216 BC* (Oxford, Osprey Publishing, 1994), p.73.
4. Ibid, p.73.
5. Peter Connolly, *Greece and Rome at War* (London, Macdonald Phoebus Limited, 1981), p.188; J. F. Lazenby, *Hannibal's War: A Military History of the Second Punic War* (Norman: University of Oklahoma Press, 1998), pp.79–81.
6. Polybius, 3.107.
7. Mosig and Belhassen, "Cannae Revisited," pp.4–5.
8. Polybius, 3.106.4.
9. Nic Fields, *The Roman Army in the Punic Wars 264–146 BC* (Oxford, Osprey Publishing, 2007), p.41.
10. Celts and Gauls are considered the same for the purposes of discussion, although Gaul usually means continental Celts; see Victor Davis Hanson, *Carnage and Culture* (New York, Doubleday, 2001), p.100.
11. Polybius, 3.114.3.
12. Ibid, 3.114.4.
13. Gregory Daly, *Cannae: The Experience of Battle in the Second Punic War* (London, Routledge, 2002), p.91.
14. Peter Connolly, *Hannibal and the Enemies of Rome* (London, Macdonald Educational, 1978), p.40.
15. Ibid.
16. Daly, *Cannae*, p.91.
17. Ibid, p.89.
18. Ibid, p.89.
19. Connolly, *Greece and Rome at War*, p.76.
20. Livy, *The War with Hannibal Books XXI–XXX of The History of Rome from its Foundation*, trans. by Aubrey De Selincourt (New York, Penguin Books, 1978), 22.48, p.147.
21. Polybius, 3.114.4.
22. Hanson, *Carnage and Culture*, p.99.
23. Nic Fields, email Sept 8, 2008.
24. Connolly, *Hannibal*, p.40. Livy does state that the mercenaries were grumbling over pay, but this detail has in general been dismissed.
25. Adrian Goldsworthy, *Cannae: Hannibal's Greatest Victory* (London, Phoenix, 2007), p.80.

26. Polybius, 3.110.3.

27. Ibid, 3.110.7.

28. Ibid, 3.110.9.

29. Ibid, 3.110.13–14.

30. Connolly, *Greece and Rome at War*, p.184.

31. Polybius, 3.112.9.

32. Ibid, 3.111

33. Paullus would have been familiar with Xenophon's *Anabasis*, which narrated how the Athenian led his 10,000 Greek mercenaries as well as camp followers across Persian lands in retreat in 400 BC. The book detailed how Xenophon often had to disengage from superior enemy forces in various terrains, which he did successfully despite the more numerous light armed cavalry and infantry troops of the pursuing enemy.

34. Polybius, 3.112.6.

35. Ibid, 3.113.1–2.

36. Fields, *The Roman Army,* p.37.

37. Polybius, 3.113.4.

38. Connolly, *Greece and Rome at War*, p.184.

39. Daly, *Cannae*, p.57.

40. Goldsworthy, *Cannae*, p.99; Lazenby, *Hannibal's War*, pp.79–80.

41. Lazenby, *Hannibal's War*, p.80.

42. Connolly, *Greece and Rome at War*, pp.184–87.

43. Mosig and Belhassen, "Cannae Revisited," p.10.

44. Fields, *The Roman Army*, p.49.

45. Goldsworthy, *Cannae*, p.76.

46. Lazenby, *Hannibal's War*, p.80.

47. Mosig and Belhassen, "Cannae Revisited," p.9.

48. Daly, *Cannae*, p.146.

49. Polybius, 3.113.7–11.

50. Ibid, 3.114.5.

52. Connolly, *Greece and Rome at War*, pp.184–87.

52. Polybius, 3.114.5.

53. Lazenby, *Hannibal's War*, p.77.

54. Polybius, 3.113.6–8.

55. Connolly, *Greece and Rome at War*, p.186.

56. Daly, *Cannae*, pp.108–9.

57. Lazenby, *Hannibal's War*, p.81.

58. Ibid, p.82.

59. Hans Delbrück, *Warfare in Antiquity: History of the Art of War*, trans. by Walter J. Renfroe, Jr. (Lincoln, University of Nebraska Press, 1990), pp.316, 322.

60. Goldsworthy, *Roman Warfare* (London: Cassel and Co., 2002), pp.74–75 and *Cannae*, pp.88–89.

61. Nic Fields proposes that they were formed in blocks as swordsmen, based on Polybius' text, email Sept 14, 2008

62. Lazenby, *Hannibal's War*, pp.81-82.

63. Ibid, pp.80–82.

64. Nic Fields, email Sept 11, 2008.

65. Polybius, 3.115.8.

66. Ibid, 3.115.4.

67. Ibid, 3.115.

68. Ibid, 3.115.6.

69. Ibid, 3115.6–7.

70. Mosig and Belhassen, "Cannae Revisited," p.11.

71. Delbrück, *Warfare in Antiquity*, p. 317.

72. Polybius, 3.115.9–10.

73. Ibid, 3.116.3.

74. Ibid, 3.115.5-7.

75. Lazenby, *Hannibal's War*, p.83.

76. F. W. Walbank, *A Historical Commentary on Polybius* (Oxford, Oxford University Press, 1970), p.447.

77. Theodore Ayrault Dodge, *Hannibal: A History of the Art of War Among the Carthaginians and Romans Down to the Battle of Pydna, 168 BC, With a Detailed Account of the Second Punic War*, Vol. 2 (London, Greenhill Books, 1993), pp.368, 373.

78. Lazenby, *Hannibal's War*, p.83.

79. Polybius, 3.115.11.

80. Ibid, 3.116.7.

81. Ibid, 3.116.10–11.

82. Ibid, 3.116.

83. Ibid, 3.116.

84. Lazenby, *Hannibal's War*, p.84.

85. Mosig and Belhassen, "Cannae Revisited," p.13.

86. Polybius, 3.117.

ZAMA

1. Lazenby, *Hannibal's War*, p.218.
2. Delbrück, *Warfare in Antiquity,* pp.372–73.
3. Mosig and Belhassen, "Revision and Reconstruction in the Second Punic War: Zama – Whose Victory," *International Journal of the Humanities*, Vol. 5, No. 9 (2007), p.3.
4. Ibid, p.3.
5. Livy, 30.28.4. http://mcadams.posc.mu.edu/txt/ah/Livy/Livy30.html
6. Lazenby, *Hannibal's War*, p.210.
7. Ibid, p.203.
8. Ibid, p.221.
9. Livy, 29.25.1–3.
10. Lazenby, *Hannibal's War*, p.203.
11. Mosig and Belhassen, "Zama," p.2.
12. Polybius, 15.4.4–5.
13. Lazenby, *Hannibal's War*, p.215.
14. Polybius, 15.3.5–7.
15. Ibid, 15.5.11.
16. Ibid, 15.5.5–11.
17. Ibid, 15.6.3.
18. Ibid, 15.7.
19. Ibid, 15.8.
20. Ibid, 15.8.
21. Mosig and Belhassen, "Zama," p.4.
22. Polybius, 3.9.7–10.
23. B. H. Liddell Hart, *Scipio Africanus: Greater Than Napoleon* (London, Greenhill Books, 1992), p.175.
24. Polybius, 18.30.6–11.
25. John Warry, *Warfare in the Classical World* (New York, St Martin's Press, 1980), p.111.
26. J. E. Lendon, *Soldiers and and Ghosts* (New Haven, Yale University Press, 2005), p.181. See Hans van Wees, *Greek Warfare: Myths and Realities* (London, Gerald Duckworth & Co., 2004) for an interpretation of ancient warfare based on individual combat rather than a uniform engagement.
27. Polybius, 15.9.7.
28. Lazenby writes that 40 *velites* were attached per maniple in *Hannibal's War*, p.221.
29. Polybius, 15.11.2–4.
30. Delbrück, *Warfare in Antiquity*, p.372.
31. For a more detailed look at the use of elephants in ancient warfare, see Konstantin Nossov, *War Elephants* (Oxford, Osprey Publishing, 2008). For an account of the elephants crossing the alps, see Sir Gavin de Beer, *Alps and Elephants: Hannibal's March* (New York, E. P. Dutton & Company, 1956), or John Prevas, *Hannibal Crosses the Alps: The Enigma Re-Examined* (New York, Sarpedon, 1998).
32. F. E. Adcock, *The Greek and Macedonian Art of War* (Berkeley, University of California Press, 1957), pp.55–56.
33. Delbrück, *Warfare in Antiquity*, p.371.
34. Mosig and Belhassen, "Zama," p.4.
35. Polybius, 15.11.1.
36. Liddell Hart, *Scipio Africanus*, p.177.
37. Fields, *The Roman Army in the Punic Wars*, p.84.
38. Ibid, p.81.
39. Delbrück, *Warfare in Antiquity*, p.370.
40. Polybius, 15.10.2–4.
41. Ibid, 15.11.4–12.
42. Mosig and Belhassen, "Zama," p.4.
43. Polybius, 15.12.3–5.
44. Mosig and Belhassen, "Zama," p.4. See also Delbrück, *Warfare in Antiquity*, p.372.
45. Polybius, 15.12.5–7.
46. Delbrück, *Warfare in Antiquity*, p.373.
47. Lazenby, *Hannibal's War*, p.223 believes the correct translation to say: "...since the antagonists did not use spears but swords."
48. Polybius, 15.12.8–9; 15.13.1–5.
49. Ibid,, 15.13.5–9.
50. Mosig and Belhassen, "Zama," p.5.
51. Polybius, 15.13.7–8
52. Liddell Hart, *Scipio Africanus*, p.181.
53. Lazenby, *Hannibal's War*, p.224.
54. Polybius, 15.14.1–9.
55. Mosig and Belhassen, "Zama," p.5.

56. Polybius, 15.14.7–9.
57. Steven James, *Zama: The Infantry Battle Revisited* (June 2005), http://www.fenrir.dk/history/index.php?title=Zama:_The_Infantry_Battle_Revisited
58. Lazenby, *Hannibal's War*, p.225.

THE TEUTOBURG FOREST

1. For an excellent reconstruction (in German) of the battle see Dr. G. Rosenfeldt, *Die Varusschlacht: Versuch einer Rekonstruktion der Ereignisse Neufassung* (Hamburg, 2006), http://www.harald-rosenfeldt.de/grosenfeldt/Home.html
2. Peter S. Wells, *The Battle That Stopped Rome: Emperor Augustus, Arminius, and the Slaughter of the Legions in the Teutoburg Forest* (New York, Norton & Company, 2003), pp.155–56.
3. Ibid, pp.162–63 and Adrian Murdoch, *Rome's Greatest Defeat: Massacre in the Teutoburg Forest* (Stroud, Sutton Publishing, 2006), pp.110–15.
4. Approximately 5,200 men per legion, a cohort of infantry between 480 and 800 men, and an *ala* of cavalry 480–768 strong. Mixed cohorts of infantry and cavalry ranged from 600 to 1040. The standard strength of a legion had significantly increased since the battles of Cannae and Zama.
5. Peter Connolly, *The Roman Army* (London, Macdonald Educational Limited, 1976), pp.27, 41.
6. Ibid, p.41.
7. John Warry, *Warfare in the Classical World* (New York, St Martin's Press, 1980), p.135.
8. Ross Cowan, *Roman Battle Tactics 109 BC–AD 313* (Oxford, Osprey Publishing, 2007), p.6.
9. Warry, *Warfare in the Classical World*, p.187.
10. Lawrence Keppie, *The Making of the Roman Army From Republic to Empire* (New York, Barnes & Noble, 1984), pp.182–83.
11. Tacitus, *Germania*, 1.4.1–5, http://www.sacred-texts.com/cla/tac/g01000.htm
12. Wells, *The Battle That Stopped Rome*, pp.159–60.
13. Ibid, pp.143,152.
14. Fergus M. Bordewich, "The Ambush That Changed History: An amateur archaeologist discovers the field where wily Germanic warriors halted the spread of the Roman Empire," *Smithsonian Magazine* (September 2005), p.3, http://www.smithsonianmag.com/history-archaeology/ambush.html
15. J. F. C. Fuller, edited by John Terraine, *The Decisive Battles of the Western World and Their Influence Upon History*, Vol. 1 (St Albans, Paladin-Granada Publishing, 1970), p.169.
16. Tacitus, *Germania*, 4.7.6.
17. Wells, *The Battle That Stopped Rome*, p.145.
18. Tacitus, *Germania*, 1.6.1–5.
19. Ibid, 4.6.7–8.
20. Ibid, 4.6.9–15.
21. Ibid, 1.7.4
22. Ibid, 4.7.7.
23. C. Velleius Paterculus, *The Roman History*, 2.118.4, http://penelope.uchicago.edu/Thayer/E/Roman/Texts/Velleius_Paterculus/2D*.html#117
24. Cassius Dio, *The Roman History*, 56.19.1, http://penelope.uchicago.edu/Thayer/E/Roman/Texts/Cassius_Dio/56*.html#18
25. Brian Todd Carey, *Warfare in the Ancient World* (Barnsley, Pen & Sword, 2005), p.125. Delbrück argues for 12,000–18,000 (*History of the Art of War*, p.75).
26. Cassius Dio, *The Roman History*, 56.19.5.
27. Ibid, 56.20.1.
28. Hans Delbrück, *The Barbarian Invasions: History Of The Art Of War* (Lincoln, University of Nebraska Press, 1990), p.74.
29. Cassius Dio, *The Roman History*, 56.20.1.
30. Ibid, 56.20.3-4.
31. Delbrück, *The Barbarian Invasions*, p.75.
32. Cassius Dio, *The Roman History*, 56.21.1.
33. Ibid, 56.21.2.
34. Ibid, 56.21.4–5; 56.22.1–2.
35. Paterculus, *The Roman History*, 2.119.4.
36. Ibid, 2.119.2.

37. Florus, *Epitome of Roman History*, 2.30, http://en.wikisource.org/wiki/Epitome_of_Roman_History/Book_2#30

38. Adrian Goldsworthy, *In the Name of Rome: The Men Who Won the Roman Empire*, (London, Phoenix, 2003), p.295.

39. Seutonius, *The Lives of the Twelve Caesars*, Augustus, 23.5–6, http://penelope.uchicago.edu/Thayer/E/Roman/Texts/Suetonius/12Caesars/Augustus*.html#23

40. New Ulm web site: http://www.ci.new-ulm.mn.us/index.asp?Type=B_BASIC&SEC={A192FEAF-A538-4CE4-81CB-02E7B069D398}

ADRIANOPLE

1. Furthermore, subsequent mounted Roman armies would often fight dismounted and still be able to hold off successive charges from elite Persian cavalry. See Simon MacDowall, *Adrianople AD 378 – The Goths Crush Rome's Legions* (Oxford, Osprey Publishing, 2001), p.88.

2. John Keegan, *A History of Warfare* (New York, Alfred A. Knopf, 1993), p.185.

3. MacDowall, *Adrianople AD 378*, pp.8–9.

4. John Julius Norwich, *Byzantium: The Early Centuries* (New York, Alfred A. Knopf, 1989), p.107. Although considered heresy by the Catholic Church, Arianism was part of a wide theological debate between Christians at this time. An Arian bishop baptized Constantine the Great.

5. Ammianus Marcellinus, *The Roman History of Ammianus Marcellinus During the Reigns of The Emperors Constantius, Julian, Jovianus, Valentinian, and Valens*, trans. C. D. Yonge (London: G. Bell & Sons, 1911), 31.12. Ammianus Marcellinus is our most reliable source on the battle of Adrianople. He was a contemporary of the events and had even served as a Roman officer in the mid-4th century. His description of the battles have the authenticity of an eye-witness.

6. Norwich, *Byzantium*, p.98.

7. The essence of Arian doctrine was as follows: "Jesus Christ was not co-eternal and of one substance with God the Father, but had been created by Him at a specific time as His Instrument for the salvation of the world." See Norwich, *Byzantium*, p.52.

8. Ammianus Marcellinus, 22.5.

9. Ibid, 31.14

10. Ibid, 31.14.

11. MacDowall, *Adrianople AD 378*, p.37.

12. Ammianus Marcellinus, 31.4

13. Ibid, 31.4.

14. Ibid, 31.5.

15. MacDowall, *Adrianople AD 378*, p.45.

16. Ibid, p.56.

17. Ibid, pp.56–57.

18. Ammianus Marcellinus, 31.11.

19. Ibid, 31.12

20. Ibid.

21. Ibid.

22. Ibid.

23. MacDowell, *Adrianople AD 378*, p.71.

24. Ammianus Marcellinus, 31.12.

25. Ibid, 31.12.

26. The Gothic wagon laager was probably a series of wagon groupings rather than a single great circle of wagons. MacDowell, *Adrianople AD 378*, pp.68–69.

27. Ammianus Marcellinus, 31.12.

28. Ibid.

29. Ibid.

30. Ibid.

31. Ibid.

32. The Roman cavalry were in part Arabians whom Valens had recruited from Syria. Delbrück, *The Barbarian Invasions*, p.274.

33. Ammianus Marcellinus, 31.13.

34. It had also been suggested that Victor, the Catholic *Magister Equitum*, may have purposefully abandoned Valens, who was an Arian. MacDowell, *Adrianople AD 378*, p.88.

35. Ammianus Marcellinus, 31.13.

36. Ibid.

37. Ibid.

38. Ibid.

39. MacDowell, *Adrianople*, p.80.

40. Ibid, p.80.

41. Ammianus Marcellinus, 31.13.

42. Ibid.

43. MacDowell, *Adrianople*, p.80.

44. Keegan, *A History of Warfare*, p.185.

45. Thomas E. Griess, *The West Point Military History Series: Ancient and Medieval Warfare* (New York, Avery Publishing Group, 1984), p.88.

PLISKA

1. John Haldon, *Byzantium at War* (Oxford, Osprey Publishing, 2002), p.29.

2. C. Mango, "Historical Introduction," in Bryer & Herrin, eds., *Iconoclasm*, (Centre for Byzantine Studies, University of Birmingham, 1977), pp.2–3.

3. Steven Runciman, *A History of the First Bulgarian Empire* (London, G. Bell & Sons, 1930), p.50.

4. Scriptor Incertus, http://en.wikisource.org/wiki/Scriptor_Incertus

5. Warren Treadgold, *The Byzantine Revival* (Palo Alto, Stanford University Press, 1988), p.157.

6. Haldon, *Byzantium at War*, p.19.

7. Soon to be crowned as the Holy Roman Emperor Charlemagne.

8. Runciman, *History of the First Bulgarian Empire*, pp.50–51.

9. Pannonia was an ancient province of the Roman Empire, consisting mostly of the western half of present-day Hungary.

10. Runciman, *History of the First Bulgarian Empire*, pp.51–52.

11. J. B. Bury, *A History of the Eastern Roman Empire from the fall of Irene to the accession of Basil I (802-867)* (London: Macmillan & Co., 1912), p.340.

12. Treadgold places this event in March 809, near the time of the death of the Caliph Harun (Treadgold, *The Byzantine Revival*, p.157).

13. Ibid, p. 157.

14. Bury, *A History of the Eastern Roman Empire*, p.341.

15. Treadgold, *The Byzantine Revival*, p.157.

16. Ibid, p.157.

17. Ibid, p.158.

18. Ibid, p.160.

19. Ibid, p.162.

20. Ibid, p.168.

21. Theophanes is a hostile source whose monastery must have been particularly hard hit by the tax reforms. See Theophanes Confessor, *Chronographia/Chapter 61*, http://en.wikisource.org/wiki/Chronographia/Chapter_61

22. Treadgold, *The Byzantine Revival*, p.170.

23. Heine Baekkelund, *Byzantium: Beyond The Golden Gate* (Nottingham, BL Publishing, 2005), p.75.

24. David Nicolle, *Attila and the Nomadic Hordes* (Oxford, Osprey Publishing Ltd., 1990), p.58.

25. Scriptor Incertus, (http://en.wikisource.org/wiki/Scriptor_Incertus).

26. Treadgold, *The Byzantine Revival*, p.171.

27. Theophanes Confessor, *Chronographia/Chapter 61*, (http://en.wikisource.org/wiki/Chronographia/Chapter_61).

28. Scriptor Incertus, (http://en.wikisource.org/wiki/Scriptor_Incertus).

29. Ibid.

30. Theophanes Confessor, *Chronographia/Chapter 61*, (http://en.wikisource.org/wiki/Chronographia/Chapter_61).

31. Runciman, *History of the First Bulgarian Empire*, p.56.

32. Scriptor Incertus, (http://en.wikisource.org/wiki/Scriptor_Incertus).

33. Runciman, *History of the First Bulgarian Empire*, p.56.

34. The matter is more thoroughly discussed by Bury, *A History of the Eastern Roman Empire*, p.344.

35. Scriptor Incertus, (http://en.wikisource.org/wiki/Scriptor_Incertus).

36. Theophanes Confessor,

(http://en.wikisource.org/wiki/Chronographia/Chapter_61).

37. Runciman, *History of the First Bulgarian Empire*, p.56.

38. This is possibly a reference to Stauracius' pleas to break through the palisades and out of the valley.

39. Scriptor Incertus, (http://en.wikisource.org/wiki/Scriptor_Incertus).

40. Ibid.

41. Theophanes Confessor, (http://en.wikisource.org/wiki/Chronographia/Chapter_61).

42. Bury, *A History of the Eastern Roman Empire*, p.344.

43. Joannes Zonaras, *Epitome historiarum*, ed. by L. Dindorfii, 6 vols, Lipsiae (BT) (1858–75), Chapter 24, p.1.

44. Constantine Mannases was a Byzantine chronicler of the 12th century.

45. *Mannases Chronicle*, (1335–1340, Apostolic Library, The Vatican), p.143.

46. Bury, *A History of the Eastern Roman Empire*, p.344

47. Theophanes Confessor, *Chronographia/Chapter 61*, (http://en.wikisource.org/wiki/Chronographia/Chapter_61).

48. It will be remembered that Nicephorus' officers had pleaded with him to attack the palisades and it seems that this would have been prudent due to Krum's evident lack of manpower.

49. Scriptor Incertus, (http://en.wikisource.org/wiki/Scriptor_Incertus).

50. John Julius Norwich, *Byzantium: The Apogee* (New York, Alfred A. Knopf, 1991), p.8.

51. Scriptor Incertus, (http://en.wikisource.org/wiki/Scriptor_Incertus).

52. Treadgold, *The Byzantine Revival*, p.174.

53. Zonaras, *Epitome historiarum*, p.1.

54. Treadgold, *The Byzantine Revival*, p.175.

55. Theophanes Confessor, (http://en.wikisource.org/wiki/Chronographia/Chapter_61)

HATTIN

1. David Nicolle, *Hattin 1187: Saladin's Greatest Victory* (Oxford, Osprey Publishing, 1993), p.11.

2. Joshua Prawler, *Crusader Institutions* (Oxford, Clarendon Press, 1980), p.487.

3. Nicolle, *Hattin 1187*, pp.60–61.

4. Stanley Lane-Poole, *Saladin: All Powerful Sultan and the Uniter of Islam* (New York, Cooper Square Press, 2002), p.209.

5. Nicolle, *Hattin 1187*, p.43.

6. Prawler, *Crusader Institutions*, p.488.

7. James Reston, *Warriors of God: Richard the Lionheart and Saladin in the Third Crusade* (New York, Random House, 2001), p.47.

8. Stephen O'Shea, *Sea of Faith: the Shared Story of Christianity and Islam in the Medieval Mediterranean World*, (New York, Walker & Company, 2006), p.192.

9. Nicolle, *Hattin 1187*, p.8.

10. Prawler, *Crusader Institutions*, p.487.

11. Ibid, p.487.

12. Ibid, p.487.

13. Nicolle, *Hattin 1187*, p.58.

14. Prawler, *Crusader Institutions*, p.492.

15. Nicolle, *Hattin 1187*, p.16.

16. Ibid, p.25.

17. Ibid, pp.29–30.

18. Ibid, pp.30, 35.

19. Baha al-Din Ibn Shaddad, *The Rare and Excellent History of Saladin*, trans. by D. S. Richards (Aldershot, Ashgate, 2002).

20. Ibid, p.73.

21. Prawler, *Crusader Institutions*, p.488.

22. Ibn Shaddad, *The Rare and Excellent History of Saladin*, p.73.

23. O'Shea, *Sea of Faith*, p.192.

24. Prawler, *Crusader Institutions*, p.492.

25. Ibn Shaddad, *The Rare and Excellent History of Saladin*, p.73.

26. Prawler, *Crusader Institutions*, p.492.

27. Reston, *Warriors of God*, p.51.

28. Lane-Poole, *Saladin*, pp.208–9.
29. O'Shea, *Sea of Faith*, p.193.
30. Prawler, *Crusader Institutions*, p.493.
31. Ibn Shaddad, *The Rare and Excellent History of Saladin*, p.73.
32. Prawler, *Crusader Institutions*, p.496.
33. Ibid, p.496.
34. Ibn Shaddad, *The Rare and Excellent History of Saladin*, p.73.
35. Ibid, p.73.
36. Prawler, *Crusader Institutions*, p.497.
37. Ibn Shaddad, *The Rare and Excellent History of Saladin*, p.74.
38. Nicolle, *Hattin 1187*, p.68-69.
39. Prawler, *Crusader Institutions*, p.497.
40. Ibid, p.498.
41. Ibid, p.499.
42. Ibn Shaddad, *The Rare and Excellent History of Saladin*, p.74.
43. Prawler, *Crusader Institutions*, p.499.
44. Lane-Poole, *Saladin*, p.211.
45. Prawler, *Crusader Institutions*, p.499.
46. Ibid, p.500.
47. Lane-Poole, *Saladin*, p.212.
48. Nicolle, *Hattin 1187*, p.76.
49. Ibn Shaddad, *The Rare and Excellent History of Saladin*, p.74.
50. Nicolle, *Hattin 1187*, p.73.
51. O'Shea, *Sea of Faith*, p.199.
52. Lane-Poole writes of 200 (*Saladin*, p.21) and Nicolle (*Hattin 1187*, p.79) says 230 were killed.
53. O'Shea, *Sea of Faith*, p.200.
54. Ibid, p.199.
55. Reston, *Warriors of God*, p.57.

TANNENBERG

1. For an excellent account of the Crusaders in Northern Europe, see Eric Christiansen, *The Northern Crusades* (Minneapolis, University of Minnesota Press, 1980).
2. William Urban, *The Teutonic Knights: A Military History* (London, Greenhill Books, 2003), p.195.
3. Hans Delbrück, *Medieval Warfare: History of the Art of War*, trans. by Walter J. Renfroe, Jr. (Lincoln, University of Nebraska Press, 1990), p.523.
4. Urban, *The Teutonic Knights*, p.219.
5. Ibid, p.220.
6. Ibid, p.198.
7. Ibid, pp.196–7.
8. Ibid, p.202.
9. Ibid, p.202.
10. Delbrück, *Medieval Warfare*, p.523.
11. Urban, *The Teutonic Knights*, p.202.
12. Stephen Turnbull, *Tannenberg 1410* (Oxford, Osprey Publishing, 2003), pp.25–29.
13. Ibid, pp.25–29.
14. Ibid, pp.25–29.
15. Ibid, p.34.
16. Ibid, p.35.
17. Delbrück, *Medieval Warfare*, p.524.
18. Urban, *The Teutonic Knights*, pp.212–3.
19. Ibid, p.214; Turnbull, *Tannenberg 1410*, p.45.
20. Urban, *The Teutonic Knights*, pp.198–99.

NÖRDLINGEN

1. Hans Delbrück, *The Dawn of Modern Warfare: History of the Art of War*, trans. by Walter J. Renfoe (Lincoln, University of Nebraska Press, 1990), p.115.
2. John Childs, *Warfare in the Seventeenth Century* (London, Cassell, 2001), pp.21, 33.
3. Ibid, p.21.
4. For an account of Lützen see Richard Brzezinski *Lützen 1632: Climax of the Thirty Years' War* (Oxford, Osprey Publishing, 2001). For German speakers see Dr. Oscar Fraas, *Die Nördlinger Schlacht am 27. August 1634* (Nördlingen, Verlag F. Steinmeier, 1983).
5. Christon I. Archer et al., *World History of Warfare*

(Lincoln, University of Nebraska Press, 2002), pp.284, 298–99.

6. Bernhard von Sachsen-Weimar had been Adolphus' second-in-command and had taken over command in the aftermath of his commander's death at Lützen,

7. Childs, *Warfare in the Seventeenth Century*, p.70; Delbrück prefers 40,000 (*The Dawn of Modern Warfare*, p.211).

8. Delbrück, *The Dawn of Modern Warfare*, p.210.

9. Thomas M. Barker, *The Military Intellectual and Battle: Raimondo Montecuccoli and the Thirty Years' War* (New York, State University of New York Press, 1975), pp.198–99.

10. Ibid, p.200.

11. Ibid, p.200.

12. Ibid, pp.200–1.

13. Ibid, p.201.

14. Ibid, pp.202–3.

15. Ibid, p.203.

16. Richard Bonney, *The Thirty Years' War 1618–1649* (Oxford, Osprey Publishing, 2002), p.53.

17. Ibid, p.56.

18. Ibid, p.56.

12. Ibid, p.64.

13. Ibid, p.56.

14. Ibid, pp.56–57.

15. Ibid, pp.58–59.

16. Ibid, p.58.

17. Ibid, p.60.

18. Ibid, pp.52–53.

19. Ibid, p.60.

20. Ibid, p.64.

21. Ibid, p.61.

22. Ibid, p.63.

23. Ibid, pp.64–65.

24. Ibid, p.69.

25. Ibid, pp.69–71.

26. Chandler, *The Campaigns of Napoleon*, p.490.

27. Chandler, *Jena 1806*, p.72.

28. Chandler, *The Campaigns of Napoleon*, p.492.

29. Ibid, pp.492–4.

30. Chandler, *Jena 1806*, p.76.

31. Chandler, *The Campaigns of Napoleon*, p.494.

32. Ibid, p.494.

33. Ibid, p.495.

34. Chandler, *Jena 1806*, pp.77–78.

35. Chandler, *The Campaigns of Napoleon*, p.488.

JENA-AUERSTADT

1. David Chandler, *The Campaigns of Napoleon* (New York: The Macmillan Company 1966), p.456.

2. David Chandler, *Jena 1806: Napoleon Destroys Prussia*, (Oxford, Osprey Publishing Ltd, 1993), pp.11–12

3. Ibid, p.17.

4. Ibid, p.20.

5. Ibid, p.23.

6. Ibid, p.47.

7. Chandler, *The Campaigns of Napoleon*, p.479.

8. Chandler, *Jena 1806*, p.24.

9. Ibid, p.47.

10. Ibid, pp.48–52.

11. Ibid, p.52.

THE ALAMO

1. Stephen L. Hardin, *The Alamo 1836: Santa Anna's Texas Campaign* (Oxford, Osprey Publishing, 2001), p.7.

2. Ibid, p.15.

3. Ibid, p.17.

4. Ibid, p.18.

5. Ibid, p.19.

6. Ibid, p.22.

7. Ibid, p.23.

8. Ibid, p.25.

9. Ibid, p.27.

10. http://www.thealamo.org/susanna_dickinson_hanning.htm

11. http://www.tsl.state.tx.us/treasures/republic/alamo/travis-full-text.html
12. Hardin, *The Alamo 1836*, pp.34–35.
13. Ibid, p.37.
14. The composition of the forces is taken from Hardin, *The Alamo 1836*.
15. http://www.lone-star.net/mall/texasinfo/alamo-battle.htm
16. http://www.thealamo.org/susanna_dickinson_hanning.htm
17. http://www.lone-star.net/mall/texasinfo/alamo-battle.htm
18. http://en.wikipedia.org/wiki/Battle_of_the_ Alamo

JUGDULLUCK

1. Peter Hopkirk, *The Great Game – The Struggle for Empire in Central Asia* (New York, Kodansha America, 1992), p.111.
42. Patrick A. Macrory, *The Fierce Pawns* (Philadelphia, J. B. Lippincott, 1966), p.45.
3. Hopkirk, *The Great Game*, p.181.
4. Macrory, *The Fierce Pawns*, p.60.
5. John H. Waller, *Beyond The Khyber Pass – The Road to British Disaster in the First Afghan War* (Austin, University of Texas Press, 1990), pp.124–25.
6. Ibid, p.78.
7. Hopkirk, *The Great Game*, p.168.
8. Macrory, *The Fierce Pawns*, p.85.
9. Ibid, p.94.
10. Ibid, p.94.
11. Waller, *Beyond The Khyber Pass*, p.124.
12. Ibid, 147.
13. Macrory, *The Fierce Pawns*, p.122.
14. Ibid, p.122.
15. Waller, *Beyond The Khyber Pass*, p.156.
16. Ibid, p.126.
17. Ibid, p.127.
18. Macrory, *The Fierce Pawns*, pp.139–140.
19. Waller, *Beyond The Khyber Pass*, p.157.
20. Macrory, *The Fierce Pawns*, p.165.
21. Ibid, p.166.
22. Waller, *Beyond The Khyber Pass*, p.189.
23. Macrory, *The Fierce Pawns*, p.166.
24. Ibid, p.167.
25. Ibid, p.168.
26. Ibid, p.169.
27. Waller, *Beyond The Khyber Pass*, p.196.
28. Ibid, p.181.
29. Ibid, pp.182–83.
30. Macrory, *The Fierce Pawns*, p.183.
31. Waller, *Beyond The Khyber Pass*, p.181.
32. Hopkirk, *The Great Game*, p.241.
33. Macrory, *The Fierce Pawns*, p.178.
34. Ibid, p.179.
35. Waller, *Beyond The Khyber Pass*, p.187.
36. Ibid, p.214.
37. Macrory, *The Fierce Pawns*, p.210.
38. Ibid, p.236.
39. Hopkirk, *The Great Game*, p.256.
40. Waller, *Beyond The Khyber Pass*, p.237.
41. Macrory, *The Fierce Pawns*, p.252.
42. Ibid, p.253.
43. Ibid, p.252.
44. Ibid, p.255.
45. Ibid, p.256.
46. Lady Florentia Sale, *A Journal of the Disasters in Afghanistan* (Franklin: Tantallon Press, 2002), p.160.
47. Hopkirk, *The Great Game*, p.261.
48. Waller, *Beyond The Khyber Pass*, p.246.
49. Lady Florentia Sale, *A Journal of the First Afghan War*, Ed. Patrick Macrory. (Oxford: Oxford University Press, 2003), p.99.
50. Macrory, *The Fierce Pawns*, p.261.
51. Ibid, p.267.
52. Ibid, p.269.
53. Ibid, p.272.
54. Ibid, p.277.
55. Ibid, p.278.
56. Macrory, *The Fierce Pawns*, p.280.

57. Ibid, p.281.
58. Waller, *Beyond The Khyber Pass*, p.254.
59. Macrory, *The Fierce Pawns*, p.290.
60. Hopkirk, *The Great Game*, p.272.
61. Macrory, *The Fierce Pawns*, p.333.

CAMERONE

1. James W. Ryan, *Camerone: The French Foreign Legion's Greatest Battle* (Westport, Praeger Westport, 1996), p.xx.
2. Ryan, *Camerone*, p. xxviii says the distance to be about 110 miles.
3. Colin Rickards, *The Hand of Captain Danjou: Camerone and the French Foreign Legion in Mexico, 30 April 1863* (Ramsbury, The Crowoods Press, 2005), p.111.
4. Ibid, p.115.
5. Ibid, p.121.
6. Ibid, p.123.
7. See René Chartrand, *The Mexican Adventure 1861–67* (London, Osprey Publishing, 1994) for a breakdown of Mexican and foreign troops.
8. Ibid, p.125.
9. Ibid, pp.126–27.
10. Ryan, *Camerone*, p.36.
11. Rickards, *The Hand of Captain Danjou*, p.127.
12. The description is based on Ryan's sketches in *Camerone*.
13. Rickards, *The Hand of Captain Danjou*, p.127.
14. Ibid, p.128.
15. Ibid, p.128.
16. Ibid, p.130.
17. Ibid, p.131.
18. Ibid, p.134.
19. Ryan, *Camerone*, p.79.
20. Rickards, *The Hand of Captain Danjou*, p.137.
21. Ibid, p.137.
22. Ibid, pp.137–8.
23. Ibid, p.138.
24. Ibid, p.138.
25. Ibid, p.139.
26. Ibid, p.141.
27. Ibid, pp.141–2.
28. Ibid, p.143.
29. Ryan, *Camerone*, p.95.
30. Rickards, *The Hand of Captain Danjou*, p.161.
31. John Robert Young, *The French Foreign Legion: The Inside Story of the World-Famous Fighting Force* (London, Thames and Hudson, 1984), p.17.

LITTLE BIG HORN

1. Peter Panzeri, *Little Big Horn 1876: Custer's Last Stand* (Oxford, Osprey Publishing,1995), pp.12–13.
2. Ibid, p.13.
3. Robert Utley, "Custer Battlefield – National Monument Montana", http://www.nps.gov/history/history/online_books/hh/1b/index.htm
4. Panzeri, *Little Big Horn*, p.47.
5. Ibid, p.41 and Utley, "Custer Battlefield."
6. Panzeri, *Little Big Horn*, p.50 and Utley, "Custer Battlefield."
7. Panzeri, *Little Big Horn*, p.50.
8. Ibid, p.62.
9. Ibid, p.64.
10. Utley, "Custer Battlefield."
11. "The Battle of the Little Bighorn, 1876", http://www.eyewitnesstohistory.com/custer.htm
12. Utley's "Custer Battlefield."
13. Andrew Curry, "Custer's Bluster – His courageous last stand may be a figment", http://www.usnews.com/usnews/doubleissue/mysteries/custer.htm
14. Archives of the West (1874–1877), "The Battle of Little Bighorn. An Eyewitness Account by the Lakota Chief Red Horse recorded in pictographs and text at the Cheyenne River Reservation, 1881", http://www.pbs.org/weta/thewest/resources/archives/six/bighorn.htm

ISANDLWANA

1. Ian Knight, *Isandlwana 1879* (Oxford, Osprey Publishing, 2002), p.11.

2. Ian Knight and Ian Castle, *Zulu War* (Oxford, Osprey Publishing, 2004), pp.146, 152.

3. Ibid.

4. Ibid.

5. Ibid.

6. Knight, *Isandlwana 1879*, p.42.

7. Ibid, p.51.

8. Ibid, p.49.

9. Ibid, p.56.

10. General Horace Smith-Dorrien, *Memories of Forty-Eight Years Service*, http://www.richthofen.com/smith-dorrien/dorrien01b.htm

11. Frank Emery, *The 24th Regiment at Isandhlwana: The Zulu War 1879* (Halesowen, Reliance Printing Works, 1978), pp.10–11. An eclipse did in fact occur that day.

12. Smith-Dorrien, *Memories of Forty-Eight Years Service*.

OPERATION *DINGO*

1. Lieutenant Colonel Stuart Pettis, "The Role of Airpower in the Rhodesian Bush War, 1965–1980," *Air & Space Power Journal* (June 2, 2008), p.1.

2. Peter Abbott and Manuel Ribeiro Rodrigues, *Modern African Wars (2): Angola and Mozambique*, (London, Osprey Publishing, 1988).

3. Pettis ("The Role of Air Power," p.4) stipulates no larger than 100 men. Lohman and MacPherson argue for 8–15-men sized units in general. See Major Charles M. Lohman and Major Robert I. MacPherson, *Rhodesia: Tactical Victory, Strategic Defeat,* War Since 1945 Seminar and Symposium, (Marine Corps Command and Staff College, Marine Corps Development and Education Command, June 7, 1983), p.27.

4. Lohman, *Rhodesia: Tactical Victory*, p.2.

5. Ibid, p.23.

6. Peter Abbott and Philip Botham, *Modern African Wars (1): Rhodesia 1965–80* (London, Osprey Publishing, 1986), p.17.

7. Cocks, *Fire Force*.

8. Barbara Cole, *The Elite: The Story of the Rhodesian Special Air Service* (Transeki, Three Knights, 1984), pp.174, 176. The author has the most detailed account of Operation *Dingo*.

9. Ibid, p.170.

10. Ibid, p.170.

11. Robert MacKenzie, "Fast Strike on Chimoio," *Soldier of Fortune* (January 1994), p.42.

12. Dr. J. R.T. Wood: *Fire Force: Helicopter Warfare in Rhodesia: 1962–1980*: http://www.jrtwood.com/article_fireforce.asp

13. Mike McDonald, "Operation Dingo Zulu One Chimoio November 23 1977", http://www.therli.com/D_Gallery_War.asp

14. MacKenzie, "Fast Strike," p.42.

15. Cole, *The Elite*, p.176.

16. MacKenzie, "Fast Strike," p.43.

17. Cole, *The Elite*, p.178.

18. McDonald, "Operation Dingo Zulu One," p.1.

19. MacKenzie, "Fast Strike," p.83.

20. Ibid, p.43.

21. Cole, *The Elite*, p.181.

22. MacKenzie, "Fast Strike," p.43.

23. McDonald, "Operation Dingo Zulu One," p.2.

24. Robert MacKenzie, "Fast Strike on Chimoio II: Mopping up Mugabe's Minions," *Soldier of Fortune* (February 1977), p.44.

25. Cole, *The Elite*, p.184.

26. MacKenzie, "Fast Strike II," p.44.

27. Cole, *The Elite*, p.183.

28. Ibid, p.184.

29. MacKenzie, "Fast Strike II," p.45.

30. Cole, *The Elite*, p.187; Robert MacKenzie, "Fast Strike," p.71.

31 Cole, *The Elite*, p.188.

GROZNY

1. Jeffrey Burds, "The Soviet War against 'Fifth Columnists': The Case of Chechnya, 1942–4," *Journal of Contemporary History*, Vol. 42, No. 2 (2007), pp.267–314. Anthony James Joes in *Urban Guerrilla Warfare* (Lexington, University Press of Kentucky, 2007, p.133), stipulates one third of nearly 600,000 Chechens died.

2. Ibid.

3. Joes, *Urban Guerrilla Warfare*, p.133.

4. Ibid, p.134.

5. Dr Theodore Karasik, "Chechen Clan Military Tactics and Russian Warfare," published in Central Asia-Caucasus Institute Analyst (March 15, 2000 issue of the CACI Analyst), http://www.cacianalyst.org/?q=node/353

6. Timothy Thomas, "The Battle of Grozny: Deadly Classroom for Urban Combat," *Parameters, US Army War College Quarterly* (Summer 1999), p.2, http://www.carlisle.army.mil/usawc/Parameters/99summer

7. Ib Faurby, 'The Battle(s) of Grozny," Royal Danish Defence College in cooperation with Märta-Lisa Magnusson, University of Southern Denmark. Published in *Baltic Defence Review*, No. 2, (1999), pp.75–87.

8. Joes, *Urban Guerrilla Warfare*, p.136.

9. Ibid, p.137.

10. Ibid, p.137.

11. Thomas, "Battle of Grozny," pp.5–6.

12. Brett C. Jenkinson, *Tactical Observations From The Grozny Combat Experience – a thesis* (Fort Leavenworth, US Army Command and General Staff College, 2002), p.40.

13. Faurby, "The Battle(s) of Grozny," p.4.

14. Jenkinson, *Tactical Observations*, p.47.

15. Timothy Jackson, *David Slays Goliath: A Chechen Perspective on the War in Chechnya (1994–1996)*, (Marine Corps Warfighting Lab, 2000), http://smallwarsjournal.com/documents/davidgoliath.pdf

16. Thomas, "Battle of Grozny," p.2. See http://www.youtube.com/watch?v=PYUTkIZCS

KY for scenes of battle-scarred Grozny.

17. David P. Dilegge, "View from the Wolves' Den – The Chechens and Urban Operations", http://smallwarsjournal.com/documents/wolvesden.htm

18. http://www.youtube.com/watch?v=Mf3atpkQP_M&feature=related

19. Ibid

20. Faurby, "The Battle(s) of Grozny, "p.5.

21. Martin Andrew, "Efficient Reading Strategy: The Russian Experience Of Urban Combat – Some Lessons From Central Asia," http://www.ditc.net.au/erm/russia.pdf

22. Lester W. Grau, "Russian-Manufactured Armored Vehicle Vulnerability in Urban Combat: The Chechnya Experience" (Fort Leavenworth, Foreign Military Studies Office). This article originally appeared in *Red Thrust Star* (January 1997), p.4, http://www.fas.org/man/dod-101/sys/land/row/rusav.htm

23. Jackson, *David Slays Goliath*, pp.14–15.

24. Faurby, "The Battle(s) of Grozny," p.5.

25. Thomas, "Battle of Grozny," p.2.

26. Joes, *Urban Guerrilla Warfare*, p.146.

27. Dilegge, "View from the Wolves' Den."

28. Faurby, "The Battle(s) of Grozny," p.6.

29. Wayne Masden, "Did NSA Help Russia Target Dudayev?," *Covert Action Quarterly*, No. 61 (1997) pp.47–49.

QALA-I-JANGI

1. Data from CIA, World Factbook, https://www.cia.gov/library/publications/the-world-factbook/geos/af.html

2. For a history of Afghanistan, see Mir Bahmanyar, *Afghanistan Cave Complexes* (Oxford, Osprey Publishing, 2004).

3. "US Gives Taliban Millions for Poppy Ban," http://www.historycommons.org/context.jsp?item=a0501talibanaid

4. See Bahmanyar *Afghanistan Cave Complexes*,

Shadow Warriors (Oxford, Osprey 2005) and *SEALs* (with Chris Osman, Oxford, Osprey, 2008), for detailed accounts of special operations missions in Afghanistan.

5. Adam Porter, "Secret History? Overseas documentary alleges war crimes in Afghanistan," *In These Times* (August 2, 2002), http://www.inthesetimes.com/issue/26/20/news1.shtml

6. "Afghan Massacre: The Convoy of Death": http://video.google.com/videoplay?docid=-8763367484184611493

7. Global Security biography of Abdul Rashid Dostum at http://www.globalsecurity.org/military/world/afghanistan/dostum.htm. The number of prisoners ranges between 300 and 600. Damien Lewis in *Bloody Heroes* (London, Century, 2006, p.166*)* writes of 600.

8. Center for Cooperative Research, "The Massacre at Qala-i-Jangi in Mazar-i-Sharif", http://66.159.17.51/cooperativeresearch/www/uswarcrimes/uswarcrimesinafghanistan/mazaarmassacre.html

9. Porter, "Secret History" and "USA versus John Phillip Walker Lindh," Crim. No. 02-37-A, Proffer of Facts in Support of Defendant's Suppression Motion, p.2.

10. Physicians for Human Rights, "PHR Calls for Probe into Removal of Mass Grave in Afghanistan" (December 12, 2008), http://afghanistan.phrblog.org/tag/general-abdul-rashid-dostum/; http://www.globalsecurity.org/military/world/afghanistan/dostum.htm; "Dasht-i-Leili Massacre": http://en.wikipedia.org/wiki/Dasht-i-Leili_massacre; Afghanistan Conflict Monitor, "UN Confirms Afghan Mass Grave Site Disturbed" (December 12, 2008): http://www.afghanconflictmonitor.org/2008/12/un-confirms-afghan-mass-grave-site-disturbed.html

See the videos of Taliban surrender and Qala-i-Jangi prisoner uprising at: "Afghan Massacre: The Convoy of Death" and National Geographic's "Taliban Uprising", http://channel.nationalgeographic.com/series/critical-situation/2951/Videos#tab-Videos/02820_00

11. Lewis, *Bloody Heroes*, p.164.

12. Ibid, p.167.

13. Ibid, p.167.

14. Wikipedia, "Battle of Qala-i-Jangi", http://en.wikipedia.org/wiki/Battle_of_Qala-i-Jangi

15. Alex Perry, "Inside The Battle At Qala-I-Jangi," *Time* (December 10, 2001), p.1.

16. Luke Harding, Simon Tisdall, Nicholas Watt, and Richard Norton-Taylor, "Fatal Errors that Led to Massacre ," *Guardian Saturday* (December 1, 200), http://www.guardian.co.uk/Archive/Article/0,4273,4311227,00.html

17. Carlotta Gall, "A Nation Challenged at Mazar-i-Sharif; Conflicting Tales Paint Blurry Picture of Siege" (November 20, 2001), http://www.nytimes.com/2001/11/20/world/nation-challenged-mazar-sharif-conflicting-tales-paint-blurry-picture-siege.html

18. Porter, "USA versus JPWL," p.5.

19. Luke Harding et al, "Fatal Errors."

20. Perry, "Inside the Battle," p.1.

21. Porter, "USA versus JPWL," p.6.

22. Ibid, p.6.

23. Lewis, *Bloody Heroes*, p.175.

24. Ibid, p.178.

25. "Massacre at Qala-i-Jangi," p.5.

26. Perry, "Inside The Battle At Qala-I-Jangi," p.2.

27. Ibid, p.2.

28. Legion of Valor, http://www.legionofvalor.com/citation_parse.php?uid=1103567760

29. National Geographic, "Taliban Uprising."

30 . Perry, "Inside The Battle," p.5.

31. National Geographic, "Taliban Uprising."

32. "USA versus JPWL," p.9.

33. Wikipedia, "Yaser Esam Hamdi":

http://en.wikipedia.org/wiki/Yaser_Esam_Hamdi

34. "Afghan Massacre: The Convoy of Death."

35. Carlotta Gall, "A Nation Challenged: The Surrender; Last Holdouts In Uprising Give Up Fort Published," *New York Times* (December 2, 2001).

36. Home of Heroes: http://www.homeofheroes.com/valor/08_WOT/dsc_mitchell.html

37. US Army Public Affairs, "Afghanistan SF leader gets first DSC since Vietnam" (November 14, 2003).

11. Herwig, p.72.

12. Carl von Clausewitz, *On War*, trans by Michel Howard and Peter Paret (Princeton, Princeton University Press, 1979), p.80.

13   National Geographic, "Taliban Uprising."

CONCLUSION

1.   Lt. Col. Robert L. Bateman, "Cause for relief: why Presidents no longer fire Generals," *Armed Forces Journal* (June 2008).

2.   http://news.yahoo.com/s/time/20090512/us_time /08599189755500;_ylt=AsOSHqaQMLexRr2Sk 7qh5rys0NUE;_ylu=X3oDMTJoNm1oZG0zBG Fzc2V0A3RpbWUvMjAwOTA1MTIvMDg1O TkxODk3NTU1MDAEY3BvcwMxBHBvcwMy BHNlYwN5bl90b3Bfc3RvcnkEc2xrA3doeXRoZ XBlbnRhZw--

3.   Macrory, *The Fierce Pawns*, p.230.

4.   Richard F. Hamilton and Holger H. Herwig, *Decisions for War, 1914–1917*, (Cambridge University Press, 2004), p.72.

5.   General Fieldmarshal Count Alfred von Schlieffen, *Cannae*, Authorized Translation, US Army Combined Arms Center, http://www-cgsc.army.mil/carl/resources/csi/ Cannae/cannae.asp

6.   Ibid.

7.   Ibid.

8.   "World War I Casualty and Death Tables": http://www.pbs.org/greatwar/resources/casdeath_ pop.html

9.   Colonel Michael R. Matheny, "The Roots of Modern American Operational Art," p.1, http://www.au.af.mil/au/awc/awcgate/army- usawc/modern_operations.pdf

10. Schlieffen, *Cannae*.

BIBLIOGRAPHY

CANNAE

Appian's Roman History. Ed. Horace White. London: William Heinemann; New York: The Macmillan Co.

Bagnall, Nigel. *The Punic Wars 264-146 BC*. Essential Histories. Oxford: Osprey Publishing Inc., 2002.

Belhassen, Imene and Yozan D. Mosig. Revision and Reconstruction in the Punic Wars: Cannae Revisited. *International Journal of the Humanities*, Vol 4 Issue 2. pp.103-110.

Connolly, Peter. *Greece and Rome at War*. London: Macdonald Phoebus Ltd., 1981.

Connolly, Peter. *Hannibal and the Enemies of Rome*. London: Macdonald Educational, 1978.

Daly, Gregory. *Cannae: The Experience of Battle in the Second Punic War*. London: Routledge, 2002.

Dodge, Theodore Ayrault. *Hannibal: A History of the Art of War among the Carthaginians and Romans down to the Battle of Pydna, 168 BC, with a Detailed Account of the Second Punic War, Volume II*. London: Greenhill Books, 1993.

Goldsworthy, Adrian. *Cannae: Hannibal's Greatest Victory*. London: Phoenix, 2007.

Goldsworthy, Adrian. *Roman Warfare*. London: Cassel and Co., 2002.

Hanson, Victor Davis. *Carnage and Culture*. New York: Doubleday, 2001.

Healy, Mark. *Cannae 216 BC: Hannibal smashes Rome's Army*. Campaign 36. Oxford: Osprey Publishing Inc., 1994.

Livy. *The War with Hannibal*. Trans. Aubrey de Selincourt. Ed. Betty Radice. New York: Penguin Books, 1965.

Yozan D. Mosig and Imene Belhassen. "Revision and Reconstruction in the Punic Wars: Cannae Revisited," *The International Journal of the Humanities*, Vol. 4, No. 2, 2006.

Polybius. *The Rise of the Roman Empire*. Trans. Ian Scott-Kilvert. London: Penguin Books, 1979.

Walbank, F.W. *A Historical Commentary on Polybius*. Oxford: University Press, 1970.

CANNAE/ZAMA

Abbott, Jacob. *Hannibal Warrior and Statesman*. New York: D. M. Mac Lellan Book Compan, 1917.

Adcock, F. E. *The Roman Art of War Under the Republic*. Cambridge: Harvard University Press, 1940.

Baker, G. P. *Hannibal*. New York: Dodd, Mead & Company, 1930.

Campbell, Duncan B. *Ancient Siege Warfare Persians, Greeks, Carthaginians and Romans 546–146 BC*. Elite 121. Oxford: Osprey Publishing Ltd., 2005

Carey, Brian Todd. *Hannibal's Last Battle: Zama and the Fall of Carthage*. Barnsley: Pen & Sword Books Ltd., 2007.

Cary, M. and H. H. Scullard. *A History of Rome down to the reign of Constantine*. 3rd ed. New York: St. Martin's Press, 1975.

Creasy, Sir Edward S. *The Fifteen Decisive Battles of the World*. London: J. M. Dent & Sons; New York: Dutton, 1962.

Davis Hanson, Victor. *Carnage and Culture: Landmark Battles in the Rise of Western Power*. New York: Doubleday, 2001.

de Beer, Sir Gavin. *Hannibal: Challenging Rome's Supremacy*. New York: The Viking Press, 1969.

Delbrück, Hans. *Warfare in Antiquity*. Trans. Walter J. Renfroe, Jr. London: Bison Books; Lincoln: University of Nebraska Press, 1990.

Errington, R. M. *The Dawn of Empire: Rome's Rise to World Power*. Ithaca: Cornell University Press, 1972.

Fields, Nic. *The Roman Armies of the Punic Wars 264-146 BC*. Battle Orders 27. Oxford: Osprey Publishing, 2007.

Frantz, Gunther. *Die Vernichtungsschlacht in Friegsgeschichtlichen Beispielen*. Berlin: E. S. Mittler & Son, 1928.

Goldsworthy, Adrian. *The Fall of Carthage: The Punic Wars 265–146 BC*. London: Cassel, 2003.

Junkelmann, Marcus. *Die Legionen des Augustus: Der römische Soldat im archäologischen Experiment*. Mainz am Rhein: Verlag Philipp von Zabern, 1986.

Lazenby, J. F. *Hannibal's War*. Norman: University of Oklahoma Press, 1998.

Lazenby, J. F. *The First Punic War*. Stanford: Stanford University Press, 1996.

Liddell Hart, B. H. *Strategy*. 2nd ed. 1954. New York: Frederick A. Praeger, 1968.

Macdougall, Lt.-Col. P.L. *The Campaigns of Hannibal: Arranged amd Critically Considered Expressly for the use of Students of Military History*. London: Longman, Brown, Green, Longmans and Roberts, 1858.

Warfare in the Ancient World. Ed. General Sir John Hackett. New York: Facts on File, 1989.

Watson, G. R. *The Roman Soldier*. Ithaca: Cornell University Press, 1969.

Wise, Terence. *Armies of the Carthaginian Wars 265-146 BC*. Men-at-Arms 121. London: Osprey Publishing, 1982.

ZAMA

Adcock, F. E. *The Greek and Macedonian Art of War*. Berkeley: University of California Press, 1957.

Belhassen, Imene and Yozan D. Mosig. "Revision and Reconstruction in the Second Punic War: Zama – Whose Victory?" *The International Journal of the Humanities*, Vol. 5. No. 9, 2007: pp.103–110.

de Beer, Sir Gavin. *Alps and Elephants: Hannibal's March*. New York: E.P. Dutton and Company, 1956.

James, Steven. "Zama: the Infantry Battle Revisited." June 2005.
http://www.fenrir.dk/history/index.php?title=Zama:_The_Infantry_Battle_Revisited

Lendon, J. E. *Soldiers & Ghosts: A History of Battle in Classical Antiquity*. New Haven: Yale University Press, 2005.

Liddell Hart, B.H. *Scipio Africanus: Greater than Napoleon*. London: Greenhill Books; California: Presidio Press, 1992.

Livy. *The History of Rome*. Trans. Rev. Canon Roberts. Ed. Ernest Rhys. London: J. M. Dent and Sons, 1905.

Nossov, Konstantin. *War Elephants*. New Vanguard 150. Oxford: Osprey Publishing, 2008.

Polybius. *The Histories*. Trans. W.R. Paton. Cambridge: Loeb Classical Library, 1922. 2 Sept. 2008 <http://penelope.uchicago.edu/Thayer/E/Roman/Texts/Polybius/3*.html>.

Prevas, John. *Hannibal Crosses the Alps: The Enigma Re-examined*. Rockville Centre: Sarpedon, 1998.

van Wees, Hans. *Greek Warfare: Myths and Realities*. London: Gerald Duckworth & Co., 2004.

Warry, John. *Warfare in the Classical World*. New York: St Martin's Press, 1980.

THE TEUTOBURGER FOREST

Bordewich, Fergus M. "The Ambush that Changed History: An amateur archaeologist discovers the field where wily Germanic warriors halted the spread of the Roman Empire." *Smithsonian Magazine*. Sept. 2005.
http://www.smithsonianmag.com/history-archaeology/ambush.htm

Carey, Brian Todd. *Warfare in the Ancient World*. Barnsley: Pen & Sword, 2005.

Cassius Dio. *Roman History*. Trans. Earnest Cary. Cambridge: Loeb Classical Library, 1914. 19 Sept. 2008
<http://penelope.uchicago.edu/Thayer/E/Roman/Texts/Cassius_Dio/56*.html#18>.

Clunn, Tony. *The Quest for the Lost Roman Legions: Discovering the Varus Battlefield*. New York: Savas Beatie; Staplehurst: Spellmount, 2005.

Connolly, Peter. *The Roman Army*. London: Macdonal Educational Ltd., 1976.

Cowan, Ross. *Roman Battle Tactics 109 BC – AD 313*. Elite 155. Oxford: Osprey Publishing, 2007.

Delbrück, Hans. *Warfare in Antiquity*. Trans. Walter J. Renfroe, Jr. Lincoln: University of Nebraska Press, 1990.

Florus. *Two Books of Epitomes from Titus Livius of all wars of 700 years*. Trans. John Selby Watson. 1889. 21 Sept. 2008

Fuller, J. F. C. *The Decisive Battles of the Western World and Their Influence Upon History*. Ed.

John Terraine. St. Albans: Paladin-Granada Publishing Ltd., 1970.

Goldsworthy, Adrian. *In the Name of Rome: The Men Who Won the Roman Empire*. London: Phoenix, 2003.

"Hermann on the Prairie." *New Ulm: A City of Charm and Tradition*. 15 Dec. 2008. <http://www.ci.new-ulm.mn.us/index.asp?Type=B_BASIC&SEC={A192FEAF-A538-4CE4-81CB-02E7B069D398}>.

Keppie, Lawrence. *The Making of the Roman Army from Republic to Empire*. New Jersey: Barnes & Noble Books, 1984.

Murdoch, Adrian. *Rome's Greatest Defeat: Massacre in the Teutoburg Forest*. Stroud: Sutton Publishing Limited, 2006.

Rosenfeldt, Dr. G. "Die Varusschlact: Versuch einer Rekonstruktion der Ereignisse." 16 Sept. 2008. *Schriften im Selbstverlag*. 2006.

Suetonius. *The Lives of the Twelve Caesars*. Trans. J.C. Rolfe. Cambridge: Loeb Classical Library, 1914.

Tacitus. *Germany*. Ed. Moses Hadas. Trans. Alfred Church and William Brodribb. 1942. New York: Random House Inc., 2003.

Velleius Paterculus, C. *The Roman History*. Trans. Frederick W. Shipley. Cambridge: Loeb Classical Library, 1924. 14 Sept. 2008. http://penelope.uchicago.edu/Thayer/E/Roman/Texts/Velleius_Paterculus/2D*.html #117

Warry, John. *Classical Warfare in the Classical World*. New York: St. Martin's Press, 1980.

Wells, Peter S. *The Battle that Stopped Rome*. New York: W. W. Norton & Company, Ltd., 2002.

Wiegels, Rainer and Winfried Woesler. *Arminius und die Varusschlacht*. Paderborn: Ferdinand Schöningh, 1995.

ADRIANOPLE

Ammianus Marcellinus. *The Roman History of Ammianus Marcellinus During the Reigns of the Emperors Constantinus, Julian, Jovianus, Valentinian and Valens*. Trans. C. D. Yonge (London: G. Bell & Sons, 1911).

Cowan, Ross. *Imperial Roman Legionary AD 161–284*. Warrior 72. Oxford: Osprey Publishing Ltd., 2003.

Delbrück, Hans. *The Barbarian Invasions*. Trans. Walter J. Renfroe Jr. Lincoln: University of Nebraska Press, 1980.

Greiss, Thomas E. *The West Point Military History Series: Ancient and Medieval Warfare*. New York: Avery Publishing Group, 1984.

Keegan, John. *A History of Warfare*. New York: Alfred A. Knopf, 1993.

MacDowall, Simon. *Adrianople AD 378*. Campaign 84. Oxford: Osprey Publishing Ltd., 2001.

MacDowall, Simon. *Late Roman Cavalryman AD 236–565*. Warrior 15. Oxford: Osprey Publishing Ltd., 1995.

MacDowall, Simon. *Late Roman Infantryman AD 236–565*. Warrior 9. London: Osprey Publishing Ltd., 1994.

Norwich, John Julius. *Byzantium: The Early Centuries*. New York: Alfred A. Knopf, 1989.

Simkins, Michael. *The Roman Army from Hadrian to Constantine*. Men-at-Arms 93. London: Osprey Publishing Ltd., 1979.

PLISKA

Baekkelund, Heine. *Byzantium: Beyond The Golden Gate*. Nottingham: BL Publishing, 2005.

Bury, J. B. *A History of the Eastern Roman Empire from the fall of Irene to the accession of Basil I (802–867)*. London: Macmillan & Co., 1912.

Haldon, John. *Byzantium at War AD 600–1453*. Essential Histories 33. Oxford: Osprey Publishing Ltd., 2002.

Mango, C. "Historical Introduction," in Bryer & Herrin, eds., *Iconoclasm*. Centre for Byzantine Studies, University of Birmingham, 1977.

Mannases Chronicle. 1335–1340, Apostolic Library, The Vatican.

Nicolle, David. *Attila and the Nomadic Hordes*. Elite 30. Oxford: Osprey Publishing Ltd. 1990.

Nicolle, David. *Hungary and the fall of Eastern Europe 1000–1568*. Men-at-Arms 195. London: Osprey Publishing Ltd., 1988.

Norwich, John Julius. *Byzantium: The Apogee*. New York: Alfred A. Knopf, 1992.

Oman, Charles. *The Dark Ages 476–918*. London: Rivingtons, 1923.

Runciman, Steven. *A History of the First Bulgarian Empire*. London: G. Bell & Sons, 1930.

Treadgold, Warren. *The Byzantine Revival*. Stanford: Stanford University Press, 1988.

HATTIN

Gabrieli, Francesco. *Arab Historians of the Crusades*. Trans. E. J. Costello. New York: Barnes & Noble Books, 1969.

Lane-Poole, Stanley. *Saladin: All Powerful Sultan and the United of Islam*. New York: Cooper Square Press, 2002.

Nicholson, Helen. *Knight Templar 1120–1312*. Warrior 91. Oxford: Osprey Publishing Ltd., 2003.

Nicolle, David. *Hattin 1187: Saladin's Greatest Victory*. Campaign 19. Oxford: Osprey Publishing Ltd, 1993.

Nicolle, David. *Knight of Outremer 1187–1344 AD*. Warrior 18. Oxford: Osprey Publishing Ltd., 1996.

Nicolle, David. *Saladin and the Saracens*. Men-at-Arms 171. London: Osprey Publishing Ltd., 1986.

Nicolle, David. *The Armies of Islam 7th–11th Centuries*. London: Osprey Publishing Ltd., 1982.

O'Shea, Stephen. *Sea of Faith: the Shared Story of Christianity and Islam in the Medieval Mediterranean World*. New York: Random House, 2001.

Prawler, Joshua. *Crusader Institutions*. Oxford: Clarendon Press, 1980.

Reston, James. *Warriors of God: Richard the Lionheart and Saladin in the Third Crusade*. New York: Random House, 2001.

Shaddād, Bahā al-Dᵕin Ibn. *The Rare and Excellent History of Saladin*. Trans. D.S. Richards. Hampshire: Ashgate, 2002.

TANNENBERG

Christiansen, Eric. *The Northern Crusades*. Minneapolis: University of Minnesota Press, 1980.

Delbrück, Hans. *Medieval Warfare*. Trans. Walter J. Renfroe, Jr. 1982. London: Bison Books; Lincoln: University of Nebraska Press, 1990.

Ekdahl, Sven. *Das Solbuch des Deutschen Ordens 1410/1411*. Cologne: Bohlau Verlag, 1988.

Ekdahl, Sven. *Die "Banderia Prutenorum" des Jan Dlugosz – eine Quelle zur Schlacht bei Tannenberg 1410*. Gottingen: Vandenhoeck & Ruprecht, 1976.

Ekdahl, Sven. *Die Schlact bei Tannenberg*. Berlin: Duncker & Humblot, 1982.

Turnbull, Stephen. *Tannenberg 1410*. Campaign 122. Oxford: Osprey Publishing, 2003.

Urban, William. *The Teutonic Knights*. London: Greenhill Books, 2003.

NÖRDLINGEN

Archer, Christon I., John R. Ferris, Holger H. Herwig and Timothy H. E. Travers. *World History of Warfare*. Lincoln: University of Nebraska Press, 2002.

Asch, Ronald G. *The Thirty Years War: The Holy Roman Empire and Europe, 1618–48*. New York: St. Martin's Press, 1997.

Barker, Thomas M. *The Military Intellectual and Battle: Raimon Do Montecuccoli and the Thrity Years War*. Albany: University of New York Press, 1975.

Bonney, Richard. *The Thirty Years' War 1618–1648*. Essential Histories 29. Oxford: Osprey Publishing, 2002.

Brezezinski, Richard. *Lützen 1632*. Campaign 68. Oxford: Osprey Publishing, 2001.

Childs, John. *Warfare in the Seventeenth Century*. London: Cassel, 2001.

Craig, Gordon A. *The Politics of the Prussian Army 1640-1945*. Oxford: Oxford University Press, 1955.

Delbrück, Hans. *The Dawn of Modern Warfare*. Lincoln: University of Nebraska Press, 1990.

Fraas, Dr. Oscar. *Die Nördlingen Schlacht*. 1869. Nördlingen: Verlag F. Steinmeier, 1983.

Guthrie, William P. *Battles of the Thirty Years War*. Westport: Greenwood Press, 2002.

Wedgwood, C. V. *The Thirty Years War*. London: The Folio Society, 1999.

Weigley, Russell F. *The Age of Battles: The Quest for Decisie Warfare from Breitenfeld to Waterloo*. Bloomington: Indiana University Press, 1991.

JENA-AUERSTÄDT

A Guide to the Battlefields of Europe. 2 vols. Ed. David Chandler. Philadelphia: Chilton Books, 1965.

Abbott, John S. C. *The History of Napoleon Bonaparte*. Vol. 2. New York: Harper & Brothers Publishers, 1855.

Chandler, David G. *The Campaigns of Napoleon*. New York: The Macmillian Company, 1966.

Chandler, David G. *Jena 1806: Napoleon destroys Prussia*. Campaign 20. Oxford: Osprey Publishing Ltd., 1993.

Connelly, Owen. *Blundering to Glory: Napoleon's Military Campaign*. Wilmington: SR Books, 1987.

Hofschröer, Peter. *Prussian Cavalry of the Napoleonic Wars (1): 1792–1807*. Men-at-Arms 162. London: Osprey Publishing Ltd., 1985.

Hofschröer, Peter. *Prussian Line Infantry 1792–1815*. Men-at-Arms 152. London: Osprey Publishing Ltd., 1984.

Jany, Curt. *Geschichte der Preussischen Armee*. Vol. 2. Osnabrück: Biblio Verlag, 1967.

Lachouque, Henry. *The Anatomy of Glory: Napoleon and his Guard a study in leadership*. Trans. Anne S. K. Brown. Providence: Brown University Press; London: Lunc Humphries, 1962.

Muir, Rory. *Tactics and the Experience of Battle in the Age of Napoleon*. New Haven: Yale University Press, 1998.

Rothenberg, Gunther E. *The Art of Warfare in the Age of Napoleon*. Bloomington: Indiana University Press, 1978.

ALAMO
Hardin, Stephen L. *The Alamo 1836*. Campaign 89. Oxford: Osprey Publishing, 2001.

JUGDULLUCK
Barr Smith, Robert. *To the Last Cartridge: From the Siege of Constantinople to Vietnam's Ia Drang Valley*. New York: Avon Books, 1994.

Barthorp, Michael. *The North-West Frontier: British Indi and Afghanistan. A Pictoral History 1839–1947*. Poole and Dorset: Blandford Press, 1982.

Farwell, Byron. *Queen Victoria's Little Wars*. 1972. New York: W. W. Norton & Company, 1985.

Hopkirk, Peter. *The Great Game – the Struggle for Empire in Central Asia*. New York: Kodansha America Inc., 1992.

Macrory, Patrick A. *The Fierce Pawns*. Philadelphia: J. B. Lippincott Company, 1966.

Sale, Lady Florentia. *A Journal of the Disasters in Afghanistan*. Franklin: Tantallon Press, 2002.

Sale, Lady Florentia. *A Journal of the First Afghan War*. Ed. Patrick Macrory. Oxford: Oxford University Press, 2003.

Venning, Annabel. *Following the Drum: The Lives of Army Wives and Daughters*. London: Headline Book Publishing, 2005.

Waller, John H. *Beyond the Khyber Pass: The Road to British Disaster in the First Afghan War*. Austin: University of Texas Press, 1990.

Wilkinson-Latham, Robert. *North-West Frontier 1837–1947*. Men-at-Arms. London: Osprey Publishing Ltd., 1977.

CAMERONE
Chartrand, René, *The Mexican Adventure 1861–67*. Men-at-Arms 272. London: Osprey Publishing, 1994.

Rickards, Colin, *The Hand of Captain Danjou: Camerone and the French Foreign Legion in Mexico, 30 April 1863*. Ramsbury: The Crowoods Press, 2005.

Ryan, James W., *Camerone: The French Foreign Legion's Greatest Battle*. Westport: Praeger Westport, 1996.

Young, John Robert, *The French Foreign Legion: The Inside Story of the World-Famous Fighting Force*. London: Thames and Hudson, 1984.

LITTLE BIG HORN

Panzeri, Peter. *Little Big Horn 1876*. Campaign 39. Oxford: Osprey Publishing, 1995.

Wood, W. J. *Leaders and Battles: the Art of Military Leadership*. Novato: Presidio Press, 1984.

ISANDLWANA

Barthorp, Michael. *The Zulu War*. Dorset: Blandford Press, 1984.

Callwell, Col. C. E. *Small Wars: Their Priciples and Practice*. Lincoln: University of Nebraska Press, 1996.

Castle, Ian and Ian Knight. *Zulu War*. Oxford: Osprey Publishing, 2004.

Edgerton, Robert B. *Africa's Armies From Honor to Infamy*. Cambridge: Westview Press, 2002.

Emery, Frank. *The 24th Regiment at Isandhlwana XXIV*. Halesowen: Reliance Printing Works, 1978.

Knight, Ian. *Isandlwana 1879*. Campaign 111. Oxford: Osprey Publishing, 2002.

Morris, Donald R. *The Washing of the Spears*. London: Jonathan Cape Ltd., 1966.

Wilkinson-Latham, Christopher. *Uniforms & Weapons of the Zulu War*. London: B.T. Batsford Ltd., 1978.

OPERATION *DINGO*

Abbot, Peter and Manuel Ribeiro Rodrigues, *Modern African Wars (2): Angola and Mozambique*. Men-at-Arms 202. London: Osprey Publishing, 1988.

Abbot, Peter and Philip Botham. *Modern Africa Wars (1): Rhodesia 1965–80*. Men-at-Arms 183. London: Osprey Publishing Ltd., 1986.

Cole, Barabara. *The Elite: The Story of the Rhodesian Special Air Service*. Transeki: Three Knights, 1984.

Lohman, Major Charles M. and Major Robert I. MacPherson. *Rhodesia: Tactical Victory, Strategic Defeat*. War Since 1945 Seminar and Symposium. Marine Corps Command and Staff College, Marine Corps Development and Education Command, June 7, 1983.

MacKenzie, Robert. "Fast Strike on Chimoio," *Soldier of Fortune*. January 1994.

Mackenzie, Robert. "Fast Strike on Chimoio II: Mopping up Mugabe's Minions," *Soldier of Fortune*. February 1977.

Pettis, Lt. Col Stuart. "The Role of Airpower in the Rhodesian Bush War, 1965–1980," *Air & Space Power Journal*. June 2, 2008.

GROZNY

Burds, Jeffrey. "The Soviet War against 'Fifth Columnists': The Case of Chechnya, 1942–4." *Journal of Contemporary History* 42.2 (2007): pp.267–314.

Faurby, Ib. "The Battle(s) of Grozny." *Baltic Defence Review*, No. 2. 1999.

Jackson, Timothy. David Slays Goliath: A Chechen Perspective on the War in Chechnya (1994–1996). Marine Corps Warfighting Lab, 2000. http://smallwarsjournal.com/documents/davidgoliath.pdf

Jenkinson, Brett C. *Tactical Observations From the Grozny Combat Experience – A thesis*. Fort Leavenworth, US Army Command and General Staff College, 2002.

Joes, Anthony James. *Urban Guerilla Warfare*. Lexington: University Press of Kentucky, 2007.

Karasik, Dr. Theodore. "Chechen Clan Military Tactics and Russian Warfare." *CACI Analyst*. 15 Mar 2000, http://www.cacianalyst.org/?q=node/353.

Masden, Wayne. "Did NSA Help Russia Target Dudayev?" *Covert Action Quarterly*, No 61, 1997.

Thomas, Timothy. "The Battle of Grozny: Deadly Classroom for Urban Combat." *Parameters*. Summer 1999.

QALA-I-JANGI

Bahmanyar, Mir. *Afghanistan Cave Complexes*. Fortress 26. Oxford: Osprey Publishing Ltd., 2004.

Bahmanyar, Mir. *Shadow Warriors: A History of the US Army Rangers*. Oxford: Osprey Publishing Ltd., 2006.

Bahmanyar, Mir. and Chris Osman. *SEALs: The US Navy's Elite Fighting Force*. Oxford: Osprey Publishing Ltd., 2008.

Kukis, Mark. *"My Heart Became Attached"*. Washington: Brassey's, Inc., 2003

Lewis, Damien. *Bloody Heroes*. London: Century, 2006.

Perry, Alex. "Inside the Battle at Qala-I-Jangi," *Time*. December 10, 2001.

Porter, Adam. "Secret History? Overseas documentary alleges war crimes in Afghanistan," *In These Times*. August 2, 2002.
http://www.inthesetimes.com/issue/26/20/news1.shtml

Radak, Jesselyn. *The Canary in the Coalmine: Blowing the Whistle in the Case of "American Taliban" Joohn Walker Lindh*. Self-published, 2006

Romero, Anthony D. and Dina Temple-Raston. *In Defense of Our America*. New York: William Morrow, 2007.

CONCLUSION

Aron, Raymond. *Clausewitz Philosopher of War*. Trans. Christine Booker and Norman Stone. New Jersey: Prentice Hall, 1985. Trans. of *Penser la Guerre, Clausewitz*. 1976.

Bateman, Lt Col Robert L. "Cause for relief: why Presidents no longer fire Generals," *Armed Forces Journal*. June 2008.

Goerlitz, Walter. *History of the German General Staff 1657-1945*. Trans. Brian Battershaw. Boulder: Westview Press, 1985.

Hamilton, Richard F. and Holger H. Herwig, *Decisions for War 1914–1917*. Cambridge University Press, 2004.

Howard, Michael. *Clausewitz*. Oxford: Oxford University Press, 1985.

Macksey, Kenneth. *From Triumph to Disaster: The Fatal Flaws of German Generalship from Moltke to Guderian*. London: Greenhill Books; Pennsylvania: Stackpole Books, 1996.

Paret, Peter. *Clausewitz and the State: The man, his theories and his times*. 1976. Princeton: Princeton University Press, 1985.

Paret, Peter. *Understanding War: Essays on Clausewitz and the History of Military Power*. Princeton: Princeton University Press, 1992.

Simpson, Keith. *History of the German Army*. Greenwich: Bison Books, 1985.

von Clausewitz, Carl. *On War*. Ed. and Trans. Michael Howard and Peter Paret. Princeton: Princeton University Press, 1984.

Willems, Emilio. *A Way of Life and Death*. Nashville: Vanderbilt University Press, 1986.

GENERAL

Alexander, Bevin. *How Great Generals Win*. New York: W. W. Norton & Company, Inc., 1993.

Alexander, Bevin. *How Wars are Won: The 13 Rules of War from Ancient Greece to the War on Terror*. New York: Three Rivers Press, 2002.

Chaliand, Gérard. *The Art of War in World History*. Berkeley: University of California Press, 1994.

David, Saul. *Military Blunders: The how and why of military failure*. New York: Caroll & Graf Publishers Inc., 1998.

Dawson, Christopher. *Mission to Asia*. Toronto: University of Toronto Press, 1980.

Duffy, Christopher. *The Military Experience in the Age of Reason*. New York: Atheneum, 1988.

Dupuy, R. Ernest and Trevor N. Dupuy. *The Encyclopedia of Military History from 3500 BC to the present*. 2nd ed. New York: Harper and Row, 1986.

Eggenberger, David. *An Encyclopedia of Battles: Accounts of Over 1560 Battles form 1479 B.C. to the Present*. 1967. New York: Dover Publications Inc, 1985

Harbottie, Thomas. *Dictonary of Battles from 7443 B.C. to the Present*. Revised George Bruce. New York: Stein and Day, 1975.

Jones, Archer. *The Art of War in the Western World*. Oxford: Oxford University Press, 1987.

Lamb, Harold. *The March of the Barbarians*. New York: The Literary Guild of America, Inc., 1940.

Liddel Hart, B. H. *Great Captains Unveiled*. 1927. London: Greenhill Books; California: Presidio Press, 1989.

Makers of Modern Strategy from Machiavelli to the Nuclear Age. Ed. Peter Paret. New Jersey: Princeton University Press, 1986.

Mitchell, Lieut. Col. William A. *Outlines of the World's Military History*. Washington D.C.: National Service Publishing Co., 1931.

Montross, Lynn. *War Through the Ages*. 3rd ed. New York: Harper and Row, Publishers, 1960.

Oman, C. W. C. *A History of the Art of War in the Sixteenth Century*. New York: E. P. Dutton and Company Inc., ?

Oman, C. W. C. *The Art of War in the Middle Ages A.D. 378-1515*. Ithaca: Cornell University Press, 1953.

Perrett, John. *Against All Odds! Dramatic Last Stand Actions*. 1995. London: Cassel and Co., 2001.

Poole, H. John. *Tactics of the Crescent Moon: Militant Muslim Combat Methods*. North Carolina: Posterity Press, 2004.